UNWELCOME STRANGERS

STUDIES IN JEWISH HISTORY

Jehuda Reinharz, General Editor

WILHELM MARR
The Patriarch of Antisemitism
MOSHE ZIMMERMANN

CHAIM WEIZMANN
The Making of a Zionist Leader, paperback edition
JEHUDA REINHARZ

UNWELCOME STRANGERS
East European Jews in Imperial Germany
JACK WERTHEIMER

THE JEWS OF PARIS AND THE "FINAL SOLUTION"
Communal Response and Internal Conflicts, 1940–1944
JACQUES ADLER

A CLASH OF HEROES
Brandeis, Weizmann, and American Zionism
BEN HALPERN

THE MAKING OF CZECH JEWRY
National Conflict and Jewish Society in Bohemia, 1870–1918
HILLEL J. KIEVAL

OTHER VOLUMES ARE IN PREPARATION

UNWELCOME STRANGERS

East European Jews

in Imperial Germany

JACK WERTHEIMER

New York   Oxford
OXFORD UNIVERSITY PRESS
1987

Oxford University Press

Oxford   New York   Toronto
Delhi   Bombay   Calcutta   Madras   Karachi
Petaling Jaya   Singapore   Hong Kong   Tokyo
Nairobi   Dar es Salaam   Cape Town
Melbourne   Auckland

and associated companies in
Beirut   Berlin   Ibadan   Nicosia

Library of Congress Cataloging-in-Publication Data
Wertheimer, Jack.
Unwelcome strangers. (Studies in Jewish history)
Bibliography: p.   Includes index.
1. Jews, East European—Germany—History.   2. Jews—Germany—
History—1800–1933.   3. Jews—Germany—Politics and government.
4. Germany—Ethnic relations.   I. Title.   II. Series.
DS135.G33W435   1987   943′.004924   86-18208
ISBN 0-19-504893-8

1 3 5 7 9 8 6 4 2

Printed in the United States of America
on acid-free paper

For Rebecca

Acknowledgments

Many teachers, colleagues, and relatives have aided me during the dozen years it has taken to prepare this study. Through this public acknowledgment of their efforts, I wish to express my deep appreciation for their direct and indirect contributions to this book.

From my first days as a graduate student to the present, when I teach at the institution over which he presides as chancellor, Professor Ismar Schorsch has been a generous mentor and colleague. Even when he no longer taught at Columbia University, he graciously volunteered to guide my research and sponsor my doctoral dissertation. In subsequent years, he has continued to take an active interest in my work. Through the model of his own engaged scholarship, his firm yet always constructive criticism, and his insightful responses to my work, he has shaped not only this book, but my outlook as a historian and teacher.

As a graduate student at Columbia University, I also benefited from contact with other outstanding scholars. Professor Zvi Ankori introduced me to the broad sweep of Jewish history, while attuning me to the value of examining subgroups within Jewish society. Professor Naomi Cohen sparked an interest in American Jewish history that has remained with me. In his capacity as the second reader of my doctoral dissertation, Professor Fritz Stern urged me to continue my research in German archives; this book has been enriched considerably because I followed his advice. The constructive suggestions offered by professors Sigmund Diamond,

Paula Hyman, and Joseph Rothschild during my doctoral defense helped me transform my dissertation into a book.

Many friends and colleagues aided me as I prepared this manuscript for publication. Professors Benjamin Gampel, Paula Hyman, and Marion Kaplan have served as critics of my writing; their close readings of my essays and sections of this book have enabled me to improve the clarity of my thought and prose. Other colleagues have provided me with information and guidance when I turned to them with queries; I especially note the help of professors Robert Liberles, Michael Meyer, Monika Richarz, Paul Ritterband, Marsha Rozenblit, and Michael Stanislawski. At an early stage of my research, Dr. Yehoyakim Doron of Kibbutz Gan Shmuel shared useful bibliographic references with me. And as my work neared completion, I received the cooperation and support of Professor Jehuda Reinharz, the editor of Oxford's series on Jewish history. Thanks to his efficiency and sensitivity, the decision to accept my manuscript proceeded smoothly. I thank him and the staff of Oxford University Press for their helpful suggestions.

At different stages, I received research grants from several foundations. As a graduate student I was awarded fellowships by the National Foundation for Jewish Culture and the Memorial Foundation for Jewish Culture. A subsequent research trip to archives in the Federal Republic of Germany was supported by the German Academic Exchange Service (DAAD). I particularly want to note the timely assistance of the Leo Baeck Institute: when in the spring of 1978 I learned that access to archives in the German Democratic Republic would be granted, the president of the Institute, Dr. Max Gruenewald, and the executive director, Dr. Fred Grubel, arranged within days for me to receive a travel grant. To me this expeditious and generous assistance characterizes the Institute's commitment to scholarship. Finally, I wish to thank the National Endowment for the Humanities for a summer grant that made it possible for me to organize and write the most demanding chapter of this book.

Several other institutions facilitated my research. I wish to pay tribute to the numerous individuals at archives and libraries in East and West Germany, Israel, and the United States who offered their friendly assistance and guidance. During all the years I have worked on this manuscript, I have been employed either on a part-time or full-time basis at the Jewish Theological Seminary of America. I thank Professor Gerson D. Cohen, now chancellor emeritus, for bringing me to the Seminary and taking an interest in my work. Thanks to my happy working relationship with colleagues and students, the Seminary has been an ideal environment for research and reflection on the modern Jewish experience.

Although I have left them for last, I recognize that members of my family played the most decisive role in shaping my work. My parents, observant and engaged Jews, heeded the biblical command to teach their children the religion and ways of Israel. Through their example, they taught me to concern myself with the welfare and fate of the Jewish people. I know that my parents' own immigrant experience attuned me to some of the issues raised in this book. In particular, their active involvement in a synagogue that attracted Jews from a wide variety of backgrounds exposed me to one of the central questions addressed by this book: How do Jews of different cultures forge a community and intermingle amicably?

It saddens me that my mother, who passed away a few years ago, did not live to witness the publication of this book. I am grateful that my father can enjoy this fulfillment of my work.

My wife, Rebecca, has contributed tangibly to this volume by typing and proofreading manuscripts as well as helping me to clarify my thinking and writing. Even more important, her ongoing confidence and gentle encouragement helped me persevere during the many years of work on this project. I dedicate this book to Rebecca in appreciation for her companionship, empathic support, and wise counsel.

Contents

UNWELCOME STRANGERS

Introduction

German Jewry's encounter with East European Jews, the meeting of *Yekkes* and *Ostjuden,*[1] has assumed near mythic significance in the modern Jewish imagination. According to popular accounts, these two segments of a once unified Ashkenazic Jewry had been riven into two distinctive and mutually exclusive camps by the time they met in the late nineteenth and early twentieth centuries: one consisted of emancipated, bourgeois Germans of the Mosaic Persuasion who considered themselves secure and safe in their homeland; the other was comprised of ghettoized, impoverished Caftan Jews forced to choose between a miserable existence in the East or migration westward in search of new opportunities. Confronted by their eastern brethren, German Jews, it is alleged, responded with arrogance and condescension. At best, they patronized *Ostjuden,* regarding the latter as backward, superstitious, dirty—and certainly inferior in culture and breeding. At worst, German Jews harbored a profound antipathy toward their coreligionists that smacked of Jewish self-hatred, if not anti-Semitism. Indeed, the very term *Yekke* is often used in written works and daily conversation as a shorthand for snobbishness and heartless meticulousness, whereas the term *Ostjude* evokes images of Jews victimized by their own kind.

This perception of how East European Jews fared at the hands of their German coreligionists has by now gained such wide currency that the mere utterance of the term *Ostjude* conjures up a whole complex of Jewish behavior. Works on

3

every imaginable theme, but especially books and articles on past or present tensions in Jewish communal life, refer to the plight of the *Ostjude* in Germany. Whether the discussion revolves around relations between native and immigrant coreligionists, Uptown and Downtown Jews, or "privileged Jews" and "Jews without money," the former are reminded of the deplorable example set by German Jewry and the latter win sympathy, for they, like the *Ostjuden,* are victims of unkind and condescending coreligionists. To cite two examples from a rich selection of possibilities: in an essay on difficulties between Sephardic and Ashkenazic Jews in contemporary Israel, a relationship that has at times exploded violently, one learns that "whatever the tensions . . . they do not approach the attitude of German Jews toward the so-called *Ostjuden . . .* in the late 19th and early 20th centuries"; and in a book describing the reception accorded to *German* Jews who fled from Hitler's *Reich* to England, a historian likens the response of Anglo Jewry to

> the perennial attitude of the established Jews towards the *Ostjuden*—using *Ostjuden* in its widest sense—the attitude of German Jews themselves to their fellows fleeing from Russia and Poland, of the Italian Jews to their brethren driven from Spain by the Inquisition, and, of course, of the Sephardim of Stuart times toward the Ashkenzi from Hamburg.

Though the author of these lines is alert to the fact that many native Jewries have disdained refugee coreligionists, his remarks, nonetheless, typify the casual employment of the term *Ostjuden* "in its widest sense"—as a code word.[2]

In the above examples, and in dozens of others that may be adduced, there is an underlying concern with the *attitudes* of German Jewry toward the *Ostjuden.* And, indeed, the sparse historical research on this subject has also focused almost exclusively on attitudinal issues—to the point of turning a very real historical meeting into a symbolic act. Often works do not even refer to the meeting of actual people, but to the clash of abstractions: What did *the Ostjude* symbolize to German Jews? How did *the* German Jew conceive of the *Ostjude?* And, to use the formulation of the most recent work on the subject, what place did "the East European Jew" occupy in "German Jewish consciousness"?[3] While all of these questions are interesting and worthwhile, it is remarkable how little attention has focused on a related question: How did German Jews *act* when confronted by East European Jews? Surely, the attitudes of German Jewry constituted only one dimension of their response to eastern coreligionists. Just as the history of anti-Semitism—or any other prejudice—is not merely a catalogue of stereotypes, but a narrative of actions such as defamation, discrimination, persecution, and annihilation, so the history of intergroup relations also must discuss *overt* behavior.

Even this approach, however, is unduly narrow because it examines the relationship of German and Eastern Jews in a vacuum. It tells us little about the environment in which both groups met: What were the political, legal, social, and economic realities that shaped their responses to one another? What possibilities were even available to them? Moreover, it limits discussion to internal relations within the Jewish community, thereby suggesting that the fate of Jews depends entirely upon the behavior of their fellow Jews. In the extreme, this has led some observers to attribute such importance to the German Jewish response that they explain the continuing movement of Eastern Jews through and out of Germany as a reaction to the ill will displayed by native Jews.[4]

The present study aims to examine the encounter of German and East European Jews within the context of modern German history. It is predicated on the assumption that this meeting was profoundly conditioned by a specific historical moment, national context, and social reality. Accordingly, it first analyzes the status of foreign Jews in German society and the conditions of immigrant life before turning to an analysis of interrelations within the Jewish community. The book opens with a discussion of German responses to Jewish migrants from Eastern Europe. Successive chapters characterize the unusual challenges confronted by German policy makers, the nature of public debates over Eastern Jews, and the specific methods devised by governments to cope with East European Jews. The book's second section traces the absorption of Jewish migrants into German life by delineating the demographic, occupational, and social patterns of the newcomers and assessing how well they were integrated into society at large. And the final section portrays the complex interaction between natives and foreigners within the Jewish community. How did the uniquely Central European communal structure affect relations between both groups of Jews? How did German and Eastern Jews relate to one another on a day-to-day basis? And how did the central institutions of native Jewry respond to the political and social problems posed by alien Jews?

Since the history of Eastern Jews in modern Germany spans over three centuries and is studded with turning points, it is not possible for one work to cover the entire subject. The present volume focuses on developments during one specific historical era—the period between the completion of German unification and the onset of World War I. These years hold a threefold significance. First, and most important, they represented a time when Germany was administered by one form of governmental system—the structure of the Second German Empire *(Reich)*. Accordingly, we can examine the experiences of Eastern Jews in a Germany that ruled continuously over the same territorial expanse and employed a uniform legal and administrative structure to cope with foreigners. (Both before German unification and after the outbreak of World War I, territorial and legal conditions were different from those during the years 1871–1914.) Second, the era covered by this book coincides with the period of Jewish mass migration from Eastern Europe. We therefore are able to scrutinize German responses at a time when leaders were forced to confront the most severe problems posed by migrating Jews; and we may then compare developments in Germany with those in other countries that simultaneously absorbed Eastern Jews. Third, by concentrating on the Second *Reich,* it is possible to study German Jewry during one of its most creative and dynamic periods. For just as Jews in Germany had acquired complete legal emancipation, they were confronted with a series of fresh challenges—not the least of which was the need to absorb foreign coreligionists. By focusing on the era after 1871, we may therefore learn more about the nature and quality of Jewish emancipation in modern Germany.

The present study concludes with the year 1914 because an entirely new chapter in the history of East European Jews in Germany opened during World War I. As a result of new, wartime needs, governments reversed long-standing policies toward such Jews. As soon as the war began, Jewish subjects of enemy states, especially Russia, were either incarcerated or expelled, whereas subjects of allied states such as Austro-Hungary were invited to join the German or Austrian armies. More important, as the war progressed, the government began to recruit East European Jews to help man German industries. Rejecting a decades-old policy of barring foreign Jews from engaging in heavy industry, Germany first sought volunteers and later forced laborers among the Jews of Eastern Europe. By virtue of their status as recruits, their swelled numbers, and their newfound assertiveness, these Eastern Jews raised an entirely new set of issues for German governments and native Jews. This was the genesis of the so-called *Ostjudenfrage* that agitated Germans during and after World War I.[5]

That problem—and indeed the very term *Ostjuden*—does not appear in the pages of this work. For the term *Ostjuden,* though casually imposed onto the entire history of Eastern Jews in Germany, simply was not employed before World War I in reference to foreign Jews residing in the *Reich.* As we shall see, contemporary Germans—both Gentiles and Jews—did not shrink from hurling epithets at Eastern Jews, calling them *"Schnorrers,"* "Pollacks," and "Polish pigs." In public discussions, they employed more neutral terms such as *Ausländer* (foreigners), or they simply referred to the newcomers as Russian or Galician Jews. But the term *Ostjuden* only gained wide currency as a term referring to Eastern Jews *in Germany* when writers began to bemoan the *Ostjudengefahr* (threat) or *Ostjudenfrage* (problem) during World War I. Equally important, this book eschews the term *Ostjuden* because even after it came into vogue, people applied it as a subjective category. Germans decided, often arbitrarily, who was an *Ostjude.* Some native Jews in southern Germany, for example, viewed Prussian coreligionists as *Ostjuden,* a classification that mortified the latter. In short, the term *Ostjuden* is too subjective and anachronistic to serve our purposes.[6]

The present study is concerned with East European Jews—that is, subjects of the Russian Empire, the Austro-Hungarian monarchy, and the Rumanian state. We shall see that foreign nationality proved decisive in deciding the fate of these Jews. Neither epithets nor stereotypes determined how foreigners in general, and Eastern Jews in particular, were treated. Rather, their status in Imperial Germany depended entirely on an objective legal category—citizenship.

By placing such emphasis upon the status of Eastern Jews, this book will focus far more attention on the German environment than on the immigrants themselves: this is a book about the world that integrated Eastern Jews, rather than the lives these Jews made in Germany. One reason for such an emphasis is that, as we shall see, it was not possible for the newcomers to create a vibrant subcommunity with its own distinctive institutions and culture. Rather than inhabit a ghetto world of their own, Eastern Jews either were forced to integrate rapidly into German life or were driven out of the country. It therefore is not possible to write a conventional immigration history for this group.

More important, this book intentionally focuses upon responses to Eastern Jews out of the conviction that the multifaceted issues raised by Jewish immigration illuminate broader themes in the history of Germany and its Jews. The treatment of foreigners in Germany constitutes one such theme. In the postwar era, historians have examined German responses to aliens as a means to understand the aggressive and xenophobic behavior of the Nazi regime. Such research has since taken on greater urgency as the growing population of "guest workers" in the Federal Republic has raised a host of social problems and reawakened latent prejudices toward aliens.[7] In the search for antecedents to contemporary debates over foreign workers, recent works have focused particularly on the importation of recruited Polish laborers during the Imperial era and of forced laborers during both world wars. There are, as we will see, even greater parallels between the tribulations of Eastern European Jews and the trials of *Gastarbeiter* in present-day Germany. For though Jews constituted but a small segment of the total population of foreigners in Imperial Germany, their experience tells us much about the ongoing difficulty of Germans with strangers in their midst.

A second issue raised by our study concerns the pervasiveness and intensity of anti-Semitism in the *Kaiserreich*. This subject has especially preoccupied scholars who have sought the historical origins of Nazi Germany's ferocious anti-Semitism. Some historians have interpreted the actions of German anti-Semites in earlier eras as rehearsals for the Nazi onslaught. Others claim that political anti-Semitism failed during the *Kaiserreich* and only achieved success with the crises brought on by World War I; the Nazi triumph therefore did not represent the culmination of earlier efforts, but a revolutionary break from the failed efforts of earlier political anti-Semites.[8] By examining the treatment of Eastern Jews in Imperial Germany, it is possible to reconsider these questions from a novel vantage point. As foreigners lacking citizenship, Eastern Jews in the *Reich* did not enjoy the same legal protections as their native coreligionists. Their treatment serves as a kind of litmus test that reveals how government officials, and not only parliamentarians, regarded Jews. Feeling free to act with impunity against Jewish aliens, German officials betrayed their stereotypical and biased views of all Jews. An examination of official behavior regarding immigrant Jews reveals a great deal about the spread of anti-Semitism to the highest echelons of government, a development that requires us to reconsider the limits of Jewish acceptance in the era of emancipation. For the vulnerability of foreign Jews raised questions about the security of all Jews in Imperial Germany.

The experience of immigrant Jews also sheds light on German Jewry in other important ways. As noted by the historian Steven Aschheim, the *Ostjude* served as a vital symbol for German Jews: "The power [of *Ostjuden*] as cultural symbols made them essential ingredients of German Jewish self-definition. Their changing image always reflected the complex and often contradictory face of German Jewry."[9] This self-contradictory behavior was expressed through both rejection and idealization of the mythical *Ostjude*. Even more important, it was expressed through complex interactions with very real East European Jews. At times, such encounters resulted in condescending and abusive behavior by German Jews toward their social inferiors from the East; but on the whole, organized German Jewry acted responsibly and charitably toward refugee coreligionists fleeing from Eastern Europe. Contrary to the professed ideology of emancipation encapsulated in the phrase

"German citizens of the Mosaic Persuasion," German Jews exhibited a concern for needy fellow Jews that belied their official indifference to the plight of Jews of foreign nationality. By examining the official responses of organized German Jewry to the influx of East European Jews we have the opportunity to reconsider some of the most widely studied questions of recent German-Jewish historiography: What was the self-definition of German Jewry? And how did emancipation affect Jewish solidarity?

Finally, our account also seeks to place the experience of Eastern Jews in Imperial Germany into a comparative international framework. In the past two decades, Jewish historians have developed a significant literature on the settlement of East European Jews in Western lands.[10] It is now possible to ascertain how German government officials reacted to Jewish mass migration as compared to their counterparts in England, France, and the United States. We can also contrast the immigrant populations of New York's Lower East Side, London's East End, and Paris' Pletzel with the settlements of Eastern Jews in Germany. And we can ascertain whether German Jewry actually treated Jewish immigrants from the East more abusively than did other native Jews. In our concluding chapter, we will begin the necessary process of writing a comparative history of the Jewish mass migration from Eastern Europe, a movement that profoundly reshaped Jewish communities around the world.

In brief, this book aims to shed light on several issues of broader historical importance. It underscores Germany's ongoing difficulties with aliens, East Europeans, "guest" populations, and Jews. And it reexamines the status and self-perception of Jews in pre–Nazi Germany, the politics and posture of emancipated Jews, and the behavior of protected, "privileged" Jews when confronted by vulnerable and less fortunate coreligionists. The experience of East European Jews in Imperial Germany deserves attention because it intersected with some of the most troubling issues in modern German and Jewish history.

I

THE GERMAN STATE

1

The Challenge of Jewish Mass Migration

In the last two years of the 1860s, a few thousand Russian Jews crossed into Prussia seeking relief from cholera epidemics and famines that were wreaking havoc in the western part of the Tsarist Empire. Desperately ill and malnourished, the refugees deluged their German coreligionists with pleas for economic assistance and medical attention. The latter responded by launching numerous ad hoc committees that collected funds throughout Germany and then funneled their receipts to Jewish communities along the frontier; these, in turn, provided relief to the needy. In time, the immediate crisis passed. Many of the Russian Jews remained in Prussia or traveled farther west, some as far as the New World. And the ad hoc committees, convinced that their mission had ended, folded their operations. No contemporary could have anticipated that the Russian refugees of 1868–69 represented the vanguard of a Jewish mass migration from the East that would transform the course of modern Jewish history.[1]

Over the next half-century, the momentum of Jewish emigration from Russia steadily increased. During the 1870s perhaps 40,000 to 50,000 Jews migrated westward. After the pogroms of 1881, however, the trickle turned into a flood as tens of thousands abandoned their homes annually. Victimized by successive pogroms and economic strangulation in the Pale, Russian Jews swept across the frontier, seeking freedom and opportunity in the West. The pace of migration further accelerated when Jews were expelled from Moscow and Saint Petersburg

11

in 1891; and when, at the beginning of the new century, tsarist Russia was wracked, first, by war with Japan and, shortly thereafter, revolution in 1905, a torrent of Jews streamed westward. By the early twentieth century, over 100,000 such refugees emigrated each year, so that by 1914 at least two and a half million Russian Jews had settled in Western countries, including England, France, Canada, Argentina, and principally the United States.[2]

Concurrently, Jews from the Austro-Hungarian Empire and Rumania also were on the move. In the face of economic boycotts and rising unemployment at the end of the nineteenth century, Jews emigrated from the Polish sectors of the Hapsburg Empire. Rumanian Jews, too, made their way west after their country denied them citizenship and introduced blatantly anti-Jewish policies. Between 1870 and the outbreak of World War I, over 400,000 Jews left their homes in the Galician, Bohemian, Moravian, Hungarian, and Rumanian lands to seek a new future in Western countries, while an even larger number migrated *within* the Austro-Hungarian Empire.[3]

Whereas anti-Semitism and impoverization provided the push to drive Jews *from* Eastern Europe, emigrants were also drawn *to* Western lands. They were lured by the promise of economic opportunity in the more industrialized West and the knowledge that their fellow Jews in England, France, Germany, and the New World countries enjoyed comparatively greater freedom and prosperity. The promise of toleration and opportunity, therefore, also attracted adventuresome Jews to seek their fortunes in new environments.[4]

This mass flight created serious problems for Western governments. For one thing, Jewish emigration from the East was unregulated and showed no signs of abating. As a consequence, governments were compelled to reassess the efficacy of existing laws in protecting native populations from undesirable aliens. Moreover, particularly in times of economic crisis, leaders were petitioned by labor and business lobbyists to curb the influx of newcomers, contending that immigrants drained the economy, harmed the interests of native workers, and created a host of social evils. Inevitably, anti-Semites joined the fray by focusing on the distinctively Jewish characteristics of unwanted aliens. Thus, wherever they settled in appreciable numbers, newly arrived Jews from the East sparked far-reaching and disruptive public controversies over attitudes and policies toward aliens.[5]

The German Setting

More than any other country, Germany was vulnerable to Jewish mass migration by virtue of its proximity to the Tsarist and Hapsburg empires. The *Reich* was a natural destination for Jewish emigrants both because most travelers had to pass through it on their way west and also because even penniless refugees could travel to Germany by foot or carriage, whereas one had to book passage on a ship in order to reach England or the New World. German leaders, therefore, could ill afford to ignore Jewish migrants. They were compelled to deal with the problem or risk inundation by a mass migration of Eastern Jews.

In developing policies to cope with this influx, government leaders were constrained by a variety of peculiarly German circumstances. To begin with, political developments at the onset of Jewish mass migration forced leaders to consider new ways of coping with Jewish foreigners. For precisely in the early years of Jewish emigration from Russia, the North German Confederation and, shortly thereafter, the newly unified German Empire granted Jews total legal equality. One consequence of this development was the cancellation of previous disabilities suffered by foreign Jews in Germany. Already on November 1, 1867, the Constitution of the North German League annulled all discriminatory residence laws (Article 3, paragraph 3), such as those directed against itinerant Jewish beggars from abroad. On July 3, 1869, religious discrimination was forbidden, and hence laws that had previously singled out Jews for special treatment were no longer permissible. To cite one casualty of this law, Prussia could not enforce a stipulation in its Jewry Law of 1847 that required foreign Jews—but no other aliens— seeking employment as religious functionaries, artisan apprentices, and house domestics to apply for a special work permit from the Ministry of Interior. Most important, the new *Reich* Citizenship Law of 1871 outlined naturalization procedures applicable to all foreigners, thereby eliminating the special demands placed upon Jews seeking citizenship (Article 7). Thus, the emancipation of German Jewry also benefited foreign Jews in the *Reich,* and required government officials to formulate new policies to cope with unwanted aliens.[6]

In the early 1890s, another legal development further limited the scope of options available to government leaders. After strenuous debates, Germany signed trade agreements with Austro-Hungary and Russia that granted most-favored-nation status to those states. Article 19 of Chancellor Caprivi's controversial new treaty with the Dual Monarchy permitted subjects of Austria to move about freely in Germany and conduct their commercial activities free of harassment. This smoothed the way for the entry of Galician, Bohemian, Moravian, and Hungarian Jews traveling to Germany on business. The 1894 trade treaty with Russia was even more explicit. It stipulated that

> the citizens of both parties of the Treaty . . . are to enjoy the same privileges of trade and business rights as natives *[Inländer].* In the other partner's territory they are to have no greater or lesser restrictions. They should have the same rights, privileges, freedoms, favors, exemptions, as do the citizens of the most favored states.

According to a spokesman for the German Foreign Ministry, these agreements protected subjects of treaty states from wholesale or class discrimination. German states were forbidden to seal their borders to Russians or Austrians as a group; they could only prevent individuals from immigrating. As a result of these commercial pacts, the only way to keep out East European Jews as a class was through passage of a law forbidding all foreign Jews—including those from Western countries—from entering Germany. The *Reich,* however, never enacted such a law, because it would have been impractical to enforce, unfeasible to legislate, and ultimately unnecessary since other measures achieved the desired result.[7]

It was impractical to seal the borders to Jews because Germany had a vested economic interest in allowing Jewish refugees into the *Reich.* For Germany—and especially its shipping companies—hoped to benefit from the lucrative business of transporting Eastern Jews to England and America via the ports of Hamburg and Bremen. The sheer number of Jewish transmigrants embarking from German ports was staggering, exceeding 700,000 during the peak years between 1905 and 1914; in the four years immediately preceding World War I, 128,879 Jewish travelers departed from the port of Hamburg and 102,417 from Bremen. According to one estimate, Jews accounted for half the passengers on Germany's growing commercial fleet, a figure that is not unrealistic when we consider that of the 5.8 million non-Germans who embarked from the North Sea ports between 1871 and 1914, thirty-eight percent were Russians and fifty-one percent were Austrians; Jews constituted a significant portion of the latter and the preponderant majority of the former. Given their desire to expand the *Reich*'s commercial operations and secure Germany's place on the seas, authorities could ill afford to prevent foreign Jews from entering the country.[8]

The extent of German interest in encouraging Jewish transmigrant traffic is illustrated by some of the policies pursued by governments and shipping firms. For example, according to Prussian decrees in force between the 1890s and the outbreak of World War I, no Russian transmigrant was officially allowed into Germany without a proper pass, a ticket for passage out of the country, plus an additional sum of money. (Each person over ten years of age had to posses 400 mark, and children needed 100 mark.) Significantly, individuals holding tickets on German ships were exempted from this rule and permitted into the *Reich* even if they possessed less money. Perhaps the most revealing episode in the campaign to develop the transmigrant traffic occurred in 1893 when the eastern-most states of the *Reich* sealed their borders in response to cholera epidemics in Eastern Europe. Led by the Hamburg America Line, German shipping companies successfully lobbied for a reversal of this policy, arguing that Jewish transmigrants posed no health risk to the German populace. To further allay fears, shipping firms expended significant sums of money to erect special transport centers in key German cities and vast barrack areas in port cities; such facilities were designed to isolate Jewish travelers from the German populace and thereby eliminate objections to the temporary presence of these Jews on German soil. Clearly, German governments and commercial interests were desirous of benefiting from the Jewish traffic. But while they strove to expedite transmigrants through the country, they could not entirely prevent these travelers from serving as a wedge that opened German borders to Jewish immigrants.[9]

In addition to the economic interests that kept Germany's frontiers open to Jews, there was also a practical reason why governments failed to bar Jewish migrants. Put simply, despite several attempts to tighten supervision at the frontiers, German officials could not manage to stem the flow of illegal migrants across the borders; the smuggling of human and other cargo continued unabated despite the best efforts of frontier guards. German officials repeatedly introduced new measures to tighten border controls. In June 1879, the kaiser personally ordered stricter curbs on travelers from Russia; yet three years later, the Prussian minister of interior reported that tighter passport supervision had not prevented a large number of Russians from entering anyway. Briefly, between 1885 and 1890

Germany successfully sealed its eastern borders, but once the government decided to import Polish seasonal workers, it again found it impossible to separate desirable laborers and transmigrants from undesirable aliens seeking to enter the *Reich*. Even though one-tenth of all Prussian *Gendarmes* were stationed at the borders during the hectic period of Russian Jewish emigration in 1904–05, manpower was insufficient to turn back all unwanted refugees. Neither rules requiring workers to carry identification cards nor the threat of six months in prison and a 1,000-mark fine imposed on smugglers dammed the flow of illegal migrants from the East.[10]

Jewish migrants entered the *Reich* illegally because they feared they could not satisfy the demands of German border guards. How many Jews, after all, possessed even enough money to purchase ship tickets, let alone several hundred mark to cover their family's expenses en route? Most emigrants also embarked on their journey without proper travel papers. According to the Russian emigrant Selig Brodetsky, "The cost of a [Russian] passport was about 15 roubles, about 1.10 s. od. per person. One could cross the Atlantic for £5 and later £2, and the additional expenditure for passports was prohibitive, especially as the documents were of little use abroad." Unable to obtain Russian travel documents, Jewish migrants sought ways to enter Germany by stealth.[11]

By their nature, such activities were not well publicized, but memoir literature abounds with examples of Polish Jews who smuggled their way into the *Reich*. Ignatz Waghalter, for instance, recalled in his memoir how, as a poor youth without the means to purchase a passport, he was brought across the Prussian border by professional smugglers; significantly, Waghalter noted that Russian Cossack patrols proved more an obstacle than German border guards. Israel Sieff described his father's entry into Germany hidden among corn sacks. And the most famous illegal immigrant to Germany, Rosa Luxemburg, first crossed into Prussia hidden under straw. Perhaps nothing better highlights the state of affairs than the case of a Russian Jew who insisted on paying smugglers a large sum of money to transport his family across the frontier illicitly, even though all possessed perfectly legal travel papers; when asked why, he replied, dumbfounded, that he thought one entered Prussia only by stealth![12]

The movement of aliens into Germany was facilitated by both professional smugglers and corrupt border guards who were eager to profit from the illegal transport of human cargo across the frontier. But even without the cooperation of guards, one could enter Germany with the aid of the thousands of individuals who regularly traversed the border to conduct their business. The closest supervision could not prevent impoverished Poles and Jews from finding poorly guarded frontier areas. As long as migrants were willing to risk their lives in order to move westward (and a significant number of such travelers died during their passage), sealing the frontier proved impossible.[13]

The consequence of these circumstances was that Germany could not rely upon comprehensive immigration restrictions to stem the flow of Jewish migrants from the East. It was necessary to keep the borders open to Jews both because commercial treaties with the Tsarist and Hapsburg empires mandated freedom of movement for business people and because the *Reich*'s economic interests were served by permitting Jewish transmigrants to enter the country in order to sail on

German ships. In addition, it was impossible to seal the frontier in such a manner that smuggling would cease. And finally, as we shall see, governments opposed efforts to legislate a ban solely on Jewish immigration. Thus, Germany was forced to find other means to control the influx of Eastern Jews.

The Role of State Bureaucracies

The burden of coping with the Jewish mass migration fell upon government administrators in the individual German states *(Länder)*, the authorities empowered by law to regulate resident aliens in the *Reich*. According to Germany's constitution, matters of citizenship came under the jurisdiction of each *Land:* state officials, therefore, could naturalize aliens as well as strip natives of their citizenship. Moreover, state governments enjoyed wide latitude in supervising the activities of foreigners inhabiting their territories. Despite continuing efforts to centralize and coordinate policies toward foreigners on a national level, the status of East European Jews and all other aliens in Germany was fundamentally determined by administrative bureaucracies in the various German states.

Not surprisingly, in view of Imperial Germany's highly bureacratic structure, the regulation of foreigners was overseen by a hierarchy of officials in every state. At the apex of each bureaucracy stood the minister of interior, assisted by ministerial underlings. The minister, in collaboration with colleagues holding other portfolios in the state government, as well as his counterparts in other *Länder*, designed policies toward foreigners and supervised the execution of his directives: his ministry interpreted laws, formulated measures to curb aliens, and served as the final arbiter when the case of a particular foreigner was appealed. Officials in ministries of interior then transmitted directives to provincial governors, who in turn communicated with regional officials. And at the bottom of this structure, a host of local police and juridical authorities carried out policies on a day-to-day basis. While the titles bestowed upon officials varied from one state to the next, and the extent of state supervision differed depending on the size of the state and its population of aliens, bureaucrats and police officials governed the lives of foreigners throughout the *Reich*.[14]

From the moment foreigners set foot on German soil, they were subject to the orders of state authorities. As noted above, a variety of regulations determined whether an alien was permitted to cross the border: *Gendarmes* barred certain categories of aliens and required passports, identification cards, and other kinds of papers from prospective travelers. Once permitted to enter the country, aliens remained under tight supervision throughout their stay. At each stop of their journey, they were expected to notify local police officials of their whereabouts and were compelled to obtain an official residence permit, which varied in duration from a few days to years. State laws required aliens to inform police whenever they changed their place of residence in a locality or moved out of the area. Such regulations facilitated police surveillance of foreigners, an extensive enterprise in Imperial Germany, and provided readily available information on the whereabouts of all foreigners. Equally important, local authorities could curb foreigners simply by failing to renew their residence permits. Without such documents, foreigners were subject to immediate expulsion from a state.[15]

Once they had obtained the proper authorization, foreigners were restricted by a wide range of laws and policies limiting their freedom of action. These included curbs on the occupations and economic activities of certain categories of aliens either within an entire state or solely in certain territories of a state. In some areas, local ordinances even required employers to seek native workers rather than hire noncitizens. Furthermore, the social and political activities of foreigners were regulated. To cite but two examples: laws of public assembly forbade groups from conducting public meetings in a language other than German, and other laws prevented aliens from participating in any way in the German political process.[16]

State authorities assumed additional influence over the lives of foreign residents by virtue of their jurisdiction over matters of citizenship. The *Reich*'s 1871 "Law Regarding the Acquisition and Loss of Citizenship" empowered German states to grant naturalization and also deprive a native of his citizenship. In truth, German nationality was defined by citizenship in a particular state (Article 1), and hence it was more accurate to speak of Bavarian or Prussian citizens than of German citizenship. The law of 1871 outlined three methods for acquiring citizenship: First, foreign women married to Germans automatically assumed the nationality of their husbands (Article 5). (Conversely, German women lost their citizenship upon marrying a foreigner [Article 13, section 5].) Second, a foreigner holding a federal, state, or local administrative office or doing service for a church, school, or community automatically was eligible for naturalization (Article 9). And, third, foreigners could also apply for citizenship to the local district or provincial administration provided that they supplied proof of the following: their freedom to become a German under the law of their country of origin, their ownership of a home in the district where they applied, their unblemished civic record, and their ability to support all dependents (Article 9). In contrast to the first two methods, which provided for almost automatic naturalization, the latter process necessitated a longer naturalization procedure; the law, however, did not require a minimum period of residence prior to the acquisition of citizenship.[17]

On the surface, Germany's naturalization laws set forth rather straightforward means to acquire citizenship; in reality, however, it proved exceedingly difficult for some categories of foreign residents to become Germans. For by empowering states to administer naturalization procedures, the law insured a highly decentralized and potentially arbitrary administration of citizenship policies. Each state wielded wide discretionary powers to bestow citizenship as it saw fit. As one ministerial official noted candidly in a private letter, "It is recognized that [stipulations in the naturalization law] represent the minimal qualifications and that it remains for the various states to impose even stricter requirements for naturalization." As a consequence, it was not unusual for state governments to reject naturalization applications from aliens who had resided in Germany for *decades*.[18]

As long as a foreigner lacked citizenship in Germany, he or she was vulnerable to the most potent measure available to state governments—expulsion. German states were empowered by law to expel aliens who participated in criminal activities such as gambling or pimping, or engaged in any behavior that endan-

gered "public interests" or "security." Taking full advantage of this vague formulation, government officials expelled any alien they deemed *lästig*—troublesome. Since the latter was a highly subjective category, officials enjoyed the freedom
to expel anyone they defined as "troublesome." During the course of the Imperial
era, tens of thousands of temporary residents in Germany were issued expulsion
orders when a local official decided that their presence was no longer desirable;
thousands more were driven from the country in periodic *mass* expulsions that
punctuated the history of modern Germany.[19]

The resort to expulsion is perhaps the most blatant indication of the extent to
which state governments during the Imperial era continued to rely upon a structure
for coping with aliens that had existed for centuries prior to German unification.
Under the federal system established by Bismarck, individual states retained their
prerogatives to supervise matters of citizenship and define policies toward aliens
in their midst; the federal government, by contrast, enjoyed only minimal jurisdiction over such matters. Furthermore, when they exercised authority over foreigners, states employed traditional instruments of policy: they policed the activities
of foreigners by requiring aliens to obtain residence permits, they discouraged
immigration by making it difficult to acquire naturalization, and they controlled
foreign populations by subjecting unwanted aliens to expulsion. Thus, government
officials could rely upon traditional measures to curb aliens; the challenge, however, was to formulate differentiated policies to deal with the diverse populations
of foreigners in the *Reich*.

Alien Populations in Imperial Germany

In setting their policies to cope with East European Jews, state authorities did not
work in a vacuum. Germany, after all, contained a significant population of foreigners, with the preponderant majority—over ninety percent—not Jewish. In addition, Jews represented only a small contingent within the massive population of
East Europeans in the *Reich*. It would appear, therefore, that governments could
simply apply the same policies to Jews from the East that they had devised to
control the far larger population of Polish Catholics. And, in truth, Jewish and
Gentile foreigners in Imperial Germany often were regulated by the same policies.
But the differences in the treatment of East European Jews and other aliens were
even more pronounced. To understand how and why this was the case, we must
first examine the general condition of foreigners in Imperial Germany.

For much of the nineteenth century, government officials were more preoccupied with the loss of Germans through emigration than by the increase of foreigners through immigration. The arrival of newcomers in Germany barely offset the
population loss sustained when natives abandoned their homes to seek opportunities in the New World. Matters began to change only in the closing decades of
the century. Between 1871 and 1875, Germany gained 75,000 more inhabitants
through migration than it lost. After a brief hiatus during the ensuing years of
economic dislocation, immigration once again gained momentum. From 1885 to
1910, the excess of immigrants over emigrants grew to half a million. In absolute

terms, the alien population increased from 270,000 in 1871 to 1,260,000 by 1910, the time of the last prewar census. (Since the census was conducted in December, a time when many seasonal workers were required to return temporarily to their homelands, these figures understate the actual size of foreign populations in the *Reich*.) The preponderant majority of these aliens were drawn from the Austro-Hungarian Empire (667,000 in 1910), followed by the Netherlands (144,000), Russia (138,000), and Italy (104,000). But given the overwhelmingly Slavic character of Germany's alien population, discussions about foreigners focused mainly upon Poles.[20]

The causes for Polish migration to the *Reich* were largely economic. It has been estimated that an industrial worker in Russian Poland earned an average wage twenty-five percent lower than the poorest-paid workers in Germany, Silesian coal miners. Yet, while economic hardship impelled some Poles to migrate, new economic opportunities also drew them to Germany. During the last decades of the nineteenth century, a labor vacuum developed in the *Reich* due to the loss of German workers to overseas migration. Especially in the agricultural northeast of Prussia and in industrial zones of the Ruhr, a critical labor shortage arose. Facing economic catastrophe, captains of industry and government leaders concluded that only cheap and abundant foreign workers could satisfy Germany's labor needs. They therefore launched a massive program to import seasonal workers.[21]

This policy is stunning when we consider the nationality of the recruits. Initially after German unification, the majority came from West European countries—especially Italy, Holland, Switzerland, and France. By 1880, however, half were drawn from the Austro-Hungarian and Russian empires, and by the first decade of the twentieth century, these empires contributed close to seventy-five percent of the foreigners in the *Reich*. Remarkably, all this occurred while Germany was simultaneously waging a campaign to *reduce* Polish influence! Yet even as Germany grappled with its "Polish Problem," it recruited hundreds of thousands of Polish workers. Moreover, these laborers were channeled to precisely the areas that long had been the locus of a determined Germanization policy. And the final irony was that the very Junkers and industrialists who displayed such pronounced anti-Polish and xenophobic tendencies lobbied hardest for the importation of foreign workers from the East.[22]

By importing Slavic workers, Germany exacerbated its already severe "Polish Problem." Roughly ten percent of Prussia's citizens at any time between 1870 and 1910 were Polish speakers. In Germany, as a whole, Poles accounted for five percent of the citizenry. These Poles of Prussian citizenship were then augmented by a vast number of Russian and Austrian subjects who were recruited as seasonal laborers. While originally confined to the four eastern provinces of Prussia, they quickly penetrated into western parts of the *Reich*. The handful of Poles in Rhineland-Westphalia in 1880 grew to 30,000 a decade later; and in 1910 they numbered between 300,000 and 420,000 souls. Taken together, this huge population of Polish-speaking Prussian citizens combined with imported Slavic workers became the object of German national fears.[23]

From the earliest years of the empire, governments introduced measures to weaken Polish national sentiment. The *Kulturkampf* launched in July 1871 was in part directed at the large Polish-speaking Catholic population of Prussia. During the years of this struggle, schools located in Polish-speaking areas were reformed. In 1873, for example, provincial governors began to require the employment of German as the language of instruction in *Volksschulen*. A more vigorous Germanization policy was launched in 1885–86: after expelling 20,000 unnaturalized Poles, Prussia established a land purchase commission to buy up Polish-owned estates and then turn properties over to German settlers. Initially, the government earmarked one hundred million mark for this scheme, but by 1913 it added over a half billion more mark to the fund. The government also fostered Germanization by expropriating properties owned by Prussian Poles, preventing Poles from working on construction sites in Prussia, and granting economic inducements to German settlers. These policies were eventually also extended to western parts of Germany when, in 1899, Polish miners were required to demonstrate their proficiency in German in order to get a job in the Ruhr. Thus, language too became a weapon in the nationality struggle. Gradually, Polish was no longer accepted as a legitimate language in court proceedings, commercial transactions, educational programs, or civic meetings. (The Prussian *Landtag* even debated whether postal workers were required to deliver mail addressed in Polish.) In sum, this Germanization policy was nothing less than a repudiation of the constitutional equality granted to all Prussians since the state encouraged discrimination against its Polish-speaking citizens.[24]

Not surprisingly, seasonal workers imported from Galicia and Russia fared even worse than Prussian Poles, for their legal status as aliens provided even less protection from anti-Polish campaigns. Within a decade and a half after German unification, Prussia ruthlessly expelled 20,000 Poles. Thereafter, governments imposed strict controls on Polish migrants. After deciding that Germany needed such laborers, the Prussian cabinet agreed to admit Poles only on a seasonal basis, stipulating that they could sojourn in the country only from April to November, and for the rest of each year they had to return to their homes across the frontier. Though governments subsequently shortened this period of forced repatriation, the general policy of admitting Poles only on a seasonal basis remained in effect. Furthermore, governments prevented seasonal workers from taking advantage of Germany's insatiable labor needs by strictly supervising the recruitment of workers in such a manner that it was possible to ferret out anyone who attempted to change jobs in order to boost his wages. Through such measures, state officials attempted to balance the contradictory demands of nationalism and economic self-interest: they admitted East Europeans only under strict supervision and on the condition that Poles would remain in the country temporarily; they tolerated Poles as seasonal workers, but not as immigrants.[25]

The foregoing remarks on the condition of Polish migrants in Germany help clarify how the experience of East European Jews and Gentiles in the *Reich* differed. To begin with the most critical distinction, the two groups played entirely different economic roles. Whereas Gentiles from Russia, Poland, and the Austro-Hungarian lands were admitted to Germany for their economic utility, Eastern Jews generally were defined as "troublesome." Catholic Poles were primarily agricultural and industrial workers recruited by German agents in Russia and Galicia. East European Jews, by contrast, migrated westward on their own and did not engage in heavy labor. In fact, German recruiters in the East were ordered to shun Jewish volunteers. Moreover, in the *Reich,* officials subjected Polish seasonal laborers to numerous work rules and regulations—none of which applied to Jews. Very simply, however much Germans disliked Poles, they needed them to facilitate agricultural and industrial production. East European Jews, by contrast, were judged incapable of hard labor—and, for that matter, were deemed too lazy to do any serious work. According to a common stereotype repeated by the police commissioner of Berlin, Eastern Jews earn a living through "haggling and begging, and have an aversion to every sort of respectable work."[26]

Perhaps nothing better highlights the divergent experiences of Catholic Poles and Eastern Jews in Germany than the fact that the very Junkers and industrialists who lobbied most actively for the admission of Polish seasonal workers supported measures to seal German frontiers to foreign Jews and expel those already in the country. Also, the areas that imported the largest number of Polish workers, Prussia's eastern provinces, barred foreign Jews with greater stringency than any other areas in the entire *Reich.* The economic utility of Polish workers clearly set them apart from East European Jews and necessitated a different government policy toward each group.[27]

Equally important, the two groups also differed in the types of residence each sought. Whereas most Poles were seasonal workers who resided in Germany only on a temporary basis and returned to their homelands annually, Eastern Jews constituted a far more variegated population, one that included four distinct subgroups: (1) the largest by far consisted of transmigrants who moved through Germany in ever-increasing numbers on their way from Russia, Rumania, and Austro-Hungary to other Western lands; (2) a second group was made up of transients who sought to remain in the country temporarily, either to find work, to absorb German culture, or to raise funds by begging for help from German Jews; (3) still another distinct group was formed by young Jews from the East who studied in Germany's renowned institutions of higher learning; (4) and, finally, immigrant Jews attempted to establish themselves as permanent residents, and even citizens, of the *Reich.* By contrast, those Gentiles from Eastern Europe who arrived in Germany as transmigrants, transients, students, and immigrants—and there certainly were Poles, Russians, Austro-Hungarians, and Rumanians in each of these categories—were overshadowed by the far larger populations of Prussian Poles and Slavic seasonal workers.

Existing government policies toward aliens in general, and toward Poles in particular, simply could not cope with the multiple and distinctive questions raised by foreign Jews in Germany: How could officials encourage Jews to transmigrate through the *Reich* from Russia, Austro-Hungary, and Rumania on their way west, yet at the same time bar such travelers from lingering and even settling in the country? By what mechanisms could governments filter out undesirable "troublemakers" from the population of Eastern Jews who resided in Germany temporarily as legitimate business people, students, and intellectuals? Would the relatively large representation of Russian Jews at German institutions of higher learning harm the quality of those schools, or would it enrich the process of education by adding diversity to the student body? And how could governments determine whether potential Jewish immigrants would prove an asset to Germany by virtue of their skills and knowledge, or a burdensome population of unproductive and unassimil- able foreigners? The arrival of East European Jews in the Second *Reich* challenged German leaders to address these difficult questions.

2

Public Debates Over
Eastern Jews

The multifaceted questions raised by Jewish migrants from Eastern Europe attracted considerable public attention throughout the history of the Second Empire. Given the dimensions of this mass migration and the attendant problems it created, it is understandable that German political and government leaders should have devoted attention to East European Jews: after all, no sovereign state can permit the unregulated movement of tens and even hundreds of thousands of foreigners across its national frontiers; and no responsible government can ignore the presence of migrants who seek to do business, acquire an education, or find permanent haven within its territory. But as public debates unfolded, it became clear that the objective issues raised by Jewish migrants were confused with a variety of subjective German fears and concerns. To begin with, the thinking of responsible officials was colored by stereotypical perceptions of Eastern Jews: government officials viewed such Jews through the prism of prejudice and bigotry, thereby reducing chances for a thoughtful and dispassionate resolution to the problems posed by Jewish migrants. Second, it proved virtually impossible in public discussions to separate the question of Jewish migration from Germany's broader "Jewish Problem"; debates over Eastern Jews invariably deteriorated into freewheeling anti-Semitic attacks upon all Jews. And, third, once the issue of Jewish migration was injected into the public arena, it became entangled with a variety of other political and economic considerations. To understand the nature of public discourse over

Jewish immigration, we must begin by sketching the political context of debates over Eastern Jews.

The Terms of Debate

Official Pronouncements

The terms of debate about East European Jews in Germany were set by government officials who, both in private meetings and public debates, explicitly characterized such migrants as an "unwanted element." In the perception of German cabinet ministers, migrant Jews constituted a "nuisance" *(Landplage)* because they swarmed across the border and required constant supervision.[1] But this relatively restrained, albeit irritated, response to Eastern Jews often gave way to ugly denunciations and dire warnings uttered by Germany's highest officials. Chancellors, cabinet ministers, state bureaucrats, and parliamentarians castigated Eastern Jews as a threat to Germany. The danger, according to official views, lay not only in the sheer quantity of emigrating Eastern Jews, but in the quality of these migrants. German leaders thereby defined the problem of Eastern Jews as a matter that went far beyond supervising and controlling an unregulated migration; rather, they represented their task as an act of saving their country from a horde of dangerous invaders bent on subverting the economic, political, and social life of the *Reich.*

The propensity of government leaders to stereotype Eastern Jews as a menace was evident already in the public and private comments of the Empire's first chancellor, Otto von Bismarck. In one of his first public addresses, he declared before the United Diet on June 26, 1847, that Russian Jews threatened to migrate into Germany in massive numbers. In later years, he stressed the lack of "German education" *(Bildung)* of those who "come here to enrich themselves." Bismarck also viewed Jews still in the East as "one of the three elements in Russia which agitate for war: the press, the Poles, and the Jews. The press only insofar as it is influenced by Poles and Jews, or is served by them. The Jews who in the Russian press and elsewhere participate in the cry for war. . . ." In these few public remarks, and his more frequent private comments on the dangers posed by Jews from the East, Bismarck adumbrated many of the major charges that were to be hurled against Eastern Jews during the history of the Empire: he portrayed such Jews as backward, prone to political subversiveness, and motivated to immigrate solely by the desire for financial gain in Germany; and he pictured such Jews as ever poised to pour across the German frontier.[2]

Bismarck's cabinet ministers further elaborated upon these themes. They justified expulsions of foreign Jews from Berlin in 1884 on the grounds that Jewish refugees were bearers of "Nihilistic" and social democratic ideologies. Robert von Puttkamer, Prussia's minister of interior, informed the Reichstag that Jews and Poles deserved expulsion "in consideration of the political security of our states . . . and in order to care for the German essence and culture." In the 1880s, government officials routinely depicted Polish Jews as deserters, renegades, traitors. As Puttkamer put it, not only have they already abandoned Russia, but they will also refuse to serve Germany, especially its army. Thus, during the Bismarckian era, government officials publicly denounced Eastern Jews in stereotypical terms, picturing them as untrustworthy deserters and revolutionaries, on the one hand, and as beggars, on the other.[3]

Although such perceptions hardly disappeared, German leaders muted their criticism of Eastern Jews during the last decade of the nineteenth century. The change in tone had much to do with domestic considerations: The 1890s were a time when governments sought to rally support for commercial treaties with the Hapsburg and Tsarist empires that would facilitate the free movement of foreign merchants in Germany; accordingly, this was hardly the time to inflame public opinion against East Europeans. In addition, it was during this period that governments embarked on a program to recruit foreign seasonal workers; it was therefore advantageous to downplay xenophobia. Moreover, the population of immigrant Jews in the *Reich* had only recently been reduced significantly by severe expulsions during the mid-1880s, and consequently such Jews posed less of an objective problem.[4]

By the early years of the new century, official attitudes changed dramatically. In response to the upsurge of revolutionary activities in Russia that culminated in 1905, German leaders grew increasingly anxious. Cabinet ministers advised the Reichstag of the anarchistic and revolutionary propensities of Russian Jewish students. Chancellor von Bülow lumped all such students together with "Mandelstamm and Silberfarb," two well-known Russian Jews recently expelled from Berlin for revolutionary activities. And government officials routinely linked foreign Jewish students with "bomb throwing," anarchism, and revolution. In a letter to his cousin "Nicky," the kaiser affirmed his conviction that Jews were "the leaders of the revolt" against the tsar. Echoing these views in public, Prussia's minister of interior, Bethmann-Hollweg, stated in the Prussian Diet that only the blind do not recognize "the passive and active role of the Jews in the Russian revolution." As the historian Robert C. Williams concluded, "For many Germans, 'Russian,' 'radical,' and 'eastern Jew' became linked together after 1905 as a single type of undesirable."[5]

Although Russian Jews were especially associated with radicalism during this period, images of Eastern Jews as beggars persisted. Chancellor von Bülow, in fact, fused the two stereotypes when he warned in a Reichstag address of February 29, 1904, that Germany "will not be led by the nose by such *Schnorrers* and conspirators." Other politicians urging harsher treatment of Jewish immigrants also utilized these stereotypes. "Pushy beggars" and "Galician *Schnorrers*" were widely employed code words for Eastern Jews in Imperial Germany.[6]

The association of Jews with begging led government officials to assume that Jewish *Schnorrers* carried diseases and epidemics into Germany. Almost from the onset of Jewish mass migration, authorities took steps to protect Germans from Jewish travelers from the East. In 1882, they ordered all future transmigrants to undergo delousing prior to their entering the country. Eventually, even train carriages carrying Jewish migrants were ordered steamed after every trip between the eastern frontier and German ports. And officials arranged for the speedy passage of migrants through the country in sealed trains that stopped only in designated and quarantined station areas. Yet even with these precautions, when epidemics did strike in German cities, Eastern Jews drew the blame. After a cholera epidemic in Hamburg, local authorities introduced new regulations in 1892 that forbade the housing of transmigrants in Hamburg proper and required the construction of special barracks far removed from other port facilities. Such steps were taken despite the findings of Hamburg's senate that absolved transmigrants of responsibility for the epidemics. "Polish Jews" were also held responsible for an epidemic that struck two years later in Marburg, even though no Eastern Jews had passed through the city for months prior to the outbreak. Perceptions, however, proved more significant than the reality and, accordingly, government officials continued to link Eastern Jews with vermin and plague—an association that was to have a long and catastrophic history in Germany.[7]

While it is well known that anti-Semites in Germany employed stereotypes depicting Eastern Jews—and, for that matter, all Jews—as "*Schnorrers* and conspirators," the participation of government officials in broadcasting these images has received less attention. It is therefore appropriate to inquire as to the significance of such intemperate official pronouncements about Eastern Jews. To begin with, it must be stated that officials did not invent these stereotypes; rather, they drew upon existing perceptions and fears. German cartoonists and wits routinely invoked stereotypes of Eastern Jews as beggars, opportunists, and revolutionaries to liven up their humorous sketches. In publicly denouncing Eastern Jews as *Schnorrers*, government officials thus echoed well-established views about the nature of such Jews.[8]

This is not to suggest that German leaders merely invoked stereotypes in order to manipulate public opinion and to rally popular support for their policies toward such Jews. On the contrary, there is ample evidence to suggest that officials sincerely believed that Eastern Jews constituted a menace and were unsavory characters. In private meetings and correspondence, they routinely referred to Eastern Jews as "troublesome," "undesirable," and a "danger." When, for example, the Prussian cabinet met in 1905 to discuss recent revolutionary developments in Russia and to determine official policies toward Russian immigrants and students residing in Berlin, not one minister demurred from the repeated assertions that such Jews were fundamentally radicals; the political subversiveness of Russian Jews was simply taken for granted. Similar assumptions are evident in government correspondence over the proper disposition of cases involving foreigners. Departing from their usual dry and matter-of-fact bureaucratic style, officials frequently incorporated judgmental remarks about Eastern Jews in their memoranda. We have already referred to the Berlin police commissioner's assertion that Russian Jews regularly engaged in haggling and avoided respectable work; other officials interjected remarks in their reports that highlighted the need to protect native Germans "from further damage by foreign Jews," and warned of the "danger of being flooded with the culturally and economically lowest Jewish element that grows in neighboring countries." These few examples must stand for many other unflattering references scattered throughout official papers. They illustrate the extent to which government officials were captives of stereotypical thinking.[9]

To be sure, such bigotry was not directed exclusively at Jews from the East; government leaders frequently expressed themselves in xenophobic and stereotypical terms when they spoke about all foreigners—and especially when they described Poles. In fact, they often applied similar stereotypes to Gentiles and Jews from Eastern Europe. Government spokesmen described both groups as products of the backward East, speakers of inferior languages, and elements of subversion. Count Herbert Bismarck's statement that "Polish is not a language of culture *[keine Kultursprache]* like German" summed up feelings about the Yiddish language as well; and references to the Polish language as "wretchedly degenerate," "an unviable product," and "an inferior sort of tongue" could be applied equally to Yiddish, according to German bigots. Yet, whereas both groups of East Europeans suffered from the contempt of German leaders, the latter still regarded Catholic Poles and Eastern Jews as distinct groups. Despite their alleged similarities in cultural outlook and political radicalism, they were assigned different economic roles: Poles, with their brute strength, deserved to be exploited as imported laborers. Eastern Jews, by contrast, were characterized as exploiters; they were regarded as parasitical *Schnorrers.*[10]

Perhaps the most important aspect of such stereotyping lay not in the fact that government officials succumbed to prejudice, but that they freely aired their views in public. Instead of seeking to calm fears and allay suspicions, the responsible leaders of Germany vented their irrational prejudices. By so doing, they lent credibility to prevailing stereotypes of Eastern Jews and, even more important, legitimized the act of publicly defaming the character of such Jews. The bigoted approach of government leaders reduced chances for a judicious and fair resolution to the problem of Jewish migration because it defined Eastern Jews as a menace to the physical, economic, and political health of German society. Through their intemperate public remarks, government leaders fostered an air of hysteria, rather than calm. Their scare tactics set the tone for public debate over Eastern Jews.

The Strategy of Anti-Semites

Public discourse about Jewish mass migration was further inflamed by the rhetoric of outspoken anti-Semites. Opponents of Jewish equality, after all, could not ignore the movement of vast numbers of foreign Jews through the *Reich,* for if they regarded native Jews as a menace, they surely would oppose a wave of migration that threatened to enlarge the population of Jews in Germany. Not surprisingly, anti-Semitic publicists and politicians mounted a campaign of vilification against Eastern Jews. This campaign, however, added several new components to the public debate over Eastern Jews.

One of the first, and certainly most influential, anti-Semites to address the issue of Jewish immigration from the East was the distinguished German historian Heinrich von Treitschke. At the height of a major resurgence of anti-Semitism, Treitschke lent his academic prestige, his influence as editor of a respected journal, and his considerable polemical skills to a wide-ranging critique of Jews in Germany, both natives and foreigners. Treitschke launched his attack in articles published between November 1879 and January 1880 in the *Preussische Jahr-bücher*.[11] From the outset he hammered away at his key theme:

> What we demand from our Jewish fellow-citizens is simple: that they become Germans, regard themselves simply as Germans, without prejudice to their faith.

The sins of German Jewry included cupidity, materialism, dishonest business practices, undue influence on the German press, and, most significantly, alienation from German culture.

> Ours is a young nation. Our country still lacks national style, instinctive pride, a firmly developed individuality; that is the reason why we are defenseless against alien manners for so long. But we are in the process of acquiring these qualities, and we can only wish that our Jews recognize in time the change which is now occurring in Germany. . . .

Treitschke demanded that all German Jews become German. He recognized, however, that "there will always be Jews who are nothing else but German-speaking Orientals."

In the course of this powerful challenge hurled at German Jewry, Treitschke injected the issue of Jewish immigration.

> Our country is invaded year after year by multitudes of assiduous trouser-selling youths from the inexhaustible cradle of Poland, whose children and grandchildren are to be the future rulers of Germany's exchanges and press. This immigration grows visibly in numbers and the question becomes more and more serious how this alien nation can be assimilated. . . . We Germans . . . have to deal with Jews of the Polish branch, which bears deep scars of centuries of Christian tyranny. According to experience, they are alien to the European, and especially to the German national character.

In these brief sentences, and in subsequent articles, Treitschke elaborated upon the prevailing critique of East European Jews by stressing their insatiable economic and social opportunism. His image of poor immigrant Jews intent on rapidly enriching themselves at Germany's expense was particularly disturbing. Compared to these exploitative foreign invaders, *Schnorrers* seemed almost benign; for Treitschke's "trouser-sellers" were obsessed with the goal of climbing to the pinnacle of wealth and power while trampling Germans underfoot along the way.

Yet how, we may ask, could Treitschke predict the future success of Polish Jews in the *Reich?* How could the *Praeceptor Germanie* confidently state that the "children and grandchildren" of Jews currently immigrating from the East would ultimately reign as "the future rulers of Germany's exchanges and press"? Why should he have prophesied such a development? In truth, the historian was not foretelling the future, but describing the present. From Treitschke's perspective, Polish Jews already *were* active in German banking and journalism. The Jews in question, however, were not recent immigrants from the East, but former residents of Prussia's eastern provinces who had migrated from Posen to Germany's expanding cities. These upstarts, the geographically and socioeconomically mobile elements of *German* Jewry, were the targets of Treitschke's withering critique.

By linking these German Jews with trouser-peddlers from the East, Treitschke

could substantiate his broader contentions about the fundamentally alien and un-
assimilable character of native Jewry. He therefore repeatedly strove to depict
German Jews as recent immigrants from Poland. Writing about the differences
between Jews in the *Reich* as compared to those in England and France, he described the latter as primarily of Spanish descent, whereas "we Germans . . .
have to deal with Jews of the Polish branch." Responding to the Prussian Diet's
debate over a widely disseminated Anti-Semitic Petition, he wrote on December
10, 1880, that "the limitation of Jewish immigration would be a palliative of only
little efficacy," for the true problem lay in the alien nature of *German Jews.*
Treitschke stated his position most explicitly in his final rejoinder to his critics. In
an article entitled "The Jewish Immigration in Prussia," published in 1883, he
repeatedly identified Posen and Russian Jews as the same entity. He concluded
that there has been "during the past decades a strong movement from East to
West by Polish Jews of Prussia, Austria, and Russia," thus reiterating his contention that Prussian Jews were as Polish as their Austrian and Russian coreligionists.
In this regard, Treitschke the polemicist merely expanded upon his own earlier
historical writings, for in his *History of Germany in the Nineteenth Century,* he
had already described Jews residing in Posen during the first half of the century
as "mostly of Polish origin." "There was nothing German about these people
with their stinking caftans and their obligatory lovelocks, except their detestable
speech." [12]

Treitschke's intentional confusion of East Prussian with Polish Jews was well
understood by his German defenders. When the Jewish statistician Solomon Neumann marshalled data to refute Treitschke's allegations about massive Jewish immigration to Germany prior to 1880, the noted political economist Adolf Wagner
argued that Neumann had entirely missed the point; concern about Jewish migration stems from the movement of Jews from "eastern parts of Germany." Similarly, the anti-Semitic historian of Posen, Eugen von Bergmann, also wrote of
"Polish Jews" from Posen and West Prussia, and he too blurred the lines between
Jewish citizens of Prussia and Polish Jews. Defenders of Treitschke, then, recognized the true meaning of his emphasis on the Polishness of German Jews. [13]

Treitschke's remarks about the character of Eastern and German Jews inspired
numerous imitators. In the three decades after the historian's essay appeared—
and, indeed, into the Nazi era—anti-Semitic writers embellished his image of
rapacious Eastern Jews. To cite just a few examples: In 1895, a member of the
Center Party, Deputy Euler, informed the Reichstag of Jews "who formerly collected rags in Russia and then came to Germany and took only the golden and
silver types of jobs, rarely touching the copper and nickel ones." During debates
over a pending trade treaty, another deputy referred to "Jewish businessmen who
first came across the borders as peddlers with a sack on their shoulders, but who,
in a few years, have not only been naturalized by us, but also have enriched
themselves at our expense." The *Badische Landeszeitung* employed similar imagery when it decried the disproportionate role played in Berlin's social and medical circles by Jews who "immigrated as adventurers from Poland and Russia."
And, in the *Preussische Jahrbücher,* Robert Hessen wrote about the typical cycle
that occurs regularly in eastern Germany: when German Jews migrate westward,

their pants-selling coreligionists are lured from the East to fill the vacuum; with the aid of native Jews, the new immigrants establish themselves; and when they in time migrate to western Germany, a new wave of Polish Jews will fill their places. Thus, in the decades after Treitschke's polemic against Jewish immigration, "trouser-selling youths" from Poland developed an increasingly well-defined profile in the imagination of anti-Semites.[14]

The historian's identification of German Jews as thinly disguised Polish *Schnorrers* also entered the stock repertoire of anti-Semites. Perhaps the most elaborate explication of this allegation was penned by a pseudonymous author, now thought to have been Morritz Busch, Bismarck's press secretary. Taking up Treitschke's theme, the author provided the following account of how Eastern Jews operate in Germany: "At first they are mostly beggars, hawkers, or hustlers, supported by German Jews who facilitate their entry into the used-rag business." Gradually, these Jews rise in class and occupation by engaging in cutthroat and crooked business practices. They heed Moses Mendelssohn's advice and acquire an education *[Bildung]* for themselves and their children—not for the sake of learning, but to "play at being Germans." If their sons do not achieve success, then certainly their grandsons become big bankers and marry into the nobility. "Scratch the gold baron, the intellectual, the journalist, the cultured lady . . . and in ninety-nine out of one hundred cases you will find a true, old, dirty Semite." Germany, therefore, must protect itself against the alien "who transforms himself from a 'Pollak' " Jew and in time becomes not only a German Jew, but a German of the Mosaic Persuasion.[15]

The significance of this Treitschke-like imagery lies in its utility as a weapon in the anti-Semitic struggle against German Jews. Anti-Semites, after all, aimed to undermine Jewish legal equality on the grounds that native-born Jews constituted a group fundamentally alien to Germany. What better way of achieving this goal than by portraying German Jews as Polish immigrants in masquerade? For once the two groups were linked, it was possible to associate the characteristics of one group with the other. And, in practice, this is precisely what anti-Semites did: Even as they accused native Jews of economic crimes—cheating, manipulation, and exploitation—they pointed to foreign *Schnorrers* who either sponged off the local economy or rose from rag-peddling to riches. Even as they charged native Jews with support for parties of the Left, they portrayed Eastern Jews as revolutionaries. And even as they pictured Jews in Germany as aliens, "Orientals," and "Asiatics," they ridiculed Eastern Jews who spoke an allegedly corrupted form of German and arrived as foreigners from the East. Pointing at Eastern Jews, German anti-Semites claimed to have discovered the true nature of all Jews: scratch away the thin veneer of German culture, they crowed, and you will find that Germans of the Mosaic Persuasion actually are barely disguised Polish Jews. Caricaturists explicitly portrayed this hidden truth by depicting the "metamorphosis" of the Polish rag-peddler "Moische Pisch": upon entering Germany, this mythical quick-change artist transformed himself into the haberdasher "Moritz Wasserstrahl"; and then, when he had sufficiently enriched himself in the *Reich,* he moved on to France in order to open a house of couture under the name "Maurice LaFontaine"! Beware of the external pose assumed by Jews, warned anti-Semites, for underneath their superficial facades, all Jews are merely unsavory Polish rag-peddlers. The latter are not worse than their Western coreligionists; they simply display overtly the contemptible characteristics of all Jewry.[16]

By repeatedly harping on the identity of character between native and foreign Jews, anti-Semitic propagandists strove to use Eastern Jews as pawns in their far larger struggle against German Jewry. In pursuit of their ultimate goal of undermining the legal equality of native-born Jews, anti-Semites were eager to exploit the issue of Jewish immigration to their own benefit. But in pursuing this strategy, anti-Semites viciously attacked the character of Eastern Jews, branding them as ruthless exploiters and menacing invaders. Such stereotyping made it difficult for anyone to discuss the very real issues raised by Jewish migrants in a dispassionate fashion. Moreover, by blurring all distinctions between native and immigrant Jews in Germany, anti-Semites added an additional and complicating dimension to debates about Eastern Jews. It was difficult for participants in such debates to separate the question of Jewish immigration from Germany's broader Jewish Problem. Due to the intemperate outburst of anti-Semitic deputies, parliamentary debates about Eastern Jews invariably deteriorated into free-for-all diatribes against all Jews. Thus, anti-Semites critically shaped both the tone and character of public discourse over Eastern Jews: they disseminated inflammatory stereotypes of such Jews and they intertwined Germany's broader Jewish Question with the specific issue of Jewish immigration.

Restrictionist Campaigns

The efforts of anti-Semitic publicists and commentators to defame the character of Eastern and native Jews provided the propaganda to buttress a far more ambitious campaign—the promotion of a legal ban on all Jewish immigration. Under the leadership of Germany's self-proclaimed political anti-Semites, efforts were launched throughout the history of the Second Empire to win government approval for policies that singled out foreign Jews from the larger population of aliens in the *Reich*. The goal of this anti-Semitic program was twofold: it aimed to bar all foreign Jews from crossing the *Reich*'s frontiers and it pressed for harsher curbs on alien Jews already residing within the *Reich*.

These restrictionist campaigns punctuated each of the major eruptions of political anti-Semitism during the Imperial era: (1) the period from 1879 to 1881, when political anti-Semitism first emerged; (2) virtually the entire decade of the 1890s, when anti-Semitic parties in the Reichstag enjoyed their period of greatest electoral and political success; and (3) the years immediately preceding the outbreak of World War I, when new coalitions of the Right embraced anti-Semitism as a unifying cause. In each instance, political anti-Semites campaigned openly for stricter curbs on foreign Jews.

The earliest widespread agitation against Jewish immigration to the recently unified *Reich* occurred when an Anti-Semitic Petition was circulated between the autumn of 1880 and April 1881. Signed by approximately 225,000 Germans, supported by the emerging leadership of the new anti-Semitic movement, Förster, Liebermann von Sonnenberg, Henrici, and Stöcker, and distributed to government, civic, and business leaders, the petition demanded that Bismarck implement four new policies toward Jews in Germany; (1) "all immigration of foreign Jews must be totally restricted or at least limited"; (2) Jews should be barred from holding administrative offices; (3) schools must maintain their Christian character; (4) a religious census should be renewed. Clearly, the first and last demands related to the issue of Jewish immigration. As the *Staatsburger-Zeitung* explained, Germans were growing concerned about the number of Jews in their midst—and rightfully so, since the *Reich* contained more Jews than sixteen European countries combined; moreover, these Jews were flocking to Berlin in order to seize control of the nation's financial markets. For this reason, the newspaper argued, "the immigration of Jewish *Schnorrers* must be checked." [17]

During the five years immediately following the circulation of the Anti-Semitic Petition, governments carried out two of the anti-Semites' demands. Already by 1882, government statistical handbooks resumed publishing data on the religious confession of the German population. (Census returns had always included confessional questions, but statistical works based on the 1875 national census had omitted references to confession.) Thereafter, data on the demographic growth of every religious group were available for public scrutiny, thus simplifying the task of keeping track of Jewish immigration and population trends. And from the early 1880s, under the direct prodding of Bismarck, German states tightened their supervision of foreign Jews, a program that culminated in the expulsion of 10,000 Polish Jews from Prussia between 1884 and 1886. While it is not possible to determine the precise relationship between these altered policies and the demands of anti-Semites, the sequence of developments certainly seems to suggest a causal relationship. In the words of Leopold Auerbach, a noted contemporary writer: "The government put into effect demands number one and four . . . in subsequent years. Whether the Petition stimulated this or whether other factors brought this about is not known for certain." We shall see in the next chapter that "other factors" did indeed play a role, but the Petition nonetheless may have influenced government behavior. [18]

The next, and most protracted, stage of restrictionist agitation occurred during the last decade of the nineteenth century. Due to the severe measures initiated by Prussia and imitated by other states, which culminated in mass expulsions, it simply would have been superfluous to push for restrictionism during the 1880s. But by the early 1890s, circumstances had changed: as one historian has described it, this was the period when anti-Semitic political parties were under pressure to demonstrate that they could "produce some palpable success, show some sign of a future solution to the Jewish question through parliamentary action." [19] The anti-Semitic *Fraktion* of the Reichstag, led by Liebermann von Sonnenberg, hoped that its proposals to restrict Jewish immigration would win it parliamentary legitimacy and success. Accordingly, during every Reichstag session between 1893 and 1902 at least one such resolution was proposed, and in each case the demands were uniform: the *Reich* should ban all future Jewish immigration; states must expel foreign Jews currently in the country; and Germany must prohibit the naturalization of Jews in the future. Significantly, these bills singled out only Jews for such treatment and did not distinguish between Jews from Western European and

Eastern European countries; rather they urged a comprehensive ban on all Jews.[20]

The foremost ally of the anti-Semitic faction in this cause was Baron Wilhelm von Hammerstein, the leader of the *Kreutzzeitung* faction of the Conservative Party. As editor of the *Kreutzzeitung,* the organ of reactionary Junkers, Hammerstein was able to enlarge the base of support for restrictionist legislation by appealing to voters who were not constituents of the anti-Semitic parties. In most cases, however, even the support of some German Conservatives was not sufficient to get restrictionist bills out of committee and into debate before the entire Reichstag.[21]

A major exception to this pattern of political isolation occurred in the year 1895. In the early 1890s, the Conservative Party had begun to flirt with political anti-Semitism and had even adopted a positive stance toward official anti-Semitism in its 1892 Tivoli Program. As a result, during the years 1893 and 1894, Conservative deputies supplemented the usual anti-Semitic resolutions with several separate restrictionist proposals of their own. In 1893, Otto von Manteuffel, chairman of the Conservative Party, joined Hammerstein in co-sponsoring a bill restricting Jewish immigration. The stage was thus set for a major Reichstag debate. In the ensuing vote, deputies resoundingly defeated the Conservative bill by a tally of 167 to 51; thirty-nine Conservative Party deputies joined with the anti-Semitic faction in support of a ban on Jewish immigration, and the progressive parties, the Poles, the Catholic Center, and the SPD rejected the bill either out of opposition to anti-Semitism or concern lest the Reichstag follow up with laws restricting Polish or Catholic immigration. After this defeat, the Conservatives did not sponsor their own restrictionist bills again; instead, those deputies who wished to curb Jewish immigration co-sponsored resolutions introduced by anti-Semitic deputies. In time such proposals evoked so little interest that even deputies of the anti-Semitic faction introduced them only sporadically after 1902, and then only in a lackluster fashion. When, for example, the Reichstag took up such a bill in 1909, only half the anti-Semitic deputies even bothered to attend the vote.[22]

In the last years before the outbreak of World War I, a new constellation of anti-Semitic forces emerged within the parties of the Right. As analyzed by the historian Werner T. Angress, these forces coalesced after the national elections of 1912. Anti-Semitism, he writes,

> was transform[ed] from its random manifestations in the past and as such was closely tied in with the changes that occurred within the political Right during the decade preceding the war. Never before had a serious attempt been made to orchestrate anti-Semitism, to use it consistently as a political tactic and to make it the one common denominator of a still precarious alliance of right-wing forces. . . . Thanks to the new agitators, the traditional Right was drawn into the witches' cauldron of racism.[23]

The brunt of these new efforts was not felt until the war years, when Jews in the military were subjected to a special census; but already during the decade before 1914, new alliances were forged between various right-wing groups opposed to Jewish immigrants. Now, in addition to the anti-Semitic political parties, lobbies such as the Pan-German League threw their support behind restrictionism. The league's chairman in the prewar years, Heinrich Class, authored the notorious *Kaiserbuch,* which urged Germany to seal its borders to Jews and expel all alien Jews as part of a larger program to revoke Jewish emancipation. Other lobbies also joined the fray.[24]

The prime target of restrictionist campaigns during the prewar years were Russian Jewish students enrolled at universities and technical schools throughout Germany. A constellation of anti-Semitic student organizations, racist professors, xenophobic professional societies, and political anti-Semites joined to pressure state governments to solve the *"Ausländerfrage,"* a euphemism for the noticeable presence of Jewish students from Russia. Petitions were sent to ministries of education in the various German states and bills were introduced into state parliaments urging quotas that would uniquely affect Russian Jews. These efforts came to a head in 1909, when the Reichstag debated whether foreign students were endangering Germany's competitive edge in industrial production. In December 1909, deputies representing the anti-Semitic faction and the Conservative Party introduced a resolution urging the Reichstag to protect "the national and economic interests of our *Volk* from the dangerous advances of foreigners at German institutions of higher learning." In response to these demands and the lobbying of other groups, state governments enacted severe new policies to curb Jewish students from Russia first at technical schools and later at universities. By the eve of the war, these quotas and regulations prevented newly arrived Russian Jews from matriculating at German institutions of higher learning and severely demoralized students who were already enrolled.[25]

While the resolution of the *Ausländerfrage* at institutions of higher learning surely heartened restrictionists, those groups that sought to enact legislation aimed at Jewish immigrants never achieved their goals during the Imperial era. What, we may ask, was the significance of these restrictionist campaigns if all bills aimed at banning Jewish immigration went down to defeat? It is a mistake to assume that these efforts had no impact because restrictionism was mainly promoted by political anti-Semites who could not rally sufficient support to enact a comprehensive ban on Jewish immigration. Though the parliamentary anti-Semites suffered defeat within the Reichstag, they won concrete, albeit limited, victories in other arenas—especially on the state and local level. As a result of their efforts, localities throughout the *Reich* scrutinized their populations of Eastern Jews, and in some cases instituted severe curbs on the newcomers. In Munich, for example, the local branch of the anti-Semitic Christian-Social Party submitted a petition in late 1904 urging the municipal government to ban Jewish immigrants. Petitioners claimed that Bavaria was "welcoming foreign Jews with open arms, so that it is no wonder that they regard it as a second Canaan." At the instigation of Councilman Herrmann, a member of the Center Party, the municipal government took up the question of whether to pass a law singling out foreign Jews for expulsion. While Herrmann's proposal was defeated by a vote of thirty to nineteen, another resolution carried that called for close inspection of foreigners on the part of physicians, school administrators, and police authorities. Thus, even when restrictionist bills failed, Eastern Jews found themselves under closer scrutiny.[26]

The efforts of anti-Semitic restrictionists also had other important, albeit less tangible, consequences. It is not unreasonable to assume that their campaigns emboldened individuals and groups who felt threatened by the economic competition of Eastern Jews to air their grievances in public. To cite just three examples: In 1894, 150,000 leaflets were distributed in the Rhineland attacking a company selling farm implements on the grounds that it was run by a "Galician swindler"; prior to his arrival in Germany, this Eastern Jew had allegedly "sold cheap goods in a bazaar." Another leaflet attacked owners of a firm selling similar implements as "two Talmud Jews from Tarnopol" who knew nothing about their business. Not surprisingly, these leaflets were distributed by Germans who resented the competition of Galician Jews. Two decades later, the association of German Shoe Merchants petitioned for the expulsion of Galician old-clothes dealers whose "swindling business practices" had robbed innocent Germans. The expulsion of Galicians would, of course, benefit members of the association. On some occasions, worker organizations also protested the unfair competition of foreign Jews: in 1900 the General Bavarian Workers Convention petitioned the government to expel Rumanian Jews who were flooding into the state; after some investigation, however, the government could locate only two such Rumanian Jews who posed an economic threat. Significantly, these protests resulted in government investigations and closer supervision of Eastern Jews.[27]

Perhaps the most far-reaching consequence of the restrictionist campaign, however, lay in its impact on public discourse concerning Eastern Jews. By harping incessantly on the Jewish menace and repeatedly proposing bills aimed solely at foreign Jews, political anti-Semites kept the issue of Jewish immigration alive as a specific issue distinct from all other immigration questions. Their agitation surely lent comfort to state officials intent on dealing harshly with Jewish immigrants. And their efforts successfully kept Eastern Jews and their friends on the defensive. For by constantly raising the specter of uncontrolled Jewish immigration, parliamentary anti-Semites forced Jewish and Gentile friends of Eastern Jews into a self-defeating defense: ever conscious that the slightest rise in Jewish immigration would be interpreted by anti-Semites as the onset of a tidal wave that would engulf the *Reich,* defenders of Eastern Jews consistently downplayed the size of Jewish immigration and in the process implicitly accepted the assumption that Jewish immigrants were a bane to Germany. This, too, represented a victory for restrictionists.

The Spectrum of Political Opinion

German political opinion was divided over the demands put forth by restrictionists. Though no political party was prepared to argue that Eastern Jews constituted a boon to Germany and therefore should be welcomed, some parties vigorously fought restrictionists and challenged governments to justify their harsh treatment of foreign Jews. During Reichstag debates over Eastern Jews, parties generally adopted positions conforming to their views on the larger Jewish Problem: parties on the Right were antagonistic to foreign Jews, the Center Party sometimes supported restrictionism and at other times defended Jewish immigrants, and the parties of the Left generally defended the interest of Eastern Jews just as they championed the rights of native Jews. To be sure, the Polish and Center parties had additional reasons for opposing restrictionism because of its possible adverse effect on Catholic Poles. Nevertheless, parliamentary anti-Semites succeeded so well in confusing the issue of Jewish immigration with the larger Jewish Question, that parties were forced to confront political anti-Semitism when they participated in debates over Jewish immigration.

Before surveying the posture of German political parties vis-à-vis Eastern Jews, a word in in order about the occasions of public debates over Jewish immigrants. As already noted, such debates were generally provoked by parliamentary anti-Semites who sought to pressure either the Reichstag or local state governments to ban Jewish immigration and curb alien Jews already in the country. But at other times debates were prompted by parliamentary deputies who regarded existing government policies as too severe. This was particularly the case during the frequent mass expulsions of Eastern Jews that punctuated the history of the Second Empire. In 1884–86 and 1904–06, when the most far-reaching expulsions were launched, several political parties insisted that governments explain their policies. Similarly, when governments cracked down on Jewish university students from Russia, several political parties held state officials accountable for their actions.

On one occasion, Eastern Jews even became the focus of controversy during a debate that ostensibly had little to do with them. In 1894 Chancellor Caprivi sought approval for a new trade treaty with Russia. Hoping to undermine the pending agreement, Conservative and anti-Semitic parties injected the question of Jewish migration into parliamentary debates. Claiming that the treaty's protection of commercial travelers (Article 1) would open the floodgates to Jewish hawkers from Russia, opponents of the agreement hoped to frighten the Reichstag into scuttling the treaty. The opening salvo in this debate was fired in an unsigned article entitled "The Russian Trade Agreement—a National Danger" that appeared in the right-wing *Grenzboten*. The author of this piece warned of an invasion of ruthless Jewish businessmen poised to overrun the Reich, "seize the last bit of German property," and destroy the German middle class. Indeed, wrote this polemicist, permitting Russian Jews to enter the country "would be inhumane to German children." In the ensuing Reichstag debate, there developed an identity of interest between attitudes toward the Russian tariff and Jewish immigration: deputies either opposed or accepted both. Only government officials departed from this pattern, for in order to win passage of their legislation, they downplayed the dangers posed by Jews from the East.[28]

In this debate and all others, the most consistent antagonists of Eastern Jews in Germany were the anti-Semitic parties. Since the propaganda and the legislative efforts of these parties have already been described earlier in this chapter, only a few additional remarks about the role of anti-Semitic politicians need to be added in the present context. It is appropriate to note the central role assumed by Liebermann von Sonnenberg in all Reichstag debates about Eastern Jews during the last decade of the nineteenth and the first decade of the twentieth centuries. Sonnenberg was in the forefront of all efforts to win passage of a law banning Jewish immigration. And when such efforts failed, he threw his considerable energies into the fight to curb "foreigners" from institutions of higher learning. But unlike many other deputies who employed euphemistic circumlocutions when they spoke of the dangers posed by "foreigners" at German universities and *Hochschulen,* Leibermann von Sonnenberg directly accused "Russian Jews at German universities of spreading revolutionary propaganda and studying dynamite at our technical schools." Such direct attacks upon Jews certainly put the Jewish Problem on the agenda of German parliaments. But precisely because anti-Semitic deputies sought to use foreign Jews as a vehicle to undermine the status of native Jews, they weakened the case against the former: for their outrageous diatribes against all Jews deflected public attention from the specific issue of Jewish migration to the broader question of Jewish emancipation in Germany.[29]

Deputies of the German Conservative Party constituted the most faithful allies of the anti-Semites in debates about Eastern Jews. While the party generally did not endorse such a position officially (with the exception of the era of the mid-1890s), some of its members, led by Baron Wilhelm von Hammerstein, spoke out in favor of tough restrictions on Jewish immigrants. During the expulsion of Eastern Jews from Berlin in 1884 and the broader expulsions from Prussia in the ensuing two years, Hammerstein and his ultra-conservative newspaper, the *Kreutzzeitung,* defended the banishment of alien Jews. A decade later, Hammerstein was able to win the support of the party's chairman, Otto von Manteuffel, for legislative bills banning Jewish immigration. But even when this alliance ceased, Conservative deputies consistently defended harsh government measures taken against foreign Jews. They apparently saw no inconsistency between their support for the importation of Slavic seasonal workers and their desire to expel Polish Jews. The former policy was desirable because it provided cheap labor for the East Elbian supporters of the party, whereas the presence of Jewish migrants served the needs of no constituencies.[30]

The National Liberal Party was equally hostile toward Eastern Jews, although some of its deputies took pains to distinguish their opposition to foreign Jews from their support of the rights of native Jews. In Reichstag debates over mass expulsions, leaders of this party routinely defended government actions as necessary. In 1905, for example, Bassermann spoke of the government's need to defend Germany by expelling poor and revolutionary Jews from abroad. The tone of this party's position was captured during the Reichstag debate over the Russian tariff agreement in 1894 when Deputy Paasche spoke of the need to protect Germany from Jews, since the latter play an inordinately large role in "bankruptcy swindles, peddling, competition, and vagrancy." At the same time, Paasche noted, "We do not wish to fight the Jew solely because he is a Jew." Paasche therefore rejected legislation aimed solely at banning Jewish immigration. Deputies of the National Liberal Party, then, shied away from openly anti-Jewish actions, but they defended the right of governments to take severe actions against foreign Jews on the grounds of "national interests."[31]

The coalition against alien Jews consisting of anti-Semitic, Conservative, and National Liberal deputies was opposed by parties of the Left and generally the Center. As the representative of a religious minority, the Catholic Center Party became after the *Kulturkampf* an important, though unreliable, defender of Jewish interests. The condition of Eastern Jews in Germany was of particular concern to Center leaders in view of their anxiety over the situation of Catholic Poles. Furthermore, the party was convinced that discriminatory actions taken against native or alien Jews might serve as a prelude to attacks upon Catholics. Under the leadership of Ludwig Windhorst, the Center Party challenged the expulsion of 30,000 Christian and Jewish Poles in 1885–86 solely as a Catholic issue—that is, he opposed the expulsion of Christian Poles. A decade later, however, Ernst Lieber recognized the linkage between the fate of Eastern Jews and Polish Catholics in the *Reich*. For if governments were free to implement ruthless measures against alien Jews, they could move against Catholics as well. In his speech decrying restrictionist legislation, Lieber summed up his position:

> As a minority in the *Reich*, we have not forgotten how we were treated and for this reason alone, not to speak of higher considerations and deeper motives, we shall never lend a hand to forge weapons used today against the Jews, tomorrow against Poles, and the day after tomorrow against the Catholics. . . . Don't expect our support in making it possible for you to exult: "We got rid of the Jews. Now *bon voyage* to the Catholics!"

It was this concern for the fate of Catholic foreigners that prompted Center Party deputies in the Reichstag to challenge discriminatory measures directed against Eastern Jews. To cite one example, in 1905, when mainly Eastern Jews were expelled from Prussia, Center deputies challenged government actions. On the state and local level, however, Center politicians often spearheaded efforts to harass immigrant Jews, just as they indulged in other anti-Semitic activities.[32]

The parties of the Left proved far more consistent as champions of beleaguered Jewish immigrants. When the Prussian Diet debated the Anti-Semitic Petition in the early 1880s, progressive speakers led by Rudolf von Virchow denounced all talk of a Jewish "mass migration" as a "fable." Five years later, when Prussia expelled large numbers of Gentile and Jewish Poles, Heinrich Rickert denounced the expulsions and specifically charged the Prussian government with anti-Semitism. Again, in the 1890s, progressive deputies fought against immigration curbs aimed solely at Jews, arguing, as did Deputy Hermes, that it was absurd to picture the small number of Jews in Germany as a threat. And when the Prussian Diet debated the expulsions of 1905–06, the Progressive Association rebuked the government. A similar pattern of opposition obtained in the progressive parties' responses to other forms of harassment directed at foreign Jews. Deputies consistently pointed out unfair practices and forthrightly labeled them as anti-Semitic in motivation.[33]

Precisely because they interpreted attacks on immigrant Jews as fundamentally rooted in anti-Semitism, progressive deputies concerned about anti-Jewish discrimination came to the defense of foreign Jews. It is surely not accidental that progressive leaders involved with the Association for the Defense Against Anti-Semitism were particularly outspoken in behalf of Eastern Jews. During his tenure as president of this defense agency, Heinrich Rickert, the Progressive Union leader, spearheaded a Reichstag challenge of Prussia's expulsion and naturalization policies. His successors in the *Abwehrverein,* Theodor Barth and Georg Gothein, also spoke out forcefully against the mistreatment of Eastern Jews—and on occasion were among the few voices that described such Jews in positive terms. To cite one important instance, Theodor Barth published a two-part essay in his journal *Die Nation* written by the Königsberg deputy Professor Möller. Entitled "The Polish Jews," the essay enthusiastically praised Eastern Jews for their industriousness, attachment to religion, close family ties, and eagerness to embrace German culture. Möller refuted some of the most pernicious charges routinely hurled at Eastern Jews: they were not *Schnorrers,* but diligent wokers; they did not immigrate to Germany solely for economic gain, but also to study German *Wissenschaft;* and they did not remain aliens, but quickly came to identify themselves and behave as Germans. A decade later, Heinrich Rickert challenged proposed restrictionist legislation on the grounds that immigrant Jews were an asset to the German economy. He referred to the damage sustained by the *Reich*'s commerce and agriculture as a result of the 1885–86 expulsions. Thus, some progressive deputies not only objected to the abusive treatment of Eastern Jews on humanitarian grounds, but pictured such Jews as an asset to Germany.[34]

The German Social Democratic Party was more ambivalent about Jewish immigrants. Although socialist leaders labored to improve conditions for immigrant Jews, they did not always picture them in a flattering light. Such mixed attitudes arose from their general ambivalence toward Jews. The historian Paul Massing has characterized this position as follows:

> In theory and practice socialist labor was opposed to anti-Semitism. The socialists never wavered in their stand against all attempts to deprive Jews of their civil rights. . . . On the other hand, socialist labor was indifferent, if not actually hostile, toward all efforts to preserve and revitalize autonomous Jewish religious, cultural, or national traditions.

This pattern also holds true for SPD actions and attitudes regarding Eastern Jews in the *Reich.*[35]

Hostile views on Eastern Jews are already found in the writings of Karl Marx, who described Polish Jews as the "dirtiest of all races" and claimed that "they multiply like lice." SPD speakers were not openly hostile toward Eastern Jews, but frequently voiced misgivings about the culture of such Jews. According to Karl Kautsky, editor of the SPD journal *Neue Zeit,* the Kishinev pogroms were partly caused by Russian Jews themselves, for such mob attacks were reactions to the Jews' self-segregation and failure to assimilate; by maintaining a distinctive physical appearance, religion, customs, and language, Russian Jews provoked anti-Semitism. The Yiddish language was especially abhorrent to SPD writers since it raised a linguistic barrier to Jewish assimilation.As the historian Edmund Silberner has noted, socialists "attacked Yiddish but they aimed at Jewish nationality."[36]

When it came to the defense of Eastern Jews against anti-immigrant measures, however, the German Social Democratic Party could be relied upon for energetic support. During debates over restrictionism in 1895, Deputy Vogther accused the Conservative Party of anti-Semitism for sponsoring legislation that would permit the importation of Gentile Poles but ban the immigration of foreign Jews. A de-

cade later, SPD leaders such as Karl Leibknecht, August Bebel, and Eduard Bernstein, together with the leading socialist newspaper, the *Vorwärts,* publicly campaigned against police actions directed against Eastern Jews. Leibknecht and Bebel
collected survey information from Russian Jews in order to acquire hard data to
refute government officials and document the existence of official discrimination
against foreign Jews. And, on occasion, Leibknecht even intervened personally to
protect individuals from expulsion. Interestingly, the *Vorwärts* sought to educate
its readers not to regard immigrants as economic competitors. Behind this solici-
tous attitude toward foreign Jews lay more than a concern with the humane treatment of foreigners; SPD leaders were acutely conscious that governments justified
measures directed against foreign Jews, particularly those from Russia, on the
grounds that such Jews constituted a menacing cadre of revolutionaries. Under the
circumstances, the SPD was impelled to join the fray in order to stymie its right-
wing opponents.[37]

This strong SPD support for Eastern Jews proved a mixed blessing. Immigrant
Jews had long been perceived as conspirators, revolutionaries, and anarchists, a
perception that was strengthened by the efforts of the SPD to defend the newcomers. In the decade prior to the outbreak of World War I, Russian Jews, especially
students, were accused of working actively in behalf of the SPD. Chancellor von
Bülow informed his cabinet in 1907 that "many students from Austro-Hungary
misuse the rights of guests and have worked toward getting votes for Social Democratic candidates." Acting on this perception, police in various states carefully
scrutinized the activities of students and expelled any foreigner who associated in
some way with the German Socialist Party. (It was illegal for aliens to participate
in German political life.) Ironically, then, the efforts of the SPD in behalf of
Eastern Jews reinforced the image of such Jews as conspirators and leftist agitators. After all, their defenders were, as Bismarck had put it, "enemies of the
Reich."[38]

It might appear at first blush that public debates ended favorably for Eastern Jews,
considering that all restrictionist bills went down to abysmal defeat and deputies
representing the middle and left of the political spectrum could be counted upon
to challenge existing policies. In reality, however, matters were more complex.
Restrictionists were defeated not because defenders of Eastern Jews were more
powerful, but because government officials decided not to support legislation banning Jewish immigration. While we have no definitive explanations of their motives, it is reasonable to assume that German leaders did not feel a need for such
legislation because existing measures were sufficiently potent to cope with Jewish
migrants. If anything, a law singling out Jewish immigrants for special discrimination would only tarnish Germany's image as a modern, civilized state. Also,
such a law would constrain government officials, whereas the prevailing system
provided wide latitude for them to act at their own discretion. Moreover, efforts
to ameliorate the condition of Eastern Jews by challenging governments in parliamentary settings proved totally ineffective. For while those who challenged government policies managed to draw public attention to the plight of Eastern Jews,
there is no evidence that they succeeded in improving the condition of such Jews.

In a few instances individuals were saved from expulsion, but for the most part, government policies remained unaffected by parliamentary debates. In this regard, as in so many others, deputies of the Reichstag proved impotent to shape government policies.[39] What is most significant, then, about the public debates over Eastern Jews were not any concrete solutions they produced, but rather the inhospitable mood they fostered. For the terms of public debate were set by anti-Semites and others who viewed Eastern Jews as an "unwanted element." As a result, debates consistently revolved around means to protect the *Reich* from an alien invasion: Were too many Eastern Jews immigrating? Were existing measures adequate to protect the *Reich* from the invaders? How could Germany best keep these unwanted aliens at bay? This negative approach surely strengthened the hands of those who were empowered to cope with aliens in the *Reich*—officials in state ministries of interior who set the actual policies that determined the fate of Eastern Jews in Germany.

3

Administrative Solutions

During the first decade after German unification, government officials devoted scant attention to the issue of Jewish foreigners in the *Reich*. For one thing, a great many other, more pressing matters needed to be resolved. For another, the number of Eastern Jews arriving in Germany in the 1870s, though representing an upswing in immigration, did not pose a significant problem. Several states, including the border states of Saxony and Bavaria, extended their exclusionary policies from the era before unification: the former continued its ban on the naturalization of foreign Jews, and the latter refused to permit indigent Jews from Poland and Russia from even settling in its territory. Only Prussia received a significant new population due to the influx of Jews fleeing harsh conditions in northwestern Russia. While Bismarck and his Prussian ministers expressed some concern about the leniency of existing regulations and urged greater stringency in the enforcement of border controls, neither Prussia nor other German states initiated new policies regarding Jewish immigrants during the decade of the seventies.[1]

With the assasination of Tsar Alexander II on March 13, 1881, and the outbreak of waves of pogroms in Russia in the ensuing months, German governments began to pay close attention to migrating East European Jews. German ambassadors and consuls in Russia sent regular reports to their ministerial superiors about the mounting tide of disturbances sweeping across Russia and the consequent westward flight of Jews. Reports also reached German state capitals of the swell-

42

ing population of Russian Jews crossing the frontiers either directly from Russia or from staging points such as Lemberg in the Galician province of the Austro-Hungarian Empire. By the late spring of 1881, state bureaucracies began to respond to the new developments by collecting systematic information on the dimensions of Jewish immigration and formulating policies on how the newcomers were to be treated. In quick succession, new directives were issued that were to serve as the foundation of state policies for the duration of the Second Empire.[2]

Prussia Takes the Initiative, 1881–86

The moving force behind the crackdown on Eastern Jews in the *Reich* was the Prussian state. Initially this was the case primarily for geographic reasons: the mass migration of East European Jews began in Russia, and Prussia was the only German state to share a common frontier with the Tsarist Empire, specifically along its four eastern provinces of East and West Prussia, Posen, and Silesia. Thus, when the momentum of Jewish mass migration from Russia began to accelerate in the 1880s, Prussian officials were the first German bureaucrats forced to confront the problem. As the mass migration from the East continued, however, two other states—Saxony and Bavaria—were compelled to take action by virtue of their common borders with the Austro-Hungarian Empire. Though the number of Jews crossing from the Dual Monarchy into Germany paled in comparison with the populations entering from Russia, a significant number of Jewish emigrants from Galicia, Moravia, and Hungary crossed into those states. (Even some Russian Jews arrived via Austro-Hungary in order to circumvent Prussian border restrictions.) By the early twentieth century, Eastern Jews had also found their way to the more western states of Baden and Hessen. Yet even when Jewish migrants had become a problem for most large German states, Prussia continued to play the dominant role in coping with East European Jews: first, because it had to contend with the largest contingent of Jewish migrants—those from Russia; and, second, because Prussia actively lobbied within the German confederation for the adoption of its approach to the problem of Jewish mass migration. An analysis of German policies toward Eastern Jews must therefore begin with Prussian responses at the onset of mass migration in the 1880s.

Significantly, East European Jews first came under official scrutiny in Prussia at the instigation of the Russian government. In response to an official inquiry from tsarist officials and on behalf of Chancellor Bismarck, the German foreign minister wrote a letter of inquiry to Prussia's minister of interior, Robert von Puttkamer, on May 11, 1881, requesting data on the number of Russian subjects who had crossed into Prussia from the Polish sector of the Tsarist Empire. Bismarck, in turn, added his own query concerning the feasibility of preventing the naturalization of such immigrants and requested a statistical count of all Russian subjects naturalized in Prussia since the year 1848. (The latter date was selected because on December 13, 1848, Prussia had instituted new naturalization procedures.) Bismarck specifically requested separate tallies for Christians and Jews who had acquired Prussian citizenship. Two days later, Puttkamer asked the director of Prussia's statistical bureau to furnish him with data on Russian subjects residing in Prussia, including a breakdown of such individuals according to their religious confession. When the statistical office responded that there were no tallies available that differentiated Russian immigrants by religion, Puttkamer issued a series of new orders to his bureaucrats: The Prussian statistical office was henceforth required to tabulate the religious confession and nationality of all foreigners. *Regierungspräsidenten* (district governors) were ordered to provide the Ministry of Interior with detailed information, including separate breakdowns by religious confession, on the incidence of naturalization in their districts since 1848. And Prussian *Oberpräsidenten* (provincial governors) now were to provide regular reports on the exact number of Russians in their territories—including specific information on Polish Jews.[3]

The flurry of correspondence in May 1881 is of interest for a number of reasons: First, it illustrates how the tsarist government played a role as an instigator of German actions directed at Russian subjects residing in the *Reich*. From the start of Jewish mass migration from the East, tsarist officials encouraged German governments to keep a close eye on Russian Jews. In time, as we shall see, the tsarist government not only did nothing to protect its subjects from abusive German police, but, on the contrary, urged the kaiser's government to tighten its surveillance and step up its harassment of Russian Jews in the *Reich*. Second, the communications passing between Puttkamer's office and the Prussian statistical bureau sheds new light on changes in census practices after 1881. We have noted in the previous chapter how German statistical works began to include more detailed data on foreign Jews in response to demands contained in the Anti-Semitic Petition of 1879–80. But the correspondence we have cited suggests a second motive: bureaucrats needed precise information on this population in order to answer inquiries submitted by the tsarist government and Chancellor Bismarck. Thus, the inclusion of statistical data on foreign Jews was prompted by both the internal needs of state bureaucracies as well as the petitions of anti-Semites.

Most important, this correspondence reveals that officials in Berlin immediately reacted negatively to the upsurge of Jewish emigration from the East. Within weeks after the outbreak of pogroms in Russia, the Prussian government began to monitor the movement of emigrating Jews in order to prevent refugees from settling in Germany. Bismarck explicitly ennunciated his concerns at a meeting of the Prussian cabinet held on May 22. The chancellor informed his cabinet of the anti-Jewish persecutions occurring in Russia and discussed means to block Polish Jews from entering Prussia's eastern provinces. Already at this early date, just as the first wave of Russian pogroms was cresting, Bismarck portrayed Jewish refugees from the East as an "unwanted element" that must be kept out of Germany. Moreover, it was Bismarck who in 1881 proposed to drive the emigrants out of Germany and on to other Western countries. Germany, from the start, was determined not to provide a haven for migrating East European Jews. This initial response was to characterize official German attitudes throughout the era of Jewish mass migration.[4]

A few days later, on May 28, Puttkamer concretized the new policy in a directive to his *Oberpräsidenten,* which included four components: (1) "As a general rule, the naturalization of Russian subjects is to be rejected and granted only in exceptional cases.'' (2) ''The immigration of foreigners from Russia is to be carefully supervised and those aliens who appear to be troublesome *[lästig]* are to be prevented from entering Prussia.'' (3) Russians living in rural areas of the border provinces are to be subjected to close scrutiny. (4) Police authorities are to expel individuals periodically in order to rid the state of undesirable aliens. In one directive, Puttkamer set into motion a concerted policy to block immigration from Russia by exercising state prerogatives over border controls, the rights of residence, and the acquisition of citizenship.[5]

For the next three years, the measures adopted in May 1881 remained in force. The hierarchy of provincial and regional officials regularly submitted reports on the numbers of Russians in their territories (always distinguishing between the Jewish and Christian components of this popultaion) and attempted to enforce Puttkamer's directives concerning matters of residence and citizenship. It soon became evident, however, that existing measures were insufficient to stem the influx from the East. In December 1882, Puttkamer again issued a directive to his *Oberpraäsidenten* reiterating Prussian policies regarding Russian Jews and other *Überläufer* (deserters). He particularly urged authorities in the four eastern provinces to drive ''beggars, vagabonds and other troublesome individuals'' back across the frontier and ordered county officials *(Landräte)* to expel from the state all aliens who had settled in Prussia ''without having established a permanent domicile or obtained a residence permit.'' He advised his underlings that they had a year to bring matters under control.[6]

Given the impossibility of sealing the Prussian frontier and stemming the swelling tide of Jewish emigrants arriving from Russia, it became increasingly difficult for state officials to accede to Puttkamer's demands. As a consequence, the minister of interior employed additional measures to tighten the vise on Eastern Jews who had settled in Prussia. One symptom of the crackdown was Puttkamer's decision in mid-1882 regarding the status of German women who had married foreign men. Puttkamer's attention was drawn to the matter by a letter from the *Oberpräsident* of Posen that decried the rising incidence of marriage between native Jewish women and Jewish men who had recently migrated across the frontier from Russia. This practice, claimed the official, was part of a concerted effort on the part of Posen Jews to find husbands for their unmarried young women, particularly those of a poorer station. Once in the country, the Russian men failed to engage in ''honorable work,'' and therefore deserved to be expelled under Puttkamer's order of May 28, 1881. Unfortunately, lamented the Posen official, Prussian policies since 1871 had encouraged leniency toward foreign men married to German women. In response to this complaint, Puttkamer instituted a new policy for coping with such cases. He reminded the Posen *Oberpräsident* that German women forfeit their citizenship when they marry a foreigner and therefore are subject to expulsion if their husbands are deemed ''troublesome'' to the state. Thereafter, until the end of the Imperial era, Puttkamer's ruling governed Prussian policies and, accordingly, numerous German Jewish women who were married to foreign men suffered the fate of exile.[7]

Puttkamer also instituted new policies affecting Jewish applicants for Prussian citizenship. In September 1884, he tightened the screws on foreign Jews serving as synagogue functionaries. According to Article 9 of the *Reich*'s "Law for the Acquisition and Forfeiture of Citizenship" (see above, Chapter 1), religious functionaries were *guaranteed* swift naturalization by virtue of their service to German society. In order to prevent foreign Jews from benefiting from this stipulation, Puttkamer revived a long-obsolete clause in Prussia's Jewry Law of 1847 that required aliens employed by a synagogue to apply directly to the Prussian Ministry of Interior for a work permit before beginning their employment. Puttkamer's directive to his bureaucracy explicitly stated that "the acceptance of such people as religious officials is not desired." The new policy was clear: Foreign Jews seeking employment in a synagogue, unlike foreign Christians employed by churches, were not compelled to apply directly to the Ministry of Interior for a work permit. The ministry, in turn, was under orders to grant such requests only under unsual circumstances and to expel unsuccessful applicants. (In practice, hundreds of foreign Jews continued to work as synagogue functionaries—indeed, most Prussian communities could not have functioned without them—but these individuals only were granted temporary work permits and therefore could not apply for automatic citizenship as stipulated in the law.)[8]

Since it was discriminatory, the clause invoked by Puttkamer had fallen into disuse with the completion of Jewish emancipation in Germany. Writing in 1870, the German legal scholar Ludwig von Rönne had concluded that the Constitution of 1867 had canceled all discriminatory regulations, including the special requirements placed upon alien Jews by pre-emancipation laws such as Prussia's Jewry Law. Puttkamer, himself, conceded that the law of 1847 had not been enforced recently in Prussia: synagogues in Silesia and Posen, in fact, had hired aliens who had not obtained permits, and the courts did not uphold the 1847 law. But Puttkamer was determined to reinstate the law and ordered his ministry to prosecute synagogue officers who hired foreigners lacking the proper permits. By the end of 1885 several such cases came before the courts. In December of that year, the *Reichsgericht* fined synagogue elders in Beuthen for employing an Austrian subject who had failed to get a permit. And thereafter leaders of numerous other Jewish communities in Prussia were tried and penalized on similar charges. In this manner, the Prussian Ministry of Interior circumvented the *Reich*'s naturalization law, for by denying work permits to foreign Jews, bureaucrats also could keep in check the numbers of functionaries who had the right to apply for citizenship under Article 9.[9]

The most far-reaching efforts to impede the naturalization of foreign Jews and other Russian subjects residing in Prussia were launched by Puttkamer in 1885. The minister acted in response to reports submitted by his underlings that made it amply clear that significant numbers of Russians were acquiring Prussian citizenship with relative ease. In the twelve years between 1868 and 1880, 9,038 naturalization certificates were issued to Russians from the Polish part of the Tsarist Empire (another 430 were issued to individuals from other parts of Russia); of these, Jews received approximately one-third of all naturalization certificates. (All of these figures refer to individual documents, which sometimes covered more than one person—for example, when a married man was naturalized, his wife and children also acquired Prussian citizenship.) Even after Puttkamer had issued his order of May 28, 1881, imposing a ban on the naturalization of Russians, individuals continued to acquire Prussian citizenship at a rapid pace: in the four eastern provinces and Berlin, 430 Russian subjects were naturalized between the date of Puttkamer's directive and October 1, 1883—and nearly half were Jews. When Puttkamer conveyed these figures to Bismarck, the chancellor ordered his minister to strip provincial and local authorities of their jurisdiction over the naturalization of Russians and instead centralize all such decisions within the Ministry of Interior. This change was necessary, Bismarck contended, because existing policies "leave too much leeway [spielraum] for provincial authorities." Furthermore, Bismarck reiterated his demand that Russian subjects should not be granted Prussian citizenship except under extraordinary circumstances. And he also promised Puttkamer that the cabinet would take public responsibility for this new policy when the inevitable hue and cry would arise in the Prussian Diet.[10]

In explaining the necessity for this hardening of policy toward Russians, Bismarck cited the dangers posed by the newcomers. They were responsible for "strengthening the Polish element" in Germany, a population that Bismarck was seeking to Germanize. They constituted the most dangerous class of agitators in Russia. And they represented a threat to Germany since the freedom they enjoyed in the Reich gave them free reign to act out their subversiveness. Bismarck also warned Puttkamer to pay special attention to "those who do not pose a visible social or political threat because these are really the most dangerous. They are the bearers, along with the Russian Poles, of revolutionary sentiments." By distinguishing this latter group of seemingly innocent immigrants from the Russian Poles, Bismarck implicity was warning Puttkamer of the insidious nature of East European Jews.

Bismarck then added one further suggestion: he urged Puttkamer to advise his Oberpräsidenten not to permit any Russian Poles to enter Prussia. Rather than continue the existing policy of admitting migrants from the East and expelling those who proved "troublesome," Bismarck counseled a ban "on the immigration of Russian Poles." If any had to be admitted, it should be only for a specified— and clearly limited—duration. Within two weeks of receiving this memorandum from Bismarck, Puttkamer launched a systematic program to expel Russian subjects from Prussia en masse.

The rehearsal for this program was held during the preceding four years when hundreds of Russian subjects—overwhelmingly Jewish refugees—were driven from certain sectors of the Prussian state. Between May 28, 1881 (the date of Puttkamer's original orders to his Oberpräsidenten), and October 1883, over 600 Russian refugees were expelled from the provice of East Prussia, especially from the city of Königsberg. In general, governors in the four eastern provinces along the Russian frontier were most zealous in expelling refugees. At the order of the Ministry of Interior, Berlin's police commissioner adopted an equally severe policy during the summer of 1884, and within a few months had driven over 600 Russian subjects, almost all Jews, from the Prussian capital. The rationale offered to justify these decrees would be repeated for decades to come: the expulsions protected Germany "from imported Nihilistic ideas and their dissemination amongst the Social Democratic elements of the capital."[11]

Having encountered little opposition to these expulsions, Puttkamer ventured a more comprehensive solution to the problem of East Europeans in Prussia. On March 26, 1885, he ordered the expulsion of all "Russian Poles" in Prussia. And in July, a new decree extended this policy to Polish subjects of the Austro-Hungarian Empire. The mass expulsion lasted over three years because some individuals were granted long periods of time to conclude their affairs in Germany prior to departing. In general, however, most of those expelled had only a brief respite before they were forced to leave.[12]

The exact number of Poles and Jews expelled from Prussia during the 1880s has been a source of speculation. In 1888, just as the sweep came to an end, the *Allgemeine Zeitung des Judentums* estimated that around 40,000 were expelled, of which half were Jews. The noted Jewish demographer Jacob Segall ventured that 17,000 Jews were driven out of Prussia between 1880 and 1885. Most recently, Joachim Mai and Helmuth Neubach, two historians who have had access to Prussian archival records, concluded independently that approximately 30,000 East Europeans were expelled. According to Neubach, one-third of these were Jews. Approximately 13,000 Russian and Austro-Hungarian subjects were spared from expulsion due to their services to the state—especially to trade and commerce. It is not known how many of the latter were Jews.[13]

The Prussian expulsions also had repercussions in other German states. Rather than watch passively as some Poles and Jews found haven in neighboring states of the *Reich,* Prussian government officials actively pressured those states not to admit expulsion victims. Prussian ambassadors in Saxony, Bavaria, Hesse, and Baden communicated their government's concerns lest individuals deemed worthy of expulsion by Prussia find refuge and possibly even acquire citizenship in other states. (At times this correspondence referred in general terms to the "foreign elements" or "Russian and Austrian subjects" seeking to evade the consequences of expulsion, but just as often official communications specified the Jewish identity of Prussian expulsion victims.) In addition to these blanket requests for cooperation, Prussian officials also intervened when they possessed information about specific individuals who had found haven in adjoining states. They pressured their counterparts not to naturalize such individuals, but rather to expel them. In this manner, Prussian officials in the ministries of Foreign Affairs and Interior worked to export their state's policies to the rest of the *Reich.* Such pressure resulted in the issuance of new directives tightening residence and naturalization policies in other German states. Thus, Prussia's initial response to Jewish mass migration set the tone for the *Reich* as a whole.[14]

Before concluding this analysis of developments during the 1880s, a word is in order concerning the anti-Jewish thrust of Prussian policies. Until Helmuth Neubach published his trailblazing study of the expulsions of Poles and Jews from Prussia, historians of Germany had either ignored the fact that one-third of the expulsion victims were Jews or else assumed that Jews were expelled simply as an accidental consequence of the Prussian drive to oust all Poles. To his credit,

Neubach reevaluated this assumption by tracing Prussian efforts to expel Eastern Jews from the onset of the mass migration. He even concluded that "the preoccupation with Eastern Jewish migrants brought Bismarck back to the general question of Polish immigration which he had first raised already in 1871"—that is, the expulsion of Poles in the mid 1880s was a secondary consequence of Prussia's initial concern over Jewish mass migration. While this latter assertion is exaggerated given Bismarck's fear of Polish nationalism, Neubach has convincingly demonstrated that Prussian officials consciously strove to expel Eastern Jews as a means of coping with Jewish mass migration, rather than solely as a solution to Prussia's "Polish Problem." [15]

The present chapter aims to push this analysis further by placing the expulsions of the 1880s into the larger framework of German policies toward Eastern Jews. The expulsions, in fact, represented not the beginning of German responses to Jewish mass migration, but the conclusion of a first phase of governmental actions: Already in the spring of 1881, as the first pogrom victims crossed into Prussia, Bismarck and Puttkamer had ordered Prussian officials to monitor the arriving Jews and tighten border, residence, and naturalization policies. In the next years, Puttkamer specifically called for new procedures regarding German Jewish women married to Russian Jews as well as foreign Jews working as synagogue functionaries. The expulsions of the mid-1880s thus served as the culmination of a campaign aimed at clamping down on Jewish migrants. And when Jews expelled from Prussia fled to other German states, Prussian authorities worked to convince their counterparts to adopt the Prussian approach to Eastern Jews. While it is true that Christian Poles from Russia and Austro-Hungary also fared badly during this period, and in some important ways were treated in a manner similar to their Jewish compatriots,[16] it needs to be stressed that government officials remained alert to the unique challenges—both real and imagined—posed by the Jewish mass migration. We shall now see that in subsequent decades German officials continued to wield their powers to curb Eastern Jews, and as time went on they formulated ever more differentiated policies to deal with Eastern Jews, as distinct from Christian Poles.

The Evolution of State Policies

Prussia's drastic solution to the problem of Jewish mass migration, the expulsions of the 1880s, proved a palliative of only brief duration. Within a few years after the conclusion of the expulsions, policymakers were confronted with a far more complex set of problems. Already in 1890, Prussia reversed its decision to bar Poles and instead began a massive program to recruit foreign laborers from Eastern Europe as seasonal workers in agriculture and industry. A few years later, Germany signed commercial treaties with its two eastern neighbors that required it to keep its borders open to commercial travelers from Russia and Austro-Hungary. As a result of these changes, it became easier for Eastern Europeans, including Jews, to cross into the *Reich*. Simultaneously, the pressure on Jews to leave their homes in the East further intensified during the decade of the 1890s and became even more severe early in the new century. The tide of emigration constantly grew in size, reaching a peak during the years of war and upheaval in Russia between 1904 and 1906. As a consequence, German states continually were forced to reassess the efficacy of existing policies and to devise new approaches to the continuing problem of Jewish mass migration.

Border Controls

The first and most important line of defense to curb foreign Jews was the system of border controls established to cope with the mass migration. Let us recall that such controls had to balance two conflicting goals: impeding the settlement of Eastern Jews in the *Reich* while simultaneously permitting such Jews to cross into the country in order to embark on German ships for England or the New World. To meet these needs, border states—especially Prussia—established an elaborate system to concentrate Jewish refugees in control stations along the frontier and then ship them as swiftly and directly as possible to ports of embarkation on the North Sea.[17]

Prussia's system, by far the most elaborate, aimed not only to expedite the transmigrants through and out of the state, but also to minimize their contact with native Germans. Unless their funds ran out or they had been sold counterfeit tickets by one of the many unscrupulous travel agents who preyed on Jewish emigrants, the refugees were transported through the country in a matter of days. At the borders, they were concentrated in specially built barracks constructed in key towns; they were then subjected to delousing and disinfection, packed into sealed fourth-class railroad cars, and shipped on to port cities. Along the way they stopped only in carefully selected transit hostels: in Ruheleben and Charlottenburg (Berlin suburbs) for those going to Hamburg and Bremen, and in Oberhausen and Hanover for transmigrants holding tickets on ships departing from Antwerp or Rotterdam. And once in German port cities, they were housed in barracks situated at the port. The entire system thus kept them at a safe distance from the German populace.[18]

The transmigrants did, however, encounter a variety of German bureaucrats, including border guards, government supervisors, and medical personnel. According to the testimony of transmigrants, these officials treated their charges with rudeness and impatience. In her classic and best-selling account of her journey from Plotzk to Boston, Mary Antin vividly portrays the harsh treatment she, her family, and fellow passengers suffered at the hands of such officials:

> The phrases "we were told to do this" and "told to do that" occur again and again in my narrative and the most effective handling of facts could give no more vivid picture of the proceedings. We emigrants were herded, packed in cars, and driven from place to place like cattle.

Perhaps nothing better illustrates this gruff treatment than the program to delouse emigrants organized by health personnel.

> In a great field, opposite a solitary house within a large yard, our train pulled up at last, and a conductor commanded the passengers to make haste and get out.

. . . He hurried us into the one large room which made up the house, and then into the yard. Here a great many men and women in white received us, the women attending to the women and girls of the passengers, and the men to the others. This was another scene of bewildering confusion, parents losing their children, and little ones crying; baggage being thrown together in one corner of the yard, heedless of contents, which suffered in consequence; those white-clad Germans shouting commands, always accompanied with "Quick! Quick!"—the confused passengers obeying all orders like meek children, only questioning now and then what was going to be done to them. And no wonder if in some minds stories arose of people being captured by robbers, murderers and the like. Here we had been taken to a lonely place where only that house was to be seen; our things were taken away, our friends separated from us; a man came to inspect us, as if to ascertain our full value; strange-looking people driving us about like dumb animals, helpless and unresisting; children we could not see crying in a way that suggested terrible things; ourselves driven into a little room where a great kettle was boiling on a little stove; our clothes taken off, our bodies rubbed with a slippery substance that might be any bad thing; a shower of warm water let down on us without warning; again driven to another little room where we sit, wrapped in woolen blankets too large; coarse bags are brought in, their contents turned out, and we see only a cloud of steam, and hear the women's orders to dress ourselves—"Quick! Quick!" or else we'll miss—something we cannot hear. We are forced to pick up our clothes from among all the others, with the steam blinding us; we choke, cough, entreat the women to give us time; they persist, "Quick! Quick!—or we'll miss the train!—Oh, so we really won't be murdered! They are only making us ready for the rest of our journey, cleaning us of all suspicions of dangerous sickness. Thank God!

Finally, the passengers arrived in Hamburg, where they were placed in quarantine for two weeks until their ship departed. Their place of detention "turned out to be a prison." [19]

Even if we take into account that Antin's description was based on childhood impressions, it is clear that the system for delivering emigrants to ports of embarkation was not designed to cater to the needs and fears of confused refugees. On the contrary, it was intended as an efficent program to expel the "unwanted element" expeditiously. And if travelers suffered some discomfort, then perhaps they would leave the *Reich* all the more swiftly. In this manner, some two million Eastern Jews were expedited through Germany on their way to the Untied States, Canada, Argentina, England, and Western Europe between 1870 and 1914. While a special bureaucracy had to be maintained to supervise this population movement and channel it appropriately, the transmigrant traffic moved efficiently and did not overly tax government resources. The more challenging problems consisted of finding means to regulate the relatively small contingent, one that never numbered more than 70,000 souls prior to 1914, that established residence in Germany either as students, transients, or would-be immigrants. [20]

Residence and Work Permits

The principal device employed by German officials to police Eastern Jews who managed to settle in the *Reich* was the residence permit. Because all aliens were required by state laws to register with local police authorities, it was relatively easy for officials to monitor the movement of foreigners. Moreover, since aliens were forbidden to remain in the country without properly issued permits, officials could exercise great power over Eastern Jews and other foreigners by limiting the duration of permits and then swiftly expelling foreigners once their papers had lapsed.[21]

German residence policies varied widely from state to state and even from one locality to another within a state. In Prussia, for example, the most rigorous limitations on Eastern Jews were enforced in the four eastern provinces, the border territories most susceptible to an influx of Jewish migrants. Already during the 1880s, the Ministry of Interior ordered provincial governors to scrutinize the papers of all Russian Jews in their territories and expel anyone who did not have a proper pass. And, more important, officials were ordered to issue residence permits to Eastern Jews only for a very circumscribed period. This policy continued throughout the Imperial era in the four eastern provinces, as is attested by the private correspondence and discussion of Prussian officials. To cite one example from the year 1900, we may quote the description of policy offered by the *Oberpräsident* of Westphalia: "The fundamental policy to keep out all foreign Jews applies only to the eastern border districts of Prussia. In the middle and western parts of the state, the residence of foreign Jews should be rejected in general only in cases when the individual is to be expelled as troublesome." Five years later, Bethmann-Hollweg, then Prussia's minister of interior, reiterated these policies in a report to the cabinet. Describing long-standing orders, he reported that Russian Jews, unlike all other foreigners, were required to acquire a residence permit from provincial authorities, rather than the local police, if they sought residence in the four eastern provinces. The minister commended Posen and West Prussian officials in particular for their success in preventing "an undesirable population growth." At the same meeting, the trade minister elaborated on this policy by reporting that the West Prussian governor granted such permits only if the chamber of commerce assured him of the applicant's economic utility to the state. Jews who failed to receive such approval were pushed on.[22]

In practice, relatively few Jews managed to acquire such support and, accordingly, the eastern provinces expelled most Jewish migrants as a matter of course. In Silesia, for example, Galician Jews who were entitled to enter Germany by virtue of their status as commercial travelers were normally granted a residence permit for fourteen days and then expelled on the grounds that they were Galician Jews. The Oppeln district of Silesia was particularly thorough in denying residence to Eastern Jews, in marked contrast to its acceptance of hordes of imported Christian Poles engaged in mining. In other eastern provinces, residence permits were renewed for longer periods, but the overall goal was to drive out Eastern Jews with special rigor lest they attract coreligionists from the East and become a nuisance. Perhaps the best proof of the success of these policies is the fact that after the expulsions of the mid-1880s, the preponderant majority of Eastern Jews in Prussia resided in Berlin and cities even farther west, whereas earlier they had been overwhelmingly situated in the four eastern provinces.[23]

While government policies were enforced rigorously, they also allowed for sufficient flexibility to permit a selective approach to matters of residence. The above-cited West Prussian policy of granting more favorable status to individuals deemed an asset by the chamber of commerce provides one example of such governmental selectivity. There is ample evidence that in other localities, as well, Eastern Jews possessing wealth, needed talents, or valuable commercial abilities were granted residence permits without difficulty. Perhaps the most cynical exploitation of Eastern Jews for their economic utility occurred in the West Prussian city of Königsberg. During the 1890s, municipal officials decided to permit Jewish import-export agents from Russia to settle in Königsberg only on the condition that they pledge not to bring their wives or families to Germany. In 1900 several of these Russian merchants were expelled on the grounds that they had reneged on their promise by sending for their wives or by having married German women. Despite the fact that this expulsion drew attention from the German press and even an uncharacteristic protest of German policy from the Russian government, Königsberg officials insisted that a change in policy would open the way for a large influx of Russian Jews. The local *Oberpräsident* further expressed his fear lest the children of such Jews serve in the German army and thereby win the right of naturalization in Prussia. At the same time, he made clear that he objected not to the presence of the merchants, but to the immigration of their families. Despite public protests, Königsberg officials maintained their policy until the outbreak of World War I and continued to expel the dependents of Russian Jews—especially their sons. Certainly, this was a blatant case of exploiting East European Jews for economic purposes, while refusing to accept such Jews as permanent residents, let alone citizens.[24]

In other German localities, matters of residence were regulated according to other criteria. As the tide of immigration mounted during the decade prior to the Great War, some municipalities, including Bavarian Munich, Saxonian Chemnitz, and Hessian Offenbach, banned the immigration of newly arriving East European Jews, while permitting those who had arrived earlier to remain. Other localities employed economic or occupational tests to determine which Eastern Jews could maintain residence and which were to be pushed on. We have already noted the Prussian decision not to permit Eastern Jews to enter the country as seasonal laborers on the grounds that such Jews were deemed incapable of hard work. The states of Prussia, Bavaria, and Württemberg also strengthened long-standing laws prohibiting the free movement of Jewish peddlers and itinerant beggars. Such official discrimination encouraged commercial groups and labor organizations to campaign for the ouster of foreign Jews who were economic competitors. As a result, a variety of East European Jews, including merchants in Leipzig, handbag makers in Offenbach, and garment merchants in Munich were expelled by municipal officials willing to placate their constituents. Thus, the power to grant or deny residence permits provided government officials with a great deal of flexibility and selectivity in their management of Eastern Jews. In some cases, this latitude was employed to filter out economically desirable individuals from the masses of "unwanted" migrants; in other cases, the power to issue residence permits was used in a more arbitrary fashion to satisfy political or other needs.[25]

For Eastern Jews, residence policies rendered Germany a highly unstable environment because an immigrant never knew whether his residence permit would be renewed. After a few days, weeks, months, years, and, in some cases, decades, officials could simply refuse to renew a permit and a resident of Germany became a homeless refugee overnight. A perusal of German archives makes it abundantly clear that tens of thousands of foreigners resided temporarily in the country and then were ordered to leave. These individual expulsions were entirely separate from the mass sweeps that drove out hundreds or thousands at a time and therefore attracted public attention. For the most part, however, Eastern Jews and other aliens were quietly pushed out of the country at the instructions of local police authorities or state officials. To illustrate how transitory was the status of Eastern European Jews who resided in Germany, we may cite the population figures of Galician and Russian Jews living in the Hessian city of Offenbach, near Frankfurt am Main: in the year form April 1, 1912, to March 31, 1913, a period in which there was no policy to expel such Jews en masse, twenty-eight individuals were forced to leave the city out of a population of Eastern Jews that hovered between fifty-five and seventy-one souls; during virtually every month, the population of such Jews rose or declined by over ten percent. Thus, German residence policies further filtered out unwanted Jewish immigrants and assured a constant turnover in the population of Eastern Jews in the *Reich*.[26]

Naturalization

While an undetermined percentage of Eastern Jews were constantly being forced to leave the country, only to be replaced by other transient residents, another portion of the immigrant population did manage to establish longer-term residence in the country. Such individuals were potential candidates for naturalization, a change in status that would insure their permanent residence in Germany. How did state officials treat applications for naturalization submitted by these foreign Jews?

To begin with Prussia, the largest and most influential state, we have already noted the important policies instituted by Puttkamer during the 1880s. In subsequent decades, the fundamentally negative attitude of the Prussian government regarding the naturalization of East European Jews remained unchanged, even as the degree of enforcement of these policies did wax and wane over the course of time. In 1890, just two years after the conclusion of the mass expulsions and upon the onset of Prussia's new policy to import seasonal workers from the East, regional administrators were notified that the new policy toward Poles did not indicate a change in attitude toward Eastern Jews. On the contrary, "the naturalization of Polish Jews is to be rejected in conformity with the existing policy"—that is, the policy of the Puttkamer era. Two years later, in January 1892, the Prussian minister of interior warned his *Regierungspräsidenten* not to imitate the sloppy behavior of officials in other German states who were improperly lax in granting citizenship to unwanted Eastern Jews. He especially expressed concern over the activities of Jewish immigrants from Rumania who had recently arrived in Prussia as merchants. In order to tighten procedures, the minister ordered regular annual reports to be submitted every January that would clearly list every individual naturalized in Prussia and then specify the previous nationality of the new citizen *and his religious confession.* These reports, which were submitted during most subsequent years of the Imperial era, contained an explanatory note next to the name of every Jew that justified why that individual was granted citizenship. Lest there be any misunderstanding, the minister issued further orders twice during the next twelve months urging his *Regierungspräsidenten* "to take special care in handling the naturalization attempts of Russian, Galician, and Rumanian Jews and to act with restraint in granting citizenship to such Jews."[27]

It is evident from the repeated warnings issued by the Prussian ministry of interior to state officials that some Eastern Jews continued to acquire naturalization because regional and provincial authorities used their own discretion in evaluating applications for citizenship. For much of the era of the 1890s, the Ministry of Interior tried to discourage leniency toward Eastern Jews by holding officials accountable for all naturalizations occurring in their territories. When too many Jews were naturalized in a particular area, the minister of interior reprimanded the responsible governor. Presumably because such warning were insufficient, the minister of interior ruled in February 1895 that *all* naturalizations in Prussia henceforth required the prior approval of his office. But since this system proved too unwieldy for the ministry to mange, it was amended on July 4, 1899, so that only three categories of individuals applying for Prussian citizenship required the approval of the minister of interior—clergy, Poles and Moravians, and Jews. Naturalization applications from all other categories could be processed locally.[28]

The policy instituted in 1898 remained in effect for the duration of the Imperial era until the outbreak of World War I, as evidenced by the fact that bureaucrats routinely cited the July 4 order. It was now a given within Prussian bureaucratic circles that "the naturalization of foreigners of the Mosaic religion is in itself inadmissible," and when exceptions were made, they had to be approved by the minister of interior. The only significant issue of discussion had to do with exceptional categories of Eastern Jews. In mid-1900, the Prussian minister of interior ruled that the sons of Poles and Russian Jewish immigrants who had lived in the country for a long period of time (i.e., since before the expulsions of the mid-1880s) could be considered for naturalization only when they reached the age of military duty and only if they were fit for army service. Those young men deemed unfit were not entitled to receive citizenship, any more than were daughters of Jewish immigrants. At the beginning of the next decade, the minister also ruled that Christian converts of Jewish ancestry needed special approval. In summing up Prussian naturalization policies during the twenty-five years between the conclusion of the mass expulsions of the 1880s and the outbreak of World War I, the following statement of policy enunciated to the cabinet by Bethmann-Hollweg, the minister of interior, provides an apt generalization: "the naturalization of immigrant Jews is banned by administrative policies; it is possible for the children of immigrants to acquire citizenship only if they were born in Germany, are militarily fit, and are found unobjectionable by the central authorities." Exceptions were made in general only "when a particular state, economic, or communal interest can be served by the naturalization of an individual."[29]

A few case studies illustrate the human toll exacted by the gradual tightening of Prussian naturalization policies. The experience of Josef Lange, for example, highlights what Jews lost through the Puttkamer crackdown. Lange, a Russian, began work as a cantor in 1880 shortly after his arrival in eastern Prussia. Only later, local officials asked him to submit proper papers—not because they wanted him to comply with the 1847 Jewry Law requiring synagogue functionaries to obtain a work permit, but rather because they wished to expedite his naturalization. The cantor procrastinated out of fear that the tsarist government would object to the Prussian naturalization on the grounds that Lange had deserted the Russian army. Yet even without the proper papers, Lange acquired citizenship when a local bureaucrat helped him draft an appeal urging his quick naturalization. (He merited such aid because he had saved a German child from drowning!) In short, Lange's success reveals that the law of 1847 was not enforced during the early 1880s and that local officials, rather than the Ministry of Interior, granted citizenship to foreign Jews prior to the Puttkamer crackdown.[30]

The frustrated career of Oskar Schwartz illustrates the damaging impact of Puttkamer's decrees. Schwartz's father, an Austrian businessman, immigrated to Berlin in 1884. At that time he could still acquire Prussian citizenship, but declined to apply since he was a "convinced Kaiser-loving *[Kaisertreue]* Austrian [dedicated to the] Black and Yellow" flag. When his son Oskar applied for naturalization in 1900, during the course of his law studies, he received a curt rejection, for by now "the naturalization of Jews had become virtually impossible." Oskar, therefore, never became an attorney *(Rechtsanwalt)* but always remained a legal clerk *(Syndikus)*.[31]

Schwartz was comparatively lucky since his father had immigrated during the 1880s; Eastern Jews who arrived after the mass expulsions encountered a far more truculent bureaucracy. The case of Jakob Borg dramatically reveals the predicament of such Jews and the cynical manner in which Prussian officials managed matters of residence and naturalization. Borg settled in Danzig in 1887, finding work as a tobacco cutter. During his first five years in Prussia, he was frequently sent expulsion edicts that were always set aside because his skills were needed by the local tobacco company. In time, he opened his own firm and won a measure of protection from the local chamber of commerce. Early in the twentieth century, two of his sons were naturalized, but not his daughters. Borg's applications for citizenship, however, were repeatedly rejected. In August 1914, when war erupted, Borg was ordered to leave Prussia on the grounds that he was a subject of an enemy country, Russia—this despite the fact that three of his sons were fighting in the German army. Neither his own twenty-seven-year residence in Danzig nor his sons' patriotism prevented his expulsion. Rather, the *Oberpräsident* of Danzig urgently requested permission from his superiors to naturalize Borg on the grounds that Borg's expulsion would force the closing of his cigarette factory, with the result that 300 German workers would lose their jobs. Only his economic utility spared Borg from expulsion during the twenty-seven years it took him to acquire Prussian citizenship.[32]

Contemporary defenders of individuals such as Jakob Borg contended that Eastern Jews were subjected to abusive and arbitrary treatment when they applied for citizenship in Prussia. Were Eastern Jews, in fact, victims of anti-Semitic discrimination? And to what extent was it possible for foreign Jews to acquire naturalization? These questions are not answerable on the basis of published government statistics, which rarely provided information correlating the nationality with the religious confession of successful applicants. And there certainly were no published statistics on the ratio of naturalizations granted relative to the total applicant pool. This absence of official data was frequently cited by German Jewish leaders and their allies, who were convinced that officials covered up their anti-Semitic discrimination by shrouding naturalization procedures in secrecy (a state of affairs that eventually led to the establishement of a central Jewish clearinghouse for gathering information on naturalization attempts). On the basis of archival materials currently available, it is now possible to confirm the accusations of German Jewish leaders: there is ample proof that Prussian administrators were under srict orders not to grant citizenship to foreign Jews except under special circumstances—and then only with the prior approval of the Ministry of Interior. To employ the phrase routinely invoked in government correspondence, "the naturalization of foreigners of the Mosaic religion is in itself inadmissible." And in practice, officials regularly rejected East European Jews by noting in the margin of an application that the individual was unworthy of Prussian citizenship "because he is a Jew." [33]

A perusal of the statistics compiled by the Prussian Ministry of Interior for its own internal purposes provides a behind-the-scenes glimpse at the actual implementation of Prussian policies. These compilations, based on annual reports submitted by district governors between the years 1892 and the outbreak of World War I, attest to the following: (1) In every year, a few dozen Eastern Jews were granted Prussian citizenship. There was never a total ban on such naturalizations, but rather a very selective and arbitrary approach was taken when Jews applied for citizenship. (2) The data do not provide information about the ratio of naturalizations issued relative to the entire pool of Jewish applicants, but it is clear from state, regional, and local archives scattered throughout Prussia that thousands of resident aliens of Jewish confession were denied citizenship during the Imperial era because state policy discouraged the naturalization of Jews. (3) An examination of naturalizations granted during five randomly chosen years (1892, 1896, 1905, 1910, 1914) indicates that Jews constituted between one and one-half and two and one-half percent of successful applicants. Only in the year 1914 did this figure soar to nine percent, presumably in order to accommodate individuals such as Jakob Borg once war had broken out. (4) Throughout this period, approximately half of all Jews naturalized in Prussia came from Western Europe or the United States, even though the preponderant majority of foreign Jews in Prussia were of East European origin. (5) Perhaps most surprising is the fact that during these sample years, considerably more Russians than Austro-Hungarians were naturalized even though the latter predominated in the population of East European Jews and even though government officials generally treated Russians with far greater severity than other foreign Jews. (6) The acceptance of Russians must be understood in light of the general profile of Jews who successfully acquired citizenship. Between one-half and two-thirds were young bachelors of military age. Presumably, these men were second-generation immigrants whose parents were denied citizenship; but having grown up in Germany and been found militarily fit, they were granted naturalization. A second significant contingent consisted of well-to-do businessmen or physicians whose annual incomes were duly noted in the Prussian compilations. (We may tentatively suggest that when Russian Jews did establish themselves in Prussia, it was only because of their commercial success, and, accordingly, they stood a greater chance of being naturalized due to that success.) Finally, a small number of individuals apparently fit neither category but, for reasons that are unclear, still manged to acquire citizenship. These included German-born women who had forfeited their citizenship by marrying foreigners and now as widows and divorcees applied for naturalization, synagogue functionaries of modest means, converts from Judaism to Christianity, and individuals fitting no discernible category. It was this last group that best exemplified the arbitrary and serendipitous process by which foreign Jews acquired citizenship in Prussia.[34]

The policies and practices of other German states were not significantly different or more generous than those of Prussia. Saxony, the state with the second-largest population of East European Jews, had the reputation of rarely granting citizenship to Eastern Jews. Authorities were so inhospitable that, as of 1910, seventy-five percent of all Jews in the state did not possess Saxon citizenship. While this stunning figure can in part be explained by the fact that Saxony only began to permit Jews, including German Jews, into its territory during the nineteenth century, and consequently there were many newcomers among Saxonian Jewry, state policy discouraged the naturalization of Jews except under extraordinary circumstances. Between the years 1900 and 1914, when a total of 3,016 certificates of naturalization were issued by Saxony, only 79 were granted to Jews, including to immigrants from other German states—this at a time when over 10,000 foreign Jews resided in the state.[35]

In Bavaria, naturalization policies were governed by a ministerial decree issued on May 9, 1871, and subsequently reiterated often. According to this decree, it was Bavarian policy not to make the process of naturalization difficult except in regard to "elements that as a consequence of their economic, political, or national status are viewed as unwanted additions to the population." These elements included Russian and Galician Poles, as well as their Jewish compatriots. For such East Europeans, exceptions could be made only with the prior approval of the Ministry of Interior. In practice this meant, as conceded in private correspondence by a ministerial official, that "Russian Jews are normally not naturalized." And in general special approval was granted "only in rare circumstances." While government statistics on the incidence of naturalizations issued to Jews are unavailable, a perusal of several hundred naturalization files for the sample years 1900, 1905, 1910, and 1914 reveals many of the same patterns that were evident in Prussian procedures: very few Jews were granted citizenship, successful applicants generally possessed significant means, and quite a few were children of immigrants. In all cases, it took approximately two years to process Jewish applications, whereas those of non-Jews were generally approved within months; and all successful Jewish applicants had resided in Germany either for their entire lives or for at least two decades.[36]

The naturalization practices of German states with smaller populations of Eastern Jews are more difficult to assess, both because detailed records are unavailable and because, for the most part, Eastern Jews only settled in western states during the twentieth century and therefore had not maintained residence long enough to warrant naturalization before World War I. There is limited evidence, however, that chances for naturalization in these states was somewhat better than in Prussia. The *Verband der deutschen Juden* reported in 1910 that during the previous year only thirty-six percent of all Jews naturalized in German states received citizenship in Prussia, whereas on the basis of population concentrations, sixty percent should have been naturalized in Prussia. It is not surprising, therefore, that Jews rejected by Prussia migrated to other states hoping to acquire citizenship and then return to Prussia, since they were now protected from expulsion by virtue of their citizenship in a German state. This practice enraged Prussian officials, who for decades badgered their counterparts in other states not to naturalize Jews expelled from Prussia and pressed for a coordinated naturalization policy for all German states.[37]

A revision of the *Reich*'s "Law for the Acquisition and Forefeiture of Citizenship" which went into effect on January 1, 1914, finally satisfied the long-standing Prussian demand. The new law differed from its predecessor mainly in the veto power it granted to every German state over naturalizations issued in other states of the federation. According to Article 9 of the new law:

> Naturalization in a state can occur only after it has been ascertained by the *Reich* Chancellor that none of the other states has raised reservations; in the event that reservations exist, the Bundesrat is to decide the case.

In theory, states had to substantiate their objections to an applicant with clear evidence that the individual posed a danger to the nation or a state. But in practice, the new provision for coordination policy made it more difficult to acquire citizenship because it granted each state the right to cast an arbitrary veto over naturalization applications filed in other states. It was a routine occurrence when the law was in effect during the Weimar era that anti-Semitic governments in Bavaria and Hamburg vetoed the naturalization of Eastern Jews (and also Christian Poles) who had applied for citizenship in the then far more liberal Prussia on the grounds that the applicants were "culturally alien Eastern foreigners."[38]

In concluding our discussion of naturalization policies, it is important to take note of the fact that the process of applying for citizenship was in itself fraught with dangerous consequences. For when an individual filed for citizenship, he drew attention to himself. His application necessitated a review of his case and a general reassessment of his status in Germany. As a result, applicants not infrequently found themselves deemed unwanted by the state, and because no justification remained for tolerating such an individual, the applicant not only was not naturalized, but was expelled. While it is impossible to know how many foreign residents decided not to apply for citizenship out of fear that they would be penalized for their actions, contemporaries were well aware of the dangers inherent in calling attention to oneself. Describing the plight of such long-term foreign residents, Gustave Karpeles, a Moravian-born rabbi who had acquired Prussian citizenship, wrote as follows:

> There are foreign Jews who have lived and worked here for three or four decades; they have children and grandchildren. When, in the interest of their wives, their German-born children, and their grandchildren, they seek naturalization, they are informed by those who know—even by well-meaning officials—[to remain silent]. They are better off not reminding people that they are foreigners.[39]

Thus, Eastern Jews found themselves in a double bind: when they strove to acquire citizenship, they called attention to their status as foreigners and thereby risked expulsion; and when they passively accepted government policies that discouraged them from even applying for naturalization, they left themselves vulnerable to arbitrary expulsion because as aliens they could be ordered to leave the country at any time.

Mass Expulsions

As long as they denied citizenship to Eastern Jews, state governments possessed a potent instrument for ridding themselves of unwanted immigrants—explusion. While German laws granted aliens some protection, they also provided states with a means of driving them out. True, they were protected by trade agreements, and even the German criminal code *(Strafgesetzbuch)* required the fair treatment of alien criminals. Foreigners were also protected from arbitrary police searches and mail interceptions; they possessed religious freedom, provided that the public interest was not thereby harmed; and they possessed the same freedoms of the press as Germans. But there was one crucial exception to this legal protection: German states had the right to expel aliens for engaging in criminal activities or for endangering "public interests" and "security." Included in the latter were any actions deemed "troublesome" *(Lästig),* a catchall that granted bureaucrats wide latitude to expel foreigners as they saw fit. The expulsion of Eastern Jews for "troublesome" behavior became the preferred means to reduce the number of foreign Jews in Germany and to discourage potential immigrants from even bothering to settle in the *Reich.*[40]

In addition to expelling individual Eastern Jews as their residence permits expired, German states—particularly Prussia—periodically swept away groups of Eastern Jews en masse. The largest mass expulsion occurred in the 1880s when 10,000 Eastern Jews, along with some 20,000 Christian Poles, were driven out of Prussia. Thereafter, in every decade of the Imperial era—and indeed into the Weimar and Nazi eras—Eastern Jews were expelled en masse from parts of Germany. In the late 1890s, for example, there were widespread expulsions of immigrant Jews from Prussia's eastern provinces. Newspaper acounts dating from July and August 1897 carried reports concerning the expulsion of 112 out of the 800 Jews in Memel, with the victims including financially well-established Russian Jews who lost their businesses when they were forced to leave. (Significantly, some of these expulsion orders were rescinded when Memel's Jewish community protested to the Prussian minister of interior.) During the same years, there were reports concerning the expulsion of groups of Eastern Jews from other areas inside Prussia, as well as from other German states. All of these occurred at a time when Prussia was simultaneously expelling large numbers of Poles, Czechs, Russians, Danes, and Dutchmen.[41]

Early in the twentieth century, expulsion decrees were directed at recent arrivals from the Tsarist Empire. The years between 1904 and 1906 witnessed a dramatic upswing in the number of Russian Jews fleeing the chaos that had erupted in their homeland due to the war with Japan and the Revolution of 1905. While the overwhelming majority of these refugees traveled to the New World, Jewish immigrant populations in Prussian cities such as Berlin, Breslau, and Königsberg swelled. According to the police commisioner of Berlin, there were 6,500 new refugees in the capital alone. The Prussian cabinet, convinced of the subversive nature of these refugees, decided to expel all Jewish immigrants from Russian who had arrived after 1904. But as defenders of these immigrants, especially organized German Jewry, had become more outspoken in recent years, the cabinet decided on means to defuse the anticipated protest. It planned to expel only ten percent of the refugees immediately and only gradually drive out another eighty percent, while permitting ten percent to stay. The government also enlisted the support of native Jews in facilitating these expulsions by contending that an organized relief effort by German Jewry would minimize the "unavoidable cruelties" that would ensue if Jewish groups did not smooth the way for departing expulsion victims. By co-opting German Jewish groups, officials lessened the impact of protests against the expulsions.[42]

The key focus of expulsions during this period was Berlin. In 1904, several hundred Russian Jewish students were ordered to leave the city on the grounds that they were political leftists and anarchists. Then, in 1905–06, some 2,000 Russian Jewish families were expelled from the capital. Simultaneously, smaller groups of Russian Jews were driven from Breslau, Cologne, and, most especially, the eastern provinces of Prussia.[43]

While the government contended that only recent arrivals and "troublesome" individuals were victims of these actions, the press, SPD deputies, and Jewish groups marshalled evidence to contradict these claims. The *Berliner Tageblatt* carried stories about wealthy, long-term residents who were ordered to leave. In a bitter Reichstag address, August Bebel utilized this information to charge the Prussian government with using the refugee issue as a pretext for expelling all Russian Jews, regardless of their wealth and ownership of property. He cited the cases of Jewish engineers and businessmen who had amassed 10,000- and 20,000-mark accounts in their German banks and of a wealthy widow who was driven from Berlin even though her assets exceeded 80,000 mark. On the basis of data published in the liberal press, Bebel further charged that some 750 million mark were on deposit in Berlin banks in the accounts of Russian Jews. It was a sham to say that only the economically "troublesome" were ordered to leave; the wealthy, the self-sufficient, and the poor suffered equally.[44]

On the eve of World War I, Prussia began to organize yet one more mass expulsion of Eastern Jews. In 1911, the Jewish Reichstag deputy Paul Cassel protested to the Prussian Diet that expulsions were once again gaining momentum. The victims of these new decrees were primarily Jewish workers engaged in factory production or manual labor. In April 1914, 200 Galician Jews employed in cigarette production were ordered to leave Berlin with their families on the grounds that they lacked proper identification papers from the *Feldarbeiterzentrale,* the central bureau dealing with foreign workers. Most of these cigarette workers had lived in Berlin for over twenty years and had arrived well before such identification cards existed. When they applied for the proper papers, they were told that they would receive permits only to work in agriculture, not in industry. These expulsions, however, served merely as the prelude for a planned expulsion of far greater magnitude. In April 1913, the minister of interior ordered his *Oberpräsident* in Potsdam to furnish detailed information on the "Russian Jewish proletariat" congregating in Berlin and its suburbs. The minister explicitly stated his intention to use the data for an expulsion order under preparation.[45]

The prewar era also witnessed concerted actions directed at Eastern Jews engaged in petty trade. Prussian officials were especially eager to rid the Rhineland of Jewish junk dealers. Accordingly, the minister of trade requested Rhenish officials to supply data on the activities of such individuals. Similar actions were taken in Bavaria, which expelled twenty Jewish clothing dealers from Munich. While the total number of Eastern Jews expelled on the eve of World War I paled in comparison with the expulsions of the mid–1880s and even those of 1904–06, this was mainly because planned expulsions could not be carried out due to the altered situation once hostilities erupted. In the last months of 1914, thousands of Russian Jews in Germany were either expelled or interned as enemy aliens, while Austro-Hungarians gained in stature since they were regarded as potential soldiers and allies in the common war effort.[46]

An analysis of the circumstances surrounding the expulsions between the 1880s and the onset of the war reveals several important trends. First, it is evident that mass expulsion was a tool primarily employed by the state of Prussia. Whereas other states routinely expelled individuals in order to rid themselves of unwanted and "troublesome" foreigners, Prussia in addition resorted to periodic mass sweeps to drive out populations of aliens. Jewish foreigners were not the sole victims of these efforts; on the contrary, vast numbers of Poles, Russians, Ruthenians, Danes, Dutchmen, and other aliens were ousted. But expulsion served as the critical method for "managing" the mounting population of Eastern Jews in Prussia. Second, the key Jewish victims of the mass expulsions were Russian Jews, rather than Austro-Hungarians or Rumanians. Let us recall that the expulsions of the mid-1880s were initially aimed solely at Russian Jews and only as an afterthought were Galician Jews included in the edicts. In later decades, and particularly in the period from 1904–1906, Russian refugees were again the primary targets. It appears that Russians were treated in this manner both because their mass emigration from the Tsarist Empire proved a particularly unmanageable problem for Prussian border patrols and also because, as we shall see, the Russian government, unlike Austro-Hungary, remained indifferent to the abuse of its subjects in Germany. Finally, there is limited evidence that the Bismarckian expulsions served as models for subsequent administrations. In justifying their programs of mass expulsions at the turn of the century and again early in the new century, Prussian bureaucrats cited the precedent of the Bismarckian decrees of the 1880s. Thus, the severe measures enacted by Bismarck and Puttkamer continues to reverberate throughout the Imperial era.[47]

The Special Case of Students

While the various administrative policies thus far discussed affected all East European Jews in Germany, there was one contingent within this alien population that constituted a special case and therefore had to be dealt with independently—students at institutions of higher learning. To be sure, Jewish students from the East generally faced the same obstacles as other Eastern Jews in the *Reich* when they sought citizenship or long-term residence. But, whereas their status as resident aliens was regulated by general policies affecting all Eastern Jews, their proper place within the German academy required special attention. As the number of such students mounted early in the twentieth century and public demonstrations against "foreigners at institutions of higher learning" became more strident, state administrators in ministries of education addressed themselves to specific issues posed by Eastern Jews at universities and technical *Hochschulen* (colleges): Should such students be judged by the same admissions standards as native students? If they met those standards, should they be admitted in an unrestricted manner? And should they be free to enroll in any program of study and thereby derive benefit for themselves and their native lands from the high level of scientific and technical expertise available at German institutions of higher learning?[48]

The specific object of government concern was the rapidly growing contingent of Jewish students from Russia. After the imposition of a *numerus clausus* at tsarist institutions of higher learning in 1887, increasing numbers of Russian Jews came to Germany in pursuit of a higher education. Whereas in the summer semester of 1888 fewer than 60 Russian Jews matriculated at German universities, by the first years of the twentieth century this figure had risen to 600 students. A decade later, between 2,500 and 3,000 Russian Jews were enrolled at German institutions of higher learning.[49]

The émigré students were rendered even more conspicuous than these figures would suggest by their uneven geographic and academic concentrations. In 1912–13, seventy-six percent of Russian Jews at German universities congregated at five institutions—in Berlin, Breslau, Königsberg, Leipzig, and Munich. The 500 Russian Jews at Berlin's university and the 350 in Leipzig formed highly visible subgroups. More important, the overconcentration of these students in a few fields of study further highlighted their presence. Few chose the faculty of law, because they stood little chance of practicing as attorneys in Germany. Initially, philosophy was the most popular of faculties, but it lost ground because Jews could not expect to receive the teaching or civil service positions in Russia for which this discipline prepared them. As a result, a staggeringly high percentage of these students matriculated in medical and, to a lesser extent, chemistry and mathematics programs. By 1911, eight-five percent of Russian Jews at Prussian universities studied medicine. In non-Prussian universities such as Freiburg, Heidelberg, Leipzig, and Munich anywhere from eighty to ninety percent of the Russian Jews matriculated as medical students. German technical *Hochschulen* were also attractive to Russian Jews, but these institutions placed restrictions on the number of foreign students far earlier and more rigorously than the universities. The few hospitable technical *Hochschulen*, however, attracted disproportionately large numbers of Russian Jews. At Karlsruhe's technical school, for example, Russians constituted one-quarter of the total student body, one-third of mechanical engineering students, and an even larger percentage of electrical engineering students in 1910. Such disproportionate overconcentration in much-sought-after fields hardly went unnoticed.[50]

The initial German response to the growing number of Russian Jewish students consisted of heightened vigilance on the part of ministries of education, the agencies that regulated institutions of higher learning in each German state. Between 1889 and 1891, just a few years after Russia imposed educational quotas on Jews, several states began to gather statistical data and exchanged information about the Russian Jews. Bureaucracies in Prussia and Saxony, where the preponderant majority of these students enrolled, required universities to submit special reports on the number of Russian students at their institutions—listing Jews and Gentiles separately. Significantly, state officials at first ordered these reports in order to answer inquiries submitted by the Russian government, just as they had first begun to monitor Russian Jewish immigrants at the behest of the tsarist government in the early 1880s. During the 1890s, German officials also expressed concern to each other over the concentration of Russian Jews in medical faculties. In 1890, Chancellor Bismarck specifically directed Prussia's education minister to examine the number of such students who had enrolled during the previous three years—that is, since the imposition of Russian quotas—and the Bavarian government inquired of the *Reich*'s interior minister whether the influx of Russian Jews necessitated a revision of admissions policies at medical schools. This flurry of activity signified increased government awareness of the newcomers, but did not result in new policies.[51]

A sustained crackdown on Russian Jewish students began only after the turn of the century in response to the lobbying efforts of a variety of groups. One source of pressure was the tsarist government, which demanded German cooperation in the battle against Russian radicals. Germany had obliged itself to cooperate in this campaign when in 1901 it negotiated and in 1904 ratified a treaty with Russia and several other European states wherein it pledged to battle against "anarchists," a term loosely applied to all radicals, socialists, and "nihilists." German states lived up to their treaty obligations and went even further by permitting tsarist agents to operate freely within the *Reich*. The historian Barbara Vogel has argued plausibly that this highly unusual arrangements served as a simple and politically safe means to strengthen ties with Russia, since collaboration in the fight against "anarchists" cost Germany little while it united the two empires in a crusade against subversion.[52]

To a limited extent, governments had already kept a special watch on Russian students during the last two decades of the nineteenth century, but efforts intensified in 1901 when the tsarist minister of education was murdered by a Russian student who had lived in Berlin prior to the assassination. On orders from the kaiser, university and police authorities in Berlin began to cooperate actively with Russian secret agents operating in the German capital. Subsequently, Russian police were permitted to work freely in the rest of Prussia and later in other German states. Especially after the Russian Revolution of 1905, German police frequently harassed Russian students, searched their libraries and social clubs for illegal literature, and spied on their meetings.[53]

Foreign students caught engaging in revolutionary activities were subjected by police to severe and arbitrary punishment against which they had no legal recourse. In several states, police closed down students clubs and reading rooms after they discovered revolutionary literature on the premises. German officials also expelled individual Russian students for allegedly "anarchistic," "nihilistic," or simply "troublesome" conduct. Police were especially quick to punish students who appeared to contravene state laws and university regulations forbidding noncitizens from attending German political rallies or engaging in election activities. To cite just two instances of swift retribution for alleged interference in the German political process: a leader of the Bundists (a revolutionary Jewish socialist party in Poland and Russia) in Berlin suffered expulsion from Prussia when he was observed spending time in the offices of the *Vorwärts,* the press organ of Germany's Social Democratic Party; and a student named Rahel Kirsch was ordered to leave Prussia five weeks before the completion of her studies at a school of commerce on the grounds that she had attended a German May Day rally. Russian students even faced severe punishment when they demonstrated on behalf of their own interests: in 1904 428 Russians in Berlin signed a petition protesting against a recent inflammatory Reichstag speech in which Chancellor von Bülow had declared, with explicit reference to Russian Jewish students, that Germany "will not be led by the nose by such *Schnorrers* and conspirators." Within a month, Prussia expelled 116 of the petitioners, including 99 Russian Jews.[54]

Official harassment of Russian Jewish students was matched by a growing movement within the academy to limit the rights of "foreign students." During the early years of the twentieth century, student groups and professional associations began to bombard education ministers and academic administrators with petitions that called for discriminatory admissions policies, particularly at technical schools, which at the time were admitting large numbers of Russian Jews. A number of complaints recurred in these petitions.[55] Native students blamed foreign intruders for the shortage of seats in lecture halls and overcrowding in universities. They singled out Russian students as the true culprits: "the culturally inferior elements from the East pose a danger to the national character of our *Hochschulen.*" Russian students fail to master the German language, it was claimed, and consequently lower the academic quality of classes, especially when they serve as teaching and laboratory assistants. Many Russian students possess "insufficient scientific training *[Bildung]*" and, in fact, are admitted to German *Hochschulen* without having passed a competitive exam *(Konkurrenzprüfung)* or attained certification after their secondary school studies *(Reifezeugnis).* Some German institutions even admit students who had been rejected by Russian *Hochschulen*. This situation, claimed the petitioners, was unfair and insulting to native students. German institutions, however, need not exclude all foreigners, but rather they must institute selective procedures to ensure that only "those who will enrich the student body" may gain admission.[56]

Petitioners also raised several broader issues. They regarded it as the height of folly for Germany to educate foreign engineers and scientists in the most advanced techniques. These aliens surely would soon go abroad and help foreign countries develop their productive capacities to rival German industries. True, at first these students might copy German production techniques and therefore import industrial machinery from the *Reich*, but in the long run Germany was educating competitors and enemies. Furthermore, foreign students were politically unreliable: it was well known that "Slavic and Jewish students work on behalf of the Social Democrats" and are "political radicals."

The petitioners proposed a variety of changes in admissions policies to remedy the situation. Student groups urged *Hochschulen* to impose higher academic fees on foreigners, permit aliens to enroll in classes only after all Germans students had completed registration, and demand fluency in the German language as a prerequisite for study at institutions of higher learning. Some groups outside the academic world demanded a policy of "German *Hochschulen* for Germans." The Society of German Chemists, for example, urged restrictions on foreign students, excepting German-speaking students from Switzerland, Austria, and the Baltic territories of tsarist Russia—"so that the young students of our people and the German race outside of the *Reich*'s borders may enjoy unrestricted educational opportunities."

Bureaucrats in the various ministries of education responded sympathetically to these demands. During the first decade of the century, they directed virtually every institution of higher learning to impose a tuition scale that discriminated between native and alien students. Generally, foreign students were required to pay up to two or three times the normal sums for the various matriculation, laboratory, lecture, examination, and certification fees. It should be noted, however, that the new, onerous fees were levied on all foreign students and did not fall more heavily on any one national contingent.[57]

State officials also formulated a series of new admissions policies for technical schools that were directed specifically at Russians. Early in the new century, Prussia set the precedent when its education minister ordered Russian students to furnish a *Reifezeugnis* valid for admission to a Russian *Hochschule* and proof of prior study at a Russian institution of higher learning as a prerequisite for enrollment at state technical schools. In March 1902, Bavarian officials adopted the same policy, consciously modeling themselves after the Prussians and adding a new regulation that permitted foreigners to begin registration at the earliest two weeks after native students had completed selecting their courses. By September, Saxony imposed a new regulation on students planning to enroll at Dresden's technical school: Russian students needed proof of prior study at a Russian university as a prerequisite for admission; even previous enrollment at a non-Saxon *Hochschule* was deemed insufficient. In sum, Prussia, Bavaria, and Saxony henceforth would accept into their technical schools only transfer students from Russian institutions of higher learning.[58]

Education officials in other German states came under strong pressures to institute similar regulations. Ministers in the more restrictive states pressed their counterparts in more lenient ministries to conform. When representatives of education ministries gathered in July 1902, just a few months after Prussia and Bavaria had acted and shortly before Saxony would impose new restrictions, they were urged to coordinate policies toward foreign students at *Hochschulen*.[59] Bureaucrats who had not yet restricted Russian students were also pressured at home by local student groups and parliamentary deputies demanding a justification for lenient admissions policies. Even more important, *Hochschulen* that did not regulate foreign students quickly experienced a dramatic increase in the number of Russians because restrictive policies in Prussia, Bavaria, and Saxony sent students in search of institutions that remained more hospitable. The pattern is evident from the following statistics: the enrollment of Russians at the Charlottenburg (Berlin) technical school declined from 121 in 1901–02 to 55 in 1912; in Dresden, 61 Russians were enrolled in 1905–06 and only 11 by 1913–14; and in Munich, the number of Russians dwindled from 243 in 1904–05 to 123 in 1913. By contrast, the technical *Hochschulen* in Karlsruhe and Darmstadt reported the highest percentages of foreigners in their student bodies (39.4% and 38.1%, respectively, in 1907) because they had not yet curbed Russian students vigorously. Clearly, Russian Jewish students sought out educational institutions that did not bar them, and this movement increased pressures in Baden, Hesse, and other states for more restrictive policies.[60]

Officials in Baden responded by imposing new curbs. In 1902, Baden's minister of education ordered Russian students to provide proof of successful performance in a Russian competitive exam *(Konkurrenzprüfung) or* of prior study at a *Hochschule* in their homeland as a prerequisite for enrollment at Karlsruhe's technical school. He also granted native students priority during course registration. By 1905 Baden's educational authorities instituted tests to check the fluency of Russians in the German language. Unlike their counterparts in other education ministries, however, bureaucrats in Baden did not require Russian students to provide evidence that they had studied at a tsarist university prior to their admission to Karlsruhe's technical *Hochschule*.[61]

Authorities in other German states proved themselves less generous under pressure. In 1905, Braunschweig's technical *Hochschule* imposed a *numerus clausus* on foreigners that limited their number to twelve percent of the student body. Two years later, the Ministry of Interior in Hesse required all Russian students at Darmstadt's technical school to furnish a diploma from a Russian *Gymnasium and* evidence of matriculation at a Russian university before they could study in Hesse. And Stuttgart's technical college simply ceased to accept Russian students.[62]

In addition, by 1908 most states rejected students from Russian *Realschulen* and technical *Hochschulen*, even as they continued to accept those from German *Real-* and *Ober-Realschulen*. As a justification, ministers noted that studies at Russian *Realschulen* lasted only seven years, compared to the nine-year course of study at German *Realschulen;* only graduates of Russian nine-year *Gymnasia* were deemed sufficiently prepared. In fact, as bureaucrats admitted in their private correspondence, they had seized upon the difference between Russian and German *Realschulen* as a further pretext to curb Russian students.[63]

While these new regulations ostensibly affected all Russians, they were actually aimed at Russian Jews. Jewish, but not Gentile, Russians could not furnish a *Gymnasium* diploma due to anti-Semitic quotas at tsarist secondary schools. Further, it was particularly difficult for Jews to present proof of study at a Russian institution of higher learning prior to their arrival in Germany: Russian Jews went abroad precisely because the *numerus clausus* blocked them from studying in their homeland. And Jews, not Gentiles, faced special obstacles in taking competitive exams in Russia and therefore could not meet German requirements for the successful completion of a *Konkurrenzprüfung*. In short, notwithstanding the euphemistic language employed by education ministries, the new admissions policies at *Hochschulen* were primarily designed to curb one contingent of foreign students—Jewish victims of tsarist quotas.

The upshot of these new restrictions at technical schools was a rapid surge in the enrollment of Russian Jews in universities. Trends in the states of Baden and Saxony illustrate the dimensions of this widespread shift: between 1905–06 and 1913, the number of Russians (including Gentiles) leaped from 89 to 212 at Heidelberg's university and sank from 372 to 161 at Karlsruhe's *Hochschule;* during the same years, enrollments by Russian Jews at Dresden's technical college dwindled from 61 to 40, whereas at Leipzig's university they soared from 63 to 297. The move to universities gained further momentum from the ever-increasing numbers of Jews who left Russia after the 1905 revolution in quest of a higher education. By 1913, nearly 500 such students matriculated at Berlin's university alone, and contingents of Russian Jews numbering in the hundreds could be found at several other universities.[64]

The influx of these Russian Jews prompted a new round of student protests. During the year 1907, German students rallied in Jena, Leipzig, Berlin, and Darmstadt to urge the exclusion of Russian or Russian Jewish students. In the same year, the *Verein Deutscher Studenten* passed a resolution at its national convention urging the Prussian government to press other German states to keep out Russian students. Simultaneously, parliamentarians in the Reichstag and state diets urged the expulsion of foreigners from institutions of higher learning in order to protect "the national and economic interests of our *Volk* from the dangerous advances of foreigners." Behind the scenes, tsarist officials pressured German state governments to intensify their surveillance of Russian Jewish students and urged that Germany should not permit students who had been rejected by tsarist institutions to matriculate at German universities.[65]

In direct response to these secret tsarist demands and public agitation by native students, Bavaria's minister of education imposed a quota on Russians, limiting their enrollment at Munich's university to 200 students. In the future, Russians admitted under this quota would have to demonstrate proficiency in the German language and provide proof of graduation from a *Gymnasium* and of prior study at a Russian institution of higher learning. Officials, however, did not anticipate accepting new Russian students for some years to come since existing enrollments far exceeded the quota. Only after the number of Russians at Munich's university declined below the quota could authorities even consider admitting new students from Russia. Not surprisingly, due to the Bavarian crackdown, the number of Russians at Saxon and Prussian universities mounted, causing further student and official concern.[66]

Before states could react, a new round of protest demonstrations erupted at universities throughout Germany. Spearheaded by medical students who claimed that foreign students were treated too leniently, these protests soon led to a strike of clinical students at the university of Halle in January 1913. This action, in turn, prompted medical students in other universities to organize sympathy demonstrations and issue demands for quotas to reduce the number of foreigners at universities.[67]

An examination of enrollment figures at medical schools makes plain that Russian Jews were the objects of this agitation. During the period of student demonstrations, Russians constituted three-quarters of all foreigners in medical faculties, while between eighty and ninety percent of all medical students from the Tsarist Empire were Jews. It is more difficult to assess the validity of student complaints about the overcrowding caused by foreign students. A 1911 memorandum from Heidelberg's anatomical institute reports a shortage of corpses needed in dissection classes. But the observation of a contemporary authority, sent from America to study German medical schools, casts some doubt on charges that there was severe overcrowding. According to Abraham Flexner's 1911 study of clinical sections in German medical schools, "benches thronged in the early days of the semester, usually have room long before its close." During clinical demonstrations, Flexner "repeatedly heard anywhere from three to a dozen names called before a response was obtained." Evidently, overcrowding was more of a problem on registration lists than in lecture theaters and laboratories.[68]

Even though some education ministers admitted that foreigners did not deprive natives of places at universities, they instituted a variety of new restrictions to satisfy protesting students. Prussia, to take the most important state first, imposed a *numerus clausus*. As of September 24, 1913, only 900 Russian students could enroll at Prussian universities: 280 in Berlin, 80 in Bonn, 100 in Breslau, 60 in Göttingen, 120 in Halle, 140 in Königsberg, and 30 each in Marburg, Kiel, Münster, and Greifswald. These quotas were not to affect the nearly 1,100 Russian students already enrolled.[69]

Bavaria followed suit by instituting a more comprehensive quota system. No more than 400 foreigners could study at the university of Munich and no more than 150 subjects of any one state could enroll in medical schools. This translated into a limit of 80 foreigners each at the universities in Würzburg and Erlangen, no more than half of whom could study medicine. At the same time, prior enrollment at a tsarist *Hochschule* was still required of incoming Russian students.[70]

Saxony imposed no quota but it required all Russian students to have studied at a university in their native country prior to their transfer to a Saxon university. (Even two years of prior study at a German university was deemed unacceptable.) Moreover, only graduates of a Russian *Gymanasium,* not a *Real-* or *Ober-Realschule,* were accepted. Even if admitted, medical students were given no assurance that they could participate in the clinical part of the program. And Russian women could not matriculate at all; at best, they might audit courses, provided they had graduated from the best women's high schools.[71]

Officials in Baden resisted pressures to impose a *numerus clausus* or admissions requirements aimed mainly at Russian Jews. The minister of education opposed such measures on the grounds that they excluded worthy students, hurt the interests of universities, and negated "the Baden tradition" of hospitality. However, he feared that quotas and restrictions in other states would bring a flood of students to Baden. He therefore ordered rigorous testing of students to measure their fluency in German, granted priority during registration to native students, and raised fees for foreigners at medical and technical schools.[72]

The new regulations had an immediate impact at universities. Since, in most cases, quotas were exceeded even before their introduction, the flow of Jewish students from Russia virtually halted. By the summer of 1913, the number of Russians matriculating at German universities plummeted by nearly twenty percent compared to the previous year. Historical events, however, intervened before the full weight of the new restrictions could be felt. A year after most quotas were imposed, war erupted and Germans expelled or interned enemy aliens. By late 1914 debates over foreign students had ceased since Russian Jews were no longer enrolled at German institutions of higher learning.[73]

Although the outbreak of war prevented their full implementation, the policies enacted by various state governments are of importance because they represent official responses to Jewish students from the East. As was the case with the larger population of Eastern Jews in the *Reich,* Russian Jewish students were the objects of bureaucratic attention that culminated in the formulation of special government policies. These policies managed to impede Russian Jews, but not other foreigners, from studying first at *Hochschulen* and then at universities. Whereas West European and American students were unaffected by the new regulations, Russian Jews were pushed out of the academy by requirements that only they could not meet. Some states imposed quotas solely on Russians. Others placed a *numerus clausus* on all foreigners, but in practice shaped restrictions to curb only Jewish students from the Tsarist Empire: they restricted foreigners in faculties where the latter predominated, for example, medicine; they rejected graduates of Russian *Realschulen,* which affected Jews who faced quotas at tsarist *Gymnasia;* and, most critical, they insisted that only Russians provide evidence of prior study at an institution of higher learning in their homeland, a demand that most Russian Jews could not meet due to tsarist quotas. The new regulations thus reduced the complex questions posed by the presence of foreigners at German universities and the particular needs of Russian Jewish students to a simple matter of curbing unwanted Jews. As new restrictions were formulated, an official in Berlin's police department clarified the issue confronting state bureaucrats:

> Academic life must be protected from the influx of Russians, which is 90% Jewish and therefore unwanted. The well-known arrogance of Russian Jewish students is growing in direct proportion to their numbers. This deepens the antagonism between German and Russian students and will lead to new and more considerable conflict.

Though not privy to such candid private correspondence, many contemporaries understood the intention of their government's policy. "Practically, it means," wrote the *Frankfurter Zeitung,* "that Russian Jews who are as good as barred from university study in their dear fatherland now also cannot attend German universities. Because of this cruelty, we permit ourselves to speak of Russian barbarism at German *Hochschulen."* Whether state policies were barbarous or Russian, they did directly address the special issues posed by Jewish students from the East.[74]

The German Response
to Jewish Immigration:
An Assessment

In concluding this survey of government policies toward Eastern Jews, it is appropriate to underscore several critical aspects of the German response to Jewish immigration. Perhaps the most noteworthy feature of developments in Germany was the relative absence of constraints under which governments operated. The entire system of governance pertaining to foreigners granted each state bureaucracy almost unlimited power to regulate foreigners in its territories. States were empowered to approve or deny the right of residence, admit or expel aliens, extend naturalization to a foreigner or strip a native of his citizenship. At most, the laws of the *Reich* outlined general principles governing the status of foreigners, but then granted states the freedom to add their own restrictions and prohibitions.

In designing and executing their policies, state officials were also relatively unconstrained by foreign policy considerations. True, they were forced to abide by commercial treaties that permitted aliens to travel about for business purposes. But when it came to the treatment of a specific East European Jew, there was little to fear from that Jew's country of origin. The tsarist government not only did not protect Russian subjects residing in the *Reich,* but consistently encouraged German officials to treat Russian Jews ever more stringently. During the expulsions of the mid-1880s, tsarist officials only spoke out when they felt that Prussian authorities had acted too leniently or had neglected to expel some individuals. In fact, Prussian ministers openly noted the indifference of Russian officials and took such apathy into account when they planned mass expulsions.[75]

The Austro-Hungarian government, by contrast, did protest Prussian policies on occasion. While the Hapsburg foreign office fully accepted the right of Prussia to expel Austro-Hungarian subjects and sympathized with the Prussian government's desire to prevent the growth of a significant population of Eastern Jews in its territory, Austrian officials at times protested the mass and indiscriminate expulsion of its subjects. This was particularly the case in the decade before the outbreak of World War I when Austrian consular officials challenged some Prussian actions. Matters came to a head in 1906 when Austria's foreign minister objected to Prussia's recent mass expulsions and threatened to raise the matter in public debate before the Austrian parliament. Significantly, in response to this protest, Prussia's minister of interior, Bethmann-Hollweg, forbade his underlings from driving out Austro-Hungarians in "mass expulsions"; instead he urged that only individuals found guilty of crimes should be deported. This exceptional protest and its results prove the rule, however: the governments of Russia, Austro-Hungary, and Rumania were indifferent to Germany's treatment of their Jewish subjects, a state of affairs that freed German officials to act with impunity toward East European Jews.[76]

Unquestionably, the most intensive meddling in state affairs came from Prussian state officials. From the first years of the new empire, Bismarck already tried to influence ministers in the various German states to follow Prussia's lead and treat aliens severely. Throughout the Imperial era, Prussian consuls and officials in the foreign ministry bombarded their colleagues in other German states, urging those states to crack down on Eastern Jews. Prussian officials were particularly incensed over the ability of some Jews expelled from Prussia to find haven and even acquire citizenship in other states of the federation and then return to Prussia as protected German citizens. As we have noted, pressure exerted by Prussian officials often led to intensified vigilance in other German states and eventually culminated in the passage of a new stipulation in the *Reich*'s "Law for the Acquisition and Forfeiture of Citizenship" that granted states veto power over naturalizations performed in other states. Prussia, by virtue of its size and immediate concern with Jewish mass migration, thus was the most important state in the resolution of German policies toward Eastern Jews.

It is far more difficult to assess the impact of German lobbyists on the policies of their governments. There certainly is evidence that local governments were attuned to the protests of their constituents: in some cases, foreigners were expelled because native Germans wished to free themselves of business competitors; and, in other cases, individuals were spared from expulsions when local business associations came to their defense, pleading their indispensability to the local economy. It is more difficult to measure the impact of lobbyists on state officials. The decision to impose quotas and other restrictions on Russian students was undoubtedly hastened by the demands of German students and technical groups. And the constant tirades of anti-Semitic politicians surely served to keep the issue of Jewish migration in the consciousness of government officials. But there is no evidence that policies such as the imposition of severe restrictions in Prussia's eastern provinces, or bans on the naturalization of Eastern Jews, or even the repeated mass expulsions came in response to specific lobbying efforts. Rather, it appears that these initiatives were launched by the highest state officials at their own behest.

The enormous power wielded by state officials in determining the fate of Eastern Jews was often exercised in an arbitrary and cynical manner. While it is entirely understandable that German government officials wished to protect Germany from the unrestricted migration of aliens across the *Reich*'s frontiers, the manner in which this influx was checked left much room for abuse. At best, individual Eastern Jews were deemed acceptable only if their presence in some manner contributed to "state interests." But the moment a local police official or state bureaucrat determined that an Eastern Jew no longer served state interests, the Jew was harassed and deported. The destructiveness of official responses, then, lay not in efforts to stem Jewish immigration but in the arbitrary and cynical manipulation of Eastern Jews.

Indeed, the entire system for coping with foreigners in general, and Eastern Jews in particular, was designed to exploit aliens, a state of affairs that permitted bigotry and abusiveness to flourish unchecked. Local police officials and entire state bureaucracies were permitted, with barely any constraints, to treat Eastern Jews as they saw fit. The efforts of Jannina Berson, a Russian Jewish student, to protest her imprisonment and expulsion by Prussian police well illustrates the defenselessness of Eastern Jews in the *Reich*. In response to Berson's formal protest, Bethmann-Hollweg, the minister of interior, ruled that Berson had no legal recourse since expulsion was an administrative prerogative that aliens could not challenge. Not surprisingly, at least some officials were corrupted by their absolute power to control the fate of Eastern Jews. A newspaper report from the year 1910 recounts the abysmal experience of a Russian Jew who resided in Posen. Every day a local police officer demanded to see the Jew's passport on an average of five or six times—even though the officer well knew that the papers were good for a year. When the Jew protested to district officials, Posen's *Regierungspräsident* ordered the policeman to desist from harassing the foreigner. The policeman, in turn, successfully sued for slander and the Russian Jew was sentenced to a three-month prison term. Such a system inevitably encouraged petty officials to tyrannize defenseless aliens.[77]

Policies toward Eastern Jews also gave free reign to the expression of anti-Semitism. Repeatedly, government officials decided the fate of an individual foreigner on the basis of his or her religious confession. In denying an application for naturalization, officials merely had to note the unacceptability of the applicant on the grounds that "he is a Jew." Such discrimination was then routinely justified by resorting to stereotypes about the subversive or rapacious character of Eastern Jews. But while it was one thing for government officials privately to harbor bigoted and stereotypical views of Eastern Jews, it was another to act upon such prejudices. Their discrimination against Eastern Jews in areas where they wielded vast discretionary powers—in cases of residence policies, naturalization procedures, expulsion decisions—incriminated state officials in the anti-Semitism of the Imperial era. At a time when native Jews were officially emancipated (protected as citizens under the law), government officials discriminated with impunity against a population of unprotected, unemancipated Jews residing in the *Reich*— East European immigrants. In this manner, state bureaucrats were accomplices in the spread and further development of anti-Semitism during the era of Jewish emancipation.[78]

The consequences for German Jewry of such official anti-Semitism will be discussed below (see Chapter 9); in the present context, however, we may note the impact of such policies upon Eastern Jews. Some benefited from the inconsistencies of state policies. They found ways to maintain long-term residence by moving from one state to the next or even from a more stringent to a more lenient locality within a state. But, for the most part, Eastern Jews suffered as victims of arbitrary and cynical policies. Their sojourn in the *Reich* depended on the whims of local and state officials: after residing in Germany for decades, they could be deported, suddenly deprived of their homes, businesses, and social networks. East European Jews in Germany thus enjoyed few legal protections. Like all Jews who lived under medieval conditions, they were dependent upon the tolerance and protection offered by government officials, a state of affairs that profoundly affected their social behavior and relations with native Jewry, themes to which we now turn.

II

THE
EAST EUROPEAN JEWS

4

Demographic Characteristics

During the many public and private debates over immigration policy, the character of East European Jews was an issue of central concern. Those who favored tighter curbs on Jewish immigration contended that Eastern Jews constituted both a quantitative and qualitative menace to Germany. They pictured Eastern Jews as a horde of potential invaders massing at the *Reich*'s frontiers, awaiting the opportunity to swarm into the country in uncountable numbers. Once in the country, it was alleged, alien Jews would live as parasites and subversives, exploiting Germany's economy and seeking to undermine its political system. But what was the true character of Jewish immigrants in Imperial Germany? Were Eastern Jews settling in the country in mass numbers? Did they live as "*Schnorrers* and conspirators"? And to what extent were they integrated into German society? In short, what was the correlation between the actual—as distinct from the perceived—demographic, occupational, and social characteristics of East European Jews in the Second German Empire?

In addressing these questions, it is necessary to distinguish between transmigrants passing through the *Reich* and resident aliens who settled in the country. The former constituted by far the larger contingent, numbering in the vicinity of two million individuals. As we have already seen in Chapter 3, German officials established an elaborate apparatus to insure their continued movement from the eastern frontiers to the North Sea ports. Due to German safeguards, the overwhelming majority of Jewish emigrants from the East swiftly moved through and out of the country. By contrast, only a small contingent of Eastern Jews managed to secure at least temporary permission to stay in the *Reich*. These residents fell into three categories—transients, students, and immigrants. Transients tarried in Germany in order to take advantage temporarily of opportunities presented by Germany. Among the most prominent transients were Yiddish and Hebrew writers, musical and theatrical performers, and visiting intellectuals; among the least prominent, but nonetheless conspicuous, were beggars who supported their families in the East by obtaining charitable contributions from German Jews. While it is impossible to know how many Eastern Jews in Germany fell into this category, transients could not have numbered more than 1,000 souls by the peak years shortly before World War I, and they were widely dispersed. University students formed yet a second population of resident aliens. Drawn overwhelmingly from the Tsarist Empire after the imposition of quotas at Russian institutions of higher learning, their numbers rose dramatically during the first decade of the twentieth century, reaching approximately 3,000 souls. And, finally, the third, and by far the largest, contingent of residents was comprised of immigrants who managed to settle in Germany and strove to remain in the country. In truth, the lines of demarcation between the four subgroups of Eastern Jews sometimes blurred: on occasion, students sought residence as immigrants upon completion of their studies; transmigrants tried to tarry rather than embark for foreign shores; transients managed to extend their stay by continually renewing their residence permits; and immigrants often found themselves driven out of the country so that they became part of the transmigrant traffic. Nonetheless, individuals in each of these four categories were identifiable to government officials since every alien in Germany was subject to strict policing.

The following three chapters present a profile of Eastern Jews who resided in Germany. In contrast to transmigrants, who rapidly traversed the *Reich* and departed, Jewish transients and immigrants were suspected by restrictionists and anti-Semites of parasitical and subversive behavior. We shall therefore confine ourselves to an analysis of these groups in order to evaluate the accuracy of German perceptions and fears.

Population Patterns

There is no systematic information on the exact numbers of East European Jews in Germany prior to 1890, the year when the *Reich*'s statistical bureau began to publish data that differentiated foreigners according to religious confession. There is, however, ample evidence of a continuous trickle of Jewish immigration into German states from the era of the Thirty Years War until the unification of the Second German Empire. Both Jewish sources and government reports attest to small-scale movement, as do the repeated efforts by local governments to halt the activities of Jewish beggars from abroad. Prussian statistics compiled during the early 1880s document the naturalization of some 3,600 Russian Jewish families in the period between 1848 and 1880, sure evidence of a limited population movement. Several hundred additional Jews from the East settled in other German states on the eve of unification, so that, for example, some 570 Eastern Jews resided in the Saxonian city of Leipzig in 1871.[1]

It was during the first fifteen years of the *Reich* that the size of these populations began to mount. By 1880, approximately 16,000 Eastern Jews inhabited the empire. The overwhelming majority of these, some 14,000–15,000, clustered in Prussia, whereas smaller numbers established themselves in Saxony and possibly Bavaria. During this early period of the *Reich*'s history, most Jewish immigrants from the East came from Russia and settled in the eastern provinces of Prussia, both in cities and small towns; by contrast, only 3,000–4,000 Eastern Jews had settled in Berlin by 1880.[2]

As Jewish mass migration accelerated during the 1880s, the number of Eastern Jews in Germany rose. By the year 1890, just a few years after the mass expulsions of the mid-1880s, some 20,000 such Jews were counted in the national census. A decade later, this population numbered some 35,000 souls. And according to the last census before World War I, there were nearly 70,000 Eastern Jews in the country on December 1, 1910. Eastern Jews then represented slightly more than one-tenth of one percent of Germany's sixty-five million inhabitants.[3]

A variety of motives prompted Eastern Jews to attempt to settle in the *Reich*. University students were attracted by the liberal admissions requirements at German institutions of higher learning, as well as the country's renown as a center of advanced study. Transients were drawn by sundry economic and cultural opportunities. For most Eastern Jews, however, chance reason determined whether they would try to settle in the *Reich*—and whether such efforts would succeed. When Jacob Thon, a Galician rabbinical student in Berlin, investigated this question early in the twentieth century by interviewing Eastern Jews in Berlin's "ghetto" area, he found that few could explain how they had come to settle there. Some arrived in Berlin with the intention of eventually continuing on to America, but lingered because they liked the city; others were lured by their relatives' success stories and promises of aid; and yet others settled in Berlin convinced that the prominent local community would help them establish new lives.[4]

Whatever their motives for seeking residence in Germany, the population of Eastern Jews in the *Reich* assumed a distinctive character by the early years of the twentieth century. Perhaps the most startling feature of this population was its preponderantly Austro-Hungarian composition: in every census conducted after 1885, Russians were in the minority, whereas the majority were drawn from the Dual Monarchy. (We have already noted that the reverse was the case prior to the expulsions of the mid-1880s.) This nationality composition is noteworthy because the mass migration of East European Jews was primarily a Russian phenomenon. Aside from Germany, no other Western country received more Jews from Austro-Hungary than Russia.[5]

A second distinguishing feature of these foreign Jewish residents was their pattern of geographic distribution. The bulk of Eastern Jews settled in only three German states—Prussia, Saxony, and Bavaria. Such was the case in the year 1880, when nearly all Eastern Jews in the *Reich* inhabited Prussia. And as late as the year 1910, 82.5% of Jewish immigrants lived in three states bordering the eastern frontier. The largest contingent settled in Prussia, home of the greatest number of German Jews. But it was in Saxony that Eastern Jews congregated in such disproportionate numbers that their relative percentage in the Jewish population of that state rose from only 15% in 1880 to 59% by 1910. While it is understandable that Eastern Jews should settle initially in border states, it would be expected that they eventually would try to infiltrate the more westerly states of Hesse, Baden, and Württemberg in greater numbers. Given the severity of policies in the eastern-most states, it is likely that Eastern Jews did not have the opportunity to move freely through Germany in order to reach other German states.[6]

Eastern Jews also assumed a discernible pattern of urban settlement. In fact, these Jews were one of the most urbanized populations in the *Reich*. By 1910, a staggering seventy-eight percent of all alien Jews resided in the forty-eight "large cities" (cities with populations exceeding 100,000 inhabitants). By contrast, only fifty percent of native Jews and only twenty-one percent of all Germans resided in the "large cities." These patterns of urban concentration were even more unusual because Eastern Jews dispersed to many German cities. In marked contrast to the propensity of East European Jews in other Western lands to settle in one major city—for example, London, Paris, Vienna, New York—barely more than one-fifth of Eastern Jews in the *Reich* resided in a single city (Berlin) by the year 1910. In this regard, Eastern Jews had a similar pattern of geographic distribution to German Jews: just as the latter never clustered in one key city, so did Eastern Jews disperse to several urban habitats. These included the Saxonian cities of Dresden and Leipzig, both of which had more immigrant than native Jews by 1910; the city of Munich in Bavaria, where Eastern Jews constituted over one-quarter of the Jewish inhabitants; and, of course, Berlin, where some 13,000 Eastern Jews resided by 1910 and comprised close to twenty percent of the Jewry in the *Reich*'s capital.[7]

Even within the large cities, these Jews tended to disperse rather than congregate in a highly visible "ghetto" area. In Berlin, for example, the city possessing the largest population of immigrant Jews, only one small quarter even remotely resembled a "ghetto" prior to World War I. Known as the *Scheunenviertel,* this area became a first stop for newly arrived immigrants seeking temporary lodgings in hotels catering to a Yiddish-speaking clientele. Streets such as the Grenadierstrasse, Dragonerstrasse, and Linienstrasse abounded in shops selling kosher food products, as well as a few small synagogue halls. Yet the *Scheunenviertel* did not long remain the home of most Eastern Jews in pre–World War I Berlin (in marked contrast to its greater vitality after the Great War). Once they found work, newcomers moved to other sections of the city. In 1910, only twenty-five percent of Eastern Jews in Berlin proper resided in the zone that encompassed the *Scheunenviertel,* whereas even larger numbers lived in other zones or in the suburbs. A contemporary observer named Klara Eschelbacher explained this dispersion by noting the absence of a key industry, such as the garment trade, to keep immigrant Jews clustered together: since they found work in many different occupations, these Jews had less of an incentive to concentrate in one area. It is equally likely that Eastern Jews shunned areas of dense concentration for fear of creating a visible target for antagonistic German officials.[8]

The foregoing overview of population growth and distribution provides sufficient information to evaluate the validity of German fears concerning a "mass immigration" from the East. Certainly, in absolute numbers, immigrant Jews posed no serious threat to German society. One can hardly refer to some 70,000 aliens out of a total German population numbering 65,000,000 as a mortal demographic threat. Moreover, it is clear that when public debates over Jewish immigration first began in the early 1880s, Eastern Jews numbered no more than 17,000–18,000 souls out of a German population of 45,000,000. No reputable statistician ever substantiated the existence of a mass influx of Jewish immigrants into Imperial Germany. On a proportional scale, however, alien Jews were overrepresented in the *Reich's* population of foreigners. Whereas Jews consistently represented a little under one percent of the *Reich's* total inhabitants, foreign Jews constituted between five and six percent of Germany's population of aliens. Furthermore, Jews were even more overrepresented among the East Europeans in the *Reich:* by 1910 over nine percent of the combined Austro-Hungarians, Russians, and Rumanians in the country were Jews.[9]

What made these foreign Jews even more visible was their concentration in urban centers. In the twentieth century, close to fifteen percent of aliens in the "large cities" were Jews; and in twenty-eight of those cities, one-tenth of all aliens were Jews. Such a distribution distorted perceptions of the actual numbers of foreign Jews. In Berlin, especially, observers could arrive at the mistaken conclusion that most foreigners were Eastern Jews. One out of three aliens in the capital city was a Jew—a fact that was undoubtedly not lost on the numerous government officials and Reichstag deputies who worked in Berlin. No doubt, the daily passage of several thousand transmigrants through Berlin lent added credence to the notion that a horde of Jewish immigrants was sweeping into the country.[10]

This deceptive situation was further complicated by the high percentage of Jews in the country's Russian population. In the twentieth century, fifteen percent of all Russians in the *Reich* were Jews. And, again, the urbanization of Russian Jews rendered them still more visible: one out of every three Russians in Germany's "large cities" was a Jew. In Berlin, the Jewish proportion of the Russian population grew from fifty-three percent in 1880 to eight-five percent in 1890, and then declined after large-scale expulsions to sixty-five percent in 1910. In other localities, Jews were equally conspicuous in Russian populations, constituting sixty-six percent in Leipzig, forty-two percent in Munich, sixty-five percent in the state of Hesse, and ninety-two percent in the city of Mainz. Small wonder, then, that the term "Russian" was used as a shorthand for "Russian Jew."[11]

What emerges from these figures is a partial source for the exaggerated fears of an impending "Jewish mass migration." The Eastern Jews' modest overrepresentation in the total population of aliens in the *Reich* was magnified by their high level of urbanization, and particularly their significant presence in Berlin. Perceptions of their actual numbers were further distorted by the constant movement of transmigrants through the country. Under these circumstances, the impression that a mass Jewish influx was in progress might have arisen. But it was an impression and not a reality. Neither on an absolute nor a relative basis did Germany receive a mass immigration of Jews. Compared to the numbers of East European Jews absorbed by other Western lands, the 70,000 who settled in the *Reich* constituted a tiny contingent.

Immigrant Demography and Native Jewry

For most opponents of Jewish immigration, however, the fact that Eastern Jews constituted a relatively small population provided little consolation. Restrictionists, after all, were concerned not only with immigrant Jews, but with their link to native coreligionists. They repeatedly drew attention to the similarity between Eastern and German Jews, and ridiculed those who attempted to distinguish between the two categories of Jews. Given this linkage, it is appropriate to examine the impact of immigrant demography upon Germany's Jews. To what extent did the immigrant population strengthen native Jewry?

The impact of immigrants upon the population of German Jewry was most blatant in those localities where newcomers constituted a significant percentage of the Jewish community. As noted above, East Europeans represented the majority of Jews in several of the largest Jewish communities in Saxony. In a number of other cities, they formed a considerable bloc: in fact, by the eve of World War I, Eastern Jews represented over twenty percent of Jewish populations in eighteen of Germany's forty-eight largest cities.[12] Yet, while it is undeniable that the presence of foreigners posed a variety of far-reaching social and communal challenges for native Jewry (see Part III of this book), the most important *demographic* consequences of Jewish immigration were more subtle, for they revolved around the rejuvenating influence of Eastern Jews upon Germany's aging and stagnating Jewish population.

One of the few contemporary writers to explore this question was the Zionist statistician Felix Theilhaber, in a book he wrote in 1911 entitled *Der Untergang der deutschen Juden* [The decline of German Jewry]. Theilhaber noted that the percentage of Jews within the larger German population progressively declined from 1.09 to .92% between 1880 and 1910. He then went on to observe that even immigration would not reverse German Jewry's demographic downturn. At best, the newcomers made it possible for the *absolute* number of Jews in the Empire to rise slightly—but not enough to keep up with the proportionate growth of the Gentile population. Without the influx of foreign Jews, the relative percentage of Jews in the *Reich* would have sunk to .82% of the total population. Immigration, therefore, was a factor—albeit a modest one—in the continued demographic vitality of Jews in Germany.[13]

An examination of demographic patterns within the immigrant group further illustrates the contributions of East European Jews to the revitalization of Germany's Jewish population. To begin with, the newcomers constituted a youthful cohort. While definitive information is unavailable, the data at our disposal suggest that more immigrant Jews were between the ages of fifteen and thirty than in any other age category; between one-third and two-fifths of immigrants fell into this category. (The other age categories employed by studies were birth to fifteen, thirty to fifty, and fifty and over.) By contrast, native Jews predominantly fell into the next-older age category. While the youthful character of Eastern Jews in the *Reich* is not surprising given the general propensity of young people to uproot themselves more easily than their elders, the demographic impact of these young immigrants deserves to be noted: they lowered the average age of Germany's Jewry.[14]

Immigrants also slightly modified the gender distribution of Jews in Germany. Whereas among native Jews there were more females than males, the reverse pattern obtained among immigrant Jews. This was certainly the case during the early phases of immigration, when young men arrived who only later sent for their wives or female kin; but even as late as 1910, fifty-five percent of foreign Jews in the *Reich* were males. (For reasons that are not apparent, foreign women exceeded the population of foreign males in a few localities.) That most Jewish immigrants initially were males should not surprise us, since males generally find it easiest to migrate, particularly young men. It is noteworthy, however, that over the course of time East European Jews partially corrected this imbalance. Compared to the larger alien population in the *Reich*, Jews were far more prone to bring their womenfolk, a circumstance that can be explained by the requirement placed upon imported Gentile laborers to accept only seasonal work. Since Eastern Jews were immigrants rather than seasonal workers, they tended to bring their wives along—or at least send for their families once they had established themselves. Data compiled by Jacob Segall on Eastern Jews in Munich highlight this tendency: In the last two decades of the century, between sixty and sixty-three percent of the alien Jews of that city were males, but by 1910 sufficient numbers of females had been attracted so that the sex ratio was only fifty-four to forty-six in favor of men. Still, even with the influx of substantial numbers of Eastern women, the immigrant population was distinguished from native Jewry by the fact that men exceeded women by considerable percentages.[15]

Given the surplus of males over females among foreign Jews and the concomitant shortage of German Jewish males for native women, one would expect "mixed marriages" between foreign and German Jews to follow the demands of the "market": native women unable to find German spouses should have sought mates among foreigners. This is precisely what happened. Despite the severe penalties paid by German women who married foreign men, among Jews the overwhelming majority of marriages between natives and foreigners occurred between foreign men and native women. In Hanover, for example, all thirty-six "intermarriages" performed between 1874 and 1910 joined a foreign-born male and a native woman. Similar patterns are evident from a perusal of Jewish wedding records in communities as diverse as Altona and Munich.[16]

German marriage laws posed a host of legal obstacles for foreigners wishing to marry in the *Reich*. According to the *Reich*'s laws, foreign residents were permitted to marry only if the marriage ceremonies were legally sanctioned by the alien's country of citizenship. And here began a terrible legal imbroglio for foreign Jews, particularly subjects of the Tsarist Empire. According to Russian law, marriages and divorces performed in Germany often could not be recognized as valid because German law recognized only civil marriages, whereas Russian law

sanctioned only religious ceremonies. (German law permitted the performance c
religious rites after civil authorities had granted their approval.) Second, eve
religious rites performed in Germany were at times deemed unacceptable unde
Russian law if they were conducted by a rabbi not recognized by tsarist officials
The officiating rabbi had to hold office in the Jewish community, presumably i
the same manner as government-appointed rabbis did under the tsarist system
Furthermore, Russian authorities frequently withheld approval of marriages per
formed abroad on the grounds that the groom had been a draft evader. As
consequence of Russian objections, German officials often could not permit Rus
sian subjects to marry within the *Reich*. This legal tangle might have been avoide
had Russia (and Austria) signed the Hague Convention of June 12, 1902, whic
permitted an alien's country of residence (in this case Germany) to waive religiou
requirements stipulated by the country of origin (Russia, in this case). The tsari
government, however, did not sign the convention, and it is not clear whethe
German authorities waived such requirements for resident aliens who originate
from signatory countries such as Rumania and Hungary. In practice, it was there
fore exceedingly difficult for Russian Jews to get married or divorced in Germany
In this regard, subjects of the Austro-Hungarian Empire were a bit more fortunate
but even these Jews often encountered bureaucratic obstacles when they notifie
officials in the Dual Monarchy of their intentions to marry in Germany.[17]

As a result, immigrant Jews generally returned to their country of origin i
order to marry or divorce. Since such a trip was not always feasible, temporar
means were found to circumvent the law. Russian Jews, for example, often wei
married by German rabbis willing to perform religious ceremonies without a civ
permit. When it was convenient at a later point, the groom traveled to Russia an
registered the marriage; and the tsarist government, in turn, dated the marriag
from the time of the religious wedding ceremony. At times, however, these prac
tices brought about an anarchic state of affairs. An incident recalled by Samm
Gronemann, a Berlin attorney who frequently came into contact with Eastern Jew
due to his strong Zionist involvements, well sums up the bizarre situations tha
could arise: After a Russian couple was married by a local rabbi in Berlin, th
groom returned to the Tsarist Empire to register his marriage. Upon his return, h
discovered that his "wife" had married another Russian Jew before the first mai
riage had been recorded in Russia. Gronemann was called in at this point to ai
bitrate the case. But before he could arrive at a decision, the problem resolve
itself: the woman "married" yet a third Russian Jew and the first two "husbands
washed their hands of the entire matter![18]

Despite the legal obstacles placed in their way, a high percentage of alien Jew
was married. Many, of course, had married prior to their emigration; the male
simply preceded their wives. Others returned to their homes in the East to choos
a spouse. In any event, Eastern Jews in Germany tended to be married—and i
relatively greater number than native Jews. Thus, in Hanover, Munich, and th
state of Hesse, three localities for which data are available, immigrant Jews dis
played a high rate of marriage that was in excess of the rates among native Jews
Fragmentary data also suggest that Hungarian immigrants were most likely t

arrive with their families, whereas Russian Jews were most likely to arrive as bachelors or without their spouses.[19]

Jewish immigrants also tended to have considerably larger families than native Jews. While data on the fertility of Eastern Jews throughout the *Reich* do not exist, it is possible to draw some tentative conclusions on the basis of the few localities for which such information is available. In the year 1910, for example, there were in Berlin an average of 2.93 children under the age of fifteen for each Jewish woman from the East, as compared to 1.23 such children for German-born Jewish women. On the basis of even more limited data from the state of Hesse, we can establish that in 1910 there were 1.22 children under fifteen years of age for all Jewish immigrant women, as compared to 1.16 children for all German Jewish women. In Munich there were in 1910 1.47 children under fifteen for foreign Jewish women who were married and only .76 for the comparable group of native Jewish women. These figures admittedly provide only the crudest of measures in that they do not differentiate between married and unmarried women, or take age into account. Furthermore, they do not indicate how many children were born in Germany, rather than immigrated with their parents. Fortunately, statistics compiled from the birth records of the Jewish community of Hanover provided clear evidence of the high birthrate common among immigrant women in at least one German city. In 1910, for example, nearly half (forty-eight percent) of the babies born to Jews in Hanover were delivered by immigrant women, even though only one-fifth of all Hanover Jews were foreigners. (No information is available on the impact of the migration experience on the fertility of women— for example, did immigrant women continue to have a high fertility rate once in the *Reich* or did Eastern women produce many children only prior to their immigration?) Despite the crude nature of these data and the impossibility of measuring the impact of the German environment on immigrant fertility, it is possible to discern an overall tendency: Jewish families from the East were larger than the families of native-born Jews.[20]

The impressionistic preceptions of contemporaries further attest to this demographic pattern. Writing on the eve of World War I, two contemporary observers, Klara Eschelbacher and Felix Theilhaber, independently noted that families of recent immigrants tended to be larger than families of native Jews. Both writers hastened to add, however, that immigrants arriving at a young age, and especially those who married in Germany, tended to conform to the patterns of native Jewry and limit the size of their families. Unfortunately, it is impossible to reconstruct the fertility patterns of different immigrant and second-generation subpopulations, but there is little reason to doubt that Eastern Jews increasingly imitated their German coreligionists—particularly because this was their pattern in other areas of human endeavor. Thus, whereas the immigrants were able to add to the population of Jewish children in the *Reich*, they could not reverse the decline of Jewish fertility in Germany.[21]

Still, over the short term, immigrants played a modest role in rejuvenating the demography of Jews in Germany. They lowered the age composition by constituting a younger population; they provided spouses for some German Jews, especially for some native women who could not find mates among the relatively smaller population of native-born Jewish males; and they helped offset the general decline of fertility among German Jews. Given the fact that Eastern Jews comprised only twelve percent of Germany's Jews, their demographic impact was limited. Nonetheless, from the perspective of anti-Semites who opposed the presence of any Jews in Germany, these subtle contributions to the demographic revitalization of Jewish life in Germany could not have been welcome.[22]

Immigrant Demography:
The Role of German Policies

In assessing the demographic character of Eastern Jews in Germany, it is necessary to recognize the interplay between the immigrants and the German environment. One aspect of this interaction was evidenced by the impact of Eastern Jews on the demography of Germany's Jewish and East European populations. But, in turn, the German environment critically shaped the demographic patterns of the newcomers. State policies limited the growth of Jewish immigration, influenced the residential choices of the newcomers, and even subtly affected marital and fertility patterns by creating a climate of instability and insecurity.

The most overt consequence of government policies was manifested in the changing population figures for Eastern Jews in the *Reich*. In periods when states either expelled foreign Jews in large numbers or refused to issue them residence permits, the number of immigrant Jews plummeted. Thus, during the 1880s, there was virtually no growth in the population of Eastern Jews in the *Reich* even though transmigration from the East continued unabated throughout the decade. Conversely, when governments grew more lax and granted residence permits more freely, the population of Eastern Jews expanded during the 1890s. In short, government policies, rather than the flow of emigrants from the East, determined how many foreign Jews resided in Germany at a given time.[23]

Government actions and preferences also played a critical role in shaping the national composition of Eastern Jews in the *Reich*. Prior to the Puttkamer decrees, Russians represented the preponderant majority of alien Jews throughout Prussia; in Berlin, for example, sixty-eight percent of foreign Jews were from the Tsarist Empire. A decade later, and in every subsequent census, Russians constituted a minority of Eastern Jews in Prussia. By 1905, they had dwindled to little more than one-third of the alien Jews in that state. In fact, of all the states and cities for which relevant data exist, only Hesse in the twentieth century was populated by more Russian than Austro-Hungarian Jews; and this was largely so because Hesse took in Russian Jews who had been expelled from Prussia. The low ratio of Russians relative to Austro-Hungarian Jews is particularly noteworthy given the overwhelmingly Russian character of Jewish transmigration through the *Reich*.[24]

To be sure, this anomalous population distribution may also have been affected by cultural affinities between Austro-Hungarians and Germans. The Dual Monarchy, after all, was within the orbit of Germany's cultural influence, thereby predisposing Jews from that empire to attempt to settle in Germany rather than try to continue on to England or the New World. But even when we take cultural affinities into account, we only understand why Austro-Hungarian Jews should have preferred to settle in the *Reich*—not why Russian Jews would have avoided Germany. To illustrate the startlingly low number of Russian Jews in the *Reich,* we need only note that the latter population remained stagnant during the quarter-century from 1880-1905 (it rose by barely 2,000 over the 11,500 individuals who had been in Germany in 1880); by contrast, the population of Austro-Hungarian Jews grew sevenfold. Government hostility toward Russian Jews clearly accounts for this pattern. As we have noted already, governments were quick to send Russian Jews packing.[25]

Government policies also shaped the geographic distribution of Eastern Jews who took up residence in Germany. We have noted that throughout the history of the Second Empire the three states bordering on Russia and the Dual Monarchy contained the bulk of Eastern Jews in Germany. The geographic proximity of these states to the East made them logical destinations for Polish Jews. But expulsion and residence policies eventually discouraged Eastern Jews from settling in Prussia. Whereas 80% of the approximately 17,000 Jewish aliens in Germany resided in Prussia a decade after unification, only 60% lived there in 1910. This stands in marked contrast to the stable 65% of German Jewry that resided in Prussia throughout the history of the Second Empire. Conversely, Saxony's failure to control Jewish immigration rigidly accounts for its stable share of Eastern Jews: in 1880 this share amounted to 5.8% of all alien Jews in Germany; and after the Prussian expulsions it rose to 13.7% in 1890, a level at which it remained until World War I. Government policies, then, played a role in determining how Eastern Jews distributed themselves geographically.[26]

Even within the Prussian state, regulations wrought changes in the population concentration of immigrant Jews. This is most evident in the dramatic decline betweeen 1880 and 1910 in the number of foreign Jews residing in the eastern provinces. In 1880, East and West Prussia, Posen, and Silesia together contained nearly three-quarters of all Eastern Jews in Prussia. Three decades later, only eleven percent of such immigrants resided in these provinces. Although native Jews also migrated out of eastern Prussia during this era, the decline in their number was not nearly as precipitous. (Forty-one percent of Prussian Jews lived in the eastern provinces in 1880, as compared to twenty-four percent in 1910.) The particular hostility of provincial governors as well as the efforts of state officials to bar Eastern Jews from border regions of Prussia account for the altered geographic distribution.[27]

In the more central areas of Germany, the growth and decline of the population of Eastern Jews were at times directly influenced by expulsions. The number of foreign Jews in Berlin, for example, grew by only two percent between 1905 and 1910, a period that also witnessed a twenty-three percent increase of Eastern Jews in all of Prussia. There can be little doubt that expulsions from Berlin in the years 1904–06 accounted for the slow rate of growth in the Prussian capital. By contrast, the number of Russian Jews in the Hessian city of Offenbach rose dramatically because it took in Jews expelled from neighboring Frankfurt am Main.[28]

In a subtle manner, government measures were even partially responsible for the marked tendency of Eastern Jews to concentrate in large urban centers rather than in rural or small-town settings. We have noted the tendency among immigrants of the 1870s and early 1880s to settle in small towns and villages along the eastern frontier of Prussia.[29] After this group was expelled in the mid-1880s, new immigrants had little incentive to settle in the same areas, both because government policies were particularly harsh in the eastern provinces and because agricultural and industrial labor was forbidden to Polish Jews. Conversely, urban centers provided newcomers with economic opportunities and anonymity—something Eastern Jews needed to evade capricious officials. Thus, the high urbanization rate of immigrant Jews needs to be understood in the context of overall government actions.

In sum, the patterns of settlement displayed by Eastern Jews in Germany suggests a crucial cycle of interaction between government policies and immigrant demography. Government measures were predicated upon fears of an imminent mass invasion of Jews from the East. In response to such fears, a variety of measures were employed to uproot Eastern Jews. Ironically, such policies often drove new immigrants to settle in areas where they were individually more anonymous but collectively more conspicuous. And so, Eastern Jews appeared more numerous than they actually were. While their low level of growth should have occasioned confidence that government measures were successfully curbing Jewish immigration, their overrepresentation in several key states and cities may have distorted their demographic profile—and heightened fears.

5

Economic Pursuits

The economic activities of Eastern Jews were no less shrouded in myth than the dimensions of their "mass immigration." According to prevalent stereotypes, immigrant Jews parasitically feasted on the German economy while contributing nothing to their host country. The prototypical Eastern Jew, of course, was the *"Schnorrer."* Cartoonists merely had to sketch a beggar garbed in black to evoke an image of the Eastern Jew. And when demagogues inveighed against *Schnorrers,* their audiences knew that immigrant Jews were the objects of scorn. The reverse side of this stereotype was the Eastern Jew who exploited Germans either by hawking junk—as did contemptible "pants-sellers"—or seizing control of lucrative and powerful economic positions—as did pushy Jewish financiers. What, however, was the relationship between these common stereotypes and the actual economic behavior of immigrant Jews?

Answers to this question can be gleaned from two types of sources: statistics compiled by German governments and the nonquantifiable observations of contemporaries. We will begin by examining the data published in official statistical works, which provide rich information on the occupational structure of foreign Jews in a limited number of German localities—the cities of Berlin, Munich, and Hanover and the entire state of Hesse—during the decade prior to World War I.[1] Since these areas contained only one-quarter of all Eastern Jews in the *Reich,* we will then move on to "impressionistic" and unquantified sources to learn about the economic pursuits of Eastern Jews in other localities.

Occupational Structure

It is evident from government statistics that Eastern Jews in the *Reich* were an industrious people. Compared to native Jews, immigrants had a high rate of employment. In Berlin, sixty-one percent of all adult Jews from Eastern Europe were economically employed, compared to forty-five percent of adults in the population of native Jews. And when only male adults are counted, this figure rises higher: fully eighty-three percent of Eastern Jews were employed, as compared to sixty-eight percent of their German counterparts. Similar patterns obtained in other areas. In Hesse, fewer than five to six percent of Jewish men from Russia and Austria were not employed, whereas in Hanover, barely four percent of the heads of families and single adults did not work. Close to eighty percent of alien Jews in Munich were also employed. In sum, then, these data contradict popular images of Eastern Jews as parasitical *Schnorrers*.[2]

Furthermore, there is reason to doubt suggestions that most immigrant Jews were impoverished. Reporting to his cabinet in 1905, Minister of Interior Beth-mann-Hollweg even conceded that some Jewish immigrants "come with means." August Bebel compiled a list of Eastern Jews who owned bank accounts containing tens of thousands of mark, some of whom lived off their wealth. Given the pattern of state policies to deport unwanted Eastern Jews, it is difficult to believe that impoverished immigrants could survive for long in Germany without arousing the attention of government officials. While some *Schnorrers* did manage to elude police briefly, they inevitably were caught and deported. All available evidence suggests that state police weeded out commercially successful Jewish migrants from the larger mass of Jewish travelers. As Werner Fraustädter noted during the Weimar era: "the Jewish transmigration had an outspoken proletarian character, while the immigration to Germany had a middle-class one." Hence, it is reasonable to conclude that the preponderant majority of immigrant Jews in Germany were neither *Schnorrers* nor impoverished.[3]

What, then, were their economic pursuits? A few government publications provide limited answers to this question by dividing Eastern Jews into five broad occupational categories conventionally employed by German statisticians: (1) agriculture, (2) industry, (3) commerce and transport, (4) domestic service, (5) public service and the professions. In all the localities for which data are available, it is evident that Eastern Jews concentrated overwhelmingly in only two of these categories—industry and commerce. Hardly any engaged in agriculture, and only limited numbers worked either as domestics or in the free professions. It is not entirely clear, however, whether more Eastern Jews were attracted to commerce or industry. Statistical works provide a mixed picture: those covering Munich and Hanover list business as the most common occupation of Eastern Jews, whereas in works on Berlin and Hesse, industrial labor is the main pursuit of immigrant

Jews. The latter data, however, need to be evaluated with care since we know from contemporary sources that a considerable number of artisans also engaged in hawking their own wares: they may have been listed officially as workers, but in practice they engaged in petty trade. Furthermore, we have a wealth of nonquantifiable evidence that attests to a wide range of commercial activities pursued by Eastern Jews, ranging from peddling old clothing in the Rhineland, to importing and exporting lumber in eastern Prussia, to fur trading in Saxony. In the absence of definitive evidence, we can only estimate that forty-five to fifty percent of Eastern Jews in Germany engaged in some form of commerce, while some thirty-five to forty percent worked as manual laborers.[4]

These patterns of distribution varied according to the nationality of immigrant Jews as well as the era of their settlement in the *Reich*. All statistical data indicate, for example, that Russian Jews had a greater tendency to work in industry, while Galicians were more apt to choose commercial occupations. We can only speculate on the reasons for these differences. It may be that Austro-Hungarians adjusted more easily to the language and social rituals necessary for doing business because they came from within the orbit of German cultural influence. And, conversely, most emigrants from the Tsarist Empire were proletarians.[5]

Whatever the reason for these national preferences, it is also clear that the occupational structure of Eastern Jews in the *Reich* shifted over time to include more working-class immigrants. While precise statistics are unavailable, reports on the occupations of Eastern Jews expelled during the 1880s indicate that immigrant Jews were preponderantly engaged in commercial occupations. According to reports on the expulsions from Berlin in 1884, only 50 out of the 574 Russian and Polish Jews driven from the capital worked as artisans—tailors, cigar-makers, and so on—and the rest engaged in business or the free professions. Similarly, in the statewide expulsions from Prussia in 1885–86, the same pattern obtained. More than half of the 5,000 alien Jews driven from East Prussia were in commerce, one quarter were workers, and the rest were religious functionaries or students. In other border areas Jews were heavily involved in the liquor trade and the import-export business. In Königsberg and Danzig, most expulsion victims were shopkeepers and wealthy merchants, and only a relatively few supported themselves as workers. While it is evident that certain categories of useful Jews were spared during the expulsions, these exemptions were granted equally to workers and merchants in critical occupations. It is therefore reasonable to assume that a cross section of Eastern Jews suffered expulsion, and this population included considerably more business people than artisans.[6]

A variety of sources attest to a gradual rise in the number of artisans and laborers around the turn of the century. This pattern is evident both from the observations of contemporaries as well as from government memoranda on expulsion victims. Reflecting on this development, the contemporary observer Klara Eschelbacher noted a propensity on the part of Eastern Jews to seek jobs in manual labor only after they had acclimated to life in Germany: initially they worked as peddlers and hawkers even if they had little experience with petty trade in the East; but once they learned some German, they diversified more easily and found work in light industry. As a result, the occupational profile of Eastern Jews in Germany took on a more pronounced proletarian character during the fifteen years prior to World War I.[7]

Despite these gradual changes, the occupational structure of Eastern Jews in the *Reich* remained singular when compared to that of fellow Jewish emigrants who settled in other Western lands. In England and the United States, to cite two critical examples, close to seventy percent of Jewish immigrants engaged in industrial labor, working as tailors, bootmakers, cigarette-makers, and so on, and only a minority earned a living through peddling. By contrast, close to half the immigrant Jews in the *Reich* engaged in some form of commerce, with only a smaller contingent engaged in labor.[8]

The causes for this unusual occupational distribution lie in the interplay between three variables—government policies, the needs of Germany's economy, and the predisposition of the immigrants. To begin with, governmental measures made it possible for certain types of Jewish immigrants to reside in the country, even as they drove other types onward. Aside from general prohibitions forbidding foreigners to engage in specific fields—for example, the civil service and law— state policies forbade the employment of Eastern Jews as seasonal laborers either in heavy industry or agriculture. In some periods, administrations even sought to discourage their employment as synagogue officials, apprentices, and domestics. By contrast, German trade treaties compelled governments to admit commercial travelers freely, a circumstance that enabled Jewish business people to enter the *Reich* and move about unmolested. In sum, then, government policies served as a mechanism for selecting certain categories of Jewish migrants over others.[9]

Second, Germany's economy employed the skills and talents of only certain types of Eastern Jews. The country could make use of individuals with the requisite linguistic attainments and business connections to organize trade with its eastern neighbors. These included Russian timber merchants and Galician furriers as well as a variety of other economic middlemen. It also provided opportunities for petty merchants and hawkers. By contrast, the garment industry, the major employer of immigrant Jews in other Western lands, did not require the services of large numbers of Eastern Jews in Germany.[10]

Finally, Eastern Jews arrived in the *Reich* predisposed to select certain kinds of work. Like immigrant Jews in other countries, they shied away from heavy industry because their experience with manual labor had been confined to artisan trades. They also tended, as is the case with immigrants in general, to take marginal jobs, entering fields of enterprise shunned by natives. And for peculiarly Jewish reasons, they preferred work that allowed for self-employment. Such work was particularly valued by Sabbath observers who did not have to rely upon the tolerance of employers in order to rest on the Jewish Sabbath. But even for those willing to work on Saturday (according to Eschelbacher, there were many) it was still preferable to work for oneself rather than risk working for a potentially unsympathetic and even anti-Semitic boss. Hence, in Germany, as elsewhere, immigrant Jews "placed great emphasis on being a *balabos far sich* [their own boss]."[11]

In sum, the occupational structure of immigrant Jews was determined both by the German environment as well as by the predisposition of the newcomers.

Sometimes these factors reinforced each other, as when state measures and Jewish predilections contributed to the low number of immigrant Jews in heavy industry and agriculture. In other cases, however, German policies and economic needs "selected" certain types of immigrants, a process that accounts for the concentration of Eastern Jews in commerce rather than industry. But because German policies toward Eastern Jews were not governed by an overall economic master plan or overseen by a single centralized bureaucracy, a variety of factors shaped the occupational structure of immigrant Jews in the *Reich*.

The Economic Role of Eastern Jews

Having established the overall pattern of immigrant occupations, it is necessary to examine specific economic pursuits in greater detail. What does it mean, after all, that a plurality of Eastern Jews engaged in commerce, if we do not know whether most plied their wares as international merchants or as itinerant peddlers? What products did Eastern Jews actually sell or produce? On what scale did they operate? Did they specialize in the delivery of specific goods and services? And what was their socioeconomic class?

Merchants and Traders

In light of the entrepreneurial interests of many immigrant Jews, it is appropriate to begin a survey of their economic pursuits with a look at business people—and specifically at types of commerce in which they specialized. Perhaps, the best known was the fur trade. For centuries, Jews had come from Galicia, especially Lemberg, to trade in furs at the Leipzig fairs. By the third quarter of the nineteenth century, municipal officials introduced measures to encourage some Jewish traders to settle permanently in Leipzig. In contrast to German administrations elsewhere, the Leipzig municipality even relaxed its naturalization policies so that fur dealers could acquire Saxonian citizenship. But with the resurgence of anti-Semitism in the 1880s, Jewish immigration was curbed. Those Galician Jews who had established residence in Leipzig continued to play an active role in the fur trade, so much so that fifteen of the twenty-nine fur concerns owned by Jews were still controlled by immigrants from the East at the turn of the century. In this fashion, Galician Jews served as a major conduit of trade in furs between Germany and the East.[12]

Russian Jews played an equally useful role in the development of trade between the Tsarist and German empires, serving as import-export agents of grain, textiles, and lumber. Nothing better attests to their contribution than the repeated efforts of chambers of commerce and trade associations to shield these merchants from Prussian expulsions. In the mid-1880s, for example, groups in Königsberg, Memel, Danzig, and Berlin petitioned Prussian authorities to revoke expulsion decrees and readmit Russian Jews who had already been deported. Their motives were overtly explained in their petitions: the expulsion of Russian Jewish merchants had created a trade slump. According to one estimate, the tonnage of merchandise crossing the Russo-German border had dropped from 85,000 tons during the first four months of 1885 to 20,000 tons in the comparable period of 1886. To stem these losses, government officials rescinded expulsion orders and developed policies that made it possible for commercially useful aliens to remain in the country. Until the end of the Imperial era, the same cycle recurred: mass expulsions were met with protests by commercial lobbyists who tried to protect their own interests by rescuing Russian Jews from deportation. Clearly, the immigrants would not have received this kind of support had they been perceived solely as business competitors or economic parasites.[13]

Not all immigrant businessmen were international traders, of course. In fact, most Eastern Jews who engaged in commerce were associated with several types of petty trade. These included the distribution of eggs, a business in which Galician Jews handled over seventy percent of Berlin's market by 1910, as well as the sale of cigarettes, which was largely in the hands of immigrant tobacconists and hawkers. The most common enterprise of Eastern Jews who sold merchandise was the trade in secondhand goods. This was particularly evident in Berlin, where Galician Jews dominated the used clothing and furniture businesses by 1910 and where Jews from the Hapsburg Empire also enjoyed a near monopoly over the remnant market. In other large cities, the same patterns were evident: in Hanover, more foreign Jews engaged in the junk business than in any other economic enterprise; in Munich, virtually all Jewish remnant dealers were immigrants; and in the Rhineland, a sufficient number of Eastern Jews plied their trade as peddlers of used merchandise to warrant an expulsion decree specifically aimed at them.[14]

While "Polish pants-sellers" served as the objects of much derision and caricature, they sometimes parlayed their peddling into large business enterprises and frequently operated out of respectable shops. Yet even where such success was not possible, Eastern Jews probably were attracted to the secondhand trade because it did not require the outlay of much start-up capital and did not compete with existing German businesses. Most important, peddling and other forms of commerce provided Eastern Jews with the independence that comes from self-employment.[15] In a city like Berlin, close to two-thirds of Russian and Austrian Jews in commercial occupations were self-employed. Given the discrimination and insecurity they suffered in Germany, it is understandable that Eastern Jews would be attracted to commercial occupations, however petty, since they allowed for mobility and independence.

Workers

Eastern Jews who engaged in manual labor also assumed some distinctive patterns of economic behavior. For one thing, like their counterparts in commerce, they gravitated to peripheral jobs, thereby acting as pioneers in a few industries. This pattern was particularly evident among those immigrant Jews who manufactured cigarettes. In the decade prior to German unification, a small number of Russian Jews helped popularize cigarette smoking by manufacturing inexpensive products at a time when few German concerns produced cigarettes. In cities such as Berlin, Munich, and Offenbach, Russian Jews virtually monopolized the craft of hand-rolling cigarettes and producing a cigarette far less expensively than did machines.

As the nineteenth century progressed, this small-scale business employed increasing numbers of Russian Jews who either opened their own family-run concerns or worked for large industrial firms employing hundreds of cigarette-rollers.[16]

The near-monopoly of Jewish workers over the manual production of cigarettes was broken by the Berlin expulsions of 1904–06, when hundreds of Russian Jewish cigarette-makers were deported. Since manufacturers did not anticipate the quick return of these skilled workers, they recruited native women to fill the labor vaccuum. But as these women gained facility at their work, they began to demand higher wages, which in turn drove up the price of cigarettes. As a consequence, machine-produced products became more competitive and the industry gradually mechanized. Still, when a new wave of Russian Jews arrived during the last years before World War I, they gravitated to some of the larger cigarette concerns— Garbatty-Rosenthal, Muratti, Manoli, and other factories. By 1913, Eastern Jews— mainly women and older men—represented twenty percent of the work force at the large cigarette factories in Berlin. In absolute numbers this meant that well over 200 families of Eastern Jews supported themselves through cigarette production in Berlin alone, a number augmented by immigrant workers in Munich, Offenbach, and other cities. A half-century after they had pioneered in Germany's cigarette production, Russian Jews continued to find significant employment in this industry.[17]

By contrast, only a handful of working-class Jews from the Hapsburg Empire engaged in cigarette production. Instead, these Jews gravitated to the garment industry. While a few of these worked as tailors, most produced specialty items such as furs, shoes, laces, hats, and handbags. These workers were also distinguished for their relatively high rate of self-employment: in Berlin over forty percent and in Munich nearly one-third of the Jewish garment workers from Eastern Europe were self-employed or worked for immediate relatives.[18]

The garment industry attracted Eastern Jews for a variety of reasons. Unlike heavy industries which were forbidden to hire foreign Jews, the needle trades did not discriminate against the newcomers. In addition, some Eastern Jews undoubtedly had already worked in this field prior to their emigration and therefore possessed sufficient skills to find employment. Equally important, the needle trades provided opportunities for self-employment, since much of the piecework could be performed at home.[19]

Given the attractiveness of the garment industry and the fact that large majorities of Eastern Jews in other Western lands occupied themselves in manufacturing clothing, it is noteworthy that even more immigrant Jews in the *Reich* did not concentrate in this field. True, in Berlin and Hesse most Eastern Jews employed in industrial occupations manufactured articles of clothing (between fifty and sixty percent), but these constituted a minority of the immigrant Jews in those localities. And in other cities such as Munich and Hanover, the majority of immigrant Jews who performed manual labor did not work in the garment industry. Noting the *relative* insignificance of the garment industry as an employer of Eastern Jews in Germany, Klara Eschelbacher made the following observations:

> This fact is explicable first of all because the garment industry in Berlin, especially in ready-made clothing, is very large and Eastern Jews are not visible in it

due to their small numbers. They play no role in tailoring because this trade which in England and America is identified as "Jewish" was established long before the immigration increased and became steady. This work also is dependent on the intensive use of machinery and a wide division of labor. Therefore, it is possible to employ unskilled labor. . . .

Hence, while the garment industry employed an important segment of working-class Jews from the East, only a small minority of Jewish immigrants in Germany was involved in an industry that was the primary employer of East European Jews who settled in other Western lands.[20]

In addition to the needle trades, several other fields employed immigrant Jews as skilled craftsmen, technicians, and menial workers. In some cases the newcomers pioneered in emerging industries, as was the case with Galician Jews who monopolized the newly mechanized dry-cleaning business in Munich, as well as the small number of Eastern Jews who worked as technicians in the developing field of commercial photography. Still others were sufficiently skilled in new metallurgical techniques to warrant special protection from expulsions early in the twentieth century. The rest gravitated to an assortment of jobs as smiths, cabinet-makers, bakers, cobblers, and clockmakers. In virtually all cases, working-class immigrants concentrated in light industry.[21]

There is one major exception to this rule: for a little over one year, Eastern Jews were recruited on an experimental basis to work as miners in Upper Silesia. At the initiative of local Jewish groups, a program was launched in 1912 to import Galician and Russian Jews to labor as pit workers in coal mines. Performing the lowest-paying labor in such mines (workers earned a monthly salary of 70 to 100 mark), approximately 400 Jewish men were permitted to work as seasonal laborers. Due to the gruelling work and difficult living conditions, over fifty percent of participants quickly dropped out. But despite this high rate of attrition, the experiment was significant because it represented the first effort to recruit Jews from the East to work for German industry. Hoping that this program would put an end to discriminatory policies practiced by recruiters of seasonal labor, organizers aimed to set a precedent that would expand the opportunities of Eastern Jews in Germany. Ironically, while the Upper Silesian experiment was quickly dismantled, the general program to import Jewish workers did take hold during World War I when tens of thousands of Jews were conscripted in the East as forced laborers for heavy industry.[22]

In concluding this brief examination of the work performed by Eastern Jews engaged in industrial labor, it is appropriate to inquire as to the class orientation of these individuals. Did such laborers identify with the working class? Did they develop a labor movement of their own or even join German associations of workers? The limited evidence at our disposal suggests a generally harmonious relationship between working-class Jews from the East and the larger German labor movement. Unlike labor movements in other Western lands, German trade unionists did not urge their governments to restrict Jewish immigration. For their parts, immigrant Jews cooperated with their fellow workers by joining trade unions and participating in strikes. Despite their small size and wide dispersal, working-class immigrants were even able to form a few labor groups of their own. To be sure, these cells mainly suported the Bund, the major labor movement of Jews still in Eastern Europe, and avoided involvement with German political and labor issues. On occasion, however, Bundists in the *Reich* pledged to stand "shoulder to shoulder with German workers."[23]

There were occasional exceptions to this peaceful relationship, the most noteworthy occurring in the city of Offenbach. In late 1908 German workers urged the municipal government to ban future Jewish immigrants on the grounds that the newcomers were competing unfairly by accepting low wages. The protesters noted, however, that they were prepared to relent if immigrant Jews would join forces with native laborers. Commenting on these developments, the local SPD newspaper identified three circumstances lying at the root of this conflict: (1) the recent arrival of Eastern Jews who were attempting to establish permanent residence in Offenbach (previous groups had merely stayed until they had earned sufficient money to move on); (2) the recent expulsions from Prussia that had driven Russian Jews from cities such as neighboring Frankfurt am Main to seek refuge in Offenbach; (3) the efforts of some Russian Jews to open their own factories and recruit coreligionists in the East, rather than employ native German workers. Despite the heightened tensions, the local SPD remained sympathetic to Eastern Jews, and native workers strove for ways to reconcile their differences with Jewish immigrants.[24]

The brief controversy in Offenbach highlights a central characteristic of Jewish immigrants who engaged in manual production—namely, their propensity to seek opportunities to escape from proletarian labor. One of the chief causes of the Offenbach crisis, after all, was the effort of Russian Jewish workers to open their own factories. In Offenbach, as elsewhere, working-class immigrants engaged in a variety of entrepreneurial activities: some supplemented their incomes by peddling goods of their own making and others recruited relatives from the East in order to maintain family-run factories. It appears that immigrant workers aspired to escape from the working class rather than improve the lot of proletarians.[25]

Even when such mobility was not possible in the first generation, immigrant parents encouraged their offspring to rise beyond their poor origins. Writing of Eastern Jews in Berlin's "ghetto" area, Klara Eschelbacher emphasized the efforts of immigrant parents to provide a good education for their children.

> The children of immigrants are not differentiated from the offspring of German-born Jews in their choices of occupations. Eastern Jews encourage . . . their children to make something of themselves. They well understand that children may not choose the same occupation as their fathers. At an early age, their children develop ambition and strive for wealth and status.

In this regard, Eastern Jews in the *Reich* behaved in much the same fashion as fellow emigrants who settled in other Western countries: they encouraged their offspring to enter white-collar occupations. As the sociologist Will Herberg put it in describing immigrant Jews in the United States: "The Jewish factory worker was a 'man of one generation: neither the son nor the father of workers'; his father had been a petty merchant or artisan and his son was to become a businessman or professional." This too was characteristic of East European Jews who settled in Germany.[26]

While it is not possible at present to trace the patterns of mobility of Jewish immigrants of the first and second generation, the case histories of a few individuals suggests that upward mobility was, indeed, possible for working-class individuals. One of the largest cigarette factories in Dresden was owned by a one-time Lithuanian yeshiva student who first sold hand-rolled cigarettes to German soldiers stationed in Halberstadt. Josef Lange became a successful synagogue functionary only after an early apprenticeship as a glazier and peddler of leather bags. And the actor Alexander Granach first began work in Germany as a baker. For Eastern Jews who managed to stay in the *Reich* for a significant amount of time, it was possible to achieve a measure of economic and class mobility.[27]

The Free Professions

Perhaps the greatest degree of upward mobility was achieved by immigrants who deliberately came to Germany hoping to succeed on the basis of their talents or professional skills. The most prominent individuals of this type were artists and musicians. The *Reich*'s concert halls and conservatories echoed to the music of violinists such as Joseph Joachim (an immigrant of an earlier period), Leopold von Auer, Adolf Brodsky, and Jacob Grün; pianists like Nicholas and Joseph Rubinstein (brothers of Anton); and opera singers on the order of the Galician Josef Mann. On the German stage Rudolph Schildkraut and Ludwig Barnay performed as William Tell, Hamlet, and Wallenstein; Emanuel Richter from Galicia was known as the "father of the Berlin style" of naturalistic acting; and Jenny Gross of Hungary and Maria Orska of Russia were leading actresses. Painters, portraitists, and sculptors of distinction studied and exhibited in Germany, including Moritz Adler, Josef Engel, Jakob Glasner, Moritz Gotlieb, and Leo Nickelson; Max Klein of Hungary was commissioned to sculpt the Fontane memorial in the Tiergarten; and Marc Chagall mounted one of his most important early exhibitions in Berlin. The Hungarian Jew Samuel Fischer built a publishing house acclaimed for introducing some of the greatest young writers to the German literary scene. Even in the academic world, a small group of scholars from the East made their marks—especially philologists and Semiticists. And political journals lent a platform to intellectuals such as Ephraim Frisch, Fritz Mauthner, and Rosa Luxemburg. None of these individuals, as we shall see, had any contact with the larger immigrant community (or, for that matter, with organized German Jewry); on the contrary, most found ways to acquire citizenship in Germany or other Western countries. But before they achieved success and acquired naturalization, they shared much the same fate as other Eastern Jews in the *Reich*.[28]

A second group of immigrant Jews that parlayed their skills and talents into successful careers in Germany consisted of rabbis and synagogue functionaries. Due to a serious shortage of native-born religious leaders and instructors, German Jewry relied heavily on immigrant Jews. The role of Eastern Jews in the German rabbinate is clearly attested in reports issued by the three major rabbinical schools—the orthodox Hildesheimer *Rabbinerseminar*, the liberal *Hochschule* (both in Berlin), and the moderately liberal *Therologisches Seminar* (in Breslau). During the Imperial era, these institutions ordained over forty Jews of East European origin who then went on to serve in German pulpits. Within this group, more traditional rabbis fared best in obtaining pulpits in Germany: of the Eastern Jews ordained by the *Hochschule*, only eleven percent served in German pulpits, compared to thirty percent and thirty-six percent, respectively, of Eastern-born rabbis produced by the *Rabbinerseminar* and Breslau *Seminar*. Even more important, Orthodox rabbis stood a far greater chance of obtaining a pulpit in a large city, whereas most Breslau graduates were forced to take congregations in rural areas. At best, the latter were able in time to graduate from rural congregations to pulpits situated in larger cities. A few case studies will illustrate these general patterns: In Frankfurt am Main, both the secessionist orthodox congregation originally established by Samson Raphael Hirsch as well as the nonsecessionist Orthodox congregations were led by Hungarian-born rabbis (the Breuer family in the former case, and Marcus Horowitz and Anton Nobel in the latter). In other large cities, such as Hamburg and Karlsruhe, Orthodox congregations were headed by rabbis born in the East (mainly Hungarians) in the late nineteenth century. By contrast, liberal rabbis of Eastern origin were consigned to remote locations and, at best, apprenticed in the boondocks for years before they were hired by more centrally located congregations. To cite the experiences of two Breslau graduates: Solomon Fried of Hungary only served in the smaller communities of Mersenheim, Ratibor, and Ulm; his colleague Nathan Porges was more fortunate to work his way from Mannheim to Leipzig (with stops at Bohemian congregations on the way). There is also evidence that a rabbi's country of origin affected his professional opportunities. Hungarians, whether liberal or orthodox, were highly successful in obtaining pulpits, while Galicians faced the poorest prospects. The chances of Bohemians, Moravians, and Russians were only fair.[29]

Such selectivity was not exercised in the hiring of cantors. As Gustave Karpeles, an informed contemporary, observed in 1892, "without Polish cantors, it would be impossible" for German congregations to function. This reliance upon foreign-born functionaries had characterized German congregations for several centuries, but by the end of the nineteenth century, the shortage of cantors and teachers was particularly acute. One measure of this dependence can be found in the frantic advertisements placed in newspapers by German congregations when between 150 and 200 cantors were deported from Prussia in the mid-1880s; the vacant positions were not filled until a new group of cantors arrived from the East. At the end of the century, the chairman of Berlin's Jewish community testified in court that the capital's Jewry was "totally dependent upon Slavs in filling cantorial posts." The preponderance of East European cantors was also evident in the overwhelmingly foreign character of the student body attracted by a newly established cantorial school, as well as in the inordinately large role played by Eastern Jews in the national Cantor's Society.[30]

Since almost all cantors also served as religious instructors, immigrant Jews played a central role in religious education. Already in 1879, a survey concluded that numerous Polish and Russian teachers worked in Jewish schools in Posen, West Prussia, and Pomerania. Three decades and several expulsions later, thirty-three out of fifty-six Jewish teachers in West Prussia were Russian-born. Whereas Jewish communities in the south and west of Germany were better able to produce their own teachers, the Polish religious instructor was a fixture in most Prussian communities. The needs were particularly great in Prussia because at the time of German unification the state contained over 600 communities, for the most part in rural areas. Mostly poor, these communities could not afford to pay salaries that would induce native Jews to serve in rural outposts.[31]

Jewish communities also provided occupational opportunities for other types of Eastern Jews. Immigrants were particularly irreplaceable as ritual slaughterers. In addition, they served in sundry positions as administrators, librarians, and communal archivists. They were prominently represented on the faculties of rabbinical seminaries: the dean of the orthodox *Rabbinerseminar* was the Hungarian David Zvi Hoffmann; the Prague-born, Budapest-educated Zecharias Frankel headed the Breslau *Seminar,* while its faculty boasted scholars from the East such as Michael Guttman; and several Hungarians also taught at the liberal *Hoschschule*—Ignatz Maybaum, Eduard Baneth, and Adolph Büchler. (The orthodox secessionists in Frankfurt also employed Hungarians in their school system.) On occasion, Eastern Jews also served as *Stiftsrabbiner, Klausrabbiner,* and *Dayanim* (rabbinic judges and scholars in residence). Finally, Jewish journalism was also enriched by the efforts of foreign-born Jews: Leo Winz edited *Ost und West,* and Nahum Goldmann's Russian-born father ran the communal newspaper in Frankfurt; the Hamburg *Israelitisches Familienblatt* was published by a naturalized Russian-born Jew; and the key founders of a Jewish statistical bureau and its central organ, the *Zeitschrift für Demographie und Statistik der Juden,* were primarily Eastern Jews— Alfred Nossig, Martin Buber, Berthold Feiwel, and Chaim Weizmann.[32]

We may conclude that Eastern Jews succeeded in the free professions either because they could fill a manpower shortage in the Jewish communities or because their artistic talents secured a place for them in the German cultural world. The professions most attractive to native Jews, however, were difficult for aliens to penetrate. Hence, immigrant and native Jews in the free professions concentrated in different areas. In Berlin only a handful of the 500 Jewish attorneys, 3 of the 196 higher officials, and seven percent of the Jewish health workers originated in the East. On the other hand, immigrants were overrepresented in communal service and the arts: forty percent of all religious officials *(Geistliche)* and close to one-quarter of all Jewish writers, artists, and actors were Eastern Jews. In Munich, these divergences were even greater: hardly any immigrants were lawyers, but between one-quarter and one-half of all Jewish writers, editors, artists, actors, and musicians were aliens.[33]

Women's Occupations

Although much of the preceding discussion applies equally to the occupations of both sexes, there were several important divergences in the occupational structures of immigrant men and women. To begin with, women were far more concentrated in industrial labor. In Berlin and Hesse, nearly twice as many females worked in industry than in commerce. By contrast, immigrant men were nearly equally divided between these two categories of employment. Female workers were also less diversified than their male counterparts: in Berlin and Hesse nearly all of women workers produced either tobacco or garment products. Finally, working-class women were also far less likely than their menfolk to be self-employed; rather, they worked in family-run concerns.[34]

The reverse pattern obtained with women engaged in commerce: in this field they showed a marked tendency to work for themselves. In Berlin, for example, half of the women in commerce were self-employed. They often owned and ran hostels and restaurants. And they also worked independently as peddlers, hawking eggs and secondhand merchandise in much the same manner as their male counterparts.[35]

Jewish women from the East also found domestic service a major source of employment. In the entire *Reich,* according to Klara Eschelbacher, there were in 1910 approximately 565 Eastern Jewish women engaged in domestic service. Of these, 460 worked as live-in maids and the rest performed household chores but did not reside at their place of work. Data from Berlin indicate that these domestics were overwhelmingly drawn from Galicia, but there is insufficient information to generalize about the rest of the *Reich.* There is also limited evidence that German Jews served as the primary employers of these women. Some regarded domestic service as an ideal opportunity to Germanize immigrant coreligionists while simultaneously satisfying a felt need of German Jewry for more domestics. In fact, several proposals were put forth at the turn of the century to form a society specifically to train girls from the East in the skills of domestic service. Declaiming on this subject, Hermann Markower, a prominent communal leader in Berlin, spoke at the opening of a special elementary school in Memel designed to educate the children of Russian Jews: "We need not ladies, but maids. And if you can promise me that the girl students will become domestics, then I can pledge you 100,000 mark!"[36]

The role of German Jews as employers of immigrant coreligionists in domestic service raises a final issue pertaining to the economic pursuits of Eastern Jews: To what extent were immigrant Jews integrated into the economic life of native Jewry? This question was raised repeatedly by anti-Semites who argued that native Jewry recruited coreligionists in the East and provided them with employment. Those who suspected Jews of conspiratorial behavior even saw the success of some Eastern Jews as part of a master plan for Jews to seize control of the German economy. It is therefore appropriate to reflect on the relationship between the economic activities of immigrant and native Jews.

In truth, the anti-Semitic argument was not entirely without foundation. The occupational distribution of Jewish natives and aliens bore some remarkable resemblances. To observe these parallels, it is merely necessary to compare the occupational structure of alien Jews with those of other groups in Germany, such as native Jews, the general German populace, and the contingent of aliens in the *Reich.* None of these groups shared an identical pattern of occupational distribution, but native and immigrant Jews were most alike in their vocational choices. Significantly, both groups shared a propensity for choosing commercial vocations over any other form of economic activity, a tendency that was idiosyncratic to Jews. Gentile natives and foreigners were predominantly engaged in agricultural or industrial labor.[37]

This congruence between the occupational structures of native and immigrant Jews was unparalleled in any other country that received a sizeable influx of East European Jews. In the United States, for example, sixty percent of Russian Jews worked in manufacturing and only twenty-one percent in trade at the beginning of the twentieth century. By contrast, nearly sixty percent of the native Jews in America engaged in wholesale or retail commerce. Similarly, in England and France, native and immigrant Jews diverged sharply in occupational structure.[38]

The parallel occupational structures of native and immigrant Jews in Germany do not, however, demonstrate a partnership, let alone a conspiracy, between the two types of Jews. In some cases, immigrant Jews, such as religious functionaries, were employed by German Jews. But there is no evidence that this was a wide-scale pattern; on the contrary, a notably high percentage of Eastern Jews was self-employed. Moreover, our findings concerning the shared propensity of native and immigrant Jews for commerce do not take into account the vast economic and class differences separating these Jewish populations. If anti-Semites were obsessed with the similarities between both groups, German Jews were preoccupied with the gaps dividing them from immigrant Jews. With much discomfort and some irritation they asked: What commonality united native entrepreneurs with impoverished peddlers who earned a living by hawking eggs, cigarettes, or used clothing?[39] What had established natives to do with newly arrived immigrants? What social denominators did bourgeois German citizens share with unrefined aliens from the East? Where anti-Semites saw an identity of economic interests, native Jews saw deep economic, class, and social chasms separating them from Eastern Jews.

6

Organizational Activities

In addition to their fears that Eastern Jews constituted a demographic and economic threat, opponents of Jewish immigration also perceived the newcomers as a politically subversive element. Let us recall the public warning uttered by Germany's chancellor in 1905, portraying immigrant Jews as *"Schnorrers* and conspirators."* The immigrants, it was often alleged, formed a cohesive population within the *Reich* that supported radical political causes. In order to evaluate these allegations, the following chapter will survey the organizational activities of Eastern Jews in the *Reich* both for the purposes of identifying their political allegiances, as well as to map the contours of their formal social networks.

Transients

The Radical Intellectuals

Let us begin with the smallest contingent, the transients, whose stay in Germany was of the shortest duration. Undoubtedly the most famous, as well as notorious, of all Jewish transients in the *Reich* were radical intellectuals. The best known of this intelligentsia contributed to the Social Democratic Party, particularly to its press organs. The Russians included Eugene Leviné, Wilhelm Buchholz, Leo Jogisches, Alexander Stein, Alexander "Parvus" Helphand, and, of course, Rosa Luxemburg. From the Hapsburg monarchy came the brothers Adolf and Heinrich Braun, Max Beer, and Friedrich Stampfer. Interestingly, the two contingents stood on diametrically opposite ends of the socialist spectrum: almost all the Russians were radicals, whereas the Austro-Hungarians favored Revisionism. Rosa Luxemburg and "Parvus" made their reputations as hostile critics of Revisionism; Stampfer and Heinrich Braun supported Eduard Bernstein's faction. (Braun even regarded "Red Rosa" as an *agent provocateur*.)[1]

The primary vehicles of communication available to these radical intellectuals were the various socialist newspapers and journals published in Germany. Serving as editors and journalists for SPD periodicals, the foreigners could place their imprint on radical discourse in the *Reich*. In Saxony, the SPD press was particularly dependent on the contributions of "Parvus," Luxemburg, and Stampfer. And in Berlin, Buchholz and Adolf Braun played a central role as editors of the *Vorwärts*. Not surprisingly, some native socialists resented the influence of foreigners. Giving vent to such resentments, one German socialist complained of the "unpleasant tone in the party press produced by the male and female immigration from the East." (The radicalism of Luxemburg proved especially galling.) Another writer, Gustave Noske, the right-wing SPD leader, accused Jewish Marxists from the East of "transforming socialism into a dogma and platitudes into articles of faith"; they developed a "secret science" that "remained incomprehensible to the German workers."[2]

Perhaps because of their greater moderation, the Austro-Hungarians were accepted more readily into the party. The Russians, however, remained outsiders. Their role was to serve as "intermediaries between two worlds," the worlds of German and Russian social democracy. Alexander Helphand, for example, edited both SPD newspapers for distribution in Germany, as well as issues of Lenin's *Iskra*. His home literally served as a meeting ground for revolutionaries from both empires. Rosa Luxemburg was simultaneously involved with the German, Polish, and Russian socialist parties. And after the Bolshevik/Menshevik split, Alexander Stein worked for the SPD while keeping in touch with the Mensheviks and editing their *Russiches Bulletin*. William Buchholz edited the *Vorwärts* in Berlin while also participating in the smuggling of illegal literature into Russia. After other Russian revolutionaries had been expelled from Germany, he served as secretary of the Russian Socialist Workers Party in Berlin. Through such activities, the Russians especially served as a link between German and foreign socialist movements.[3]

Socially, however, they remained isolated from their German comrades. This was particularly true of Russian radicals, who formed a variety of support groups in Germany. As early as 1894, a "League of Russian Social Democrats Abroad" established a branch in Berlin. When Russian social democracy splintered, each faction established branches in Germany, ranging from a "Group to Support *Iskra*" to Menshevik cells, Bundist societies, and a "Neutral Group of Social Democrats in Berlin." On the surface, these societies were primarily occupied with the production of propaganda that would be smuggled into the Tsarist Empire. But they also served a vital social function by providing gathering places for lonely Russian émigrés in an alien land.[4]

Though little is known about the activities of these small and short-lived groups, we can gain some insight about their programs from the memoirs of Alexander Granach. The Galician actor describes a tiny anarchist circle which he joined during his first years in Germany around the year 1905. Most of the members consisted of Russian Jews who had recently arrived in Berlin and were engaged in cigarette manufacturing. The group lived in a communal fashion, sharing in the performance of chores and in the allocation of resources. Members attended a congregation of Free Thinkers on Sundays. And as a cover for their radical agenda, they called their society "The Worker's Friend." Ostensibly gathering for cultural programs such as the presentation of plays, they met nightly to listen to antibourgeois poetry. Later they founded a Jacob Gordin Society (named after the Yiddish playwright) where they heard lectures on literary themes, held dances, and performed some Yiddish plays. Apparently, their interest in radical politics waned quickly and they now preferred to meet for social and cultural purposes.[5]

A striking feature of this group was its attendance of Sunday church services and its concomitant alienation from Berlin's thriving Jewish community. Like most subgroups of Jewish transients from the East, the radical intellectuals maintained no formal connection to native Jewry—or, for that matter, to any German group. This was, in part, the consequence of a profound alienation felt by the émigrés when they came into contact with what they perceived as the parochialism of the Jewish community and the nationalist arrogance of German society. But a sense of isolation was also bred by the frequent expulsions endured by the émigrés. Both Austro-Hungarians and Russians were regularly driven from one German state to the next after their political activities were discovered. Sometimes, large groups of radicals were expelled at a single stroke. Other times, individuals were deported: "Parvus," a Russian, was driven out of Prussia and Saxony, while the Austrian Heinrich Braun was forced to leave Prussia. Only those émigrés who found a way to secure citizenship in a German state were protected from arbitrary expulsion. Hence, Rosa Luxemburg could enjoy relative freedom of action because of her "marriage of convenience" to a German, while Wilhelm Buchholz could play a pivotal role between Russian and German socialists because he was born to German parents who resided in Russia. Most of the radicals, however, lived too precariously in Germany and were too engrossed in East European politics to sink deep roots in the country.[6]

Hebraists, Yiddishists, Zionists

Germany also attracted an entirely different kind of Jewish intellectual from the East—the avant-garde of contemporary Hebrew and Yiddish writers. Initially such individuals came to spend a brief period of time studying at a German university or taking in the cultural life of the *Reich*. Already in the 1890s, the poet Saul Tchernichowsky (a Russian) and the essayist Simon Bernfeld (a Galician) came to study. At the turn of the century, young Zionists such as Leo Motzkin, Shmaryahu

Levin, Nahman Syrkin, Mordechai Ehrenpreis, and Osias Thon came to Berlin as students. They represented the vanguard of a Zionist student body that would attract more visiting Jewish ideologues and intellectuals, for they constituted a well-educated and sophisticated audience before whom new ideas and literary approaches could be tested.[7]

The growing importance of Germany as a center of the Zionist movement, as well as for young Russian Jews seeking an education abroad due to anti-Semitic quotas in the Tsarist Empire, encouraged even more intellectuals from the East to spend some time visiting in the *Reich*. On his first evening in Berlin sometime in the year 1903, Itamar Ben Avi, the son of the Hebrew lexicographer Eliezer Ben Yehuda, encountered a virtual "who's who" of Zionist leaders, Yiddishists, and Hebraists at the Cafe Monopol. They included the artist Ephraim Lilien, the journalist Berthold Feiwel, the leader of German Zionism Arthur Hantke, the folklorist Heinrich Loewe, the Hebrew author Reuben Breinin, the journalist and historian of Zionism Nahum Sokolow, the Zionist organizer Shymaryahu Levin, and the two Yiddish authors Sholom Aleichem and Sholem Asch. (With the exception of Hantke and Loewe, all were either Galicians or Russians.) These literary figures, in turn, attracted other writers passing through the capital city, such as David Frischman, A. Hermoni, Samuel Abba Horodetsky, Shai Ish Hurwicz, Jakob Kahan, Zalman Schneur, and Jacob Simchoni. Their haunt, the Cafe Monopol, became known as the regular gathering place for writers from the East: the Hebraists sat in one corner and within easy glaring distance sat the Yiddishists. Even the waiters picked up a smattering of Hebrew.[8]

Like the radical intellectuals, these Jewish literati were profoundly isolated from German society. While they struggled to create a vital Jewish literature, few Germans, whether Gentile or Jewish, had the slightest interest in a modern literature written in a Jewish language. A few of these writers even ventured to launch periodicals in the Hebrew language that might appeal to Jewish readers in Germany, but such efforts came to naught. Although numerous Hebrew journals were published in Germany, none attracted more than a handful of readers in the *Reich*. Instead, they were directed at Jews still in the East. Symptomatic of this gap between the visiting literati and their German Jewish counterparts was the reception extended to the first annual congress of the "Association for Hebrew Language and Culture" held in 1909. Organizers chose Berlin as the site of this congress because of its large and distinguished Jewish community. But hardly any native Jews bothered to attend, and the few official representatives of the local Jewish community addressed the congress in German![9]

Only a few of these visiting writers established a rapport with some circles of native Jews. The artist Ephraim Lillien married a German-born woman; Samuel Agnon found sponsors willing to support his work when he arrived in Germany shortly before the outbreak of World War I; and Micha Josef Berdichevsky apparently gained sufficient respect in Germany so that his stories were frequently published in the largest German Jewish newspaper and he was eventually buried in the honorary row of Berlin's Jewish cemetery in Weissensee. Significantly, all three eschewed involvement with the insulated circle of Hebraists in Berlin, a circle that lived on the periphery of Jewish society.[10]

The isolation of these visiting intellectuals from the East had important consequences for German Jewry, for it was precisely these writers who did much to shape East European Jewry's perceptions of the German Jew. Russian Zionists such as Chaim Weizmann, Schmaryahu Levin, and Jacob Klatzkin railed against the self-satisfied and deluded Jews whom they encountered in Germany. Indeed, the memoirs of these transient intellectuals have fixed the image of German Jews as *the* personification of the self-hating, assimilated Jew. In 1905, Klatzkin penned perhaps the most biting portrait of German Jewry in a bitter satire entitled "Germans of the Mosaic Persuasion." Directed specifically at the Orthodox Jews in Frankfurt am Main, Klatzkin's critique presented the stereotypical German Jew: For the German of the Mosaic Persuasion, everything was a duty, nothing an opportunity for human kindness. German Jews were contemptuous of their East European coreligionists. True, they contributed charity to refugees, but only on the condition that the poor would move on—"people like you are capable of bringing great danger upon us; go back to the place you came from." According to Klatzkin, this attitude derived from a kind of social Darwinist outlook common among German Jews: "He who does not have, is not worthy of having; he is a *Shlemiel*. He who has, deserves more; he is smart, capable." From their vantage point at the periphery of German society, visiting Hebraists and Yiddishists formed a negative view of native Jewry that they actively disseminated.[11]

Wandering Beggars

Ironically, Klatzkin's *Shlemiels,* itinerant beggars, maintained far closer contacts with native Jews than did most other transient Jews from the East. At least since the onset of the Thirty Years War, Polish *Betteljuden* had come to Germany to seek financial support from their more affluent German coreligionists. They were received into the homes of German Jews with a mixture of sympathy and annoyance, a response that was captured in the following Judeo-German ditty quoted by Johannes Buxtdorf already in 1643:

> The first day he is a guest.
> The second day he is a pest.
> The third day is his last.

Despite the elaborate efforts of Jewish communities to eradicate itinerant begging, *Betteljuden* continued to arrive from the East. Quite simply, these beggars came because their need was sufficiently great and because they continued to find hospitable and generous support from native Jews.[12]

Several types of wandering beggars appeared regularly. One type consisted of Hassidic "wonder rabbis" who journeyed mainly to rural Jewish communities—particularly in eastern Prussia—seeking to attract followers and benefactors by performing miraculous acts. A second type consisted of individuals whose claim for financial support was based on their distinguished *Yichus*, their rabbinic lineage. And a third type was comprised of beggars carrying letters from their local rabbis attesting to their designation as official fund-raisers for worthy institutions of learning, needy synagogues, or impoverished widows or orphans in the East.

The German Jewish press regularly carried articles exposing some of these individuals as swindlers and frauds. The *Allgemeine Zeitung des Judentums* even "uncovered" what it described as an "international scheme to swindle" unsuspecting German Jews. It is therefore difficult to believe that native Jews did not see through these individuals and know, as did Rahel Strauss, that most of the money collected by these beggars "flowed into their own pockets." [13]

Yet despite the frequent warnings and the elaborate programs established by the organized leadership of native Jews to centralize the distribution of charity through officially sanctioned philanthropic funds, itinerant beggars continued coming to Germany throughout the Imperial era. One factor for the persistence of this phenomenon was the ongoing economic crisis endured by Jews in the East. But a second factor was the continuing generosity of individual Jews in Germany who provided these beggars with support in contravention to the official policy of communities. [14]

While such behavior does not conform to stereotypes of the mean-spirited German Jew promoted by some embittered Eastern Jews who resided in the *Reich*, there is evidence that some "Germans of the Mosaic Persuasion"—particularly in rural areas—welcomed *Betteljuden* into their homes. In part, such behavior can be ascribed to altruism and concern for fellow Jews. But the itinerant beggars also served a useful function for Jews in isolated areas. They provided small-town Jews with news, anecdotes, a touch of the exotic, and some interesting morsels of Jewish learning. In his memoirs, Sammy Gronemann describes how itinerant beggars traveling through rural Pomerania knew that in exchange for a few religious homilies, they would be fed and housed. According to Rahel Strauss, every Jewish family in her mother's hometown (in Posen) made an effort to have a Sabbath "guest." In fact, on one of the frequent occasions when her grandfather entertained guests from the East, a visiting Hungarian played matchmaker and introduced Strauss' parents to each other. Thus, despite their constant wanderings, itinerant beggars were involved in the life of the Jewish community far more than other transients from the East. [15]

Students [16]

The largest contingent of transient Jews from the East consisted of students enrolled at German institutions of higher learning. Numbering close to 3,000 souls on the eve of World War I, these students were overwhelmingly drawn from the Tsarist Empire, where anti-Semitic quotas had prevented them from studying at Russian universities. Like other Jewish transients, they came to Germany in order to partake of the *Reich*'s cultural and educational opportunities. And, like the émigré intellectuals, they stood at the periphery of German society, maintaining little social contact with native Jews or Gentiles. The experience of students, however, was vastly different from that of other transients because of the rich subculture they were able to create in the *Reich*. In virtually every city housing a major institution of higher learning, Jewish students from the East organized networks of clubs and societies to meet their social needs and express their political concerns.

Ideological Factionalism

The impulse of Russian Jewish students to organize their own societies in Germany was evident already from the onset of the Imperial era. In mid-October 1870, students, manual laborers, and tradesmen from Russia founded the *Amicitia (Ahvah)* Society in Berlin for the purposes of mutual aid, cultural edification, and support for needy coreligionists still in the East. No sooner was the society founded than ideological differences shattered its unity. A controversy erupted over the national identity of the society: Was the group to identify itself as a "Russian Polish" or merely a "Russian" society? If the latter term were to be employed, then the group would implicitly legitimize Russian hegemony over Poland; by contrast, use of the former term would grant implicit recognition to Polish separatism—that is, Polish nationalism. Within a half-year, this issue proved so nettlesome that the majority of the members broke away to found the "Russian Jewish Society, *Concordia.*" The new society strove to foster a love of the Russian "Fatherland" among all Russian Jews by urging the latter to abandon the Yiddish "jargon" and assimilate into Russian society.[17]

The divisive history of this early society foreshadowed many of the difficulties that were to beset clubs established by Jewish students from the East in successive decades. Originally founded to serve as support groups for lonely émigré students, these societies either disintegrated or splintered due to political conflicts. Ironically, the issues that prompted conflicts had little to do with realities faced by the students in Germany. Rather, groups that were primarily established to help students cope with life in Germany were torn asunder by ideological considerations of significance only in Eastern Europe.

The conflict within the *Amicitia* Society illustrates that the key lines of division during the last decades of the nineteenth century concerned tensions between Russian and Polish nationalists. At the university in Munich, for example, two Polish societies, *Polonia* and the Scientific Society of Polish Students, countered propaganda issued by a range of Russian nationalist groups. Neither the Russian nor the Polish bloc displayed any interest in the preservation of Jewish culture, even though most of their members were of Jewish origin. Typical of this bias was the decision of the Russian Reading Room in Berlin to display only one Jewish newspaper, the Russian-language journal *Voschod.* When, in the early 1890s, some members urged the library to subscribe to Hebrew periodicals, a violent debate ensued. According to Shmaryahu Levin, the leader of the nascent group of Jewish nationalists, there were some "Jewish students who thought it their duty to express their abhorrence of nationalist chauvinism by refusing admission to the Hebrew press. The *Hamelitz* and *Hazephirah*, they argued, were reactionary by virtue of their language alone." Such Jewish students "proclaimed themselves Russians, and violently repudiated anything that bound them to their own race and people."[18]

Gradually during the 1890s there was a discernible shift in the allegiances of these émigré students from support for various forms of East European nationalism to more radical causes. During the two decades prior to World War I, the major ideological rivals were socialist revolutionaries and Jewish nationalists—with each faction containing numerous splinter groups. In part, the increasing success of these groups reflected the general radicalization of the Russian Jewish intelligentsia after the pogroms of 1881. But the students in Germany were especially drawn to radicalism because of their bitter experiences with the tsarist *numerus clausus*. It is no wonder that students forced to study abroad because their own government discriminated against them were susceptible to radical propaganda.

The socialist revolutionaries in Germany were divided into several factions that paralleled radical movements in Russia. These included, most prominently, Bolsheviks, Mensheviks, and Bundists. United by the common goal of establishing a new political order in Russia, these ideological movements differed substantially in their visions of the new Russian state, as well as in the degree of sympathy they held for Jewish cultural particularism. Students of Jewish origin who supported the cause of Russian social democracy had little patience for Jewish needs; they defined themselves as internationalists who, like Rosa Luxemburg, had no special sympathy for Jewish suffering. The Bundists, by contrast, evolved a program at the turn of the century that called for national cultural autonomy for Jews—as well as for other minorities in Russia. They worked for the creation of a new, postrevolutionary Russia where Jewish national identity would be encouraged by the state and where Jewish cultural institutions would be financed by the government. While it is not possible to ascertain which faction won the support of most leftists students, it is clear that the Bund was a force to be reckoned with in the student colonies. As early as 1901, a large Bundist society functioned at the technical *Hochschule* in Karlsruhe. And when representatives of Bundist groups in Western Europe held a convention in 1907, delegates were sent by "support groups" in Berlin, Coethen, Darmstadt, Friedberg, Jena, Mittweida, and Munich.[19]

The factions of the Left combatted each other fiercely as they vied to win the support of émigré students. In order to shore up morale and win new recruits, both the Bund and the Russian social democrats sent their best speakers from Russia to lecture in university towns in Western Europe. Recalling one such tour to address Russian students in Munich, Heidelberg, Karlsruhe, and Berlin, Vladimir Medem, a leading Bundist, described a hard-fought debate with the emissary of Russian social democracy, Leon Trotsky:

> The exchange lasted several hours. One of my comrades from Karlsruhe launched it with an enunciation of the national program of the Bund as adopted at the Fourth Congress in 1901. Then Trotsky offered a detailed critique, to which I gave the response. I can no longer remember the details of the debate, but I do recall that it was conducted vehemently and that both sides, as usual, left feeling satisfied with themselves. I must confess that I developed a dislike for the fellow at that time, and I have reason to believe the feeling was mutual. It was not until evening, however, that interest really mounted and certain characteristics became

apparent. Upon the completion of my lecture, a few Zionists took the floor, as did several unaffiliated youths with erratic ideas. Trotsky spoke next. He responded to the Zionists wittily and well. But then he turned on me, taking umbrage because I had "dared" to direct some caustic remarks at the Russian social democrats. I had accused them of having consistently neglected the important task of fighting anti-Semitism, and I made no secret of the fact that I considered this a grave misfortune and a serious shortcoming which must be avoided in the future. Trotsky took up the cudgels for the Russian socialists.

Thus, in a student society situated in Germany, leaders of the Bund and Russian social democracy fought to win the allegiance of Russian Jewry's educated elite.[20]

As noted by Medem, the various socialist revolutionaries were challenged by representatives of Jewish nationalist societies. Beginning in the 1890s, a variety of groups espousing Jewish nationalism—though not necessarily Zionism—were founded by Russian students in the *Reich*. Some of these were mainly concerned with the dissemination of Jewish culture and learning: the *"Bildung"* society, for example, was founded in 1896 mainly to "promote literature in the Yiddish language." Others, however, identified with the Basel program of the World Zionist Movement. In fact, students from the East established enough Zionist clubs to warrant the establishment of a national "Cartel of Zionist Students from Russia in Germany."![21]

The existence of such separate clubs is noteworthy when we consider that Zionists from the East could have linked up with German Jews who shared their ideology. After all, the federation established by native-born Zionist students admitted noncitizens to its ranks. Yet, despite their involvement with German Zionists, students from the East continued to maintain clubs whose membership was open exclusively to *Landsleit* (compatriots). Some of these, in fact, catered specifically to Rumanian or Russian students in Germany, rather than to foreign students in general. Undoubtedly, such separate groups were established to provide financial and social support to émigré students who identified with Zionism, just as similar mutual aid societies were maintained by other ideological factions. Equally important, however, these groups were needed to provide a base for the missionary activities of Zionists among the population of East European Jews studying in the *Reich*. Only Zionist societies that catered exclusively to Russians and operated within student circles could hope to compete for the allegiance of uncommitted students from the Tsarist Empire.[22]

Given their youthful passions and certainties, it is not surprising that Jewish students from the East engaged in fierce and uncompromising ideological combat. Contending factions battled to "catch souls" among new arrivals and "convert" the uncommitted. Rivalries even erupted at railroad terminals when newly arriving students from the East were "ambushed" by representatives of the various ideological factions who vied to help them adjust to the new environment—and win them over to the cause. But the most important setting of these battles occurred in meetings sponsored by the various societies. Newspapers frequently reported on the unruly behavior of socialists and Bundists who disrupted Zionist meetings; undoubtedly, the Zionists reciprocated in kind. But because socialist revolutionaries were forced to be far more circumspect at their own meetings, given the

special surveillance and harassment to which they were subjected by German police authorities, Zionist meetings became the setting for major ideological confrontations. On occasion, hundreds of students would crowd into such meetings
in order to witness the oratorical pyrotechnics displayed by some of the most
formidable Russian minds in Germany. The unfolding of one such debate was
vividly captured by the Zionist leader Shmaryahu Levin:

> One of the deadliest debaters on the Socialist side was Parvus, who even in those
> days had achieved a considerable reputation as a Marxist theoretician. He was
> present at almost every meeting. In debate he was swift and merciless . . . he
> always spoke not as if he were discussing theoretical matters, but with a terrific
> immediacy, as though the barricades were rising in the streets of Berlin, and the
> moral struggle of the classes had opened. . . . Parvus was thundering—as only
> he could—against the meaninglessness of nationalism. He cited Marx, history,
> philosophy, and then feeling that these arguments were too vague and academic
> he grabbed hold of his coat and roared: "The wool of this coat was taken from
> sheep pastured in Angora; it was spun in England; and it was woven in Lodz;
> the buttons come from Germany, the thread from Austria: is it not clear to you
> that this world is *international,* and even a miserable thing like a coat is made up
> of the labor of ten different races?" The argument and, still more, the illustration
> was effective. You could *feel* the stream of intellectual sympathy turning in Par-
> vus' direction. Hands were lifted to applaud—and then something unexpected
> happened. Parvus' coat was too small for him. In the fury of gesticulation, and
> while he pulled his coat about to illustrate his argument, he had ripped the right
> elbow, which now showed a patch of white shirt. Right opposite Parvus sat Nach-
> man Syrkin, whose eyes burned with rage and contempt. Just at the moment
> when Parvus had completed his argument, Syrkin, unable to contain himself, rose
> to his feet and shouted: "And the rip in your sleeve comes from the pogrom in
> Kiev!" The effect of that interjection was marvelous. Parvus had worked an hour
> to come to his climax of the international coat. Syrkin had undone him with a
> sentence.[23]

It is virtually impossible to determine which faction won the struggle for
"converts" or which ideology was most popular among Eastern Jews at German
universities. Not surprisingly, the few historians to deal with Russian students
abroad exaggerate the importance of their favorite groups: scholars in the German
Democratic Republic stress the vitality of Russian social democrats—especially
the Bolsheviks—while Zionist memoirists emphasize the popularity of societies
with which they affiliated. On the basis of fragmentary sources, it seems that
"Jewish national" groups attracted a larger membership than did other ideological
factions. Police files from Munich dating to the period 1905–10 indicate that Jewish national societies attracted 81 out of the 120 students in the major clubs; and
newspaper reports from Berlin tell of Zionist meetings attended by hundreds of
students. Still, these examples may be misleading, since Zionists were relatively
free to conduct their meetings while socialists were constantly harassed by the
secret police. Under the circumstances, it is little wonder that we can count relatively few radical students and Bundists. The fact that societies functioned only
briefly and often reappeared under new names, and that membership fluctuated
constantly—due to propaganda victories or simply the transience inherent in Ger-

man student life—renders it even more difficult to assess the numerical strength of each ideological faction.[24]

What is more certain is that the lines of division between socialist revolutionaries and Zionists hardened and that the students were increasingly polarized in the waning years of the Second Empire. With the imposition of quotas and other government measures designed to curb Jewish students from Russia, both factions adopted more radical positions. In late February and early March 1913, both the revolutionaries and the Zionists convened national conferences to unify their constituents in the face of government efforts to drive Russian Jews from the German academy. (See Chapter 3.) Out of these conferences emerged two new federations—one unifying students who supported Russian social democracy and the other organizing students who identified as national Jews. Both federations established press organs, propaganda machinery, and strategies to fight the new policies. Significantly, both federations also developed programs to solve the problems of Russian students in Germany by establishing new universities. By the onset of World War I, then, the students had polarized into two ideological camps that offered radical solutions to the problems of Russian Jewry at home and Russian students abroad.[25]

Life in the Russian "Colonies"

Despite their political fragmentation, Russian Jewish students in Germany managed to attain a remarkable social cohesiveness. For even as intense ideological debates divided students into rival factions, they also unified the émigrés by focusing their attention on a common concern—the future of Jewish life in the East. This preoccupation set Russian Jews apart from their fellow students and added to their sense of alienation from German society. Such feelings of estrangement were further heightened by the insularity of the students' social life as well as the cold reception extended to the Russian Jews by their German hosts. The students therefore retreated into their own "colonies," a term they used to describe the conglomeration of clubs and societies that together constituted a distinctive Russian Jewish subcommunity in virtually every German city that boasted a university or Hochschule.[26]

Newcomers from Tsarist Russia were drawn into the life of the local Russian colony almost from their first moments on German soil. Understandably, new arrivals immediately sought out fellow Russian Jews to help negotiate the first difficult days of adjustment to the new country. The newcomer required assistance locating suitable lodgings, finding his way around a strange city, and learning about university life. Yet even after their adjustment to Germany, Russian students continued to fraternize mainly within their own colonies. True, they frequented lecture halls and museums and eagerly partook of Germany's diversified cultural life. But despite these forays, they generally maintained social contacts solely within the colonies. Only among their own could they find the companionship of like-minded friends who shared similar perceptions and experiences. More practically, they could benefit from the various mutual assistance programs offered by various societies within the student colonies.[27]

Perhaps most important, Jewish students from Russia remained enmeshed in their own subculture because, as one contemporary wrote, the colonies constituted "a Pinsk or Minsk in miniature," reproducing the texture and tone of life in the Pale. As we have seen, the student colonies teemed with societies that replicated on German soil the fractious political debates dividing Jews in the East. Equally important, membership in the societies ensured young Russian Jews of steady contact with the literary and political avant-garde of the Pale. The continuous comings and goings of leading Russian revolutionaries and Zionist organizers kept students well informed about the latest political and intellectual fashions.[28]

While the sheer intensity and excitement of life in the colonies lured young Russians, the forbidding German environment also drove them into each other's company. As a practical matter, poverty limited Russian students from participating in German life. The penurious students were forced to rent shabby rooms located in working-class districts; they resorted to walking vast distances since they could not afford public transport; and they sometimes eschewed popular student haunts because they lacked the financial means to eat and drink well. Reflecting on his student days in Germany, Chaim Weizmann wrote:

> If we constituted a kind of ghetto—not a compulsory one, and not in a negative sense—it was to a large extent because most of us were practically penniless. I, with my hundred mark allowance a month—that had to cover books as well as living expenses—was among the well-to-do. But I did not eat a single meal except as somebody's guest. We lived among ourselves because we could not afford to live separately.[29]

German legal restrictions also served to bar the émigrés from popular student activities—especially those that smacked of involvement with local politics. Government officials banned foreign students from attending German political rallies and severly punished any aliens who made contact with local political organizations. It was even dangerous to subscribe to the socialist *Vorwärts*. Shmaryahu Levin noted the anomalous situation whereby "German police would regard the political activity of the foreign students not as an internal German matter to be regulated by German law but purely from the Russian point of view. More than once . . . men were punished . . . for crimes that were not crimes according to German law." In order to avoid even the appearance of impropriety, Russian students eschewed involvement with German politics.[30]

Finally, a significant psychological gap separated the foreign students from their native peers. Once again, Shmaryahu Levin may serve as our interpreter of the social realities.

> On the one side were the "native sons," deep-rooted in their land, satisfied, proud, convinced that God had created the world in order that Germany might be its leader. On the other side were the homeless aliens, young people uprooted from their native land, haunted by doubts and fears, seeking some sort of economic and social foothold in a world which was not theirs. Their outlook was misty, their plans vague, for not all of them were determined to return to Russia. The old proverb "The sated man does not understand the hungry man" applies in the psychic sense, too, and runs both ways: the sated man *does not want* to understand the hungry man, the hungry man *cannot* understand the sated man.

As a result, it was difficult for the aliens to find empathy and friendship among fellow students.[31]

This sense of alienation extended as well to native Jews. The foreign students generally did not establish close personal friendships with native coreligionists and, with the exception of some Zionists, did not even join the student clubs of native Jews. Even among the Zionists, as we have noted, most Eastern Jews participated in their own societies. As one contemporary noted: "German Jews do not join the associations founded by foreign coreligionists." And whereas the reverse may have occurred slightly more often, the multiplicity of uniquely Russian groups—even among the Zionists—suggests otherwise.[32]

Remarkably, the students were even uninvolved with fellow Eastern Jews in Germany. This fact was bemoaned by Fabius Schach, a journalist of Polish origin: "It is a crying wrong that Russian students do not take an interest in these people (the immigrants) and do nothing for them." While the last phrase is too harsh, Schach was correct in emphasizing the distance between students and immigrants from the East. In truth, the two groups inhabited worlds that rarely overlapped. They were not even of the same nationality, since most students were Russians and the immigrants were predominantly from Austro-Hungary. The immigrants, as we shall shortly see, did not share the students' intense ideological commitments. Most fundamentally, the students were removed from the issues of greatest concern to immigrants—economic survival, social adjustment, and acculturation in Germany.[33]

The students' isolation from fellow Eastern Jews in the *Reich* completed their social isolation. They lived, as Shmaryahu Levin aptly put it, "on an island, locked in and locked out."[34] In response to the stimulating discussions and warm fellowship offered by their societies, the students were absorbed in concerns far removed from German life, concerns that focused on the future of Jews in the East. Simultaneously, the foreign ways and alien preoccupations of Russian Jews impeded social contacts with their German colleagues and neighbors, thereby heightening their sense of alienation from life around them. The student colonies, indeed, served as islands—both of refuge and of isolation.

Immigrants Without a Community

In contrast to the diversified and well-organized structure enjoyed by students in their own colonies, immigrant Jews were distinguished by their inability to form a cohesive community prior to World War I. To be sure, immigrant Jews did establish a few institutions, but they failed to create a vibrant equivalent in Germany to the East European "ghettos" that emerged in other Western lands. There were no settlements comparable to London's East End or the Parisian Pletzel, let alone New York's Lower East Side.[35] Given the relatively small number of Eastern Jews in Germany and their wide dispersal, this is understandable. The institutional poverty of these Jews is noteworthy, however, because it signified their lack of cohesiveness as a social group.

We need only survey the few institutions successfully established by Eastern

Jews to observe the meagerness and deficiencies of organized immigrant life. The most distinctive of such institutions, no doubt, was the *Shtibl*—the prayer hall. In part, immigrants formed separate congregations because they felt uncomfortable with the type of religious service common in German synagogues. Writing of his first visit to a liberal congregation, a Galician alumnus of the liberal rabbinical school in Berlin described his perceptions of religious services in Berlin's Orienburgstrasse synagogue: "The people sat as if they were spectators in a theater. Most did not have prayerbooks. They listened to the choir and watched its conductor." By contrast, in the writer's hometown of Lemberg, Jews "really prayed"; their "service had a living character." Even in more traditional synagogues, immigrants did not feel at home, because of both the formality of prayer services and the differences in liturgical and cantorial customs. In fact, a key motive for the founding of immigrant congregations was the desire to replicate in Germany familiar traditions and customs prevalent in the East. Still other congregations were formed to permit *Hassidim* to avoid worshipping with *Mitnagdim* (and vice versa). Undoubtedly, social needs also prompted the creation of such synagogues: immigrants wanted a place to worship and fraternize with *Landsleit* (compatriots). Some congregations were organized as *Chevrot*—mutual aid societies, providing services ranging from medical attention, proper burial rites, care for the needs of mourners, and advice on how to adjust to the new country.[36]

These services, and the cost of maintaining prayer halls, were often supported by voluntary dues or other funds raised by the immigrants. Frequently, however, the official communities of native Jewry supported these institutions with subventions—just as they supported private prayer halls established by German Jews. This latter point is significant because it underscores the fact that immigrant Jews were not unique in establishing their own synagogues. Well before they arrived, German Jews had set the precedent of establishing prayer services to meet the needs of compatriots from particular areas *within* the *Reich*. In Leipzig, for example, congregations such as the Berliner and Hamburger *Schule* and the Dessauer, Breslauer, and Halberstadter synagogues met the needs of natives who had migrated from other German cities. Similarly, most of the thirty-five or so private congregations in Berlin by 1914 were founded by and for German Jews. These private congregations served as models for East European immigrants and legitimized the existence of *Chevrot* within the communal structure. By attending immigrant synagogues, East European Jews were not breaking with the established Jewish communities; they were still counted as members of those communities and participated in their activities.[37]

Perhaps the most alien institutions established by East European Jews were Bundist cells. Affiliated with the General Jewish Worker's Union in Lithuania, Poland, and Russia, these cells were primarily concerned with rallying working-class Jews to support the socialist movement of Jews in Eastern Europe. Prior to 1905, only a few such cells existed among students, but in the years after the Russian Revolution of 1905, more working-class Jews arrived from Russia, and Bundist cells were established in cities such as Berlin, Leipzig, Gera, Munich, Offenbach, Mannheim, Karslruhe, and Baden-Baden. From the scant evidence available, it appears that most cells remained small: only 40–50 individuals out of the 800 Eastern Jews in Mannheim attended local meetings; in Karlsruhe, meetings were attended by no more than 13 members.[38]

A partial picture of party activities emerges from the records of a Bundist group in Offenbach. According to these statutes, membership was open to all Jews, regardless of sex, who believed in the principles of the society—provided they were Russians. The group defined its objectives, as follows: (1) to support the Russian workers' movement and especially the Russian Bund; (2) to get Russian, Lithuanian, and Polish Jews in Offenbach to join the Bund; (3) to educate local members; (4) to stand "shoulder to shoulder with German workers and further proletarian interests." The statutes attest to the educational and social programs of the group—particularly in the realm of mutual aid. Clearly, the Bundists were less concerned with the class struggle in Germany than with the overthrow of the tsar. While links were forged with local SPD groups, little effort was expended on representing the interests of working-class members before their German employers. And, certainly, there was no talk of strikes in Germany. The Bundist cell was oriented to self-help at home and education regarding developments abroad.[39]

The weak program of the Bundist group in Offenbach, probably the largest such association in the *Reich,* highlights the anemic character of Bundism in Germany. Despite the presence of cells in over half a dozen cities and a potential constituency drawn from the 20,000–30,000 working-class Jews from the East who resided in the *Reich,* the Bund was organizationally and politically insignificant in Germany. It established no newspaper to communicate with party members throughout the *Reich,* it did not organize a central office to link cells, and it even failed to produce spokesmen for Bundism in Germany. The well-known Bundist S. Shelly worked as a tailor in Offenbach for a time, but in his memoirs of those years he does not try to glamorize his leadership activities or glorify the Bund's development in Germany. It may be argued that party officials could not operate openly in Germany due to police surveillance and therefore Bundist activities had to remain clandestine. But even from the safety of the United States and many years after the events, Bundist leaders such as Shelly, Vladimir Medem, and B. Hofmann (*"Zivion"*) had little to say about party successes in Germany. Immigrant Jews were too scattered throughout the *Reich* and too intimidated by the threat of expulsion to organize an effective labor movement to ameliorate their own condition.[40]

The failure of immigrants to organize effective associations for the betterment of their economic lot was matched by a similar failure to create institutions for the expression of their cultural and social interests. With few exceptions, there were no entertainment showcases or artistic forums for the presentation of Yiddish literature, drama, or poetry. Only a few theaters and cabarets such as the Jargon Theater des Centrums produced Yiddish programs in the Berlin ghetto area. It is doubtful that visiting troupes from Eastern Europe toured the country before World War I, as they did after the war. In fact, when in 1905 Pinski's *Eisik Sheftel* was performed, the *Jüdische Rundschau* panned the production for being delivered in a "mumbled High German"—probably by native Jews who knew little Yiddish.[41]

Remarkably, the immigrants did not even publish a journal or newsletter cov-

ering matters of mutual concern. While approximately twenty Hebrew and Yiddish periodicals appeared in Germany during the era of the Second Empire, none
was addressed to Eastern Jews residing in the *Reich*. All were directed at Jews
still in the East. To cite one of the most prominent such journals, the Hebrew *Ha-
Maggid* was published in East Prussia from 1856 until circa 1892, but, according
to the literary historian Meyer Waxman, "it was intended for the Jewish masses
in the Russian Empire—with news and information of all events transpiring in
both the general and Jewish world in the language they knew best." Thus, the
dispersed immigrants had no press organ to unify them, offer advice on how to
adapt to Germany, or direct them to common action.[42]

But the greatest failure of the immigrants was their inability to produce their
own leaders. No spokesmen emerged from their midst to represent their interests
before government officials or native Jews. No leaders directed their energies toward
creating a distinctive culture. And no representative organs gave voice to their
particular needs or interests. This is not to suggest that there were no East European Jews in Germany with leadership abilities. On the contrary, intellectuals such
as the Jewish thinker Martin Buber, the Heidelberg professor Hermann Schapira,
and the Galician belletrist Karl Emil Franzos exercised influence upon some sections of native Jewry. Quite a number of Austro-Hungarians and Russians became
prominent in German cultural life. And dozens of Eastern-born rabbis led German
congregations. But none took an active interest in the condition of immigrant
Jews. None spoke for the immigrants. And none tried to unite the Russian, Austro-Hungarian, and Rumanian Jews scattered throughout the country into a cohesive group. The conclusion is inescapable: with no individual leaders, representative groups, formal channels of communication, opportunities to express common
interests, cultural forums, and only a few scattered and informal associations, the
immigrants failed to create a separate community.[43]

Having surveyed the associational activities of Eastern Jews in the *Reich*, it is
now possible to evaluate charges about their radicalism and subversiveness. It is
clear from the foregoing that some Eastern Jews in the *Reich* indeed were bent on
radical revolution. Some visiting intelectuals, university students, and even a small
minority of immigrants supported radical causes. In order to further their aims and
organize their activities, they established a small network of student societies and
Bundist cells that facilitated the sharing of information and propaganda. It is equally
clear, however, that the target of these activities was the tsar, not the kaiser.
Russian social democrats and Bundists in the *Reich* were intent on improving the
lot of Jews in the East, but they offered virtually no programs to improve the lot
of Eastern Jews in Germany. This distinction was lost on restrictionists and anti-
Semites who used the charge of radicalism to arouse popular sentiment against all
Jews from the East.

Our survey also highlights the fragmented associational life of Eastern Jews in
Germany. Upon close inspection, it is evident that the newcomers were divided
into a series of subgroups whose organizational and social activities rarely intersected. On limited occasions, transients and students came into contact within the
Russian student colonies; but, for the most part, immigrants and transients shared

little in common and never joined forces for the furtherance of a mutually agreed-upon program. Equally important, within each of these categories there were even smaller associations and organizational groups that further fragmented Eastern Jews into socially isolated units. The significance of this organizational impoverishment was twofold: First, Eastern Jews did not have the institutional network to effect a program for the amelioration of their own condition. They were therefore unequipped to mount any campaign of self-defense when new government policies threatened their status in Germany. Second, the absence of competing institutions both symbolized and facilitated the absorption of immigrant Jews into the established communities of Germany Jewry. To a degree unparalleled in any other Western land, Eastern Jews in the Second Empire swiftly became members of native Jewish communities—a process, as we shall now see in the final section of this book, that caused severe communal and social strains between immigrant and native Jews.

III

THE JEWISH COMMUNITY

7

In the Maelstrom of Communal Politics

The encounter of Eastern and German Jews occurred within an institutional setting unique to Central Europe—the Jewish *Kultus-Gemeinde*. Created by German states to centralize local Jewish religious activities, *Gemeinden* embraced all Jews within their territorial authority—including foreigners. As a consequence, immigrants were compelled to join the communities of native Jews and German Jews were forced to integrate newcomers into their institutions—a state of affairs that made it impossible for native and immigrant Jews to avoid each other. *Gemeinden* thus became the locus of both cooperation and conflict between German and East European Jews in the *Reich*.

Participation in Communal Life

The German-Jewish *Kultus-Gemeinden* were built on the foundations of medieval *Kehilot* (autonomous religious corporations) and were first modified to serve the needs of absolutist states. In Imperial Germany, the *Gemeinden* were empowered to organize Jewish communal and ritual affairs. They hired rabbis and religious functionaries, maintained and built synagogues, cared for the religious needs of the community, and ran a variety of institutions—newspapers, social associations, cemeteries, libraries, health facilities, and charity funds. All of these activities were supported with tax revenues collected either by the government on behalf of the Jews or by the community with the cooperation of state tax inspectors.[1]

Every Jew, whether resident alien or German citizen, was required by state law to support the community and to become a member of the *Gemeinde* nearest to his place of legal domicile. Each male also possessed the rights inherent in membership—including the right to vote in communal elections. Individuals could lose their membership rights by falling into arrears with tax payments or by committing criminal acts. But voluntary secession from the *Gemeinde* required a formal legal proceeding in which an individual petitioned for the right to remove himself from the community.[2]

Gemeinde leadership was chosen through a process of democratic elections. All male taxpayers who had come of age and possessed an unblemished record were entitled to the franchise. They elected a representative assembly, which in turn chose an executive board (*Vorstand*), a body empowered to make major administrative and policy decisions. In general, the voting system favored the election of plutocrats who wielded the real power in the community.[3]

But the authority of these notables was circumscribed both by communal statutes and state governments. The former served as constitutions, outlining the manner in which *Gemeinden* would run their affairs. The oversight of state governments, however, was even more crucial for, fundamentally, *Gemeinden* were the creations of the state. States stipulated the manner in which communities were to be run, the scope of their activities, and the extent of their authority. Whenever new communal statutes were drafted by *Gemeinden,* they had to be submitted to state and municipal authorities for approval. And in cases of intercommunal conflicts, government officials were the final arbiters. Thus, the latitude granted by German authorities fundamentally determined how the *Gemeinden* functioned. Only in areas where laws did not specifically outline what should be done, were *Gemeinde* statutes authoritative.[4]

This was clearly the case with regard to the status of alien Jews in the community. All states required their membership in *Gemeinden,* and most governments stipulated that aliens possessed the franchise (the active vote) and could even stand for election to a communal office (the passive vote). Only when state laws remained vague and government bureaucrats took a neutral position could communal statutes deny the franchise to foreigners.

Two blatant examples should suffice to illustrate the decisive role played by state laws. In Prussia the law of July 23, 1847, continued to regulate communal affairs throughout the history of the Second Empire. Section 41 of this law stated the following:

> All male members of the Synagogue Community who are of age, have an umblemished record, make an independent living, and have not been in arrears with their communal dues for the last three years elect representatives, and these elect the Board for a six-year term of office.

Accordingly, Prussian governors repeatedly ruled that alien Jews must be granted the voting franchise. The communal statutes of Prussian *Gemeinden* reflected this state-imposed requirement: they did not discriminate between natives and aliens in regard to membership rights. Saxon laws, by contrast, failed to stipulate clearly which Jews were entitled to the voting franchise, but instead left the decision in the hands of individual communities. As a consequence, some *Gemeinden*—but not all—drafted statutes that deprived aliens of the franchise. In Leipzig, for example, elders gave "the right to participate in the elections only to male members who are of age and possess Saxon citizenship or the rights of citizenship in the city of Leipzig." Similar rules applied in Dresden. In Chemnitz, however, aliens enjoyed the passive vote until early in the twentieth century and the active vote until they were disenfranchised in 1913 (see below). The Saxon model of governmental neutrality was the exception, not the rule. In fact, the other major states populated by Eastern Jews—Baden, Bavaria, Hesse, and Württemberg—followed Prussia's example by stipulating that foreigners could vote in communal elections.[5]

A perusal of communal statutes from *Gemeinden* scattered throughout the country further indicates that few restrictions were placed on the voting rights of aliens. The Orthodox secessionist communities in Frankfurt am Main (*Israelitisches Religionsgesellschaft*), Berlin (*Adass Jisroel*), and Nuremberg also extended complete membership rights to aliens. Indeed, when a survey was undertaken by the German-Israelite Communal League (D.I.G.B.) in early 1903 regarding the rights granted to aliens by *Gemeinden*, only one of the twenty-seven communities to respond stated that alien residents were forbidden to vote—and that was Leipzig. In Kattowitz foreigners could vote and be elected to the representative assembly; they could not, however, serve on the *Vorstand*. And only two communities reported partial restrictions placed on aliens: in Chemnitz foreigners could vote but not be elected; and in Würzburg they could vote after residing in the community for five years. Elsewhere they enjoyed both active and passive voting rights. Although the number of respondents to this survey was pitifully small, the findings confirm that few *Gemeinden* forbade Eastern Jews from exercising the franchise.[6]

While it is well established, though not commonly known, that Eastern Jews were legally entitled to vote as equals in *Gemeinde* elections, it is more difficult to document the extent of their actual participation. There is no question that some Eastern Jews did vote and even were elected in communal balloting. This is evident from the fact that in several *Gemeinden* scattered throughout Germany efforts were made to strip aliens of their franchise precisely because they controlled the balance of power in elections: their votes counted too heavily. On the whole, however, it is impossible to estimate how many immigrants cast ballots in *Gemeinde* elections.[7]

The involvement of Eastern Jews in other spheres of communal life is equally evident, though not quantifiable. To begin with, quite a number of foreigners attended native synagogues. The existence of private services designed to meet the needs of immigrants ought not obscure the fact that Eastern Jews also worshipped side by side with natives. Ironically, much of the evidence for this is limited to reports describing tensions that arose because of such contact. In Bamberg a fight broke out in one synagogue because native Jews were offended by the custom of a Polish worshipper to cover his head with a prayer shawl. And in the Roonstrasse synagogue in Cologne a Galician Jew was ejected because he fell asleep during the services and therefore failed to rise during the prayer for the welfare of the kaiser! Such stories illustrate that Eastern Jews prayed in native synagogues, but provide little information on the number who did so.[8]

Eastern Jews also took advantage of educational programs provided by *Gemeinden*. While some sent their children to schools founded by immigrant *Chevrot*, a great many enrolled their children in community-run schools. In Berlin, the city with the most extensive network of *Chevrot*, hundreds of immigrant parents sent their children to *Gemeinde*-run schools. As of 1914, at least 425 Eastern Jews were enrolled in the ten communal schools within the city, and additional Russian and Galican students studied in the various schools located in the suburbs. In other German cities, Eastern Jews also opted to send their children to *Gemeinde* schools: the *Talmud Torah Realschule* in Hamburg reported that eight percent of its student body in 1898–99 was born abroad; by 1913–14 this figure had jumped to nearly fifteen percent (from twenty-three to fifty-six alien children). And at the *Philanthropin Realschule* in Frankfurt am Main, around 20 of the 250 students attending the school in the late 1880s and early 1890s were aliens. Here too we see how German laws pushed native and immigrant Jews together: due to the legal requirement that all children attend religious schools, immigrants were forced to send their children to communal schools and the *Gemeinden* had to educate the offspring of aliens.[9]

The apparent failure of immigrants to secede from *Gemeinden* further attests to their integration into the key institutions of German Jewry. Writing of the interwar period, Alexander Carlebach claimed that few Eastern Jews were receptive to secessionist Orthodoxy. (A minority of Orthodox Jews in Germany regarded the established *Gemeinden* as religiously illegitimate since they were run by adherents of Liberal Judaism; to demonstrate their disapproval, they seceded from *Gemeinden* and formed secessionist [*Austritt*] congregations.) There is no reason to assume that there was any greater receptivity to *Austritt* groups prior to World War I. Furthermore, the reports issued by the school systems of the *Israelitsches Religionsgesellschaft* of Frankfurt and the *Adass Jisroel* community in Berlin reveal that only a small number of Eastern Jews studied in these schools. In fact, many of those who did attend were sent there by parents who continued to reside in Eastern Europe or by parents—such as those of Nahum Goldmann—who remained members of the official community. There are several explanations for this refusal to withdraw from the community: secession required a formal declaration and court appearance—an act that was complicated and potentially hazardous; the *Austritt* groups were no more friendly to Eastern Jews than were official *Gemeinden;* and the newcomers may have wished to avoid antagonizing powerful philanthropic and communal leaders. While all of these reasons may be valid, Alexander Carlebach probably came closest to the mark when he argued that the newcomers eschewed secession because they simply did not understand the *Austritt* mentality.[10]

Even institutions outside of the official communal structure accepted aliens as members. The regulations of B'nai Brith fraternal lodges, the Societies for Jewish History and Literature, and the Jewish Women's League, as well as political groups such as the Zionist Federation, did not discriminate against foreigners but opened their membership to all Jews. Only a few organizations proved exceptions. The Central Union of German Citizens of the Jewish Persuasion (C.V.) did not admit foreigners, since its ideology was that of a German group fighting for the rights of *citizens*. More surprising, relief organizations such as the German Society for the Support of Needy Russians admitted only German citizens—perhaps for political reasons or else in order not to blur the patron-client relationship between German philanthropists and Russian recipients.[11]

It is difficult to judge how many Eastern Jews, in fact, joined these organizations. Klara Eschelbacher claimed that German welfare societies, professional associations, B'nai Brith lodges, and even Freemason groups in Berlin all contained immigrants from the East. Still, it is doubtful that many immigrants joined native organizations. For one thing, it probably took a while for them to feel comfortable in a German-speaking group. For another, many of these associations were essentially middle-class and liberal in their outlook and values: for these reasons an organization such as the *Jüdischer Frauenbund* attracted neither members who were religiously Orthodox nor immigrant women who were potential or former clients. Finally, and most important, the social distance that unquestionably separated native and Eastern Jews prevented the latter from joining some organizations. To cite one example, while B'nai Brith lodges were open to all Jews, new members could join only when sponsored by a fraternal brother. It is doubtful that many German Jews sponsored the admission of Eastern Jews. Still, without minimizing the social barriers obstructing the immigrants, we should note the significance of the fact that aliens could and did joint native organizations.[12]

The participation of Eastern Jews in the ideological movements of German Jewry is even more noteworthy. While the consequences of their involvement in *Gemeinde* politics will be analyzed below, in the present context we should take note of the immigrants' ability to influence ideological developments in the community—especially their strengthening of religious Orthodoxy and Zionism at the expense of Liberal Judaism. By their very presence in synagogues and meetings, they contributed to the upsurge of these minority movements; and the ballots they cast decisively tipped elections in favor of Orthodox and Zionist slates. Such bold and active participation in the most sensitive areas of German Jewish communal life was nothing short of remarkable. It attests to the power wielded by immigrants in the established institutions of native Jewry.

We need not conclude from the foregoing comments that all Eastern Jews were Orthodox or Zionist. In truth, it is impossible to generalize about the ideology and beliefs of immigrant Jews because our sources are too limited and ambiguous. The existence of *Shtibls* suggests that some newcomers were observant Jews, but it is possible that such congregations were mainly designed to transplant to Germany the kind of service with which recent immigrants felt most comfortable— regardless of their level of personal observance. Moreover, we also have statements describing many immigrants in Berlin who abandoned religious practices, worked on the Sabbath, and if they observed Jewish laws, did so merely out of habit. It is also mistaken to categorize most immigrants as Zionists. According to Klara Eschelbacher, the first generation of immigrants had only the slightest interest in Zionism. Furthermore, while several memoirs indicate that many, if not most, Zionists in some towns were Eastern Jews, this does not mean that most immigrants supported the movement. (It merely attests to the unpopularity of Zionism among native Jews.) It is not even clear whether immigrants voted for Orthodox and Zionist slates out of ideological consent or merely to register their protest against the established liberal notables. In the absence of definitive documentation, it is impossible to generalize about the beliefs or ideological commitments of the immigrants.[13]

What is not in dispute is the rapidity with which immigrant Jews were integrated into the key institution of German Jewry—the *Gemeinde*. Unlike Eastern Jews who settled in other Western lands and there established a panoply of their own organizations outside the communal structure of native Jews, immigrant Jews in Germany quickly became members òf *Gemeinden,* utilizing communal resources and participating in the electoral process. Such involvements occurred in Germany because of a unique constellation of forces pressuring both immigrants and natives to work together in one communal structure. By its very nature, the German structure of state-mandated religious communities required immigrants to join *Gemeinden* as full and, generally, equal members. In addition, the precariousness and instability of immigrant life in Germany discouraged Eastern Jews from creating viable and assertive communities of their own. All else followed from these two circumstances: without their own institutions, foreign Jews were forced to rely heavily upon *Gemeinde*-run agencies; and German Jews were required by law and political necessity to integrate the newcomers into their institutions.

The Movement to Disenfranchise Aliens

The newcomers paid a high price for their involvement. As a consequence of their active participation in *Gemeinde* affairs—and especially elections—Eastern Jews were caught in the cross fire between warring political factions. Not only did some groups actively vie for their votes, but others, particularly those whose electoral fortunes were on the decline, castigated foreign Jews for meddling in the political affairs of German Jewry. Especially in the last years before the outbreak of World War I, when electoral campaigns were most hotly contested, immigrant Jews became political pawns and the objects of a movement to disenfranchise aliens in *Gemeinde* elections.

The political context of this movement was an intensified electoral struggle that erupted on the eve of World War I between two major ideological blocs. Arrayed on one side were liberal notables who had governed most communities during the Imperial era; their challengers were leaders of a self-styled "conservative" bloc consisting of Orthodox Jews and Zionists. The former were adherents of Liberal Judaism and proponents of Jewish integration in German society. Orthodox Jews challenged these leaders in the name of traditional Judaism: whereas Orthodox Jews supported efforts to integrate into German society, they opposed the far-reaching religious reforms introduced by Liberal Judaism. They argued, instead, that one could live simultaneously as an observant Jew and a bourgeois German citizen without experiencing significant contradictions. The Zionists, by contrast, were generally closer to liberal Jews in their religious behavior and out-look but challenged the integrationist ideology of Liberal and Orthodox Judaism. Zionists criticized both groups for downplaying the national dimension of Jewish identity. Yet, despite their differences and even criticism of one another, Zionist and Orthodox groups forged a political alliance that enabled them to pose a for-midable challenge to their common liberal foes.[14]

In response to the growing electoral strength of the "conservative" bloc on the eve of World War I, liberal politicians took steps to disenfranchise foreigners in over a dozen German communities. They employed a number of strategies to achieve this end—ranging from blackmail and public defamation to the revision of voting regulations. In some cases, native Jews simply challenged election re-sults on the grounds that aliens had voted or had been elected to office. In Co-logne, for example, when a Galician Jew was elected in 1906 on the Zionist slate as a *Gemeinde* representative, a native leader petitioned the local German gover-nor to invalidate the results since the Galican had won his office with the aid of ballots cast by other foreigners. An even more dramatic election challenge was initiated in late 1912 by over forty members of the Duisburg community who argued that a recent election was invalid since the votes of numerous Galicians had been purchased. Significantly, both of these challenges were rejected by gov-ernment officials on the grounds that the charges were unfounded.[15]

Unofficial methods were often more successful in keeping Eastern Jews away from the polls. According to the *Jüdische Rundschau,* the national newspaper of German Zionists, pressure tactics were employed in at least two *Gemeinden:* in Hanover and Chemnitz the ever-present danger of expulsion was used to frighten aliens into political neutrality. While this newspaper was not an unbiased source, there is little reason to doubt that underhanded methods were used to cow alien Jews into submissiveness. After all, one word of complaint by native Jews might have brought about the expulsion of a troublesome alien.[16]

In late 1913 both of these methods—pressure tactics and election challenges—were implemented against alien Jews in Dessau. From the start, liberal represen-tatives disqualified fifteen *Gemeinde* members on the grounds that they were im-migrants. During the election campaign some liberals ran on the slogan "Germans here, 'Pollacks' there" (*"Hie Deutsche, Hie Polacken"*). Through this slogan they aimed to portray Zionism as an "alien" ideology which immigrants must eschew if they wished to be accepted. As the Zionists admitted ruefully, the strat-egy worked well: the "conservative" slate received ten to twenty votes fewer than had been anticipated because a number of aliens chose to vote "German."[17]

Underhanded means were not, however, the primary method used to deprive alien Jews of the vote. On the contrary, the voting rights controversy took place publicly and revolved around legal issues. In the community of Hamborn, com-munal elders brazenly introduced a three-tier voting system (similar to that used in Prussian elections) under which the numerically few wealthy Jews who con-tributed a third of all communal taxes had an equal say with the far more numerous poorer Jews who constituted the bottom tier of tax contributors. According to opponents of this change, the Hamborn leaders were motivated to introduce this regressive system at precisely the time (in 1911) when many other communities were adopting a more democratic "one man, one vote" system in order to limit the impact of votes cast by immigrants. Presumably, the newcomers were poor and would fall into the bottom, and least powerful, voting tier.[18]

Of all the strategies used to eliminate foreigners from the balloting, by far the boldest and most common was the revision of communal statutes so that only native Jews possessed the franchise. The first such revision was introduced already in 1897 by the *Gemeinde* in Neustadt, a city in Upper Silesia. In quick order, the local Prussian governor vetoed this proposal on the grounds that foreign residents were members of *Gemeinden* according to state laws. This unequivocal decision probably explains why a full decade elapsed before similar statute revisions were again introduced. In the intervening period, the methods discussed above were tried, but only rarely was disenfranchisement proposed. There were apparently only three exceptions to this generalization: in 1904 aliens in Chemnitz were deprived of the passive, but not the active, vote; four years later, the Synod of Jews in Baden briefly flirted with the notion of disenfranchising all aliens, but ultimately decided against taking such a drastic step; and in 1909 the *Gemeinde* of greater Stuttgart stipulated that aliens could only exercise the franchise after they had maintained residence in the city for a set time period.[19]

The voting rights controversy erupted in full force only during the two years before the outbreak of World War I. The first salvo in this battle was fired in Bochum when *Gemeinde* leaders decided to require citizenship in a German state as a prerequisite for voting. This statute revision was approved by the *Oberpräsident* of Westphalia. Emboldened by the Bochum example, other communities followed suit—especially those located in Rhineland-Westphalia. In the last days of 1912 notables in Duisburg disenfranchised foreigners, and similar steps were taken by *Gemeinden* in Cologne and Dortmund (in 1912), Danzig and Chemnitz (in 1913), Hamm and Münster (in 1914). Thus, by early 1914 several proposed statute revisions awaited government approval.[20]

In an effort to influence the final decision, as well as sway Jewish public opinion, various religious and political factions publicized legal opinions rendered by prominent attorneys. In May 1912, the liberal *Allgemeine Zeitung des Judentums* threw down the gauntlet by publishing the view of Alfred Michaelis, the author of a tome on the legal status of Jews in Prussia. Michaelis argued that the long-standing practice of extending the franchise to aliens was illegal according to Prussian law. Aliens were not members of *Gemeinden* and therefore had no right to vote. This conclusion—as well as the entire legal controversy—hinged on the proper interpretation of a law promulgated in 1847 that defined the corporate status of Jews in Prussia. According to Michaelis, the law's omission of any reference to aliens could only mean that foreigners were not considered members of the community. As a result, foreigners were not entitled to the active vote. Moreover, since one could only be elected to a communal position if one possessed the franchise, aliens also could not exercise the passive vote. In order to rectify this state of affairs, Michaelis urged a revision of the 1847 law so as to extend *Ge-*

meinde membership to aliens. As the law was presently formulated, however, aliens could not be regarded as members.[21]

The Michaelis articles represented a landmark in the history of the voting rights controversy. They were credited by Michaelis' arch-antagonist—the Zionist attorney Harry Epstein—with single-handedly convincing Westphalia's governor to approve a statute revision submitted by the Bochum *Gemeinde*. (This was the only case in which disenfranchisement was officially sanctioned by a Prussian administrator.) The repercussions of Michaelis' articles within Jewish *Gemeinden* were more complex. It is true that they served as the stock defense for statute revisions. Yet few liberals who sided with Michaelis were willing to accept his extreme position. They realized that if aliens were excluded from *Gemeinde* membership, they would not be responsible to pay communal taxes in the future and communities might even have to return large sums of past tax revenues that had been collected from foreigners. Few leaders of native Jewry were anxious to live with this prospect, let alone encourage the creation of a separate community of aliens that would function outside of the *Gemeinde* structure. Thus, while Michaelis' essays were used to justify *disenfranchisement,* his judgment about the exclusion of aliens from communal *membership* was ignored even by his followers.[22]

Michaelis' opinion evoked a storm of indignation from Orthodox and Zionist attorneys. These writers agreed with Michaelis that the law of 1847 was central to the debate. But they contended that existing practices conformed with the law: it was disenfranchisement that was patently illegal. According to these writers, the law of 1847 ignored the issue of nationality when discussing *Gemeinde* membership simply because citizenship made no difference. *Gemeinden* were "confessional organizations," and since religion was not bound by national frontiers, a Jew's place of birth was immaterial. Thus, foreigners had to be regarded as members of Jewish religious communities (*Kultus-Gemeinden*) and, as such, were entitled to all privileges. The only remaining legal question was whether aliens were also members of *Gemeinden* in territories outside of the "Old Prussian provinces" (Hanover, Kurhessen, Frankfurt am Main, Schleswig-Holstein, etc.) since the law of 1847 was not in force in those areas. Orthodox and Zionist scholars answered in the affirmative: even in these territories, laws governing Jews disregarded nationality as a prerequisite for communal membership and voting rights. In short, Prussian laws protected all Jews and prevented *Gemeinden* from stripping aliens or any other group of the franchise.[23]

This was precisely the manner in which government officials in Prussia interpreted the law. Following a decision handed down by the minister of interior on May 4, 1914, various regional administrators overturned communal statutes that had disenfranchised alien Jews. According to government officials, the law of 1847 protected all Jews: while transients were forbidden to have a say in communal affairs, "those who have lived in the community for years" may not be barred from voting. (In fact, this formulation added a new requirement—several years of residence—that had not existed before.) Moreover, other attempts to deprive Eastern Jews of the vote were also rejected. Officials in the Rhineland overruled efforts to introduce a three-tier voting system in Hamborn; and other governors found no evidence of irregularities that warranted the invalidation of election results in Duisburg and Cologne. Thus, efforts to strip alien Jews of the vote ended in abysmal failure.[24]

The Voting Rights Controversy

During the two years it took government officials to rule on the status of foreigners, *Gemeinden* were racked with controversies over voting rights, and the national press organs of German Jewry highlighted the debate. Contending factions each claimed to uphold a different lofty principle: the Orthodox and Zionists "waved the flag of 'justice' and 'democratic and religious equality,'" while their opponents spoke in the name of 'Western Culture' and 'identification with the German *Volk*' [*Volksangehörigkeit*]."[25] Before the controversy subsided, a few German Jews physically assaulted one another. Libel suits and countersuits were initiated, and communities were riven into two mutually hostile camps. Clearly, the issue touched an extremely sensitive collective nerve.

The liberals defended their proposed statute revision in the name of national pride. They pointed to the dangers posed by the continuous influx of immigrants: simply on the basis of their growing numbers, the newcomers would accumulate political power. Such a development was intolerable, argued the liberals. For one thing, native Jews cannot permit aliens to determine the future of *Gemeinden* when there was no assurance that the newcomers would remain in Germany for long and therefore had no investment in Jewish communal life. Why should transients have the right to vote on issues affecting the future of institutions in which they had so little stake? Second, how could one permit aliens who were ignorant of conditions in Germany and knew nothing of Western culture to determine the character of native religious life, forms of synagogue worship, and programs of social welfare? Finally, liberals resented the participation in the election process of individuals who had contributed little, if any, tax revenues to the community. Why should such individuals have an equal say with the financial pillars of the *Gemeinden*?[26]

While all the proponents of this position were liberals, not all liberal Jews wanted to disenfranchise aliens. Some merely demanded a minimum residence period of several years as a prerequisite for voting; this would insure that immigrants had begun to Germanize before they exercised the franchise. Other liberal Jews openly argued against any discrimination in the community and pleaded for a retention of the status quo. The liberal organizations, however, remained officially neutral. Groups such as the *Central Verein* (C.V.) and the *Liberale Vereinigung für Deutschland* were torn between the need to defend their own members from the attacks of Orthodox and Zionist groups and an unwillingness to take a stance on the principle of disenfranchisement. Thus, the C.V. defended notables in Duisburg because they were the objects of a withering critique of liberalism, but at the same time it tried to hold itself aloof from the specific actions taken in that *Gemeinde*, by pleading that it could not mix into local communal affairs. The positions of the *Deutsch-Israelitischer Gemeindebund* and the *Verband der deut-*

schen Juden were less ambiguous: they proposed a new Prussian law (to replace that of 1847) which began with the words "Every person of the Jewish faith is a member of the Synagogue *Gemeinde* in the locale where he is domiciled." These groups, which were headed by liberal notables, supported the continued acceptance of aliens as full members of the community.[27]

The defense of foreign Jews was, however, primarily waged by Orthodox and Zionist spokesmen. They pleaded for brotherhood among all Jews. As *Der Israelit* put it, "One does not have to be a confirmed Zionist to protest such a division between Jews and Jews." How could Jews who fought so hard against anti-Semitism now turn around and support discrimination against a coreligionist simply because he happened to have been born on the wrong side of the German-Russian border? Furthermore, a division between alien and native Jews only strengthened the hands of anti-Semites and was tantamount to a "denunciation of the foreigners before the government." Discrimination against aliens weakened German Jewry, which so sorely needed unity and cooperation.[28]

Zionist writers also stressed the contributions of immigrants to native Jewish life. Dr. Gerson Bloede alluded to the important role played by Polish teachers and Eastern rabbis in educating German Jews. He noted the vital infusion of new blood and energy provided by immigrants. And he pointedly reminded native Jews that a great many of them actually descended from Polish immigrants who had arrived in earlier eras. Yet now the descendants of Eastern Jews vied to outdo one another by publicly parading their German patriotism at the expense of foreign coreligionists.[29]

During the controversy some individuals—notably writers for the *Israelitisches Familienblatt* in Cologne—took a middle-of-the-road stance. One lead article in the paper, for example, dismissed the fears of liberals as groundless yet recognized the need to place some controls upon foreigners. It went on to argue that if a minimum residence period were introduced before enfranchising newcomers, then this must apply equally to German migrants, for they too are unfamiliar with the problems of their adopted *Gemeinden*. The article, at the same time, rejected the Zionist contention that there were no differences between German and Eastern Jews. Instead of marshalling "pathetic national Jewish arguments" to fight discrimination, one could find better reasons to treat Jews equally. But, by the same token, before accepting immigrants as members, one should require them to fulfill their financial and religious obligations to the community in the same way as do native Jews.[30]

Such moderation did not, however, characterize the general tone of the voting rights controversy. Public meetings held in various German cities became scenes of tense confrontations. At one such meeting in Dessau a fight broke out and a liberal candidate for the representative assembly punched a Zionist. Even more important, newspaper articles upholding one position rarely refrained from taking vicious swipes at the integrity of Jews defending the opposing point of view. Put simply, the debate consistently deteriorated into mud-slinging contests between liberals and their self-styled "conservative" opponents.[31]

Liberals, for example, fought not only for the right to strip aliens of their communal membership, but also attacked the integrity of Zionists who defended the immigrants. The liberal attorney Immanuel Saul of Duisburg was not content with defending his group's proposed statute revision; he also portrayed his Zionist opponents as motivated solely by political hatred of liberal Jews. For the sake of a propaganda victory, the Zionists blackened the name of all Jews by turning the Duisburg Affair into an international scandal (see below for more on this affair). The liberal *Geheimrat* Geiger referred to the equal rights of foreigners as "a Zionist Utopian dream," presumably because this would increase voter support for Zionism. Eugen Katz wrote in the *Allgemeine Zeitung des Judentums* that "instead of alleviating the depressed condition of Eastern Jews, and raising it through European culture . . . Zionism has the tendency of dragging German Jewry down to the level of the East." In short, the liberals took advantage of the controversy to impugn the motives of the Zionists. The latter did not really care a whit about aliens; they merely used them as a convenient instrument to flay the liberals, for the Zionists, according to their opponents, were primarily interested in increasing their own power.[32]

The Zionists retorted with equally venemous statements besmirching the character of their opponents. They jeered at liberal Jews who were so illiberal that they discriminated against their own coreligionists. They referred to statute revisions as attempts "to rob foreign Jews of the vote." And they accused liberals of hating East European Jews. Equally important, they castigated the liberals for showing such a shameful lack of responsibility toward their brothers. By implication, the Zionists accused liberal Jews of acting so irresponsibly that they had forfeited the right to lead German Jewry. Thus, Zionists used the controversy to challenge the integrity of the liberal notables standing at the helm of German Jewry.[33]

The acrimonious tone of the voting rights controversy forces us to raise a number of questions. Why, after all, should such a bitter controversy over the franchise of aliens have erupted at all? It is clear that immigrant Jews in their own right posed no direct political threat to liberal leaders. None of the *Gemeinden* embroiled in this controversy even remotely faced the prospect of foreigners outnumbering native Jews. (The only two communities that lived with this reality had never enfranchised foreigners.) No more than 20% of the Jews in any of these communities originated from abroad. (In Chemnitz the figure was 33.59%, but this community's location in Saxony, where most foreigners never had the franchise, renders it a special case.) In fact, in every *Gemeinde* aside from Duisburg the percentage of aliens fell below the average figure for communities in the "large cities" of Germany. Thus, the controversy cannot be explained as the panicky response of native Jews fearful of being overrun by foreigners.[34]

Perhaps, then, the debate was over a matter of communal policy: What is the proper way to treat aliens? But it is doubtful that this question would generate such a bitter and vituperative conflict. Even more puzzling than the intensity of emotion evoked by the debate is the complete absence of any public statements issued by the subjects of this controversy—the immigrants. Eastern Jews did not band together to fight for their rights, and one would be hard pressed to find instances of individual immigrants publicly pleading their own case. On the contrary, the entire debate was conducted by German Jews, with one native Jewish group berating the other. Finally, how are we to account for the curious behavior of liberal Jews? At the very same time as they fought to deprive Eastern Jews of the franchise, liberal Jewish organizations, such as the *Central Verein* and the *Verband de deutschen Juden,* were busy lobbying for an easing of government policies toward the very same Jews! If the liberals were as hostile toward the immigrants as suggested by Zionist writers, why did they actively work to ameliorate the condition of Eastern Jews and smooth their integration into German society?

Communal Politics

These curious aspects of the controversy lead us to the inescapable conclusion that far more than voting rights was at stake. While the debate revolved around alien Jews, it ultimately was not about foreigners at all. Rather, the immigrants were pawns in a struggle between native Jewish factions over control of the *Gemeinden.*

The genesis of this struggle may be traced to a call issued by Theodore Herzl at the Second Zionist Congress (1898) urging his followers to embark on a program of "conquest of the *Gemeinden.*" Over the short term, there was little response to this charge, and Zionists coexisted and even cooperated with liberals, albeit uneasily. The Zionists were initially contented with seeking a greater voice in communal affairs. Many of the early leaders of German Zionism were also in ideological agreement with the liberal establishment over matters such as Jewish self-defense against anti-Semitism. Zionism for these early leaders was a solution to the problems of suffering Jews in Eastern Europe, not a radical cure for the condition of German Jewry. Thus, a major rift did not initially separate liberal and Zionist Jews.[35]

With the emergence of a second generation of Zionist leaders in Germany, this relatively peaceful coexistence was shattered around the year 1910. Men such as Kurt Blumenfeld and Arthur Hantke replaced the more moderate Max Bodenheimer. The new leaders took hold of a German Zionist Federation that had consolidated its political base and now was strong enough to embark on a more ambitious course. The Young Turks immediately shifted to a new brand of Zionism— practical instead of political (a transformation that both mirrored and reinforced a similar change occuring within the World Zionist Organization). Even more important, the new leadership challenged the entire ideology of integration, an ideology that previously was accepted by all sectors of German Jewry during the age of emancipation. Because of their personal experiences with the intensified anti-Semitism of the 1890s and their dismay at the shallowness of liberal Jewry, they revolted against communal notables and voiced their disillusionment with the liberal ideology of integration.

Under Blumenfeld's leadership, the movement openly stressed Jewish nationalism. It affirmed the centrality of Palestine for German—and not only East European—Jews. And it sought every opportunity to criticize the ideology and ideologists of "assimilation." Zionist preachings inevitably collided with the ideology promoted by liberal "Germans of the Mosaic Persuasion." For the Zionist argu-

ment undermined a fundamental tenet of modern Jewish religious movements—
that native Jews were patriotic and dearly wished to integrate with their compatriots.

The battle between liberals and Zionists was fought on a number of different
fronts. Zionists campaigned to radicalize Jewish youths while liberal Jews formed
an anti-Zionist committee that regularly published advertisements in the Jewish
and German press. During important public controversies a *Kulturkampf* divided
German Jews over issues such as Werner Sombart's endorsement of Zionism, the
"battle of languages" at the newly established technical school in Haifa, and
Moritz Goldstein's public profession of despair over the ability of Jews to participate in German cultural life.

These ideological skirmishes were complemented by electoral battles on the
grass-roots level. Emboldened by evidence that they were capturing new voter
support, Zionists targeted *Gemeinden* ripe for "conquest." They entered slates in
communal elections and even formed a *Neuer Jüdischer Gemeindeverein* that ran
lists in cities such as Berlin, Königsberg, Dessau, and Chemnitz. In quite a few
localities the Zionists strengthened their positions by forging political alliances
with Orthodox groups. As the first decade of the twentieth century came to a
close, this new "conservative" bloc began to register election victories in several
Gemeinden.[36]

It is in this context that we must understand the voting rights controversy. For
both the "conservatives" as well as the liberals recognized that alien Jews represented the balance of power in many communities. Deprived of the immigrant
vote, the Zionist/Orthodox alliance stood little chance of winning elections. With
the votes of foreign Jews, however, the new alliance occasionally succeeded in
ousting liberal notables from communal office. In the face of successful "conservative" challenges and the danger that an ever-growing influx of immigrants
would permanently tip the balance toward their opponents, liberals disenfranchised alien Jews in order to fortify their own political position. At the heart of
the voting rights controversy, then, was a power struggle between contending
German Jewish political blocs.

Contemporary Zionists analyzed efforts to disenfranchise aliens in precisely
this manner—as a tactic to weaken the "conservative" bloc. Since their own
political viability was at stake, Zionists threw all of their energy into the battle.
They recognized—in the words of Harry Epstein, a leading Zionist attorney—that
their "influence in the *Gemeinden* will become nil if the vote is taken from aliens."
In private correspondence and memoranda submitted to government officials, the
Zionists argued that "only because aliens vote for the side . . . with conservative
tendencies, does the party of religious indifference want to deprive them of the
voting right." The liberals never countered this charge effectively—primarily because it was true. At best they justified disenfranchisement as a means to protect
German society from interference by aliens. But the liberals were, in fact, more
concerned with Zionist interference in communal politics. They sought to recoup
their losses by eliminating a major electoral stronghold of their "conservative"
opponents—immigrant voters.[37]

A few case studies of communities embroiled in the controversy enable us to discern the political motives prompting efforts to disenfranchisement aliens. Developments in Baden provide an early case in point. In April 1908, that state's Jewish Synod was convened to vote on the adoption of a new prayer book. Ten years in the making, the proposed *Sidur* eliminated all references to the reinstitution of sacrifices in Jerusalem, the revival of David's kingdom, and other "particularistic" prayers. When the text was circulated during the year preceding the conference, the battle lines were drawn. Most rabbis in large *Gemeinden* approved the revised prayer book, while rabbis in small towns rejected it. The delegates sent to the Synod by various communities also reflected a divided opinion. Nearly half were Orthodox or Zionist—a remarkable victory for the "conservative" bloc.[38]

When the Synod convened, several resolutions were unexpectedly introduced. One recommended that only Germans ought to possess the voting franchise. This proposal was immediately defeated, but a compromise resolution permitting certain categories of aliens to vote only if they received the approval of the *Oberrat* (the statewide body of Jews in Baden) was temporarily accepted by the Synod over the strenuous objections of Zionist, Orthodox, and even some liberal delegates. A few months later, the entire notion was dropped in the face of withering criticism.

The surfacing of this issue at a conference concerned with the introduction of a long-awaited prayer book was not fortuitous. For once the liberals saw that their delegate strength was insufficient to win the prayer book controversy, they sought a new means to shore up their position. They therefore acted to weaken the "conservative" bloc by eliminating aliens from the electoral process. In this case, however, they were too late and too weak; and by the time of the 1911 Synod, fifteen out of the twenty-one delegates were either Orthodox or Zionist.[39]

Similar events preceded the disenfranchisement bid in Chemnitz. Already in 1904 the *Gemeinde* in that Saxon city stripped its foreign members of the passive vote. In late 1913, a "conservative" group belonging to the *Neuer Jüdischer Gemeindeverein,* a Zionist political party active in several communities, for the first time mounted a serious campaign to oust the liberals. In the election, the "conservatives" captured forty percent of the vote. Promptly thereafter the liberals introduced a new regulation into the communal statutes: non-Germans now possessed the active vote only if they had resided in Chemnitz continuously for at least ten years and had regularly paid a minimum of twenty-five mark per annum in *Gemeinde* taxes. Since most aliens had only arrived during the previous decade and were not wealthy enough to be assessed twenty-five mark, they were effectively eliminated from future elections. (The regulation was not opposed by the Saxon government since state laws did not require the acceptance of aliens as equal members.)[40]

Developments in Baden and Chemnitz were paralleled in other communities. In general, communities acted to strip aliens of the franchise after "conservative" forces had scored significant electoral gains. It was not accidental that the earliest and most persistent attempts to disenfranchise foreigners occurred in Cologne (in 1902, 1906, and 1912)—the center of German Zionism and the World Zionist Organization, the home of Max Bodenheimer and David Wolffsohn. Nor was it fortuitous that a controversy over aliens erupted in Dessau after liberals barely

won a hotly contested election. And a similar pattern is evident in the most notorious instance of all, the case of the *Gemeinde* in Duisburg, where liberals attempted to save their political fortunes by altering election regulations after they
had been voted out of office. Since the Duisburg Affair became a test case for all
Prussia—and was of national and even international interest—it deserves close
scrutiny.[41]

The Duisburg Affair[42]

The prologue to the Duisburg Affair occurred during a *Gemeinde* election held in
December 1909. After a bitter campaign principally fought over proposed reforms
in prayer services, a newly formed "conservative" alliance of Orthodox and Zionist members won several seats in the *Gemeinde*'s Representative Assembly and
thereby gained sufficient strength to veto proposed liturgical reforms. Liberal leaders responded first by attempting to nullify the election results on the grounds that
one of the new representatives, a Prussian citizen, had not maintained residence
in Duisburg for a sufficient period of time. When this bid failed, they threatened
to secede from the community. They were dissuaded by the *Gemeinde* rabbi, who
urged them not to destroy the unity of the community. Significantly, this liberal
rabbi depicted opponents of reform as Jews "coming from an entirely different
environment who have no judgment or understanding concerning the needs of our
community"—that is, the "conservatives" were alien to Duisburg.[43]

When a new election was called three years later, unresolved tensions between
liberals and Zionists erupted with greater intensity. The campaign preceding this
election was particularly hard fought because an unusually large number of communal positions were vacant. Due to several deaths and resignations, five of the
nine seats in the Representative Assembly and all three alternates *(Stellvertreter)*
were up for election. The outcome of the balloting was disastrous for the liberals.
Their opponents captured all of the new positions, thereby gaining control of the
Representative Assembly. The liberals only managed to retain a hold on the board
because incumbent representatives selected its members.[44]

Stunned by their electoral loss, liberal representatives and their supporters devised a plan to undo their defeat. Their counteroffensive began on December 19,
1912, with a petition signed by fifty-five members of the *Gemeinde* urging the
Prussian district governor in Düsseldorf to overturn the results of the recently
completed election on the grounds that Orthodox leaders had perpetrated voter
fraud. According to the petitioners, Orthodox Jews were so intent on ousting liberals from office that they solicited support from Galician coreligionists residing
in Duisburg. The latter, however, did not deserve to participate in elections, for
"these elements mostly immigrated in recent years and stand apart from their
native coreligionists due to their religious requirements and way of life. . . .
They display their aloofness practically by supporting a separate prayer house
where they conduct services according to the rites of Hassidism, a movement
considered fanatical by right-minded Jews." Foreign Jews even maintain their
own ritual slaughterer, rather than support the *Gemeinde*'s *shohet*. "On the whole,

these seventy or eighty people play no role in communal affairs but are manipulated by a small minority of Orthodox Jews during election campaigns." It would be unthinkable to permit foreign Jews who have little contact with communal life and who practice a sectarian form of Judaism to decide the future of a German *Gemeinde*.[45]

The participation of Galicians in communal voting was not only unfair but inevitably led to corrupt campaign practices, contended the petitioners. Since it was easy to deceive inexperienced newcomers, Orthodox Jews spread false rumors that liberals planned to shift the Jewish Sabbath to Sunday and eliminate Hebrew from the prayer book, in order to frighten Galicians into voting against liberal candidates. When scare tactics failed to convince the foreigners, the Orthodox openly bought votes by bribing the Galicians' spiritual leader to pay his followers five mark each to vote for "conservative" candidates. The Orthodox even drove Galician voters to the polls and then instructed them how to vote. Under these circumstances of corruption, contended the liberals, the previous voting was invalid and a new election must be scheduled.

A few days after submitting their petition, and just eight days before their term of office expired, the liberal incumbents of the Representative Assembly hastily approved a revision of the *Gemeinde* statutes so as to insure a different outcome in future elections. Henceforth, the franchise was restricted to men of "German citizenship" who had resided in Duisburg for at least one year and had earned sufficient income to be assessed for communal tax. In order to justify this revision to the Prussian authorities, who had to approve all changes in communal statutes, the Duisburg notables sent a memorandum that depicted the foreign Jews in Duisburg in a negative light. It was preposterous to grant aliens "of a lower culture . . . whose hearts cannot beat in unison for Germany" the power to determine the future of a German Jewish community. The liberals also argued for a reassessment of the Jewry Law of 1847, the Prussian decree regulating communal affairs. When this law was originally drafted, the liberals contended, Jewish immigration was virtually unknown in Duisburg. "And even when an individual moved there, he came from a land of equal culture *[Kulturhöhe]* or else did not concern himself with the vote. . . ." "But all this changed with the immigration of numerous Jews out of the Eastern lands—especially Galicia. These immigrants . . . are fully alien to German Jews by virtue of their customs, outlook, and way of life. They belong to an entirely different, and comparatively inferior, culture." This cultural difference also bespeaks a social gap "which is maintained by both sides," by native and Eastern Jews in Germany; "the immigrants do not want to alter their imported, medieval customs and habits"; and even native Jews on the same social and economic level as the immigrants have nothing in common with the newcomers.[46]

There was an additional reason why the aliens had no right to vote in the elections: "these people, a goodly part of whom cannot read German—so that the Hebrew names of those for whom they should vote are written out for them in advance—voted in the two most recent elections for a silent minority that resolutely opposes participating in our religious and synagogue establishments. Some say their votes were bought." As a result, five members of the above party (the

Orthodox) were elected as representatives—four Germans and one alien. This situation was bound to deteriorate: "Immigration from the East continues. Without doubt, Galicians will surely represent the majority in future elections unless preventive measures are taken against the misuse of voting rights. . . ." There is a danger "that the *Gemeinde* will be used for their narrow interests and, more important, that the honor of many German Jews will prevent them from belonging to a community led by such elements." (Again the liberals threatened to secede.)

Finally, the Duisburg elders focused on the issue of greatest concern. The problem was not a religious one because various religious factions had always participated in the *Gemeinde* and resolved their differences through compromise.

> This would have continued had the Zionists worked within the system. But that faction has recently sought to bring its originally political opposition to the . . . majority into the religious sphere. The Duisburg Zionist group, a numerically insignificant one . . . already in the second to the last election gained the votes of Galicians. . . . This is the question: In the future should the community be led and represented by German-feeling men or by men who . . . want to revise world history to reestablish a national Judaism and who do not partake of the German national sensibility *[Volksempfinden]*, its thinking, feeling and aspirations?

With this last declaration, the liberals betrayed their agenda. For what concerned them had little to do with corrupt campaign practices and undue foreign influence in *Gemeinde* affairs. Instead, they feared the increasing strength of their political opponents. Since immigrants bolstered the "conservatives," they had to be eliminated from elections. The voting controversy in Duisburg, as elsewhere, was only incidentally over Eastern Jews. Liberals disenfranchised immigrants in order to weaken the insurgent Zionist/Orthodox camp.

Recognizing the danger, the "conservative" alliance responded forcefully to their opponents' actions. As early as December 17, 1912, they pledged to "battle against Jewish liberalism and for freedom and Judaism." They warned the liberals to back down lest a bitter struggle ensue. When liberals took the matter before government officials, the "conservatives" drafted their own memorandum. They petitioned the governor to reject the statute revision on the grounds that the law of 1847 protected aliens as equal members of the community. They stressed the destructive consequences such a distinction between Jews would have on communal unity. And they portrayed liberals as political hacks intent on rushing through a statute revision against all democratic and religious rules of procedure. Moreover, they countered damaging charges of voter fraud by attributing the allegations to "a very limited individual [who] neither reads nor writes in German or Yiddish." The Galicians were prepared to testify that no one sought or received money for voting.[47]

After conducting his own investigation, the mayor of Duisburg concluded that the election had been orderly and had met legal requirements. He informed his Prussian superiors that charges of voter fraud were baseless. True, some Orthodox and Zionist campaigners had driven their supporters to the polls, but there was no evidence to support charges of vote buying. Based on these assurances, the *Regi-*

erungspräsident of Düsseldorf ratified the election results and rejected the liberals' protest. He did not, however, rule on the proposed statute revision.[48]

Two days after this decision was handed down, the still dissatisfied liberals again hurled charges of voter fraud. Members of the Duisburg *Gemeinde* had gathered to debate new religious guidelines drafted by a synod of Liberal rabbis. An Orthodox spokesman began the proceedings by denouncing the guidelines, after which the communal rabbi spoke in defense of the revisions. The Zionist attorney Harry Epstein then took the floor and charged the rabbi "with speaking falsehoods . . . [he] does not know what truth is." In the ensuing uproar, Epstein was warmly applauded by his supporters, including Galician Jews seated in the rear of the room, and hooted by liberals. A liberal merchant named Levy Rosenthal thereupon turned to the foreign Jews and shouted in exasperation, "Silence, you Galicians, you five-mark men!" Epstein and one of the Galicians subsequently sued Rosenthal for libel, knowing that the hapless Rosenthal was in a weak position because he had repeated a charge that had already been rejected by government officials. Thus, in the heat of controversy, communal leaders humiliated one another in public, laymen branded rabbis as liars, and neighbors slapped each other with lawsuits. (When the Epstein/Rosenthal case came to trial, both Epstein's father and father-in-law stated their willingness to testify on behalf of Rosenthal against their own kin.) Clearly the community was rent into bitterly feuding factions.[49]

For reasons not immediately apparent, nearly a full year elapsed before events in Duisburg drew the attention of German Jewry. Not until November 1913 did the *Jüdische Rundschau* publicize the affair in a hard-hitting critique entitled "The Shame of Duisburg." Seizing upon the affair, the Zionist newspaper aimed to discredit the entire disenfranchisement movement by focusing on the particularly scandalous practices of liberals in Duisburg—practices that included denunciations of fellow Jews before government officials and efforts to overturn election results by changing *Gemeinde* statutes. Once exposed to national attention, the Duisburg Affair ceased to be a local dispute and became a test case for all Prussian Jewry.[50]

Ultimately, Prussian state officials resolved the affair and the larger issue of voting rights. Since both the mayor of Duisburg and the district governor in Düsseldorf had appealed to the Ministry of Interior to issue a definitive ruling, matters dragged on for a year and a half. Finally, on May 4, 1914, the minister of interior ruled that Prussia's Jewry Law extended membership to all Jews, regardless of their nationality, and that the law granted voting privileges to all members. The minister thereby acted to maintain the status quo, an unsurprising decision from a conservative bureaucrat. Following this ruling, the provincial governor of the Rhineland informed Duisburg's Representative Assembly that "there is no reason to exclude people from the franchise if they have lived in the community for years." He then quashed proposals to disenfranchise aliens and the Duisburg Affair came to an end in much the same fashion as it had begun—with the abysmal defeat of the liberals.[51]

The Duisburg Affair, and the larger controversy over voting rights which it exemplified, reveals much about the political struggles agitating German Jewry on the eve of World War I, as well as the manner in which those conflicts were expressed on the grass-roots level in smaller communities. Contrary to the common historical wisdom, which pictures liberal notables invincibly dominating *Gemeinden*, the affair demonstrates the electoral resurgence and political adroitness of "conservative" forces. The liberals' efforts to disenfranchise aliens were born of desperation, not strength. Their Zionist and Orthodox foes, by contrast, not only triumphed on the issue of voting rights, but also scored important propaganda victories.[52]

Events in Duisburg also underscore the critical role played by alien Jews in the electoral process. The immigrants often represented the balance of power in communities almost evenly divided between liberals and "conservatives." Thus, by exercising their right to vote, the immigrants wielded enormous political clout— something that would have been inconceivable had they not been members of *Gemeinden*. Nothing better illustrates the extent to which Eastern Jews were integrated into the institutional structure of German Jewry.

At the same time, the Duisburg Affair reveals the vulnerability of the newcomers. Throughout the controversy they remained silent: Galicians in Duisburg relied upon Orthodox and Zionist allies to plead their case. (Here, again, it is evident that immigrants failed to produce representative organizations or spokesmen.) Moreover, the affair revealed the extent of social tensions separating native and immigrant Jews. In the heat of this controversy, the blanket of civility was stripped away to reveal a deep reservoir of prejudice. The animosity felt by many German Jews toward their Eastern coreligionists was bared. Tensions between these two segments of Jewry had long simmered beneath the surface, but the voting rights controversy provided an opportunity for these emotions to boil over. In Duisburg, some of the most vicious calumnies were aired: the Galicians sold their votes; they were sectarians who had little to do with the mainstream of modern Jewry; by virtue of their customs, outlook, and way of life, they were fully alien to German Jewry. During the controversy, public attacks upon *"Polacken"* became increasingly common.[53]

What is significant in this struggle, then, is the manner in which immigrants, precisely because they were members of the communities, were dragged into a political fracas not of their making. The conflict over voting rights did not pit native against Eastern Jews but two different native factions against each other over the issue of communal power. In the course of this political conflict, however, ugly accusations were made, primarily by the liberals to defend their proposed statute revisions: the immigrants were unreliable, dishonest, backward, and were alien to the ways of German and native Jewish society. In short, the voting rights struggle was over native politics, but it provided an opportunity for pent-up social antagonisms to explode.

8

Social and Cultural Tensions

According to many scholarly and popular accounts, the disdainful treatment of immigrant Jews during the voting rights controversy typefied the attitudes of German Jewry as a whole toward their coreligionists from the East. German Jews, it is often claimed, "looked down on the Jews of Eastern Europe," stereotyping them as *Schnorrers*, "wild men from the uncivilized East," unkempt primitives, and superstitious religious fanatics. Only rarely did they deign to mingle with refugees or immigrants, and on such occasions they acted out of duty rather than genuine concern for needy fellow Jews.[1]

The historian wishing to document the pervasiveness of such behavior is severely limited by the paucity of sources that explicitly characterize relations between native and immigrant Jews. To be sure, a variety of anecdotes relate incidents of inhospitable behavior, social estrangement, and even cruelty; but such reports do not provide information on the frequency or intensity of hostilities within the Jewish communities. In the absence of opinion polls and survey data, we simply do not know how many German Jews harbored negative views, let alone acted upon them; and it is impossible to assess how such disdain affected day-to-day relations between immigrants and natives. Bearing these caveats in mind, we must still attempt to characterize social relations within Jewish communities, however limited our sources and problematic our generalizations. Tensions between native and immigrant Jews were too important in the history of both groups for us to ignore.

Symptoms of Hostility

The voting rights controversy provides a useful point of departure for an assessment of German Jewish prejudices. In the heat of emotional exchanges, attitudes usually expressed only in private conversations were publicly aired. As we have seen, Eastern immigrants were stereotyped as parasites feeding off the Jewish community. They were adjudged as cultural inferiors who ''import medieval customs and habits.'' Their ability to master German was doubted. And their honesty was questioned because they allegedly sold their votes. But the accusation repeated most often concerned their foreign ways: they were pictured as ''fully alien to German Jews by virtue of their customs, outlook, and way of life.'' Those who aired these charges did not invent new stereotypes, but rather drew upon a catalogue of negative images long associated with Eastern Jews. Without a venerable tradition of contempt for Eastern coreligionists, no one would have dared suddenly to declare them second-class citizens of *Gemeinden*. The voting rights controversy may be regarded as a watershed only because, under the strain of communal strife, social restraints were weakened that previously had prevented public attacks upon Eastern Jews. In the future, especially under the pressure of a sizeable new influx during World War I, such criticism was voiced ever more boldly. But even before the war, social tensions were evident.

In the waning years of the nineteenth century, responsible leaders felt the need to chastise native Jewry for its lack of brotherly love. Gustav Karpeles, for example, repeatedly used his position as editor of the *Allgemeine Zeitung des Judentums* to rebuke German Jews who ''laugh at Polish Jews in their caftans and sidelocks.'' He depicted their contemptuous behavior as follows: ''For us, all Polish Jews are from 'half Asia' *[Halbasien]*—even those who never have seen Poland. We treat them as the Spanish Jews formerly treated the German Jews; yes, . . . somewhat as the anti-Semites treat us.'' Zionist writers took up the same theme. They often denounced native Jews for viewing their Eastern coreligionists as ''foreign rabble.'' On one occasion, a Galician immigrant had the temerity to castigate native Jews. Writing in the Hamburg *Israelitisches Familienblatt*, this anonymous writer described the plight of immigrants:

> We foreign Jews . . . are little liked and even less respected. The stereotyped image of Polish Jews still rises in the minds of German Jews when one speaks of foreigners. The Galician, or Russian, or Polish *Schnorrer* still remains the yardstick for assessing the value of the alien Jew. . . . Do we foreign Jews actually deserve this disdainful treatment?

While it is always problematic to use sermonic and hortatory materials to gauge the evils they sought to correct, the fact that writers were disturbed by the behavior of German Jews attests to the presence of a social problem.[2]

The memoirs of several German Jews also depict the discomfort of natives in the presence of Eastern Jews. Children especially felt ill at ease. They feared that their peers would identify them with such foreigners—a concern they probably acquired from their parents. As Jakob Lowenberg put it: Jewish children "were ashamed that these dirty, shabbily dressed beggars, these *Polacken,* were also Jews." When a foreign Jew addressed him in Yiddish, asking for directions, the young Kurt Blumenfeld feigned that he did not understand the question because he felt embarrassed before his German schoolmates. Eastern children, in turn, sensed that there was something wrong with them, that they had something to hide. One woman working with young children reported that Galician youths were taught by their parents to state their place of origin as Austria, rather than Galicia.[3]

Undoubtedly, native children acquired their prejudices from their parents. Blumenfeld's aloofness toward the beggar, for example, may be related to the fact that his parents shunned the company of Eastern Jews. He recalls in his memoir how his fiancée was the first Eastern Jew to step foot in his parental home. This social estrangement was evident in public places as well. According to one account, German Jews "hide when they see an old-clothes peddler carrying his wares through rain and snow, lest they be seen together by non-Jews." While they may not have actually hidden, some native Jews certainly strove to avoid the company of alien Jews. Children could not have failed to note the discrimination practiced by their elders against Eastern Jews. Sammy Gronemann claimed that in Hanover, Polish Jews were denied synagogue honors—including being called to the Torah—and sometimes were prevented from sending their children to communal schools. Thus, through subtle and sometimes overt behavior, adults imparted their scorn for Eastern Jews.[4]

Occasionally, Hebrew and Yiddish newspapers published reports by Eastern Jews on the abuse they witnessed or personally experienced. One writer claimed that German Jews, "your brothers, haters, and oppressors, degrade the name of Polish Jewry." The following *cri de coeur* by Dr. Moses Eisenstadt is especially gripping.

> Our brothers, the Germans, hate their Slavic brethren, and in their hearts scorn them. They . . . will place obstacles in their paths so that they will return to their place of birth. . . . Our German brothers look upon our Slavic brethren as the Christians look upon all Jews. . . . When our German brothers say, *sotto voce,* "Polish pig" or "Russian swine" there is no way to atone for the sin of having been born in a Slavic land, just as there is no way atone for having been born of Jewish parents.

Since the intent of Eisenstadt's article was to discourage Eastern Jews from emigrating and instead urged them to work for change in Russia, his description may well have exaggerated the degree of animosity displayed by German Jews. Nevertheless, there is no reason to doubt that some native Jews were hostile and abusive toward the immigrants.[5]

The flagrant use of pejorative epithets for Eastern Jews provides further proof of social hostility. Again and again, we find German Jews referring to these immigrants as *Polacken*—"Pollacks." (In the small towns of Hesse, one spoke of *"Bolacke."*) It appears that Jews were mimicking their German neighbors, who referred to all Poles as *Polacken*. According to Alexander Granach, the term had even wider ramifications: "Berliners call all foreigners 'Pollacks.' " Yet even if this were the case, the widespread use of such an epithet attests to the deep social antagonism toward Eastern Jews: natives apparently viewed Jews from the East as Poles or foreigners and felt free to belittle them.[6]

There were also other popular epithets for Eastern Jews. In polite society, one referred to *Ausländische Juden, Osteuropaische Glaubensbrüdern* (East European coreligionists), or simply those from the *Ostländern* (the Eastern lands). (As we have already noted, one term apparently not used at all in refrence to immigrants was *"Ostjuden"*). The less flattering terms invariably associated the newcomers with begging or backwardness. Immigrants were often identified with the culture of *Halbasien*—backward Asia—simply because they came from the East. Occasionally, they were labeled *Sklaven* (Slavs). *"Polnische Schnorrer"* or *"Galizische Schnorrer"* were commonly assumed to be Eastern Jews—and vice versa. According to some accounts, the very term "Polish Jew" became anonymous with *"Schnorrer."* It did not matter whether the Easterner in question was a transmigrant, transient, itinerant peddler, productive laborer, or merchant.[7]

The identification of Eastern Jews with begging may well have stemmed from annoyance over the need to support poor Jews in Russia or impoverished refugees streaming westward. Still, even gainfully employed immigrants were depicted as beggars when their only sin was to settle in the country. Immigration to Germany was identified with parasitism. While bemoaning the poor quality of foreign-born preachers in Prussia, an article in the *Allgemeine Zeitung des Judentums* labeled such immigrants as "Polish *Schnorrers.*" There was no recognition that these men performed a vital function by taking poorly paying jobs that few natives were willing to undertake. Immigrants were also stereotyped as opportunistic renegades from Judaism: allegedly, many came to Germany in order to abandon their religion. No sooner did they cross the border than they discarded their phylacteries— and Judaism.

> These Jews may be registered with the police as Jews, but their way of living is thoroughly un-Jewish. Once these people cross the Polish border and take off their long coats, they no longer observe the Jewish law. The very people who lived so orthodox a life in Polish towns now have thrown overboard all Jewish laws.

Somehow, this too was viewed as opportunistic—as if secularism was unknown among German Jews.[8]

We find evidence of disdain in minor incidents and unintentionally revealing comments. When natives toured a school established by Jewish philanthropists in Offenbach for the purpose of educating children of immigrants, the visitors were "astounded" to find these students quiet, well behaved, and studious—contrary to all expectations. Late in the nineteenth century, when it was especially difficult to find native women willing to work as maids for Jewish families, several people urged the importation of girls from the East to work as domestics. Clearly, it was assumed that Eastern Jews were fit to fill jobs that German Jews would not deign to perform. To cite another example of such disdain, an article in the *Rheinische*

Zeitung reported on the fate of a Galician Jew who had made the mistake of falling asleep during synagogue services one Saturday morning. When the slumbering Jew failed to rise for the prayer honoring the kaiser, members of the communal board summoned a policeman and the Galician was "advised" to move on. While such incidents—and there are other examples—may seem trivial, they provide us with a glimpse of social interactions. Certainly, not all natives shared these prejudices or acted so callously, but Eastern Jews had to expect that they would encounter scornful and insensitive natives.[9]

Prejudice was not harbored by only one sector of German Jewish society. A number of anecdotes suggest that individuals of all ideological persuasions were susceptible to bigotry. That liberals stereotyped Eastern Jews is apparent from exchanges during the voting rights controversy. The Orthodox and Zionists perhaps were more inclined to tolerance since their ideological movements stressed some of the virtues of Eastern Jewry: the former still respected the learning and piety of Polish Jewry, while the latter appreciated the sense of national unity common among Jews in the East. Nevertheless, there was a difference between approved ideological dogmas and actual behavior. We find bigots in both camps: An Orthodox rabbi declared his support of expulsions because "this element means so little for the honor of Jewry"; members of the Frankfurt secessionist community felt uneasy over the election of Salamon Breuer as the successor of Samson Raphael Hirsch because the former originated from "wild Hungary"; *Der Israelit*, the leading Orthodox newspaper, felt the need to rebuke some Orthodox communities in south Germany for depriving foreigners of their rights; and even in the Orthodox *Rabbinerseminar*, Mordechai Braude was taunted by classmates for being a *"Polack."* Similarly, relations between German Zionists and Eastern Jews were marred by friction. One of the few Galicians to air his views during the voting rights controversy accused Zionists of merely using the foreigners to achieve their own political ends. Moreover, when Zionist thinkers publicly debated the relative merits of *Ostjudentum* versus *Westjudentum*, a great deal of tension between Eastern and Western Zionists surfaced. During this controversy German Zionists displayed an arrogance and condescension toward Russian and Galician Jews that differed little from the paternalism and cultural superiority often manifested by liberal Jews. Thus, disdain for Eastern Jews was not a monopoly of any one ideological faction within native Jewry.[10]

The Critique of Jewish Culture in the East

This prejudice was rooted in a profound sense of alienation from Eastern Jews. Ernst Lissauer recalled an experience that exemplified the unease he felt in the presence of Jews from the East. When he was a *Gymnasium* student, Lissauer once was approached by a man wearing a caftan and earlocks. "He asked us: 'Are there no Jews in Berlin?' and instinctively I thought to myself, 'No,' for he meant something different by the word than we did." Many German Jews felt the same revulsion at the sight of Eastern Jews. They felt estranged from those whom they met and were highly critical of Jewish society in the East, a society they viewed as corrupt and sick.[11]

Jewish newspapers in Germany frequently carried reports portraying the decay and deterioration endemic to East European Jewry. The Jews of the East, according to these articles, were backward and fanatical; they were mired in a superstitious and unenlightened culture; and most were incapable of productive work. Instead, they tenaciously held fast to outmoded religious and social values. This was especially lamentable because it obstructed their acceptance by their neighbors. If only they would modernize, Westernize, and integrate into their host societies, their situation would improve rapidly. Implicit in this critique was the assumption that the Jews themselves were, at least in part, responsible for their own misfortune.

The "spiritual decay" of Jewish society in the East was a major theme of this critique. "Our Russian coreligionists live in a situation that civilized Germans cannot imagine even in their richest fantasies," reported one contemporary observer. Fanaticism and obsessive attention to ritual prescriptions ruled. Life was devoid of love and emotion: Young people were married off before any thought was given to their means of future support. Marriages were loveless and usually arranged by parents who had little regard for the emotional needs of their children. As a result, love was thwarted and the unfortunate Eastern Jews were chained to a primitive and destructive life.[12]

It was, moreover, a society characterized by sloth and cheating. After returning from a trip to Russia, Hugo Ganz depicted the "repulsive" Jewish proletariat he encountered:

> Their laziness, their filth, their craftiness, their perpetual readiness to cheat cannot help but fill the Western European with very painful feelings and unedifying thoughts, in spite of all the teachings of history and all the desire to be just. The evil wish arises that in some painless way the world might be rid of these disagreeable objects, or the equally inhuman thought [arises] that it would really be no great pity if this part of the Polish population did not exist at all. Either we must renounce our ideas of cleanliness and honesty or find a great part of Eastern Hebrews altogether unpleasant.

Theodor Lessing recorded similar impressions of wretched filth and scandalous cheating after a trip to Galicia.[13]

Hassidic culture particularly exemplified this deterioration. A writer in the *Allgemeine Zeitung des Judentums* began an article by deploring "how far Jewry has been brought down by Hassidism." The adherents of this movement were habituated to mysticism and superstition much like addicts to opium. Their leaders, "wonder-rabbis, are enthroned and live as despots." These charlatans claim omniscience and prey upon the naiveté and primitive fears of their followers. Hassidic rabbis are "priests of darkness" who encourage Eastern Jews to live an "obscurantist and fanatical existence."[14]

However, according to most accounts, "the greatest misfortune for the Jewish population in Poland, without doubt, is the Polish rabbinate." Such men utterly failed to prepare their flock for anything other than begging in Germany, "the promised land of *Schnorrers.*'' An obituary in a leading newspaper described Israel Salanter, founder of the *Mussar* Movement (and a peripatetic inhabitant of Eastern Prussia between 1857 and 1883), as a ''third-rate mind.'' Like so many other Eastern rabbis, he leaped from one discipline to the next with little sense of order or system. Even a dependable friend of Eastern Jews, the rabbi in Memel, Isaac Rülf, felt that Eastern rabbis ''are in truth noble men but have no larger view of the world, and have no insight into worldly or cultural matters.''[15]

The single greatest cause for the disaster befalling Eastern Jewry was the traditional system of education with its nearly exclusive emphasis on Talmudic learning. ''The study of Talmud does not bring bread to the people; a knowledge of German and an enlightenment of the spirit would be better.'' The *cheder* (elementary school) and *Yeshiva* (advanced academy) systems were disastrous because they failed to train students for useful vocations and neglected to expose children to Western values and culture. Orthodox rabbis in Germany were no less critical of the *cheder* system: they urged their Eastern colleagues to reform educational institutions in a manner consistent with tradition and the holy ways of the past.[16]

Yet modern secular movements such as the Bund were also not appreciated by German Jewish leaders. (Eugen Fuchs, the director of the C.V., regarded Jewish revolutionaries as ''silly boys.'') They warned their Russian coreligionists not to join ''anarchistic'' or ''nihilistic'' groups. And they rejected the view that revolutionary movements provided any hope for Eastern Jews.[17]

Instead, Jewish leaders in Germany offered their own solutions to salvage this rapidly declining Jewry. First, Eastern Jews must learn the language of the land in which they lived. Unless they internalized the culture and language of their host country, they could never acquire citizenship. Before all else, they had to abandon Yiddish, for this tasteless ''jargon'' could not pass as a ''language of culture.'' Its continued use only impeded full integration. A few additional steps were outlined by Herman Markower, a distinguished leader of German Jewish relief efforts: He urged Eastern rabbis to discourage early marriages and to reform the educational system. Most important, ''the fruitless method of 'Learning' [Talmud] must be given up'' since it failed to prepare Jews for productive lives.[18]

Such criticism of Eastern Jewry did not originate in the nineteenth century. Already in earlier eras, German Jews wrote poems ridiculing Eastern Jews for their peculiar ways. Late in the eighteenth century a comedy entitled *Als der Sof iz Gut iz Alles Gut* depicted Polish Jews unsympathetically—as swindlers, wife deserters, ignoramuses, and so on. (By contrast, the German Jew is an upstanding, responsible individual.) With the onset of Jewish Enlightenment *(Haskala),* scorn for Eastern Jews intensified. Moses Mendelssohn, the influential spokesman for this movement, described Yiddish as ''a language of stammerers, corrupt and deformed, repulsive to those who are able to speak in a correct and elegant manner.'' His disciples castigated the ''jargon'' and culture that doomed Eastern Jews to permanent isolation from the civilized world.[19]

During the nineteenth century, the most respected leaders of German Jewry contributed to this critical evaluation of Eastern Jews. Samson Raphael Hirsch, the leader of secessionist Orthodoxy, belittled ''Polish teachers'' for introducing their students to tortuous methods of Torah study *(Pilpul).* The historian Heinrich

Graetz was even more outspoken. He found nothing of redeeming value in Hassidism and had few kind words for contemporary Eastern Jewry. Polish *Melamdim* (religious instructors) exercised a pernicious influence and spoke a language nothing short of "gibberish." In fact, Graetz even forbade the translation of his multivolume history into Yiddish since he viewed "jargon" as "the greatest shame for a people." Reform spokesmen were no less hostile toward Eastern Jews. By airing such views publicly, these leaders of native Jewry helped to legitimize prejudices. We know that in at least one famous case (the Duisburg Affair), Graetz's indictment of Hassidism was quoted to justify attacks upon adherents of this sect. If the most respected religious and scholarly authorities harbored such prejudices, what could one expect of the average layman![20]

Literary works also helped popularize a negative view of Jewish life in the East. During the 1840s a new genre, known as "ghetto literature," was developed by Jewish authors to depict the world of traditional Jewry. While many authors described this milieu with nostalgia and sympathy, others were highly critical. Hermann Schiff, a stepcousin of Heine, published a few books during the 1840s portraying the narrow-mindedness and superstition common among *shtetl* Jews. And in the late 1860s, Leo Herzberg-Frankel continued this tradition with his *Polnische Juden: Geschichte and Bilder,* a book that indicted the standard culprits: wonder-rabbis, parents who arrange early marriages, religious fanatics, and the stultifying *cheder* system. According to one literary historian, all of these writers had two principal goals: first, to inform German readers of a "little-known and despised way of life"; second, to prod Jews into correcting "those ghetto customs and attitudes which hindered progress and prevented their acceptance."[21]

The most popular "ghetto writer" during the Imperial era was Karl Emil Franzos. Born in Podolia, Russia, of Galician parents, Franzos first achieved a measure of fame as a writer on non-Jewish themes. In 1876 the first of six ghetto novels and his most successful best-seller appeared under the title *Aus Halb-Asien,* a clear enunication of his perception of the culture of East European Jewry. In the introduction to his collection of short stories, *The Jews of Barnow,* Franzos stated his purpose in writing of Galician Jewry: "These stories are not written for the purpose of holding up the Eastern Jews to obloquy or admiration, but with the object of throwing as much light as I could in dark places." According to Franzos, "Every country has the Jews it deserves—and it is not the fault of the Polish Jews that they are less civilized than their brethren in faith in England, Germany and France. At least, it is not entirely their fault." Nevertheless, the writer painted a dismal picture of this Jewry's shortcomings. The Jews of Barnow are trapped in a miserable, fanatical, religious culture. Franzos finds heroes only among those who attempt to break the bonds that shackle them to this society: young rebels secretly reading Schiller's poetry, adulterous wives having love affairs with Christians, and university-trained doctors who cannot return to traditional society once they have been exposed to modernity. In Barnow, the conventions of Jewish society literally lead to an early death, while the clandestine perusal of German literature is a necessary prelude to escape, success, and self-expression. The ghetto represents death and assimilation, an affirmation of life.[22]

Franzos was actively involved in numerous relief committees to aid Eastern

Jews. It is doubtful, however, that his literary works benefited the subjects of his tales. According to Mary L. Martin, many of his Jewish readers expressed indignation and resentment because Franzos' portrait of Galician Jewry was so critical. At the same time, there is reason to suspect that Franzos achieved success in Germany precisely because of his unsympathetic treatment of Jews in the East: his tales reinforced the basest prejudices of German Jews. He found little of redeeming value among his coreligionists in *Halb-Asien*. At best, he aimed to lead these Jews out of darkness so that they would model themselves after his true ideal—German Jewry. "He was," as Gustav Karpeles put it in an obituary for Franzos, "a German and a Jew simultaneously, and both with full knowledge and deep sensitivity. He was a 'national German' *[deutsch-national]* and despite that the best type of German Jew." Franzos succeeded because he wanted to remake the Jews of Barnow in the image of German Jewry. His readers wholeheartedly shared this wish.[23]

Toward a New Appreciation of Eastern Jews

From the turn of the twentieth century, a small number of intellectuals contested Franzos' dour evaluation of Jewish life in the East. Rather than picture Galician and Russian coreligionists as trapped in the wilds of "half-Asia," they glorified the culture of Eastern Jewry. Such writers realized that existing popular, scholarly, and journalistic accounts presented a uniformly critical assessment of Yiddish culture with the result that German Jews simply possessed no other, more positive source of information. In order to remedy this situation, some journalists strove to display the finest achievements of Eastern writers, poets, and artists so that German Jews could judge for themselves. Perhaps through education pernicious stereotypes would be eradicated.

Zionists especially encouraged such a reeducation. In 1902, the Democratic Faction founded a Jewish publishing company, the Jüdischer Verlag, for the purpose of disseminating its Zionist views as well fostering "a spiritual unity between the [Jewish] masses of the East . . . and the Jews of the West." The Verlag's founders were primarily Eastern Zionists such as Chaim Weizmann, Berthold Feiwel, Alfred Nossig, and Martin Buber, but they also included a few Germans such as Davis Trietsch. Together they strove to present a more flattering portrait of Eastern Jewry to Western audiences. Towards this end, the Verlag published translations of Yiddish stories (by Peretz) and Hebrew poems (by Bialik). It sponsored statistical studies in order to provide an accurate picture of contemporary Jewish communities. (The first such endeavor, *Jüdische Statistik,* paved the way for the founding of a Jewish Statistical Bureau that regularly published the *Zeitschrift für Demographie und Statistik der Juden.*) The intentions of the Verlag's founders were most clearly revealed in an early publication, the *Almanach* of 1902. This volume included translations of articles and poems by such Eastern titans as Ahad Ha'Am, Peretz, Tchernichowsky, Bialik, Berdichevsky, and Sholom Aleichem. The *Almanach* also contained a lengthy essay glorifying the achievements of Yiddish literature. Penned by Dr. Isidor Eliaschoff (known by the *nom de plume* Baal Machaschoves), this article evaluated the literary merits of recent Yiddish writers. The author concluded that " 'jargon' [Yiddish] is not only an instrument for the education of the Jewish masses, it is also the most appropriate tool to evoke in the Jewish intelligentsia understanding for the people and its suffering soul." Through publications such as the *Almanach,* the Jüdischer Verlag hoped to expose German readers to the cultural achievements of contemporary Eastern Jews.[24]

Other Zionist publications participated in this educational program. The *Jüdische Rundschau* protested repeatedly against the bigotry of German Jews, and especially denounced those who referred to Eastern Jews as *"Polacken."* It also defended Yiddish as a "beautiful language." Writing in 1904, Heinrich Loewe pleaded with his readers to stop using the derogatory word "jargon" when they referred to Yiddish. He castigated those who dismissed the language as *"Mauscheln"*—mumbling. (A year before the war, Fritz Mordechai Kaufmann founded-*Die Freistatt* to fight the same prejudices.)[25]

The most important press organ in this information campaign was *Ost und West.* Founded in 1901 under the auspices of the *Alliance Israélite Universèlle,* supported both by Zionist and liberal intellectuals, and edited by Leo Winz (a Jew born in the East), this monthly declared its "essential goal . . . to build bridges between the Jews of the East and Western Jewry and to make it easier for one to understand the other." In fact, by publishing only in German, the periodical clearly intended to erect a one-way bridge: *Ost und West* was concerned with enlightening one Jewry—that of Germany—about Eastern Jews. There was scant opportunity for dialogue between representatives of both Jewries.[26]

Ost und West employed a variety of approaches to further its educational mission. It published stories and poems by great Hebrew and Yiddish writers, generously reproduced drawings by artists such as Ephraim Lilien, and displayed works carved by numerous Eastern sculptors. The periodical also contained photographs of Jewish life in the East: in one tableau it presented pictures of four generations of one Russian family to illustrate the modernization of Eastern Jewry. Finally, *Ost und West* published polemics rejecting stereotypical views of Jews in the East. One article depicted Polish Jews as *the* quintessential Jews: "With the dwindling exception of Sephardic Jews, the totality of European and American Jews consider Poland as their place of origin, with the only difference consisting of the fact that one person's father left Poland one or two generations ago, while the other's six generations ago." For this reason, the Polish Jew is the "eternal Jew." And Yiddish, according to another article, "is the true *Volk* language, par excellence, of contemporary Jewry. . . . It is no arbitrary distortion and disfigurement of an existing dialect, but a full-formed *Volk* language with its own history and development. . . . It does not sound as unpleasant as the language of south German cattle traders." (The latter assertion probably alludes to German Jews active in this occupation.) The article concludes with a message persistently conveyed by *Ost und West:* educated German Jews must learn Yiddish and read Yiddish literature so that they will come to know and love the Jews of the East.[27]

Liberal periodicals also strove to educate their readers about the positive features of Jewish culture in the East. This tendency was especially evident during Gustav Karpeles' reign as editor when the the paper published translations of Yiddish and Hebrew works in order to expose readers to contemporary Yiddish and Hebraic culture. Occasionally, the paper even attempted to evoke sympathy for Eastern Jews by blurring the differences between them and German Jews. One article, for example, urged the latter to familiarize themselves with Eastern Jews: their "culture merits our attention . . . because its bearers speak our language and think in it." Presumably, then, Yiddish and German were to be regarded as the same language. Another "sympathetic" portrait of these Jews was offered by Lina Morgenstern, a leader in women's relief organizations. She noted that it is

> shocking to see many blond-haired and blue-eyed men, women, and children among the Russian refugees. It is a nice race of people. We saw women with clear white skin and rosy cheeks, red-blond hair, and deep blue eyes; children so tender that one could take them to be ur-Germans.

While such phrases reveal a cultural snobbishness that measured all people by the yardstick of German aesthetics, they nevertheless were well meant and intended to show German Jews that their coreligionists were not "half-Asians." [28]

Early in the twentieth century, several new books also sought to provide German Jewry with an appreciation for the richness of Yiddish culture. Salamon Dembitzer, for example, published a volume of his Yiddish poems, and in order to render his verses accessible to a German audience, the book was published in Latin characters. On a more ambitious scale, Martin Buber embarked on his project of "retelling" Hassidic tales so as to open the world of Hassidism to German readers and show them that this culture had much to teach modern man. And, in a different vein, some writers used their literary talents to plead for more kindness toward immigrants in Germany. A drama entitled *Exil* urged German Jews to view their Eastern coreligionists as brothers. The author of this play, Heinrich Grünau, depicted a self-deluded Jewish "Baron" who denied any ties to his employees, Jewish mine workers from the East. The hero of the play, a Mr. Weidenbaum, learns that all Jews are responsible for one another and share the common experience of exile. [29]

The promotion of a new, more positive image of Eastern Jews is generally associated with developments during the interwar period. According to most historians, there was a revival of interest in East European Jews after World War I prompted in part by the experiences of German Jewish soldiers in occupied Poland and in part by a large influx of immigrants to Germany. But, as we have seen, the groundwork for this revival already was laid before the war. From the onset of the new century, Yiddish and Hebrew works were presented to German audiences in order to reeducate native Jews as to the nature of Jewish culture in the East. Such works not only portrayed Eastern Jews in a positive light, but, even more important, they argued that such coreligionists had much to teach German Jews. This point of view certainly did not gain wide acceptance. But those who promoted it hoped that in time an appreciation for the richness of Yiddish culture would replace stereotypes of half-Asian *Schnorrers.* [30]

The Germanization of Immigrants

As this educational program unfolded, a simultaneous effort to Germanize immigrants also was progressing. Several types of aid were extended to ease the initial
transition into German society. Generally, *Gemeinde* "Poor Funds" *(Armenko-
mmissionen)* denied aid to Jews who had not lived in the community for at least
one year. Still, newcomers managed to receive funds. In 1911–12, for example,
nearly thirteen percent of the recipients of welfare funds from the Berlin *Gemeinde*
were Eastern Jews. On the whole, however, aid programs focused more on finding
work for the newcomers. The *Jüdischer Frauenbund* established job-counseling
centers for destitute women in Frankfurt am Main and Breslau. Inspired by the
motto "Work Rather than Alms," B'nai Brith lodges organized labor exchanges
in Frankfurt and Berlin already during the 1890s. On a more ambitious scale, a
"Cologne Aid Committee for Alien Jews" was founded in 1901 by local welfare
groups and women's organizations: the committee sent representatives to visit the
poor in their homes, care for the economic and social needs of immigrants, and
find jobs for the newcomers and schools for their children. By 1911, enough such
programs existed to warrant the creation by B'nai Brith of a national commission
to coordinate these programs (the *Verband der jüdischer Arbeiternachweise bei
der Grossloge*).[31]

The main efforts of native groups, however, were directed at educating the
immigrants. Special schools were founded to grant vocational training to Eastern
Jews. In 1899, the German-Israelite Community League established a worker colony in Weissensee, Berlin, to provide employment and training for Eastern Jews.
(The latter were defined as transmigrants who were being prepared for life elsewhere in the West; one wonders how many actually moved on after living in
Germany for several years.) By 1913, nearly 700 colonists had passed through
Weissensee, over three-quarters of whom were Eastern Jews. Orphans were also
brought to Germany and educated. The *Jüdischer Frauenbund* ran a home for
orphans in Isenburg (near Frankfurt), and schools for orphans were established in
Pankow (Berlin), Munich, and Frankfurt to teach academic skills, languages, and
vocational trades. Finally, a special school was erected in Offenbach for children
of immigrants. Fearing that such youths would fall into bad company and spend
their time gambling and drinking, local philanthropists in Frankfurt and Offenbach, aided by the Paris Rothschilds, paid two seminary-trained teachers to in-
struct these children in vocational as well as academic subjects.[32]

There were also special institutions to educate adult immigrants. In several
cities, native Jews founded Toynbee Halls. Named after Arnold Toynbee and
modeled after an institution in Whitechapel, London, these centers were designed
as locales "where the rich meet the poor, the educated with the uneducated to
seek a common ground between the extremes of the social spectrum." During the
first years of the twentieth century, Toynbee Halls were erected in large cities
such as Hamburg, Berlin, and Frankfurt am Main under the auspices of B'nai
Brith lodges. From the list of programs held at the Berlin hall we can get a clear
sense of the goals of such institutions: during the year 1911–12, 142 lectures were

held that dealt with Jewish history and contemporary Jewish issues, cultural history, pedogogy, natural sciences, medicine, and poetry. In addition, musical evenings and poetry readings were offered. Ostensibly, Toynbee Halls were designed for all "poor Jews," not only those from the East. But it appears that they specifically aimed to educate and Germanize foreigners; they instilled middle-class values and exposed Eastern Jews to the culture of native Jewry.[33]

Several other institutions served a similar function. The *Jüdischer Frauenbund* ran a club in Frankfurt for young women—mainly from the East. Here the newcomers were offered courses in typing, stenography, and sewing, as well as in politics and literature. Similarly, a network of Jewish Reading Rooms established by various *Gemeinden* also served as educational centers. In fact, when the Cologne *Lesehalle* was opened in 1908, it was described as a forum for presenting lectures on hygiene, the German language, and general culture to Eastern Jews. Its founders intended to turn it into a Toynbee Hall eventually. Philanthropists in Upper Silesia even organized study circles for the mine workers they helped to bring to Germany. After a day at the mines, the workers were treated to lectures on Graetz's history of the Jews![34]

While the purpose of such programs was to educate the immigrants, there also was a hidden agenda: natives aimed to Germanize the newcomers and expose them to "proper" values. More important, they attempted to remake the immigrants in their image. By reading Graetz with mine workers, they at once managed to teach the immigrants Jewish history, as well as the values implicit in Graetz's works. Thus, natives attempted to hasten the acculturation and Westernization of Eastern Jews.

In this context, it is appropriate to mention one additional—and easily overlooked—agency for aculturation, the German rabbinical school. Between 1868 and 1914 some 400 Eastern Jews attended the three rabbinical schools, thereby constituting an inordinately high percentage of the student bodies. Eastern youths constituted forty, thirty-eight, and twenty-four percent of the students at the Berlin *Hochschule,* Breslau Seminary, and Berlin *Rabbinerseminar,* respectively. During the last quarter of the nineteenth century, these figures were even higher: From its founding in 1872 until its twenty-fifth anniversary, the *Hochschule* could muster only one-third of its students from Germany; nearly sixty percent came from the East. From the 1860s through the 1880s nearly half of the enrollment at Breslau's seminary consisted of Eastern students. And the Orthodox Hildesheimer academy drew anywhere from half to one-third of its students from the East. These foreign Jews were far more advanced than their native classmates. Shmaryahu Levin recalled that "the German Jewish students were astonishingly ignorant; their knowledge was about equal to that of a *cheder* boy at home, in his second or third term." In view of their numerical strength, homogeneity, and strong Judaic backgrounds, Eastern students should have transformed rabbinical schools and, for that matter, the German rabbinate. Instead, the reverse occurred—Eastern students were thoroughly Germanized.[35]

This is not surprising given that the seminaries were intent on producing cultured and sophisticated rabbis fit to represent German Jewry. They shaped their students by demanding linguistic proficiency in German; and, more important, they encouraged students who met expectations and discouraged those who deviated from the norm. Thus, professors favored native-born students over the far more knowledgeable Easterners. Shmaryahu Levin recalls that German Jewish students "were looked upon as the leaders in the seminary *[Hochschule]*, and were treated with special tenderness by professors. Their claim to special consideration lay in their passports; they were, after all, Germans, while we others were aliens." Caesar Seligmann recalled how during his student days at Breslau he differed radically from his fellow classmates: he was the only one who had previously studied at a German university, "the only one who could dance, swim, ice-skate, and bowl." Such achievements stood him in good stead. By contrast, students from the East were pressured to fit the German mold. Describing his first visit to the *Hochschule*, Mordechai Ehrenpreis relates how the principal, Sigmund Maybaum (himself a Hungarian), criticized Eastern students for their "Austrian outlook" and warned him that Galicians had difficulties adjusting. Furthermore, by his very example, Maybaum made it amply clear to students what was required: despite his Hungarian origins, Maybaum was one of the leading preachers in Berlin and head of the *Hochschule*. He had succeeded by adopting the correct stances, including a passionate espousal of German nationalism and an equally visceral anti-Zionism. There is good reason to assume that similar values were imparted at the other rabbinical schools.[36]

By all indications, most Eastern graduates underwent a process of Germanization. They learned to speak a fluent German, eschewed controversial movements such as Zionism, and, for the most part, distanced themselves from their fellow immigrants. According to Shmaryahu Levin, Hungarian rabbis played an especially important role in what he described as "the de-Judaization of the Jews in Germany."[37] While this assessment is unfairly harsh, it is clear that the congregational activities of rabbis born in the East were not characterized by a distinctive style or outlook. Such rabbis also served as models: by their very example, they made plain that all Eastern Jews who Germanized and adopted the values of native Jewry also could achieve success.

This lesson was not lost upon the immigrants. While we are severely limited by the meager sources at our disposal, we can find symptoms of a conscious striving on the parts of Eastern Jews to disappear into German Jewish society. Here is how the Zionist Shmaryahu Levin acerbically portrayed Russian Jews in Königsberg:

> The membership was composed mostly of Hebraists and good middle-class Jews of the older school. The only "Germans" were Rabbi Bamberger and the cantor, Birnbaum, and the latter was only a naturalized German. It did not occur to me that this society could harbor a strong assimilatory movement. Yet it did. There were Jews in it who wanted to become Teutonized—and did not come in contact with Teutons. They met only Germanified Jews. And these became their models. To me the man who lives a natural national life in the midst of his own group lives an "original" or authentic life. An outsider who imitates him is living in a first translation and a third party who imitates the second is living in a second translation. It is a Russion Jew imitating a German Jew who is imitating a German.

While it is difficult to judge how widespread this tendency was, by all accounts immigrants rapidly adopted the habits of German Jews.[38]

This was particularly evident in their manner of raising children. First, immigrants bestowed highly Germanized names upon their offspring. Who could imagine, for example, that Heinemann Cassel was the son of Eastern immigrants? More important, immigrant parents provided their children with a strong German education. In Königsberg, they quickly overcame their fears and enrolled their children in public schools. Klara Eschelbacher also reports that Eastern Jews employed tutors to prepare their children for entry into a *Gymnasium*. Such efforts paid off when their offspring succeeded in the professions. To take one example, the son of a Lithuanian cantor named Türk eventually became a *Gymnasium* teacher and headed the liberal faction of the *Gemeinde*'s representative assembly in Berlin; the son clearly had Germanized and adopted the predominant religious outlook of native Jewry. According to Eschelbacher, the second generation generally integrated well into German society.[39]

We can find evidence of acculturation also among the older generation. Eschelbacher again provides valuable information on this subject. She wrote of the rapid decline in religious observance among even the first generation of immigrants in Berlin. Many Galicians worked on the Sabbath and permitted their children to write in school on the day of rest. On a more subtle level, we may find a symptom of acculturation in the scorn displayed by more settled immigrants toward recent newcomers: such contempt bespeaks an internalization of the values of native Jewry. (Certainly, it indicates also a deep sense of insecurity.) In the opinion of a journalist writing during the interwar period, Eastern Jews adapted to German life quickly before World War I—far more so than after the war.[40]

The psychological causes for this rapid acculturation are not hard to find. We have already discussed at length the pressures placed on immigrants to integrate and avoid public exposure. Newcomers learned to lead an inconspicuous life, marked by rapid integration into native society, lest their foreign manners attract the attention of police authorities. Yet we should not overlook the other motive for such behavior: Eastern Jews may have preferred to integrate and Germanize; they may well have regarded life as a Germanized Jew as a superior—not a second—"translation."[41]

The Tenacity of Prejudice

Despite the rapid acculturation of immigrants and their success in finding allies among native Jews, social tensions persisted. Acculturation is a process that takes time; and even when one immigrant cohort had Germanized, a fresh wave of newcomers raised tensions once again, since they appeared so visibly alien. Programs designed to increase respect for the culture of Eastern Jewry also met with limited success, since prejudice is not eradicated by a few publications. Despite the best intentions of individuals in both camps, relations between native and immigrant Jews continued to be marred by social tensions.

Some writers have attributed the tenacity of this prejudice to pathological behavior on the part of German Jews. According to this analysis, native Jews despised their Eastern coreligionists because they hated themselves. Such is the view of the historian Peter Gay, who claims that German Jews harbored a "selective anti-Semitism."

> This permitted German Jews to despise recent Jewish immigrants in company with Germans; nothing, after all, unites one with others more than possession of a common enemy. Moreover, Jewish anti-Semitism had a special function in the German-Jewish psychic economy: hatred of outsiders diverted self-hatred to other targets. Finally, and most important: to construct this target for Jew-hatred would, many German Jews fondly believed, disarm German anti-Semitism altogether.[42]

Though they did not use the same psychological categories, a few Eastern Jews living in Imperial Germany already noted the presence of such irrational fear and loathing. On the eve of his departure from Berlin after five years of university study, Moses Eisenstadt delivered the following explanation for "the hatred of our German brother for us, the Russian and Polish Jews":

> [He] hates us not because he hates himself—for he loves his body above all else—but rather because he hates Judaism and its literature. Naturally, he hates those of his brethren who hold fast to . . . Judaism and care about its survival. And who are these brothers if not we, the children of Russia and Poland who . . . are the "Jews among the Jews"?[43]

It is possible to collect a few statements by contemporary German Jews that might partially substantiate the charges of Eisenstadt and Gay. In 1885 Simon Bernfeld, a Jewish intellectual from Galicia who often traveled to Germany, quoted one distinguished Jewish leader as follows:

> The Poles are responsible for the upsurge of hatred directed at us; therefore, we are distancing ourselves from these people. We hope that Russian and Polish Jews will compare us to the people of Sodom and Gomorrah—and will cease coming to us.

A few years later Lion Wolff elaborated on this theme:

> The Russian Jews have multiplied in Germany like frogs . . . ; they serve as cantors, functionaries, etc. But they do not know the language of the state, and therefore they evoke a justified German hatred for Jews. . . . The first and true cause of German anti-Semitism is known to all but no one dares to reveal it: It is the coming of foreigners . . . to Germany.

Cruder yet was Max Marcuse's polemic in the scientific journal *Sexual-Probleme:* "These Jews are our complete misfortune. They . . . always bring us the ghetto atmosphere and are the worst danger for the harmony of peoples." Such an approach enabled some German Jews to shift the blame for anti-Semitism from their Gentile neighbors to the immigrants. It also bound them closer to their fellow Germans since they had a common enemy.[44]

No doubt, then, there is some truth to Eisenstadt's charge and the more sophisticated analysis offered by Gay. Some German Jews did blame the immigrants for their misfortunes; some did despise Eastern Jews for representing the Judaism that embarrassed them; and some did find a bond of unity with their German neighbors by heaping contempt on foreign Jews. But the key word here is "some." Eisenstadt and Gay merely explain the motives of the most vulgar. The crude attitudes expressed by Marcuse and Wolff are noteworthy because they were expressed in public so infrequently. Perhaps other German Jews shared similar views. *There simply is no evidence,* however, that most German Jews "despised" their Eastern coreligionists. Yes, they shunned their company and often behaved condescendingly, but they also displayed compassion for the suffering of their coreligionists. As we shall see in the next chapter, they provided various types of support—legal aid, political support, and care for the needy. While we have no way of knowing what the "average" German Jew said in the privacy of his home, we have numerous ways of documenting what German Jews said and did publicly. And from the evidence at our disposal, it appears that their actions on behalf of the immigrants were incompatible with "hatred." In the absence of compelling evidence to the contrary, we cannot diagnose a half-million German Jews as pathological self-haters. Indeed, if we wish to use psychological terminology, the concept of "ambivalence" would be more appropriate.[45]

There is no need, however, to speculate as to the *subjective* basis of this antipathy when we can locate numerous *objective* sources of friction. Prejudice toward Eastern Jews was born of social and cultural differences rather than pathology. It was in part a natural outgrowth of the unequal status of native and immigrant Jews in the eyes of the law. As early as the seventeenth and eighteenth centuries, German rulers distinguished native from immigrant Jews and demanded that the former cooperate in keeping foreigners out. In the Imperial era, governments treated Eastern Jews as inferiors: a native woman lost her citizenship if she married an alien—but not if she married a German; an Eastern Jew seeking employment in Prussia as a rabbi or teacher needed permission from the minister of interior—not so a native; and, most important, Eastern Jews were virtually without legal protection and could be harassed or expelled at the whim of a capricious official—not so native Jews, who were protected by their citizenship. It is hardly surprising under the circumstances that German Jews internalized the view of their governments that immigrants were not their equals.[46]

Disdain was also a response to the very real class differences separating natives and immigrants. German Jews comfortably ensconced in the middle class felt little affinity for the many needy Jews they encountered. What, after all, had bourgeois doctors, lawyers, and businessmen to do with homeless refugees? And even when the latter did arrive with some means and skills, their status as immigrants set them apart from longtime residents of Germany. It also need hardly surprise us that upwardly mobile Jews did not want to be identified with social inferiors and refugees.

A vast cultural abyss also separated these two types of Jews. Eastern Jews spoke either a strange language or a clumsy German. Some of the newcomers dressed differently. And they even defined their Jewishness in terms that were foreign to native Jews. Chaim Weizmann recalled an incident that illustrates this profound lack of mutual comprehension. Shortly after his arrival in Darmstadt, one of the teachers asked me what nationality I was; and when I answered, *"Ein Russicher Jude"* [a Russian Jew], he stared at me, then went off into gales of laughter. He had never heard of such a thing. A German, yes. A Russian, yes. Judaism, yes. But a Russian Jew! That was to him the height of the ridiculous.

Individuals who viewed themselves as German citizens of the Mosaic Persuasion had little in common with coreligionists with a self-identification as national Jews.[47]

But alienation was not at all that German Jews felt. Many German Jews were both embarrassed and repelled by the culture of Eastern Jews. They had little appreciation for the Yiddish language—a "jargon"—or for the "primitive" and "superstitious" Yiddish culture it expressed. Repeatedly, they exhorted their coreligionists to abandon their "backward" ways. The solution to the problem of Russian and Galician Jewry lay in *Bildung*—education in its broadest sense. Eastern Jews must reform their educational system and teach their children "practical" subjects; they must learn Western languages and literature; and they must internalize proper etiquette. By becoming *"gebildet"*—educated—they would improve their lot. Put differently, Eastern Jews suffered because they had not yet followed the path of German Jews.[48]

In fact, this critique sorely missed the mark. The actual tribulations of Jews in Eastern Europe had little to do with Yiddish culture. It is extremely doubtful that Eastern Jews suddenly could have made many new friends if only they would have Westernized. During pogroms, Westernized Jews fared no better than *shtetl* types. Were they as *"gebildet"* as German Jewry, Eastern Jews would have endured discrimination, pogroms, and economic hardship.

The inappropriateness of this critique of Yiddish culture reveals much about the perceptions of *German Jews.* In their repeated emphasis on *Bildung,* German Jews were projecting their own situation upon Eastern Jews. For the former were convinced that *their Bildung* had won them emancipation. Since the age of *Haskala* in the late eighteenth century, German Jews linked the improvement of their status to their own self-betterment. They believed that emancipation had been *earned.* Whether emancipation in fact was a reward for Jewish cultural achievement is debatable; but German Jews believed this to be the case. They then projected their own situation upon Eastern Jews and repeatedly advised their coreligionists to imitate their example.[49]

This perceived link between their own *Bildung* and emancipation also accounts for the hostility of German Jews toward immigrants. For the newcomers threatened to revive an image of the Jew that natives had worked so hard to obliterate. Anti-Semites argued that German Jews were foreign and Oriental; they had no affinity for *Deutschtum;* they lacked a sensitivity for the *Volkgeist.* German Jews countered by stressing their cultural achievements. Moses Mendelssohn, Ludwig Börne, and Heinrich Heine were heroes of German Jewry because they attested to the ability of native Jews to acculturate and contribute to German high culture. Moreover, the self-esteem of German Jews was tied to their cultural attainments. Already in the 1830s Johann Jacoby noted the connection:

> The Jews attempted to compensate for the "loss of dignity" through ambitious industry and learnedness, a striving in which the Jewish tradition of learning

encouraged them. They derived satisfaction from their intellectual prowess and their claim of superiority in this field frequently recurred in their self-reflections.

Hence, the Jewish "love affair" with education and *Bildung*.[50]

And now, suddenly, Jews came from the East who possessed neither education nor *Bildung*. They could barely speak German properly. They reminded everyone—particularly their native coreligionists—that Jews were not inherently Western or German but had to work at acquiring *Bildung*. Furthermore, the newcomers also appeared as apparitions out of an earlier era of German Jewish history, an era that native Jews wanted to forget. For Eastern Jews were unemancipated Jews who had only begun to modernize. Their presence might encourage the forces in German society that wanted to turn back the clock and revoke the emancipation of all Jews in the *Reich*.

While such fears account for the emotional intensity of tensions between natives and immigrants, the primary sources of friction were objective political, social, economic, and cultural differences. Such factors have often led to severe social strains within Jewish communities. In the Middle Ages, numerous Jewish communities attempted to protect themselves from immigrant coreligionists by passing laws to restrict newcomers. The *Herem Ha-Yishuv* (Ban of Settlement), which was designed to protect local businessmen from immigrant competitors, was a standard feature of communal statutes. More recently, native Jews in various Western countries have reacted with disdain and prejudice when less modernized Jews arrived in their communities. One can find numerous parallels to the attitudes and behavior of German Jews in the responses of their contemporary American, British, French, Dutch, Belgian, and even South American coreligionists. Antagonism has also marred relations within Jewish communities in Eastern Europe: *Hassidim* fought with *Mitnagdim*, and Lithuanian Jews mocked Galician coreligionists. The most unkind remarks of German Jews paled in comparison with the biting, sarcastic criticism hurled at the culture of East European Jewry by *Maskilim* and Yiddish authors. Disdain for fellow Jews of a different cultural background was not a monopoly of German Jewry.[51]

9

The Posture of
Organized German Jewry

Despite the severe social tensions dividing natives and immigrants within the Jewish community, organized German Jewry acted in behalf of East European Jews in the *Reich*. For while it was one thing for individual German Jews to disdain and even discriminate against foreign coreligionists, it was an entirely different matter for the organized community to accept passively governmental discrimination against immigrant Jews. The leaders of native Jewry could not ignore restrictionist proposals aimed solely at Jewish immigrants; and they could not stand by idly as state authorities and police officials treated Eastern Jews arbitrarily and harshly. With immigrant Jews under attack, the responsible leadership of German Jewry was forced to take a stance.

Before they could act in defense of immigrant coreligionists, Jewish leaders had to assess the interests of the community and devise a strategy to serve those interests. Neither activity was easy and both required time. For one thing, the issue of Jewish immigration was an exceedingly sensitive one in the Jewish community. There is no doubt that leaders of German Jewry empathized with the suffering Jews in the East and actively strove to alleviate the misery and degradation endured by those coreligionists. Most native leaders also recognized that it was necessary for Jews to leave Russia and Austro-Hungary, and they worked to facilitate a population movement from East to West. At the same time, however, some of these leaders, like other German Jews, felt uncomfortable in the presence of Eastern Jews. The former were repelled by the culture, habits, and mores of their fellow Jews. These conflicting responses to migrating Jews influenced the policies of Jewish leaders.

Moreover, like all responsible leaders, German Jewish spokesmen first had to consider the best interests of their followers. Political decisions rarely are based on altruism—especially when much is at stake. And German Jews had a great deal to lose; they were very vulnerable. Within a decade after the completion of emancipation in 1871, anti-Semitism once again was on the rise, expressing itself in new idioms and movements. Before taking a stance on Jewish immigration, native leaders had to assess the possible impact of their statements upon their own situation: Was it politically wise for Jews to challenge their governments' policies and denounce German leaders? On the other hand, could they avoid taking a stand if discrimination against immigrant Jews might presage an attack upon the equality of all Jews in the *Reich?*

But even after leaders of native Jewry decided where their interests lay, they needed effective institutions and strategies to express their views. At the onset of the Imperial era, native Jews were ill-equipped to defend themselves, let alone foreign Jews. Only gradually did German Jewry's response to anti-Semitism evolve from restrained opposition to active confrontation. Initially, efforts at organizing defense activities were hampered by fears that public agitation on behalf of Jewish interests might further isolate Jews. However, with the intensification of the anti-Semitic campaign in the early 1890s, Jewish leaders reassessed their approach to defense activities. In the face of blood libels, efforts to prohibit kosher slaughtering, election victories by anti-Semitic deputies, and the adoption of an anti-Semitic plank in the Conservative Party's Tivoli Program, it became necessary to implement a more forthright and open self-defense. Modeling themselves after some of the new lobbies established toward the end of the nineteenth century by a wide range of interest groups in Germany, native Jews organized to defend themselves. During the two decades before the outbreak of World War I, German Jewry founded new defense agencies, such as the Central Union of German Citizens of the Jewish Persuasion (C.V.) and the Association of German Jews *(Verband)*, and conceived bolder challenges to anti-Semitism.[1]

Only after they had adopted an aggressive stance regarding all manifestations of anti-Semitism in Germany could native Jews effectively fight discrimination against foreign Jews. The change in policy occurred because native Jewry perceived a link between its own fate and that of alien Jews. Recognizing that restrictionism was a cause promoted mainly by avowed anti-Semites and that the arguments of restrictionists relied heavily on the arsenal of anti-Semitic stereotypes commonly employed in the battle against native Jews, the leadership of German Jewry joined the fray and fought to protect immigrant Jews. Effective advocacy in behalf of immigrant Jews thus began only after German Jewry had organized to combat anti-Semitism.

Press Reaction

This pattern of response characterized the positions assumed by the German Jewish press. During the first two decades of the *Reich*'s history, Jewish newspapers reacted with restraint when they reported on the harsh treatment meted out to immigrant Jews. However, from the 1890s until World War I, the Jewish press consistently and forthrightly opposed government policies toward foreign coreligionists.[2]

German Jewry's premier weekly, the *Allgemeine Zeitung des Judentums (AZJ)* provides a case in point. During the early 1880s, the *AZJ* either ignored Prussian expulsions or merely provided terse reports on the number of Jews driven from specific localities. By September 1885 mild protests began to appear: the paper criticized expulsions on humanitarian grounds and challenged Puttkamer's assertion that Eastern Jews were a Polonizing or revolutionary element. In late 1885 and the beginning of the following year, articles in the *AZJ* took a new—and very peculiar—twist. In response to the contention of the Russian *Nevoe Vremja*, the Vatican *Observatore Romano*, and the Rhenish *Kölnische Zeitung*, that the expulsions were primarily aimed at Jewish beggars and not at Russians, Catholics, or Poles, the Jewish newspaper denied that the expulsions were motivated by anti-Semitism. "Anti-Semites," the *AZJ* wrote, "cannot boast of having brought about the expulsions with their yelling; for the Polish Jews are only indirectly afflicted. [They are expelled] not because they are Jews, but because they are from Poland." The *AZJ* adopted yet a third position in early 1886 when it argued that the expulsions ran counter to modern norms of civilized behavior; it also expressed sympathy for the expelled Eastern Jews. When Puttkamer claimed before the Prussian Chamber of Deputies that Eastern Jews were of little economic or social utility, the *AZJ* published one of the strongest defenses of Polish Jews issued during the entire history of the Second Empire: Eastern Jews are "hard-working, moderate and thrifty; they have close-knit families, honor the holinesss of marriage, and make sacrifices for their parents." Furthermore, the paper added, their religion places great value on education, and Polish Jews stand on a much higher cultural plane than do their Slavic neighbors. Finally, the paper accused Puttkamer of succumbing to anti-Semitic propaganda. The *AZJ* thus altered its views on the expulsions several times, but eventually did label them as anti-Semitic acts. While the reasons for these shifts in posture are not clear—perhaps Jewish editors gained courage from the strong defense of Eastern Jews published in *Die Nation* by philo-Semitic progressives—the paper was not indifferent to the plight of expulsion victims; rather, editors of the *AZJ* needed time to decide on a proper response to the new Prussian policies.[3]

Beginning with the 1890s, the *AZJ* adopted a more militant stand on issues affecting Eastern European Jews in Germany. During debates over the Russian Trade Treaty and restrictionist bills in the mid-1890s, the *AZJ* stated its position unequivocally. Unlike its timid stance during the expulsions, the paper now forthrightly chastised opponents of Jewish immigration. The paper tried to educate its readers to recognize that the mistreatment of Jewish immigrants was part of the program of political anti-Semites and the first step in a larger assault upon Jewish emancipation in Germany. Efforts to restrict Jewish immigration, it explained, were intensified because anti-Semites had failed to undermine the status of native Jews. Gustav Karpeles, editor of the *AZJ*, contended that "criticism of our Russian coreligionists is directed against us [German Jews] and this is only the start in the weakening of the principle of equal rights." Again in 1898 he warned German Jews of a new restrictionist proposal:

It would be a disastrous mistake if people on our side imagine that this only concerns foreign Jews. We are fighting for our own existence when we fight against the restrictionist proposal. Whoever does not believe this should read the commentaries of the anti-Semitic newspapers . . . and his eyes will be opened.

He went on to quote an analysis of the bill by the German Social Reform Party, an anti-Semitic group:

"Upon it we can build further: once we prevent the immigration of foreign Jews we can also hope to get rid of more and more domestic Jews."

Thus, the *AZJ* attempted to prod native Jews into a more determined defense of alien Jews by appealing to their self-interest.[4]

When new expulsions were launched between 1904 and 1906, the *AZJ* and other major newspapers candidly expressed their opposition to such policies. The Orthodox *Jüdische Presse*, which had in 1886 voiced concern only for victims who were religious functionaries, sharply condemned Prussian officials responsible for the 1905–06 expulsion. *Im deutschen Reich*, the journal of the Central Union of German Citizens of the Jewish Persuasion, expressed similar sentiments in behalf of liberal German Jews. During the twentieth century, a united Jewish press opposed the mass expulsions of Eastern Jews from the *Reich*.[5]

Jewish newspapers also criticized discriminatory actions taken against alien Jews. The Hamburg *Israelitisches Familienblatt*, for example, urged Jewish defense agencies to monitor naturalization proceedings and offer legal aid to alien Jews. The Hamburg paper, along with others, prodded Jewish groups to use their influence so that a pending Naturalization Law would make it easier for Jews to receive citizenship. Another target of criticism was the particularly severe policy practiced by Prussian governors in the eastern provinces when Jews immigrated from Russia or Austro-Hungary. Clearly, the most widely distributed Jewish newspapers firmly opposed any policies that singled out East European Jews for exceptional treatment.[6]

Jewish newspapers employed several strategies to express their opposition to restrictionism. The approach most favored was to quote opinions published in the general press or voiced by Gentile politicians that were critical of government actions. The newspapers thereby utilized a tried Jewish tradition of relying upon non-Jews to fight anti-Semitism, an approach based on the assumption that Gentile spokesmen are more effective in such battles. This tactic was also attractive because it protected these papers against charges of political dissidence: they could claim that they were merely reporting the opinions of others. The Jewish press also fought government policies by reporting on the suffering caused by official actions. While individual government officials were not rebuked directly, expressions of sympathy for the victims implicitly condemned their tormentors.[7]

Although it defended Eastern Jews, the native press made no serious attempt to replace negative stereotypes with positive images. The Jewish press rarely extolled the virtues of alien Jews or described them as an asset to Germany. Instead, newspapers merely denied that Eastern Jews posed a serious danger to the country's welfare. When demagogues warned of an impending "Jewish invasion," Jewish newspapers responded with denials: the mass immigration was a "fable"; Jews from the East were not settling in the *Reich* in appreciable numbers. Significantly, no Jewish writers argued that immigration from the East was desirable or harmless. Implicitly the German Jewish press accepted the basic premise that Eastern Jews were an "unwanted element" of little value to Germany.[8]

Jewish newspapers did, however, reject stereotypes of Eastern Jews as "beggars and conspirators." One of the most positive articles on the economic activities of these Jews attempted to refute the charge that all Russian Jews were *"Schnorrers"*; the *AZJ* argued in a lead article that this was like depicting all Italians as Figaros, and it blamed economic competitors for many of the allegations against these Jews. Despite all obstacles, the newspaper contended, immigrant Jews contribute to German trade and for that reason are attacked by agrarian interests opposed to business and commerce. Other newspaper articles rejected the association of Russian Jews with revolution. The *AZJ*, for example, cited trial statistics of Russian revolutionaries to prove that Jews were not the main participants in the 1905 revolution; and if some Jews in Russia were attracted to "nihilism," they were driven to radicalism by their mistreatment at the hands of anti-Semites.[9]

The Jewish press also tried to counter the association of Eastern Jews with backwardness. When immigrant Jews were blamed for outbreaks of cholera, newspapers investigated these allegations and publicized findings that they were innocent of spreading epidemics. The German Jewish press also denied the involvement of Eastern Jews in the spread of Polish nationalism and culture. On the contrary, the newspapers argued, such Jews do not even speak Polish, but they do speak a Germanic language—Yiddish. "In the midst of Slavic lands, they speak German still today, even if it is only a corrupted dialect." Jewish communities in Eastern Europe were portrayed as outposts of Germanism in a Polish wilderness. Under the circumstances, Eastern Jews deserved better treatment at the hands of Germans. Furthermore, the Jewish press contended, Eastern Jews are far less culturally backward than Polish Catholics and their religious practices are less superstitious than the rituals of Russian sectarians. A contemporary study by Maurice Fishberg, entitled "Materials for the Physical Anthropology of the Eastern European Jew," was cited to prove the adaptability of Eastern Jews to new environments; newspapers employed Fishberg's study to claim that Jewish immigrants would quickly adopt to Germany—and even their physical appearances would change! Finally, in one article Gustav Karpeles completely denied the charge that Eastern Jews retarded the assimilation of German Jewry:

> Experience teaches that the Russian Jews assimilate to us very quickly and already in the second generation are the same as German Jews in their thinking and

feeling. Along with the Russian dust they also shake off the repressed Russian spirit.

. . . This process of assimilation would progress even more rapidly and completely were they not constantly living under the Sword of Damocles—expulsion.

The only bar, then, to the quick assimilation of immigrant Jews was the severity of government policies.[10]

Some newspaper articles even pleaded for more liberal policies on grounds that had nothing to do with the character of Eastern Jews but with humanitarian concerns or German self-respect. Especially during the 1885-86 expulsions, the *AZJ* repeatedly warned against driving out alien Jews lest other countries retaliate by expelling German nationals. (One such article referred to the danger that Russia might expel 100,000 Prussians.) There also were pleas couched in humanitarian phrases: the Orthodox *Der Israelit* quoted biblical and rabbinic texts on the proper treatment of the "stranger in your land." During the 1906 expulsions, the *AZJ* cited America's generous acceptance of Jewish refugees and appealed on humanitarian grounds for allowing some Eastern Jews to settle in Germany. Finally, Jewish newspapers published an appeal written by Lilli Jannasch, a Gentile woman, urging Germans to aid Russian Jews in reciprocation for the extensive relief activities undertaken by German Jews to aid the needy of all confessions.[11]

These appeals and arguments had little noticeable impact on German policies or attitudes, for humanitarian pleas carried no weight in a country that was fundamentally hostile to strangers and refugees. Also, German leaders had no need to fear retaliation from states that victimized their own Jewish populations: the Russian and Hapsburg empires were unconcerned with the needs of their Jewish subjects at home, let alone abroad; and if German subjects were expelled from Eastern lands, they would be more than welcome in Germany. The Jewish press was also powerless to eradicate anti-Semitic stereotypes of Eastern Jews; it had difficulty enough freeing German Jews of prejudice. But if they failed to alter government policies, Jewish newspapers nonetheless played an important pedagogic and hortatory role. Journalists educated German Jews to recognize the link between their own interests and the fate of immigrant Jews. They repeatedly stressed that it was dangerous for native Jews to tolerate discrimination against immigrant coreligionists because such actions might undermine the emancipation of German Jewry. In addition, Jewish newspapers kept pressure on organizations such as the *Central Verein* and *Verband*, urging them to lobby in behalf of Eastern Jews.[12]

Organizational Responses

Like the German Jewish press, native Jewry's organizations shifted from a policy of indifference to active support for Eastern Jews, but at a far slower pace. Indeed, according to the prominent German diplomat Ottmar von Mohl, "all the German Jewish corporations and organs outwardly fought against [Jewish] immigration" during the early decades of the Second Empire. While there is evidence to challenge such a sweeping generalization, Mohl might have been referring to the role of the *Deutsch-Israelitscher Gemeindebund* (the German-Israelite Community League). The impetus for the founding of this organization in July 1869 partly stemmed from the desire to curb the flow of itinerant Jewish beggars into Germany. The league attempted to stop German Jews from donating charity to individual Polish *"Schnorrers"* and instead worked for the centralization of all welfare activities. The *Gemeindebund* even did not shrink from asking German police and municipal authorities to evict Jewish beggars. There is an enormous difference, however, between requesting aid to keep out beggars and sanctioning the abusive treatment of all alien Jews.[13]

The Central Union of German Citizens of the Jewish Persuasion initially was also unsympathetic to migrating Eastern Jews. One year after its founding in 1893, the C.V. sent representatives to meet with Germany's foreign secretary in order to urge stronger border safeguards against Jewish immigration. During the 1890s, the agency's press organ, *Im deutschen Reich,* rarely reported on the mistreatment of immigrant Jews. As foreigners, these Jews were of no concern to "German citizens of the Jewish persuasion." (A notable exception to this initial indifference was the intercession of C.V. leaders, who urged government officials to rescind expulsion orders in 1897.)[14]

The Prussian expulsions of 1905–06 brought about a dramatic reversal of the C.V.'s attitude toward immigrant Jews. Several articles in *Im deutschen Reich* expressed sympathy for the victims and, most significantly, recognized that the expulsions were particularly harsh on Jews. The periodical explained its concerns as follows:

> Even though no German citizen of the Jewish persuasion was involved, the C.V.
> has an interest in this matter insofar as a German government is making the right
> of residence in its state dependent upon religious confession.

In this passage, a theme occurs that was echoed in subsequent statements by the C.V. and other groups: concern for Eastern Jews was justified since German policies were implicitly anti-Semitic. The C.V. thus took up the cause of immigrant Jews as part of its program to defend *native* Jewry.[15]

Once it adopted this approach, the C.V. moved from its previous apathy—and occasional hostility—toward Eastern Jews to an active defense of their interests. It portrayed Jews who were expelled as innocent victims. And it rebuked the Austrian government for failing to defend its Jewish citizens against German policies. In 1908, *Im deutschen Reich* berated the city of Offenbach for its "inhospitable conduct" when the Hessian city denied residence permits to alien Jews. In the five years prior to World War I, C.V. protests were aimed especially at discriminatory naturalization and residence policies directed against Eastern Jews. In 1910, for example, over 1,000 members meeting in Posen passed a resolution stating that

> the expulsion of foreigners for their Jewish faith and the near total impossibility
> of Jews obtaining naturalization constitute considerable slights to the foreigners
> and to German Jews. The [assembly] requests the administration to rectify these
> slights.

With protests such as this, the C.V. expressed its conviction that discriminatory policies toward Eastern Jews represented "an insult against all Jews."[16]

German Jewry's other major defense organization, the *Verband der deutschen Juden,* did even more than protest; it organized programs to collect pertinent data on the status of Eastern Jews and lobbied to improve their lot. Perhaps because it was founded in 1904, after German Jewry had accepted the need to voice its opposition to anti-Semitism in public, the *Verband* from its inception defended Eastern Jews against discrimination. Already at its first national convention, in 1906, the *Verband* leader Eugen Fuchs protested Prussia's expulsion policies. A year later the second convention noted "the offense against German Jews in the expulsion of aliens solely because of their Jewish confession and in the near complete failure to grant citizenship to foreign Jews." At almost every national convention and regional conference, the *Verband* rebuked German governments for their unfair policies toward immigrant Jews. Equally important, the organization worked to educate German Jews as to the necessity of fighting against the mistreatment of Eastern Jews. As *Justizrat* Horowitz put it to the fifth national convention of the *Verband* in 1913:

> The conviction that one can treat foreign Jews differently from foreign Christians—namely in a worse manner—can only be gained by German [officials] from their contacts with native Jews. It is insulting to . . . [us] and Judaism to think that foreign Jews are a worse element for German states than are foreign Christians."

Thus, *Verband* leaders urged their followers to drop any illusion that the unequal treatment of foreign Jews would have no deleterious consequences for native Jewry.[17]

As German Jewry's watchdog against legal and administrative anti-Semitism, the *Verband* also kept an eye on official discrimination against alien Jews. When, in 1908, it organized over 100 permanent correspondents from every area of the *Reich* to submit data on local developments of concern to German Jewry, it also requested information on the immigration and naturalization of alien Jews. This information was published in the *Verband*'s annual reports and provided German Jewry with a means to scrutinize government actions. The material gathered by the *Verband* also supplied valuable ammunition for Jews and their allies to challenge policies: at a time when state governments tried to deal with immigrant Jews in secrecy and without accountability, data compiled by the *Verband* broke the monopoly on information enjoyed by government agencies, who only published statistics to suit their needs. When, for example, a Prussian official contended that in 1910 only 13 alien Jews were rejected for citizenship out of 104 applicants, the *Verband* could publish the names and immigration histories of 19 Jews known to it who had been rejected—thus throwing into question the government's entire set of statistics. (There is no evidence, however, that governments liberalized their policies due to such adverse publicity.)[18]

The *Verband* also appealed directly to politicians and bureaucrats, urging changes in German policies toward the immigrants. Its representatives met with the minister of interior to request his support for a law explicitly prohibiting religious discrimination in naturalization procedures. The organization also sent memoranda to Reichstag committees outlining its position on issues affecting foreign Jews. It even published prejudicial statements made by government officials that substantiated allegations of discrimination against foreign Jews. Thus, it publicized the remarks of a Prussian bureaucrat who had stated in regard to immigrant Jews that "as long as they remain Jews, they will not be naturalized; but when they convert to Christianity, then we will discuss the matter." It also circulated secret directives issued by Prussian ministers forbidding the naturalization of Jews. While its claim to have "battled without rest against the authorities" surely was hyperbolic, the *Verband* organized the most important lobbying activities to ameliorate the condition of Eastern Jews in the *Reich*.[19]

One of the issues of greatest concern to native organizations such as the *Verband* was the policy of states regarding the acquisition and loss of citizenship. Jewish groups were particularly concerned about the fate of longtime residents of Germany who were denied citizenship, as well as native women who lost their citizenship when they married a foreigner. In order to monitor naturalization practices, the *Verband* and the C.V. founded a joint commission toward the end of 1909 which gathered information by sending out questionnaires to *Gemeinde* leaders. Using data elicited in this fashion, Jewish attorneys prepared legal briefs on matters concerning naturalization. They apparently did not, however, mount test cases to challenge the legality of government practices, primarily because German law offered little protection to aliens.[20]

In the years immediately preceding the outbreak of war, Jewish lobbying activities focused on a new naturalization bill pending before the Reichstag. From the time a Reichstag committee was established to draw up this bill, the joint commission lobbied on behalf of Jewish interests. It urged the Reichstag to include two stipulations in the new law: first, the law should prohibit "any discrimination in the treatment of an application [for naturalization] based on the religious confession of the applicant or his membership in a specific religious community"; and, second, the new law should offer some protection to German women married to foreigners. (Under the existing law, these women were often subjected to expulsion along with their husbands, and they had little hope of ever returning to Germany.) The Jewish commission urged the Reichstag to permit these women to regain their German citizenship after their husbands died. The outcome of this lobbying was mixed: the Reichstag refused to legislate a prohibition against religious discrimination but did sanction a more lenient approach to German-born widows of aliens.[21]

As the new law progressively passed through various Reichstag committees, a new problem arose that affected Jewish interests: whereas the existing naturalization law granted automatic citizenship to all foreigners performing in a "church service" *(Kirchendienst)*, the revised law was worded to refer only to service in a "church" *(Kirche)*. The former term was interpreted to include synagogue service, while the latter apparently referred only to service in a Christian institution. If allowed to stand, the new wording could exclude Jewish functionaries from the automatic naturalization granted to clergymen and would place them at the mercy of government officials. Such a situation would be catastrophic for German Jewry since native communities depended heavily upon the services of foreigners: German rabbinical schools ordained significant numbers of foreign students who eventually led small and medium-size congregations; and native Jews relied upon Eastern cantors, teachers, and ritual slaughterers. Despite the grave danger this new wording posed to Jewish *Gemeinden*, it initially proved impossible to persuade the Reichstag to reword the law. Finally, in the third, and last, reading of the law, Deputy Gröber of the Center Party, an ally of Jewish groups, was able to push through a version of the bill that would protect Jewish institutions. The approved wording referred to service in "a recognized religious community" *(Religions-Gemeinschaft)*, and the threat to immigrant synagogue functionaries was averted.[22]

The *Verband* was not the only German Jewish organizations to lobby. Efforts to alter the citizenship law would have failed without the intercession of the Zionist *Volkspartei*, the Association for the Interests of Orthodox Judaism, and especially the Association of Berlin Synagogue Societies. The Berlin community often interceded with government officials to aid Eastern Jews. During the 1906 expulsions, a deputation sent by the community and the Berlin branch of the *Alliance Israélite Universelle* met with the minister of interior to plead for a reversal of the expulsion policies. In 1914, similar representations were made for cigarette workers in Berlin who had been ordered to leave the city. During the expulsions at the turn of the century, the C.V. board and communities in West Prussia, Saxony, Braunschweig, and Dortmund successfully saved some Eastern Jews from expulsion. And even during the 1885–86 expulsions, some Jewish groups directly appealed to local governors, winning reprieves for some expulsion victims. While other delegations of native Jews undoubtedly interceded in behalf of immigrant Jews, it is impossible to assess the extent of such activities since they were conducted behind the scenes.[23]

German Jewry also established a variety of institutions to aid the growing number of transmigrants. As early as 1868, Jewish communities along the border—especially the Prussian-Russian frontier—founded relief committees to collect funds from German Jews and disburse them to needy transmigrants. The Berlin office of the *Alliance Israélite Universelle*, along with other Jewish committees, coordinated these activities. They were supported by an ever-growing number of native Jewish contributors. At this stage, however, much of the leadership was still provided by local rabbis, such as Treuenfels of Stettin, Rülf of Memel, and Bamberger of Königsberg. When, during the 1880s and 1890s, the crush of transmigrants overwhelmed the meager resources of these groups, a more comprehensive network of aid organizations was established. A central office in Berlin set policies in conjunction with relief agencies in America and Western Europe. In Germany, a central bureau in Berlin coordinated the programs of fund-raising committees located in every corner of the country; it organized volunteers who aided transmigrants at each stage of their journey—in border stations, in cities along the main railway links, and in ports; and it dealt with shipping companies and government officials. The bureau also provided direct services to the migrants by arranging for medical personnel to meet the sick arriving on trains, distributing food and clothing at train stations or in hostels along the route, and erecting kosher kitchens in Hamburg and Bremen to cater to the passengers. Several groups, including the League of Jewish Women, also formed volunteer units to aid particularly vulnerable travelers: individuals traveling on their own were steered away from swindlers who preyed on refugees, and single women were met at railway stations before they fell into the hands of white-slave traffickers.[24]

In May 1901, Germany Jewry created the *Hilfsverein der deutschen Juden* to take over most of these activities. Its founders had several goals: to establish a permanent agency that would replace the numerous ad hoc committess that had sprung up haphazardly whenever an emergency arose; to negotiate with shipping lines and government officials on an ongoing basis; to regulate and coordinate all phases of the transmigration; and to compete with the central aid organizations run by French, English, and Austrian Jews. By 1905 the *Hilfsverein* was recognized by the Prussian minister of interior as the official Jewish agency overseeing transmigration. Within a decade of its founding, the *Hilfsverein* boasted nearly 20,000 members.[25]

Historians have generally dismissed the activities of these relief agencies by attributing their efforts to the desire of German Jewry to rid itself of unwanted refugees. According to such reasoning, native Jews were mainly interested in driving refugee coreligionists out of the *Reich,* and therefore their aid was motivated by selfishness rather than genuine concern. Such an appraisal completely fails to explain the massive outpouring of help extended to transmigrants by Jews throughout Germany. As early as 1869 committees collected funds to aid sick and needy migrant Jews in Russia and in Germany. Lists of contributors indicate that Jews in every corner of the country donated funds. By 1870, the *Alliance Israélite Universelle,* the international relief agency run by French Jews, had more members in Germany than in any other country—including France. German Jews contributed more money to aid refugess than did Jews in Great Britain, France, or the United States. And an army of *volunteers* met the transmigrants in order to supply them with kosher food, medical attention, clothing, advice, and information. It is simply not enough to attribute all of these activities to cynical motives, for regardless of what German Jews desired, their governments were intent on ridding the *Reich* of these Eastern Jews. The emigrants had to move on anyway, and most even preferred going to America. German Jews helped smooth the way for transmigrants and made their journey as comfortable as possible.[26]

In all of these activities, groups situated across the gamut of Jewish life displayed a unity of purpose. This is remarkable because German Jewry was divided into rival camps during the period of the Second Empire (see Chapter 7). Nonetheless, on the issue of Jewish immigration, both Orthodox and Zionist groups concurred with the positions taken by liberal organizations such as the C.V. and *Verband;* when they objected, they were concerned more with questions of emphasis than substance. The Orthodox differed mainly in their preference for a less combative Jewish stance vis-à-vis government officials. During the 1885–86 expulsions, for example, *Die Jüdische Presse,* the newspaper of Berlin's Orthodox community, joined the liberal *AZJ* in downplaying the number of Jewish victims; but by the twentieth century, this paper as well as *Der Israelit,* the mouthpiece of Orthodox Jews in Frankfurt am Main, generally were more combative. Sometimes, however, the old reticence to confront anti-Semitism reappeared. As late as 1914, *Der Israelit* still rebuked the liberal press for not giving credence to official pronouncements; they urged greater trust for government officials. Rather than engage in public protests against state policies, Orthodox groups chose to work behind the scenes, mounting relief efforts for refugees. The essentially Orthodox communities in eastern Prussia spearheaded German Jewry's fund-raising for victims of expulsions and sent delegations to intercede with local officials on behalf of those ordered to leave. In at least one city, Halberstadt, the ultra-Orthodox *Agudas Jisroel* employed an attorney to aid Eastern Jews with their legal problems. Also, Orthodox rabbis such as Hildesheimer of Berlin, Carlebach of Memel and Cologne, Rülf of Memel, and Bamberger of Königsberg worked especially hard to protect immigrant Jews. Nonetheless, the Orthodox were more eager to aid Eastern Jews than to challenge governments that victimized them.[27]

The Zionists, on the other hand, urged the Jewish community to confront government officials who mistreated Eastern Jews. They consistently ridiculed the established community for its timidity. Zionist newspapers provided the most comprehensive reportage on East European immigrants and did not hesitate to denounce government actions. The *Jüdische Volkspartei*, a Zionist political party that participated in communal elections in several German cities, also organized protests and lobbied on behalf of Jewish victims. When the Zionists created a defense organization to counter the C.V., much of the work of the newly formed Imperial Society of German Jewry dealt with aid to Eastern Jews: founded on May 1, 1913, the society became actively involved in preventing threatened expulsions from the Rhineland. It sent a prominent Berlin attorney to meet with high-level officials in the Ministry of Interior and with local authorities in Duisburg and Coblenz. It hoped to succeed where C.V. and Orthodox lobbyists had failed—an aspiration typical of the Zionist efforts on behalf of Eastern Jews.[28]

The responses of liberal, Orthodox, and Zionist organizations to the plight of immigrant Jews in part were shaped by internal ideological and political considerations. Both Orthodox and Zionist groups had much to gain by championing the cause of immigrant Jews, since they hoped to capture the votes of the newcomers. In addition, both of these factions derived a measure of legitimacy from their alliances with Jewish groups in Eastern Europe. Brotherly love alone did not account for the Zionist and Orthodox defense of the immigrants. The liberal position was, by contrast, more complex. Liberals felt that they had the most to lose from the immigration of Eastern Jews. In a number of communities, immigrant Jews tilted the balance of votes against liberal candidates, thereby enabling "conservative" slates to seize power. Moreover, it was awkward for liberals who prided themselves on their German nationalism to challenge government officials over policies toward aliens. Nevertheless, by the turn of the century, leaders of liberal Jewry publicly fought against the mistreatment of immigrant Jews. Their motives were based less on altruism than a calculated assessment of the best interests of German Jewry: in order to preserve the equal status of German Jews, it was necessary to combat discrimination practiced against any Jews in the *Reich*—including immigrant Jews. For this reason, liberal groups along with Jewish organizations spanning the religious and ideological spectrum opposed the exceptional treatment of immigrant Jews.

The emergence of such a consensus within the organizational world of German Jewry is particularly noteworthy in light of the severe pressures placed upon native Jews to distance themselves from immigrants. Throughout the history of the Second Empire, anti-Semitic polemicists and writers who professed no overt animus for Jews, warned native Jews to steer clear of Eastern immigrants. As early as 1880, one anti-Semitic writer warned that "even if a change in the general character of the Semitic element is possible, the present immigration of truly uncivilized Jews from Poland would still render this expectation illusory"—that is, Jewish immigrants were retarding the integration of Jews in Germany. In Hermann Bahr's *Judentaufen,* a collection of essays on the "Jewish Question" written by prominent intellectuals, this concern surfaced frequently. "Were it not for the continual immigration here from the East, German Jewry long ago would have been—if not fully absorbed—thoroughly assimilated," wrote Hans Heinz Ewers. He added that "Russian Polish Jews whose culture is far behind ours make it harder for *our* Jews to forget the ghetto" (Ewers' emphasis). German Jews, in short, were admonished not to mingle with or defend Eastern coreligionists lest they be tainted by such an association.[29]

Sometimes this message was imparted subtly when writers approvingly described the "correct" position assumed by some native Jews: by describing with approval the "many native Jews [who] want to have nothing to do with the foreign beggars *[Schnorrertum]* and are deeply ashamed of being Jewish," a writer in the *Kreuzzeitung* sought to teach native Jews how to behave properly. Other antagonists of Jewish immigrants professed to be working at the behest of German Jewry. One Conservative Party deputy averred "that many German Jews are truly happy to be protected from the immigration of their brothers from the East." Similarly, the leader of the Conservative Party, Manteuffel, approvingly quoted a Jew who had signed the Anti-Semitic Petition because he felt that "Eastern Jews will discredit me; I don't want them here; I am happy if Russian Jews do not come here." While these statements undoubtedly were descriptive of the attitudes of some German Jews, they were also meant to be prescriptive: "good" Germans should not associate with Eastern European Jews.[30]

In a few instances, German Jewry was even overtly warned that association with Eastern Jews would prove costly. The Anti-Semitic Petition already demanded punishment of anyone aiding Jewish immigration. Later, Jew-baiters such as Ernst Hasse of the Pan-German League attacked the solidarity of German Jews with immigrants from the East. Some anti-Semites even accused native Jews of underwriting revolutionary activities in Russia with money ostensibly collected to aid pogrom victims. In November 1905, Baron von Richthofen, the German foreign secretary, warned James Simon, a leader in Jewish philanthropic work, that German Jews must cut off all financial aid to revolutionary Jews; failure to comply, he warned, would exacerbate anti-Semitism in Germany. The message was clear: German Jews will pay for aiding Eastern Jews to improve their lot either in Germany or abroad.[31]

It was in this charged atmosphere that German Jews formulated responses to their governments' treatment of immigrant Jews. Under the circumstances, it is not surprising that individual German Jews supported restrictionism, and organizations only gradually came to the defense of immigrant Jews. By the turn of the century, however, a consensus had emerged among the major organizations and newspapers that claimed to speak for the overwhelming majority of German Jewry. Jewish religious and ideological groups spanning the spectrum—from Orthodox to liberal, from Zionist to German Citizens of the Jewish Persuasion—fought to change government policies. Jewish leaders interceded with administrators, lobbied with legislators, and gathered data to challenge official claims. Newspapers regularly rebuked the government. And Jewish groups urged the rescinding of expulsion decrees and the cessation of discriminatory naturalization and residence policies. In short, native Jews struggled to *prevent* Eastern Jews from being pushed out of Germany. Their special goal was to bring about nondiscriminatory naturalization procedures. Had they succeeded, immigrant Jews would have acquired citizenship and won immunity from expulsions. The spokesmen, defense agencies, and major press organs of German Jewry thus engaged in a struggle to make it *easier* for immigrants to remain in Germany.

The motives for this concerted effort were hardly altruistic—although enough sympathy for victims of government policies was expressed to suggest that at least some German Jewish spokesmen were genuinely moved by the plight of their Eastern coreligionists. Jewish leaders candidly defended their concern for Eastern Jews as motivated by self-interest: it served the interests of German Jews to prevent discrimination against alien coreligionists, for the unequal treatment of foreign Jews would abet the efforts of anti-Semites. Furthermore, discrimination against foreign Jews represented "an insult to all Jews." Thus, Jewish groups legitimized their defense of immigrant groups as an extension of their program to battle against all forms of religious discrimination. They were not in principle opposed to curbing aliens, but to the unequal treatment of certain categories of foreigners.[32]

This determination to oppose unfair government policies toward Eastern Jews did not translate into equal concern for the hospitable treatment of immigrant Jews within Jewish *Gemeinden*. Immigrant Jews were accepted as equal members of communities because state laws required such acceptance. And due to the necessity of combatting all forms of discrimination, native Jewry united in a common struggle to defend the interests of Eastern Jews. Nonetheless, social tensions continued to divide Jewish citizens of Germany from immigrants of an alien culture and nationality. The resulting response of German Jews to the aliens in their midst was one of deep ambivalence, a mixture of empathy and discomfort aptly summed up by a contemporary observer: "One had the desire to help the Eastern Jew when he was financially"—and, we may add here, politically—"needy; but there was no desire to greet him *Unter den Linden*."[33]

Conclusion:
A Comparative Perspective

The migration of East European Jews into Imperial Germany represented only part of a far larger population movement that redrew the map of Jewish settlement. In the period between 1870 and 1914, over two million Jews fled their homes in Austro-Hungary, Rumania, and especially Russia. The largest numbers settled in the New World, mainly in the United States, but significant populations found haven in Western Europe, South Africa, and Palestine. No matter where they settled, these Jews, by their sheer presence and numbers, posed social challenges to their host societies. In response to the arrival of Eastern Jews, governments reassessed their immigration policies; societies reconsidered their attitudes toward aliens, and created programs to spur the integration of immigrants; and native Jews reevaluated the nature of Jewish identity and group solidarity in order to clarify their relationship with coreligionists of a different culture and social standing. This broader international framework of Jewish mass migration provides a useful context within which to highlight some of the peculiarities of developments in Imperial Germany. We will therefore conclude this study by contrasting the experience of immigrant Jews in the Second *Reich* to that of East European Jews who settled in other Western lands, principally the United States, England, and France.[1]

One of the major factors shaping Germany's particular response to Jewish mass migration was the *Reich*'s geographic proximity to the multinational states of Eastern Europe. Alone among European states, the *Reich* shared common borders with both the Tsarist and Hapsburg empires, a circumstance that rendered it particularly vulnerable to migrants fleeing their homes in the East. German officials thus confronted the twofold challenge of transmigration and immigration: they needed measures to channel the tide of refugees flooding across the nation's frontiers; and they needed policies to manage those migrants who sought haven in Germany. While a number of other Western countries also were confronted with the problem of Jewish immigration, no other country faced the same threat to the integrity of its borders posed by the uncontrolled tide of Jewish transmigration.

The manner in which Germans responded to Jewish migrants was also unusual: whereas other Western countries devised national policies to cope with new immigrants, Germany developed no federal policy regarding Jewish, or any other, immigration. Because the *Reich*'s constitution granted jurisdiction over matters of citizenship to individual *Länder,* it proved impossible to develop a coordinated and centralized policy toward Jewish immigrants. States jealously protected their prerogatives and, accordingly, resisted taking steps toward formal coordination. Despite the ongoing efforts of Prussia, the largest and most powerful state, and the campaigns of several German chancellors, policies toward foreigners were regulated solely by individual states throughout the Imperial era.

By extending state jurisdiction over aliens, the *Reich*'s Constitution insured the historical continuity of German responses to foreigners. Not only did states preserve their prerogatives in regard to aliens, but they continued to employ the same instruments for controlling foreigners that had been devised during the Middle Ages. States barred aliens from settling in specific localities and forbade them from engaging in certain types of occupations; they required foreigners to renew their residence permits at regular intervals; they evaluated an alien's legal status only on a case-by-case basis, rather than through a clearly defined procedure; and they expelled all aliens deemed ''troublesome'' by police authorities. To highlight the continuities, we need only substitute the term ''Jew'' for ''alien'' in this listing of measures and we have described the treatment of Jews in medieval and early modern Germany. Because they lacked citizenship in a German state, East European Jews in the Second *Reich* were unemancipated.

Such was not the case in other Western countries. Once they entered England, France, and the United States, immigrant Jews were generally not harassed by government officials. They enjoyed freedom of movement and occupation. And after residing in the country for a set number of years and meeting a few clearly specified qualifications, they could anticipate receiving citizenship. Unless they engaged in subversive political activities, they had no need to fear summary expulsion. (England even refused to sign an international agreement to combat anarchism because the treaty called for the expulsion of anarchists, an action contrary to British law.)[2] German states, by contrast, allowed Eastern Jews and other aliens into the country and then selected desirable from undesirable individuals through ongoing expulsions.

This is not to suggest that other Western states were thoroughly hospitable toward immigrants. Both England and the United States, for example, enacted restrictionist legislation that banned or curbed specific types of aliens. Already during the 1880s, the American Congress had excluded Chinese immigrants, and in subsequent decades restrictionists enacted literacy, means, and health tests to curb unwanted immigrants. By the end of World War I, new legislation set national quotas on the numbers of immigrants permitted into the United States. English legislators anticipated such actions by passing an Aliens Act already in 1905, thereby providing the British government with a means to curb the influx of Eastern Jews, as well as other immigrants.[3] Despite the existence of these models, no German government promoted legislation to cope with the Jewish mass migration. Reichstag deputies of the anti-Semitic and Conservative parties repeatedly urged such a course of action, and some government officials openly discussed means of drafting such a law without contravening commercial treaties with the Hapsburg and Tsarist empires. In 1894, for example, the German foreign minister informed the Reichstag that no legal barriers stood in the way of a law forbidding *all* foreign Jews from entering Germany; trade treaties only prevented selective discrimination against Jewish immigrants from a particular country. In a cabinet meeting held in 1905, Chancellor von Bülow suggested that Germany should imitate English and American precedents by enacting a law excluding certain categories of unwanted immigrants.[4] Nonetheless, Germany passed no law banning Jewish or other immigrants. Rather than manage immigrants through comprehensive *legislation,* as did England and the United States, Germany employed *administrative measures* to cope with foreigners.

This unique structure for managing alien populations had several important ramifications. To begin with, the German system granted local and state bureaucrats almost unlimited power over newcomers. Since most decisions were rendered by a faceless bureaucracy, aliens in Germany had little recourse once their fate was decided. Second, since bureaucrats were only required to account for their actions to their ministerial superiors, they enjoyed a great deal of autonomy. In exercising their authority over Eastern Jews, German officials gave free expression to their xenophobia and anti-Semitism. They could act with impunity since the system for dealing with foreigners placed few checks upon them. By contrast, in England, France, and the United States, law rather than administrative fiat regulated Jewish immigrants and, accordingly, Eastern Jews were less vulnerable to arbitrary and antagonistic officials.

While Germany's structure for dealing with foreigners was not created with the intension of fostering xenophobia, it facilitated the spread of anti-alien attitudes. For by failing to develop a comprehensive and publicly announced policy, state governments made clear that foreigners could be treated arbitrarily. Officials judged each immigrant by his utility to the state, and especially its economy: if a Polish worker could help man heavy industry or agriculture, he was permitted temporary residence in Prussia; if a Jewish merchant could facilitate trade with Russia, he was allowed to reside in Königsberg; but both types of individuals were forbidden to bring their wives from the East and were denied citizenship. At its core, the German approach to aliens was exploitative: not only did Germans not conceive of their homeland as a haven for the persecuted and needy, they evaluated foreigners solely on the basis of their utility.

This cynical treatment of aliens in general, and Eastern Jews in particular, deserves consideration in the ongoing historical debates about continuity in German history. Certainly, xenophobia and anti-Semitism were not monopolized by Germans; but both prejudices were given institutional expression and legitimacy by government officials during the Imperial era. State policies marked Christians and Jews from the East for special treatment, and government officials publicly aired their bigoted views of Poles and Eastern Jews. By so doing, officials set important precedents. It is not accidental that two populations, Catholic Poles and Eastern Jews, singled out for exploitation during the Imperial era were recruited as forced laborers during World War I. And it is not accidental that stereotypes developed during the nineteenth century which pictured Poles as menial laborers and Eastern Jews as *"Schnorrers* and conspirators" were central to the imagery and policies of the Nazi era. Furthermore, contemporary debates over *Gastarbeiter* in the German Federal Republic echo similar controversies during the Imperial era. Several historians have noted parallels between the exploitation of Polish seasonal workers and today's "guest workers."[5] There are also important similarities between the *Gastarbeiter* and Eastern Jews who settled in the *Reich.* Like many contemporary "guest workers," Eastern Jews lived in the country for decades, contributed to its economy, and raised their children as Germans, but they had no assurance that they would acquire citizenship or protection from expulsion. Despite their contributions to Germany's economy and society, they were viewed as Asian invaders who deserved neither security nor toleration. Whereas present-day policies offer aliens better protection than those of the past, some contemporary Germans are reenacting their ancestors' abuse of strangers in their midst.

The character and experience of Eastern Jews in the *Reich* were profoundly shaped by Germany's unusual methods of dealing with aliens. Even though most trans-migrants passing through the *Reich* spoke Yiddish, a language akin to German, and probably were enticed by the relative affluence of the country, a smaller number settled in Germany than in most other Western countries.[6] As noted by a contemporary observer, the emigrants knew "that a Jew—especially a Russian Jew—would not find anything in Germany. They already heard enough stories about the Prussian *Gendarmes,* the notorious border stations, the expulsions from Prussia. They knew that one could never get in, let us not even mention finding work there."[7] Official measures not only limited the number of immigrants, but also selected certain types of Eastern Jews while sending others on their way through and out of the country. The preponderant majority of Eastern Jews in Germany originated in Austro-Hungary and engaged in commercial occupations. By contrast, Eastern Jews in other Western lands were predominantly from the Tsarist Empire and engaged in manual labor.[8] Finally, the inhospitable reception accorded to foreigners encouraged them to scatter to many localities rather than form a noticeable presence: conspicuousness invited expulsion.

These circumstances, in turn, were responsible for the unusually impoverished organizational life of Eastern Jews in the *Reich.* Unlike their counterparts in other Western lands, these immigrant Jews created no Jewish labor movement; at best, they formed a few Bundist cells and ideologically motivated student societies. Similarly, there were no immigrant periodicals, Yiddish theaters, or thriving cultural centers in Imperial Germany comparable to what could be found in the Pletzel of Paris, the East End of London, or the numerous "ghettos" of the New World.[9] And unlike their counterparts in other countries who took to the streets to protest unfair working conditions, price gouging by kosher butchers, and slanderous accusations by public officials, Eastern Jews in Germany—despite their more vulnerable status—never managed to organize in defense of their own interests.[10] Their geographic dispersal and insecure position fostered passivity and disunity.

A further consequence of their vulnerable status in Germany was the rapid acculturation of Eastern Jews in the *Reich*. The immigrants evinced no romantic attachment to the past, nor did they glorify the Yiddish world of their fathers. In other Western countries, there were fewer pressures to conform and greater possibilities for cultural self-expression. Hence, a Yiddish literature and culture developed in the United States, England, and, to a lesser extent, France. But in Germany, where the cost of nonconformity was prohibitive, Eastern Jews quickly abandoned the "Golden Tradition" of their ancestors.[11]

This, in part, also explains the relatively small impact of immigrants upon the culture of native Jews in Germany, as compared to other Western lands. In some countries, Eastern Jews transformed the communities of native Jews. In Germany, the reverse occurred: newcomers quickly adopted the style of their native coreligionists—even to the point of disdaining more recent immigrants. Centripetal forces pulled Eastern Jews into the vortex of Jewish communal life and changed them irrevocably. This is not to suggest that immigrants played no role in the communal life of native Jewry. On the contrary, no other Western Jewry recruited so many of its rabbis, teachers, religious functionaries, and scholars from *first-generation* immigrants.[12] But in Germany, the most prominent Eastern Jews—rabbis and other communal leaders—internalized the values of native Jewry and shunned the society of less acculturated immigrants. They behaved as highly Germanized individuals.

Despite the rapid acculturation and relatively high economic attainments of Eastern Jews in Germany, the encounter between native and immigrant Jews was marked by social tensions. As was the case in all encounters between Western and Eastern Jews, significant class and cultural differences separated the two populations. But relations were further strained by circumstances peculiar to Germany. To begin with, the legal status of immigrant Jews created a difficult situation for both groups. On the one hand, Eastern Jews stood little chance of ever acquiring citizenship—and therefore equality before the law with native Jews. This inequality inevitably obstructed normal relations. To take but one example, native parents knew that if their daughter married an immigrant, she would lose her German citizenship and face possible expulsion along with her husband and family, a state of affairs that hardly encouraged native families to welcome aliens into their midst. Moreover, it was difficult to maintain a strong sense of group solidarity when society at large, and especially the state, treated native and Eastern Jews so differently. On the other hand, natives were compelled by state laws to accept immigrants as total equals within the Jewish community. *Gemeinden* were required to enfranchise newcomers and grant them equal status in the run-ning of communal affairs. Thus, laws peculiar to Germany created the anomalous situation whereby immigrants could never attain the rights and privileges of German citizens of the Mosaic Persuasion, yet within the *Gemeinden* they had to be accepted as complete equals.

Tensions were further exacerbated by the nature of public debates over Jewish immigration. Only in Germany did restrictionists propose a ban solely on Jewish immigrants, and only in Germany were immigrant Jews exploited and harassed by police and other public officials. Under the circumstances, native Jews were compelled to act because laws and policies that singled out immigrant Jews for special treatment potentially threatened to undermine the principle of Jewish emancipation: if it was acceptable to mistreat foreign Jews, what would prevent religious discrimination in other spheres of public life? Thus, out of self-interest, leaders of native Jewry opposed restrictionist legislation and discriminatory immigration policies.[13]

This concern for the mistreatment of immigrant Jews did not, however, translate into amicable social encounters between natives and newcomers. For while it was one thing for the community to take a public stance opposing the mistreatment of immigrant coreligionists, it was an entirely different matter for German Jews to fraternize with Eastern Jews. If anything, the former wished to distance themselves from individuals who were stigmatized by public officials as *"Schnorrers* and conspirators.*"* Moreover, they wished to give the lie to charges by anti-Semites that native and immigrant Jews were identical: scratch away his thin veneer of German culture, argued anti-Semites, and you will find a dirty caftan Jew masquerading as a German citizen of the Mosaic Persuasion. Given the fact that anti-Semites stressed not only a commonality of interest but also of identity between German and Eastern Jews, it is not surprising that native Jews sought to avoid social contact with the immigrants. Thus, when German Jews acted to defend the interests of immigrant coreligionists in the arena of German politics and when they disdained Eastern Jews within the more private confines of the *Gemeinden,* their behavior was prompted by discomfort over the awkward questions Jewish immigration raised regarding their own status. Franz Rosenzweig, the great Jewish philosopher, succinctly identified what was at stake when he declared, "There is no *Ostjudenfrage,* only a *Judenfrage.*"[14] The experience of East European Jews in the Second Empire attests to the ongoing insecurity of Jewish life in Germany during the age of emancipation.

Abbreviations

Archives

ALBI   Archives of the Leo Baeck Institute.
BHA   Bayerisches Hauptstaatsarchiv, Munich.
CAHJP   Central Archives for the History of the Jewish People, Jerusalem.
CZA   Central Zionist Archives, Jerusalem.
Dresden   Sächsisches Landeshauptarchiv, Dresden.
DZA II   Deutsches Zentralarchiv, Merseburg.
GLA   Generallandesarchiv, Karlsruhe.
GStA   Geheimes Staatsarchiv Preussischer Kulturbesitz, Dahlem.

Periodicals

AZJ   *Allgemeine Zeitung des Judentums.*
BLBI   *Bulletin des Leo Baeck Instituts.*
EJ   *Encyclopedia Judaica* (Jerusalem, 1971).
Erg. 1916   *Vierteljahrshefte zur Statistik des Deutschen Reichs, Ergänzung zu 1916.*
Eschelbacher, 1920 or 1923   Klara Eschelbacher, "Die ostjüdische Einwanderungsbevölkerung der Stadt Berlin," ZfDS XVI, no. 1–6 (1920), and XVII, no. 1–3 (1923).
GB   *Geschäftberichte des Verbandes der deutschen Juden.*
IDR   *Im deutschen Reich.*
IFF   *Israelitisches Familienblatt,* Frankfurt.
IFH   *Israelitisches Familienblatt,* Hamburg.
IR   *Israelitische Rundschau.*
JP   *Jüdische Presse.*
JR   *Jüdische Rundschau.*
JSS   *Jewish Social Studies.*
KB   *Korrespondenz-Blatt des Verbandes der deutschen Juden.*
MAV   *Mitteilungen aus dem Verein zur Abwehr des Antisemitismus.*
MDIGB   *Mitteilungen des Deutsch-Israelitischen Gemeindebund.*
SBVHA   *Stenographische Berichte über die Verhandlungen des Hauses der Abgeordneten.*
SBR   *Stenographische Berichte über die Verhandlungen des Reichstags.*
SDR   *Statistik des Deutschen Reiches.*
SJDR   *Statistisches Jahrbuch für das Deutsche Reich.*
VSDR   *Vierteljahrshefte zur Statistik des Deutschen Reichs.*
YBLBI   *Leo Baeck Institute Yearbook.*
ZfDS   *Zeitschrift für Demographie und Statistik der Juden.*

Appendix:
Statistical Tables

Table I.   Eastern Jews in Major States and Cities, 1871–1910

a. Germany
b. Prussia
c. Saxony
d. Hesse
e. Berlin
f. Dresden
g. Hanover
h. Leipzig
i. Munich
j. Cities in Hesse: Mainz, Darmstadt, Offenbach, Worms.

Table II.   Foreign Jews in the Total Jewish and Alien Populations, 1910

a. In Major Provinces of Prussia and in Large German States.
b. In the "Large Cities" (Populations of more than 100,000)

Table III.   Urbanization, 1900 and 1910

a. Proportion of Jewish and Gentile Populations in the "Large Cities"
b. Jewish and Gentile Aliens from Eastern Europe

Table IV.   Jewish and Gentile Aliens from Eastern Europe (by Nationality)

a. In Germany, 1880–1910
b. In Berlin, 1880–1910
c. In Prussia, 1880–1905

Table V. Occupational Distribution

a. Natives and Aliens in Berlin, Munich, Hesse, and Hanover (c. 1910)
b. Russians, Austrians, and Rumanians in Germany (c. 1910)
c. Natives and Aliens in the "Large Cities" (c. 1910)
d. Protestants, Catholics, and Jews in Germany (1907)

TABLE I. Eastern Jews in Major States and Cities, 1871–1910

a. Germany

Year	Total Jews(a)	FJ or EJ	Russian Jews	Austrian Jews	Hungarian Jews	Other Nationalities
1871	512,153(b) 1.25%(a)					
1880	561,612(b) 1.25%(a)	FJ = 17,000–18,000(g) EJ = 16,000(g)				
1890	567,884(b) 1.04%(a)	EJ = 20,388(c)	9,897(c)	8,803(c)	1,688(c)	
1900	586,833(c) 1.04%(a)	FJ = 41,113(d) EJ = 34,360(d)	12,752(d)	12,752(d)	3,340(d)	Rumanian: 858(d)
1910	615,021(a) 0.95%(a)	FJ = 79,646(e) EJ = 70,234(e)	21,644(e)	41,512(f)	5,475(f)	Rumanian: 1,509(e) Serbian: 94(e)

FJ = Foreign Jews   EJ = Eastern Jews

(a) ZfDS, VIII (1912), p. 160.
(b) ZfDS, I, no. 1 (1905), p. 10.
(c) VSDR, II (1895), Part III, p. 111.
(d) ZfDS, I, no. 12 (1905), p. 6.
(e) VSDR, XXV (1916), p. 33.
(f) Erg., 1916, p. 13.
(g) The 1880 figures for FJ and EJ are calculated by adding the known populations of such Jews in Prussia, Saxony, and Munich to the estimated number in other areas. (Since the overwhelming majority of foreign Jews resided in Prussia, Saxony, and Munich, we have estimated that all other such Jews in Germany could not have numbered more than 1,000–2,000.) The reader is cautioned that our figure, however reasonable, is an estimate.

b. Prussia

Year	Total Jews	FJ or EJ	Russian Jews	Austrian Jews	Hungarian Jews	Other Nationalities
1880	363,790(d)	FJ = 15,165(e) EJ = 14,328(c) EJ = 14,608(h)	11,512(c) 11,364(h)	2,816(c) 3,244(h)		
1890	372,058(d)	FJ = 11,390(f) FJ = 19,304(g) EJ = 14,760(g)	8,264(g)	5,514(g)	978(g)	Rumanians: 220(g) Balkans: 4(g)
1900	392,322(d)	FJ = 21,800(l)				

TABLE I. Eastern Jews in Major States and Cities, 1871–1910 (*Continued*)

b. Prussia

Year	Total Jews	FJ or EJ	Russian Jews	Austrian Jews	Hungarian Jews	Other Nationalities
1905	409,501(d)	FJ = 38,844(a) EJ = 34,138(a)	13,185(a)	16,665(a)	3,386(a)	Bulgarian: 21(a) Rumanians: 854(a) Serbian: 27(a)
1910	415,867(i)	FJ = 48,166(b)				

FJ = Foreign Jews EJ = Eastern Jews

(a) *Statistisches Jahrbuch für den Preussischen Staat*, IV (1906), Part I, p. 17.
(b) Erg., 1916, p. 53.
(c) Solomon Neumann, *Zur Statistik der Juden in Preussen*, p. 18. (Note: not all of Prussia is included in this census.)
(d) *Statistisches Jahrbuch für den Preussischen Staat* (1908), Part I, p. 7.
(e) SBR, IX Leg., IV Session, II, p. 1284.
(f) ZfDS, VIII (1912), p. 85. (Only unnaturalized Jews are included in this figure.)
(g) AZJ, Jan. 25, 1895, p. 37. Both naturalized and unnaturalized foreign-born Jews are included in these figures.
(h) Ibid., p. 38. Only the following areas of Prussia were surveyed to arrive at these figures: East and West Prussia, Posen, Silesia, and the city of Berlin.
(i) ZfDS, VII (1911), p. 154.
(l) F. Theilhaber, *Der Untergang der deutschen Juden*, p. 23. This is an estimate made by the author on the basis of statistics on Jews who have a foreign mother tongue. Theilhaber's use of figures is often sloppy and therefore this estimate is not utilized in the text of our study. It is cited merely for the sake of thoroughness.

c. Saxony

Year	Total Jews	FJ or EJ	Russian Jews	Austrian Jews	Hungarian Jews	Other Nationalities
1880	6,518(f)	FJ = 1,000(h)				
1885	7,755(g)			526(e) A+H		
1890	9,368(f)	FJ = 2,800(h)		793(e) A+H		
1900	12,416(f)	FJ = 5,637(a)				
1905	14,697(e)	FJ = 7,778(c)	2,271(e)	4,701(e)	217(e)	
1910	17,587(e)	FJ = 10,287(b) FJ = 10,360(d) EJ = 9,642(e)	3,192(e)	6,129(e)	321(e)	

FJ = Foreign Jews EJ = Eastern Jews
A+H = Austrians plus Hungarian Jews

(a) *Kalendar und Statistisches Jahrbuch für das Königreich Sachsen* (1903), p. 6.
(b) Erg., 1916, p. 53.
(c) *Kalendar und Statistisches Jahrbuch für das Königreich Sachsen* (1908), p. 13.
(d) *Kalendar und Statistisches Jahrbuch für das Königreich Sachsen* (1913), p. 17.
(e) ZfDS, X (1914), p. 39.
(f) ZfDS, I, no. 1 (1905), p. 10
(g) Ibid., p. 36
(h) A. Diamant, *Chronik der Juden in Dresden*, p. 231. (The author claims that his figures were taken from census data. It is not clear as to where he found his data.)

d. Hesse

Year	Total Jews	FJ or EJ	Russian Jews	Austrian Jews	Hungarian Jews	Other Nationalities
1905	24,696(a)	FJ = 1,787(a)	886(a)	690(a)	74(a)	10(d)
		EJ = 1,650(a)				
1910	24,063(b)	FJ = 2,502(b)	1,606(b)	689(b)	71(d)	3(d)
		EJ = 2,369(c)				

FJ = Foreign Jews   EJ = Eastern Jews
(a) *Statistisches Handbuch für das Grossherzogtum Hessen* (1909), Part II, p. 33.
(b) ZfDS, VIII (1912), pp. 105–07.
(c) My computations are based on (c) and (e).
(d) ZfDS, VIII (1912), p. 103

e. Berlin

Year	Total Jews	FJ or EJ	Russian Jews	Austrian Jews	Hungarian Jews	Other Nationalities
1871	36,015(e)					
1880	53,916(a)	FJ = 3,662(a)	2,048(a)	957(a)		
		EJ = 3,005(a)				
1890	79,286(g)	FJ = 6,141(c)	2,427(c)	2,494(c)	569(c)	Rumanians: 214(c)
		EJ = 5,704(c)				
1895	86,152(i)	FJ = 9,403(j)				
1900	92,206(d)	FJ = 11,615(d)				
1905	98,893(i)	FJ = 18,316(b)	6,730(b)	7,900(b)	1,911(b)	Rumanians: 520(b)
		EJ = 17,061(b)				
1910	90,013(n)	FJ = 15,524(n)	3,606(n)	6,098(n)		Rumanians: 555(n)
		EJ = 10,259(n)				
1910*	137,043(f)	FJ = 21,683(f)	5,360(f)	6,770(f)		Rumanians: 825(f)
1910		FJ = 18,694(m)				
1910		FJ = 25,241(m)				

FJ = Foreign Jews   EJ = Eastern Jews
*Greater Berlin (includes Berlin proper, Charlottenburg, Neukölln, Wilmersdorf, and Schöneberg).
(a) *Statistisches Jahrbuch der Stadt Berlin*, IX, p. 8.
(b) Ibid., XXXII, pp. 30–31.
(c) Ibid., XVIII, pp. 2–3
(d) Ibid., XXVI, pp. 20–21.
(e) Solomon Neumann, *Die Fabel der jüdischen Masseneinwanderung*, p. 12.
(f) Eschelbacher, 1920, p. 4.
(g) ZfDS, I, no. 1 (1905), p. 10.
(i) ZfDS, IX (1913), p. 9.
(j) *Die Bevölkerungs-und-Wohnungs-Aufnahme in der Stadt Berlin* (1900), Part I, p. 38.
(m) Erg., 1916, p. 86.
(n) Eschelbacher, 1920, pp. 4, 7.

Source (c) specifies the following number of *"Inländer"* (presumably naturalized Jews) among the total group of alien Jews: EJ, 1,477; Russian Jews, 863; Austrian Jews, 480; Hungarians, 85; other Eastern Jews, 49. (These *Inländer* were not deducted from our figures for 1890.)

TABLE I. Eastern Jews in Major States and Cities, 1871–1910 (*Continued*)

f. Dresden

Year	Total Jews	FJ or EJ	Russian Jews	Austrian Jews	Hungarian Jews	Other Nationalities
1880	2,228(i)	FJ = 299(j)				
1890	2,595(h)	FJ = 933(j)				
1895	2,558(g)	FJ = 766(g)	189(g)	51(g) A + H		65(h)
1900	3,059(e)	FJ = 1,244(a)				
1905	3,514(d)	FJ = 3,514(d) EJ = 1,600(d)	513(d)	1,038	49(d)	115(h)
1910	3,734(c)	FJ = 1,948(b)	555(c)	1,166(c)	112(c)	150(c)

FJ = Foreign Jews   EJ = Eastern Jews
A + H = Austrians plus Hungarians
(a) *Kalender und Statistisches Jahrbuch für das Königreich Sachsen* (Dresden, 1903), p. 6.
(b) Erg., 1916, p. 86.
(c) *Statistisches Jahrbuch der Stadt Dresden für 1915*, XVII, p. 327.
(d) Ibid., *für 1914*, XIV, p. 285.
(e) Ibid., *für 1901*, III, p. 44.
(f) Ibid., *für 1904*, Part III, p. 28.
(g) Ibid., *für 1900*, p. 29.
(h) ZfDS, X (1914), pp. 40, 36.
(i) ZfDS, IV (1908), p. 142.
(j) Diamant, *Chronik der Juden in Dresden*, p. 231. The author claims that his figures are based on census returns. It is unclear where he found them.

g. Hanover

Year	Total Jews	FJ or EJ	Russian Jews	Austrian Jews	Hungarian Jews	Other Nationalities
1900	4,540(b)	FJ = 272(a)	44(a)	128(a)	14(a)	
1905	4,923(b)	FJ = 714(a)*	121(a)	434(a)	28(a)	
1910	5,155(b)	FJ = 1,002(a)	232(a)	594(a)	37(a)	
1913		FJ = 971(a) EJ = 904(a)	241(a)	624(a)	39(a)	Rumanians: 3(a)
1910	5,386(c)	FJ = 1,091(d)				

*The figures are from 1904.
EJ = Eastern Jews   FG = Foreign Jews
(a) ZfDS, X (1914), pp. 114–15. The figures are computed on the basis of this source.
(b) ZfDS, X (1914), pp. 111–12.
(c) Silbergleit, p. 24
(d) Erg., 1916, p. 86.

h. Leipzig

Year	Total Jews	FJ or EJ	Russian Jews	Austrian Jews	Hungarian Jews	Other Nationalities
1871	1,768(g)	EJ = 570(h)				
1875	2,616(k)	EJ = 731(k) EJ = 395(i)	158(i)	237(i) A + H		
1880	3,265(g)	FJ = 331(j)				
1885	3,749(d)	FJ = 931		526(e) A + H		375(e)
1890	4,136(d)	FJ = 1,296(e) FJ = 1,696(j)		793(e) A + H		485(e)

h. Leipzig

Year	Total Jews	FJ or EJ	Russian Jews	Austrian Jews	Hungarian Jews	Other Nationalities
1900	6,171(c)	FJ = 3,577(a)				
		FJ = 2,612(c)	704(l)	1,490(l)		Rumanians: 84(l)
		EJ = 2,562(a)		1,774(c) A + H		
1905	7,676(d)	FJ = 4,843(k)	1,401(f)	3,010(f)	117(f)	315(f)
1910	9,874(d)	FJ = 6,401(b)	2,006(f)	3,881(f)	148(f)	391(f)
		EJ = 6,035(b)				

EJ = Eastern Jews   FJ = Foreign Jews
A + H = Austrians plus Hungarians
(a) *Kalendar und Statistisches Jahrbuch für das Königreich Sachsen* (Dresden, 1903), p. 6.
(b) Erg., 1916, p. 86.
(c) *Ergebnisse der Volkszählung von 1 Dezember 1900 in der Stadt Leipzig* (Leipzig, 1901), pp. 92–93.
(d) ZfDS, X (1914), p. 40.
(e) Ibid., p. 42
(f) Ibid., p. 43.
(g) Ibid., p. 36.
(h) Eugen von Bergmann, *Zur Geschichte der Entwicklung deutscher, polnischer, und jüdischer Bevölkerung in der Provinz Posen seit 1824*, p. 317.
(i) Bruno Blau, *Die Entwicklung der jüdischen Bevölkerung in Deutschland, 1880–1945*, vol. II: *1880–1945* (unpublished manuscript in Yivo Archive, New York).
(j) Diamant, *Chronik der Juden in Dresden*, p. 231. The author does not reveal his source.
(k) F. Theilhaber, *Der Untergang der Deutschen Juden*, p. 18.
(l) Microfilm #154, "Auswärtiges Amt. Stuttgart 1903–1918," ALBI, New York.

i. Munich

Year	Total Jews	FJ or EJ	Russian Jews	Austrian Jews	Hungarian Jews	Other Nationalities
1880	4,144(a)	FJ = 367(b)		269(d) A + H		52(d)
1885	4,854(a)	FJ = 471(b)		304(d) A + H		94
1890	6,112(a)	FJ = 794(b)	81(d)	586(d) A + H		30(d)
1895	7,167(a)	FJ = 1,076(b)				
1900	8,739(c)	FJ = 1,705(b)				
1905	10,056(d)	FJ = 2,588(d)				
1910	11,083(b)	FJ = 3,857(b)	861(b)	1,605(b)	329(b)	235(b)
		EJ = 2,795(b)				
		FJ = 3,857(c)				

FJ = Foreign Jews   EJ = Eastern Jews
A + H = Austrians plus Hungarians
(a) ZfDS, V (1909), p. 18.
(b) ZfDS, XV (1919), p. 122.
(c) Erg., 1916, p. 86.
(d) ZfDS, III (1907), pp. 90–91.

j. Cities in Hesse *

City	Year	Total Jews	FJ or EJ	Russian Jews	Austrian Jews	Other Nationality
Mainz	1905	3101	FJ = 225	71	126	28
Mainz	1910	2926	FJ = 380	202	144	34
Darmstadt	1905	1689	FJ = 450	339	76	35

TABLE I. Eastern Jews in Major States and Cities, 1871–1910 (*Continued*)

City	Year	Total Jews	FJ or EJ		Russian Jews	Austrian Jews	Other Nationality
Darmstadt	1910	1998	FJ =	512	363	127	22
Offenbach	1905	1894	FJ =	680	330	289	61
Offenbach	1910	2361	FJ =	1131	876	200	55
Worms	1905	1307	FJ =	100	12	74	14
Worms	1910	1281	FJ =	132	17	95	20

FJ = Foreign Jews   EJ = Eastern Jews
*This entire table has been compiled from data presented in ZfDS, VIII (1912), p. 105.

TABLE II. Foreign Jews in the Total Jewish and Alien Populations, 1910

a. In Major Provinces of Prussia and in Large German States

Locality*	Total Jews (a)	FJ (d)	% of Total Jews who are FJ	Total Number of Aliens (e)	% of Alien Populaton who are Jewish
Prussia:					
East Prussia	13,027	2,108	16.18	15,004	14.05
West Prussia	13,954	412	2.95	7,087	5.81
Brandenburg	61,343	8,666	14.13	70,984	12.21
Pomerania	8,862	248	2.80	16,140	1.54
Posen	26,512	324	1.22	10,166	3.19
Silesia	44,985	2,554	5.68	105,962	2.41
Hanover	15,545	1,820	11.71	30,015	6.06
Rhineland	57,287	4,843	8.45	205,037	2.36
City of Berlin	90,013	18,694	20.77	54,046	34.59
Total: Prussia	415,926	48,166	11.58	688,788	6.99
Bavaria	55,065	7,320	13.58	134,124	5.46
Saxony	17,587	10,293	58.53	188,443	5.46
Württemberg	11,982(b)	1,156	9.65	25,851	4.47
Baden	25,896(c)	2,620	10.12	41,912	6.25
Hesse	24,063	2,494	10.36	11,328	22.02

*Listed in order generally used by German statistical publications.

FJ = Foreign Jews

(a) Unless otherwise noted, figures in this column are taken from H. Silbergleit, *Die Bevölkerung und Berufsverhältnisse der Juden im Deutschen Reich,* p. 24.
(b) ZfDS, IX (1913), p. 72
(c) ZfDS, VIII (1912), p. 15
(d) Erg., 1916, p. 53
(e) Erg., 1916, p. 53

b. In the "Large Cities" (Population of more than 100,000)

City*	Total Jews (a)	FJ (b)	% of Total Jews who are FJ	Total Number of Aliens (c)	% of Alien Populaton who are Jewish
Königsberg	4,565	1,169	25.61	2,144	54.52
Danzig	2,390(f)	276	11.55	875	31.54
Berlin (proper)	90,013(d)	15,524(d) 18,694(a)	17.25 20.77	54,046	28.72
Charlottenburg	22,508(e)	3,227	14.34	11,105	29.06
Neukölln	2,080(e)	485	23.32	4,356	11.13
Schoeneberg	11,641(e)	1,412	12.13	5,741	24.60
Wilmersdorf	9,698(e)	1,423	14.67	5,013	28.39
Stettin	2,757	108	3.92	1,374	7.86
Posen	5,605(f)	110	1.96	1,241	8.86
Breslau	20,212	1,455	7.20	6,982	20.84
Magdeburg	1,843	295	16.01	1,925	15.32
Halle	1,397	263	18.83	1,655	15.89
Erfurt	807	103	12.76	1,073	9.60
Kiel	527	110	20.87	2,271	4.84
Altona	1,824	643	35.25	4.097	15.69
Hanover	5,386	1,091	20.26	3,783	28.84
Dortmund	2,830	391	13.82	3,598	10.87
Gelsenkirchen	1,261	229	18.16	2,687	8.52
Bochum	997	81	8.12	1,399	5.79
Frankfurt a/M	26,228	3,541	13.50	11,778	30.06
Cassel	2,675	257	9.60	1,817	14.14
Wiesbaden	2,444	750	30.69	3,778	19.85
Köln	12,393	1,672	13.49	9,812	17.04
Düsseldorf	3,985	569	14.28	1,172	4.83
Essen	2,944	445	15.12	6,139	7.25
Duisburg	1,554	309	19.88	18,311	1.69
Elberfeld	1,919	289	15.06	2,559	11.29
Barmen	668	69	10.33	1,392	4.96
Aachen	1,565	131	8.37	6,574	1.99
Krefeld	1,815	97	5.34	3,078	3.15
Mülheim	664	54	8.13	4,489	1.20
Saarbrücken	1,081	146	13.51	1,437	10.16
Hamborn	356	59	16.57	17,224	0.34
Munich	11,083(g)	3,857	34.86	33,232	12.60
Nürnberg	7,815(g)	1,226	15.69	7,847	15.62
Augsburg	1,217(g)	155	12.74	2,623	5.91
Leipzig	9,874	6,406	64.83	21,946	29.19
Dresden	3,734	1,948	52.17	30,756	6.33

TABLE II. Foreign Jews in the Total Jewish and Alien Populations, 1910 (*Cont.*)

b. In the "Large Cities" (Population of more than 100,000) (*Continued*)

City*	Total Jews (a)	FJ (b)	% of Total Jews who are FJ	Total Number of Aliens (c)	% of Alien Populaton who are Jewish
Chemnitz	1,911(h)	642	33.59	17,175	3.74
Plauen	953(h)	432	45.33	8,942	4.83
Stuttgart	4,291(j)	836	19.48	6,559	12.74
Mannheim	6,402(k)	887	13.86	5,694	15.58
Karlsruhe	3,058(k)	654	21.39	3,168	20.64
Mainz	2,926	373	12.75	1,566	23.82
Braunschweig	1,774(i)	160	9.02	2,299	6.96
Bremen	1,409	679	48.19	9,552	7.11
Hamburg	18,932	3,111	16.43	27,076	11.49
Strassburg	5,780	768	13.29	4,652	16.51

*Listed in order commonly given by German statistical publications.

FJ = Foreign Jews

(a) When not otherwise stated, figures in this column are from H. Silbergleit, *Die Bevölkerung und Berufsverhältnisse der Juden im Deutschen Reich*, p. 24.

(b) When not otherwise stated, figures in this column are taken from Erg., 1916, p. 86.

(c) Erg., 1916, pp. 68–69.

(d) Eschelbacher, 1920, p. 4.

(e) ZfDS, X (1914), p. 121.

(f) ZfDS, VII (1911), p. 157.

(g) ZfDS, VIII (1912), p. 14.

(h) ZfDS, XII (1916), p. 111.

(i) SJDR, XXV (1914), p. 9.

TABLE III. Urbanization, 1900 and 1910

a. Proportion of Jewish and Gentile Populations in the "Large Cities"

	Total Population	Total Jews	Total Aliens	Alien Jews	% of Aliens who are Jewish	German Jews	% of all Jews who are FJ
Total in Germany, 1900	56,367,178(c)	586,833(c)	782,484(+)	41,113(+)	4.9(+)	545,720(d)	7.01
Total in (33) "Large Cities," 1900	9,112,989(f)	250,695(g)	182,397(+)	28,226(+)	13.4(+)	222,469(d)	15.48
% in "Large Cities," 1900	16.16	42.72	23.31	68.65		40.77	
Total in Germany, 1910	64,925,993(c)	615,021(b)	1,259,880(*)	79,646(a)	6.32(+)	535,375(d)	12.95
Total in (48) "Large Cities," 1910	13,823,348(e)	329,591(c)	398,610(*)	62,072(a)	15.57(+)	267,519(d)	18.83
% in "Large Cities," 1910	21.29	53.59	31.64	77.93		49.97	

No sign = My own computation.
(+) ZfDS, I no.12, (1905), pp. 4–8.
(*) Erg., 1916, p. 53 or 86.
(a) Erg., 1916, p. 67.
(b) See Table IIb.
(c) See Table Ia
(d) Number of "Alien Jews" subtracted from "Total Jews."
(e) Computed on basis of material on cities with populations of over 100,000 people. SJDR, XXXIII, pp. 8–9.
(f) Computed on basis of material in *Statistik des Deutschen Reichs*. X (1901) Part 1, p. 238.
(g) A. Ruppin, *The Jews of Today*, p. 101. (Note that Ruppin only gives the percentage, but not the absolute numbers. I have computed the latter on the basis of these percentages.)

Table III. Urbanization, 1900 and 1910 (*Continued*)

b. Jewish and Gentile Aliens from Eastern Europe

	Gentile Russians	Russian Jews	% of Russians who are Jews	Gentile Austrians	Austrian Jews	% of Austrians who are Jews	Gentile Hungarians	Hungarian Jews	% of Hungarians who are Jews	Gentile Rumanians	Rumanian Jews	% of Rumanians who are Jews
Total in Germany, 1900	76,461 (a)	12,752 (a)	14.29	321,367 (a)	17,410 (a)	5.14%	19,765 (a)	3,340 (a)	14.5 (a)	1,263 (a)	858 (a)	40.5 (a)
Total in "Large Cities," 1900	29,773 (b)	7,983 (b)	21.14	76,364 (b)	13,289 (b)	14.82	6,353 (b)	2,531 (b)	28.49	655 (b)	717 (b)	52.3
% in "Large Cities," 1900	38.94	62.60	—	23.76	76.33	—	32.14	75.78	—	51.86	83.57	—
Total in Germany, 1910	116,024 (d)	21,644 (e)	15.72	593,477 (d)	41,512 (e)	6.54	26,612 (d)	5,475 (e)	17.06		1,509 (d)	51.47
Total in "Large Cities," 1910	32,471 (f)	15,471 (f)	32.27	210,761 (f)	33,834 (f)	13.83	15,454 (f)	4,770 (f)	23.59	2,322 (f)	1,374 (f)	37.18
% in "Large Cities," 1910	27.99	71.48	—	35.39	81.5	—	58.07	87.12	—	91.05	91.05	—

No sign = My computation.
(a) ZfDS, I, no. 12 (1905), p. 6.
(b) Computed on the basis of data in ibid.
(c) Ibid., p. 7
(d) Computed on the basis of data in Erg., 1916. (I have subtracted the number of Jews from figures on their Gentile compatriots.)
(e) Erg., 1916, p. 13.
(f) Erg., 1916, p. 67.
— Data unavailable.

TABLE IV. Jewish and Gentile Aliens from Eastern Europe (by Nationality)

a. In Germany, 1880–1910

Year	Total Alien Pop.	Alien Jews	Jewish % of Alien Pop.	Total Russian Pop.	Russian Jews	Jewish % of Russian Pop.	Total Austrian Pop.	Austrian Jews	Jewish % of Austrians	Total Hungarian Pop.	Hungarian Jews	Jewish % of Hungarians	Total Rumanian Pop.	Rumanian Jews	Jewish % of Rumanians
1880	276,087 (a)	17,000 *	6.2	15,097 (a)											
1890	433,254 (a)	20,388 *	4.7	17,107 (a)	9,897 *	57.9	194,974 (c)	8,803 *	4.5	6,706 (c)	1,688 *	25.2	728 (c)		
1900	757,541 (c)	41,113 *	5.4	46,967 (c)	12,752 *	27.2	371,005 (c)	17,410 *	4.7	19,959 (c)	3,340 *	16.7	1,613 (c)	858 *	53.2
1905	418,679 (c)			106,639 (c)			493,872 (c)			31,949 (c)			2,535 (c)		
1910	1,236,196 (c)	79,646 *	6.4	137,697 (c)	21,644 *	15.7	593,477 (e)	41,512 (e)	6.54	26,612 (e)	5,475 (e)	17.1	2,932 (c)	1,509 *	51.5

* See Table Ia.

(a) *Vierteljahreshefte zur Statistik des Deutschen Reiches*, XI, Part I, p. 88.

(c) SJDR, XXXV, p. 10

(d) Ibid., I, p. 5

(e) Erg., 1916, p. 13.

TABLE IV. Jewish and Gentile Aliens from Eastern Europe (by Nationality) (Continued)

b. In Berlin^x, 1880–1910

Year	Total Alien Pop.	Alien Jews	Jewish % of Alien Pop.	Jewish % of German Pop.	Total Russian Pop.	Russian Jews	Jewish % of Russian Pop.	Total Austrian Pop.	Austrian Jews	Jewish % of Austrians	Total Hungarian Pop.	Hungarian Jews	Jewish % of Hungarians	Total Rumanian Pop.	Rumanian Jews	Jewish % of Rumanians
1880	6,457 (i)	3,662 *	56.7	4.8 *	3,830 (e)	2,048 *	53.5	4,692 (e)	957 *	20.4						
1890	17,750 (a)	6,141 *	34.6	5.0 *	2,416 (a)	2,042 *	84.5	8,215 (a)	2,494 *	30.4						
1895	27,087 (a)	9,403 *	34.7	5.1 *												
1900	35,027 (a)	11,651 *	33.3	4.9 *	4,167 (a)				19,760 (a) (A+H)	98.11 * (A+H)	49.7 (A+H)					
1905	48,896 (g)	18,316 *	37.5	4.8 *	9,098 (g)	6,730 *	74.	23,116 (g)	7,900 *	34.2	4,531 (g)	1,911 *	42.2	686 (g)	520 *	75.8
1910	54,046 (h)	15,524 *	28.7	4.3 *	5,569 (b)	3,606 (b)	64.8	30,822 (b)	6,098 (b)	19.8						

* See Table Ie.
^x Denotes Berlin proper, excluding the suburbs.
A+H = Austrians plus Hungarians
(a) *Statistisches Jahrbuch der Stadt Berlin,* XXVII, p. 23.
(b) *Erg.,* 1916, p. 34
(c) *Statistisches Jahrbuch der Stadt Berlin,* III, pp. 14–15.
(d) *Ibid.,* IV, p. 14
(e) *Ibid.,* IX, p. 8.
(f) *Ibid.,* XV, pp. 7–8.
(g) *Ibid.,* XXXII, pp. 30–31.
(h) *Erg.,* 1916, p. 86.
(i) *Zeitschrift des Königlich Preussischen Statistischen Bureaus,* XXXII, p. i

c. In Prussia, 1880–1905

Year	Total Alien Pop.	Alien Jews	Jewish % of Alien Pop.	Total Russian Pop.	Russian Jews	Jewish % of Russian Pop.	Total Austrian Pop.	Austrian Jews	Jewish % of Austrians	Total Hungarian Pop.	Hungarian Jews	Jewish % of Hungarians	Total Rumanian Pop.	Rumanian Jews	Jewish % of Rumanians
1880	98,958 (a)	15,165 *	15.3		11,512 *			2,816 *							
1890	164,798	19,304 *		10,347 (b)	8,264 *	79.9	46,346	5,514 *	11.9	2,846 (b)	978	34.36			
1905	524,874 (c)	38,844 *	7.4	75,796 (c)	13,185 *	17.4	210,960 (c)	16,665 *	7.9	21,450 (c)	3,386 *	15.7	1,486 (c)	854 *	57.5

*See Table Ib.

(a) SDR, XLVIII, vol. II, Section XI, p. 30.

(b) Zeitschrift des Königlich Preussischen Statistischen Bureaus, XXXII, p. i

(c) Statistisches Jahrbuch für den Preussischen Staat, I, p. 17.

TABLE V. Occupational Distribution

a. Natives and Aliens in Berlin, Munich, Hesse, and Hanover (c. 1910)

	BERLIN (1)				MUNICH (2)				HESSE (3)				HANOVER (4)			
	Total Pop. 1907	Total Jews 1907	EJ, 1910	Total Aliens (Minus EJ), 1910	Total Gentile Pop. 1907	German Jews, 1907	EJ, 1907	Total Aliens, 1910	Gentile Pop. 1907	Total Jews 1907	Russian Plus Austrian Jews, 1910	Total Aliens Minus EJ, 1910	Total Gentile Pop., 1907	Total Jews, 1907	FJ, 1913	Total Aliens 1910
Agriculture A	3,937	29	6	145	2,637	4	2	126	163,234	153	—	814	1,713	1	1	58
%	0.43	0.07	.1	0.62	0.96	0.12	0.15	0.62	29.78	1.37	—	16.20	1.47	0.04	.4	2.13
Industry A	530,165	16,593	2,934	13,741	108,436	380	315	8,787	218,324	2,239	339	2,289	52,709	462	41	633
%	58.33	41.32	47.62	59.06	39.66	11.46	24.17	43.17	39.83	20.08	29.12	45.28	45.28	20.07	16.27	23.22
Commerce & A	241,855	19,636	2,643	5,850	69,047	1,452	643	3,574	58,562	6,208	314	707	27,284	1,130	179	1,123
Transport %	26.61	48.90	42.89	25.14	25.25	43.79	49.35	17.56	10.68	55.66	26.98	14.07	23.44	49.09	71.03	41.20
Domestic A	60,448	378	231	1,076	16,654	8	8	746	5,856	27	8	130	2,850	8	7	86
Service %	6.65	0.94	3.75	4.62	6.09	0.24	0.61	3.67	1.07	0.24	0.69	2.59	2.45	0.35	2.78	3.15

Civil Service & Free Prof. A	72,471	3,519	339	2,455	32,763	396	70	1,427	42,328	530	7	252	14,003	96	13	148
%	7.97	8.76	5.63	10.55	11.98	11.94	5.3	7.01	7.72	4.75	0.60	5.01	5.01	12.03	5.16	5.43
Without Occupation A	X	X	X	X	43,883	1,076	265	5,693	59,857	1,996	496	834	17,842	605	11	678
%	X	X	X	X	16.05	32.45	20.34	20.97	10.92	17.90	42.61	16.59	15.33	26.28	4.37	24.87
Total	908,876	40,155	6,153	23,267	273,420	3,316	1,303	20,353	548,161	11,153	1,164	5,026	116,401	2,302	252	2,726

FJ = Foreign Jews
A = Absolute Number
% = Relative to entire work force
X = No data available

1. The data on the general population are taken from the occupational census of 1907, while those on aliens are based on a 1910 census. The figure on Berlin's total population excludes Jews, but includes Gentile aliens. The figures on "Total Aliens" excludes Eastern, but no other, foreign Jews. The data on "Total Jews" are based on statistics published in ZfDS, VII (1911), p. 27. The data on Gentile foreigners are computed from statistics in Erg., 1916, p. 74. Figures on East European Jews are taken from Eschelbacher, 1920, p. 17. Since the latter source does not contain figures on unemployed Eastern Jews, all data on Berlin have been computed to exclude this category. Only by so doing can a comparison be drawn between the different groups of Berlin inhabitants.

2. Because some of the data for Munich date to 1907 and others to 1910, it was not possible to deduct the number of alien Jews from the general population of foreigners. The total Jewish population was, however, subtracted from the "Total Population" and the number of foreign Jews was deducted from the "Total Jewish Population." (Note that alien Gentiles are included with the "Total Gentile Population.")

Sources: Gentile Population—Computed on the basis of statistics in SDR, vol. 207, Part VI, pp. 626–27; German and Eastern Jews—ZfDS, XII (1916), p. 35; Total Aliens—Erg., 1916, p. 76.

3. Note that the figures on the "Total Gentile Population" and the "Total Jews" include aliens. The "Total Alien Population" figures include Russian and Austrian Jews.

Sources: Gentile Population—Computed on the basis of statistics in SDR, vol. 206, Part V, pp. 254–55; Jewish Population—Ibid.; Russian and Austrian Jews—ZfDS, VII (1912), p. 106–07; Total Aliens—Erg., 1916, p. 42.

4. The number of foreign Jews was not subtracted from the figure on the "Total Alien Population" since our data on the two groups date from different years.

Sources: Total Gentile Population and Jewish Population—Computed on the basis of SDR, vol. 207, VI, pp. 603–04; Total Aliens—Erg., 1916, VI, pp. 75; Foreign Jews—ZfDS, X (1914), p. 115.

TABLE V. Occupational Distribution (Continued)

b. Russians, Austrians, and Rumanians in Germany (c. 1910)

Occupational Category		Russians (a)	Russian Jews (b) M	(c) B	(d) H	Austrians (a)	Austrian Jews (b) M	(c) B	(d) H	Rumanians (a)	Rumanian Jews (b) M	(c) B	All Aliens (a)	Alien Jews (b) M	(c) B	(d) H
Agriculture	A	69,485	2	—	—	57,322	—	—	—	24	—	—	158,404			
	%	63.56	0.54	0.26	—	15.84	—	—	—	1.23	—	—	21.32	0.1	.1	.1
Industry	A	17,850	118	—	301	219,816	151	1,864	48	498	11	—	384			
	%	16.33	32.15	50.4	38.69	60.75	19.09	47.26	12.12	25.55	32.4	36.33	51.74	23.5	47.6	30.
Commerce & Transport	A	5,432	68	—	133	39,351	523	1,784	171	431	10	—	78,402			
	%	4.97	18.6	35.6	17.0	10.9	66.1	45.2	43.2	22.1	2.94	57.4	10.55	48.0	43.	26.
Domestic Service	A	1,973	3	—	1	10,611	3	198	7	18	—	—	18,531			
	%	1.8	0.8	1.58	0.13	2.9	0.4	5.0	11.8	0.92	11.8	0.9	2.5	6.0	3.8	1.
Free Prof. & Civil Service	A	1,988	16	—	7	9,664	41	97	—	187	—	—	25,462			
	%	1.82	4.4	12.3	0.9	2.67	5.2	2.5	—	9.6	—	5.3	3.43	7.0	6.0	.7
Without Occupation	A	12,584	160	—	336	25,088	73	—	170	791	121	—	77,987			
	%	11.5	43.6		43.2	6.93	9.23		42.9	40.6	36.3		10.49	21.0	—	43.
Total		109,312	367		778	361,852	791	3,943	396	1,949	142		743,103			

M = Munich
B = Berlin
H = Hesse

Note: Occupational tables do not include the dependents of working people. Only the employed and the employable are counted. (Data on Eastern Jews in Hesse could not be controlled to exclude dependents. For this reason the "Without Occupation" category for Eastern Jews in this state is unusually large.) In addition, individuals who resided in their places of work were not included in any of these tables.

Sources: (a) Erg., 1916., pp. 22, 23, 43.
(b) Paula Odenbacher, *Die Berufe der Juden in München* (München, 1918), p. 71.
(c) Eschelbacher, 1920, p. 17.
(d) ZfDS, VIII (1912), pp. 106–07.

TABLE V

c. Natives and Aliens in the "Large Cities" (c. 1910)

Occupational Category	Gentile Population* A(1907)	%	Total Jews* A(1907)	%	Total Aliens† A(1910)	%	Percent of Eastern Jews Berlin (1910)	Percent of Eastern Jews Munich (1907)
Agriculture	13,560	1.34	514	0.22	4,066	2.13	.10	0.19
Industry	6,016,453	57.73	72,829	31.81	111,649	58.58	47.62	30.35
Commerce & Transport	2,931,604	28.13	133,777	58.43	50,297	26.39	42.89	61.95
Domestic Service	332,921	3.19	1,233	0.54	9,014	4.73	3.75	0.77
Free Prof. & Civil Service	1,000,313	9.60	20,585	8.99	15,552	8.16	5.63	6.74
Total	10,420,851		228,938		190,578		6,153	1,038

A = Absolute numbers
% = Percentage of the particular population.
Sources: *Computed on the basis of ZfDS, VII (1911), p. 88. The figures include aliens.
†Erg., 1916, p. 59.
Note that the category "Without Occupation" has been excluded from these figures.

TABLE V

d. Protestants, Catholics, and Jews in Germany (1907)

Occupational Category	Jews A	%	Protestants A	%	Catholics A	%	Percentage of Christians in Category
Agriculture	3,746	1.30	5,491,734	29.75	4,363,593	38.45	28.91
Industry	62,995	21.88	7,051,792	38.20	4,081,894	35.93	42.93
Commerce & Transport	145,606	50.56	2,274,154	12.32	1,039,554	9.15	13.02
Domestic Service	1,350	0.47	319,187	1.73	149,371	1.31	1.29
Free Prof. & Civil Service	18,848	6.55	1,153,361	6.24	448,990	4.92	5.50
No occupation	55,417	19.24	2,172,124	11.77	1,162,594	10.23	8.23
Total	287,962		18,462,353		11,360,996		

A = Absolute numbers.
% = Percentage of the religious group.
Sources: The data on Jews, Protestants, and Catholics have been compiled on the basis of SDR, vol. 203, p. 54.
Figures in the column on "Percentage of Christians in Category" are taken from ZfDS, VI (1910), p. 165.

Notes

Introduction

1. Mordechai Eliav has noted four possible etymologies for the term *Yekke*, while admitting that none is very satisfying: (1) it derives from the *Jacke*, "jacket," sported by German Jews in contrast to the caftan commonly worn by East Europeans; (2) it serves as an acronym for the Hebrew words *Yehudi Kashe Havana*, "a dim-witted Jew"; it is a derivative of (3) *Jeck* or (4) Jacob, terms that denote fools, according to German dialect. "German Jews' Share in the Building of the National Home in Palestine and the State of Israel," YBLBI, 1985, p. 261, note 23.

2. Daniel J. Elazar, "Sephardim and Ashkenazim: The Classic and Romantic Traditions in Jewish Civilization," *Judaism*, vol. 33 (Spring 1984), p. 149. Austin Stevens, *The Dispossessed* (London, 1975) pp. 119–20. For another two instances in which distinguished scholars emphasize the negativity of German Jewry, see Hannah Arendt, "Privileged Jews," JSS, vol. VIII (Jan. 1946), pp. 25–28, and Theodore S. Hamerow, "Cravat and Caftan Jews," *Commentary*, vol. 77 (May 1984), pp. 34–35.

3. Steven E. Aschheim, *Brothers and Strangers: The East European Jew in German and German Jewish Consciousness, 1800–1923* (Madison, Wisc., 1982). In the preface to his book, Aschheim graciously acknowledges the complementarity of my work with his and takes note of the different approaches we have taken. The present introduction further explicates what I hope to accomplish by examining the political and social history of East European Jews who resided in the Second Empire.

During the course of this study, we will have occasion to cite the judgment of historians such as Lloyd Gartner, Peter Gay, Shimshon Kirshenbaum, and Zosa Szajkowski regarding German Jewish attitudes toward Eastern Jews. Their writings are augmented by many "oral traditions" about the hostility of German Jews toward their Eastern coreligionists.

4. See, for example, the unpublished dissertation of Shimshon Kirshenbaum, which suggests that German Jews drove their Eastern coreligionists out of the *Reich*. (*The Immigration of Jews from Russia and Poland into Germany, France, and England in the Last Quarter of the Nineteenth Century and Their Settlements in these Countries* [in Hebrew], Hebrew University, Jerusalem, 1950. See especially p. 290.)

5. For a number of older works on Eastern Jews in Weimar Germany, see: Leon Sklarz, *Geschichte und Organisation der Ostjudenhilfe in Deutschland seit dem Jahre 1914* (Dissertation, Rostock, 1927); Werner Fraustädter, *Die ostjüdische Arbeitereinwanderung im Rheinisch-Westfälischen-Industriegebiet* (Dissertation, Frankfurt am Main, n.d.); Shalom Adler-Rudel, *Ostjuden in Deutschland, 1880–1940* (Tübingen, 1959) (written by a participant in German Jewish social programs on behalf of Eastern Jews, this oft-cited volume is more of a memoir than a scholarly monograph); and Zosa Szajkowski, "East European Jewish Workers in Germany During World War I," *Salo Baron Jubilee Volume*, II (Jerusalem, 1975). Several scholars in the Federal Republic are presently concluding research on this period as well. For some initial findings, see Ludger Heid, "East European Jewish

Workers in the Ruhr, 1915–1922," YBLBI, 1985, pp. 141–68; and Trude Maurer, "The East European Jew in the Weimar Press: Stereotype and Attempted Rebuttal," *Studies in Contemporary Jewry*, I (1984), pp. 176–98.

6. It is difficult to state categorically when a particular term came into vogue. Still, I have been repeatedly struck by the absence of the terms *Ostjuden* and *Ostjudenfrage* both in government correspondence and public papers written prior to the outbreak of World War I. When writers did employ the term *Ostjuden* before the war, it was only in reference to Jews living in the East, not to ˚migrants settling in the West. In 1910, Binjamin Segal noted that the term *Ostjuden* had *lately (in neuster Zeit)* gained currency as a term describing "the seven to eight million Jews in Russia, Poland, Galicia, Bukowina, and Romania." (*Die Entdeckungsreise des Herrn Dr. Theodor Lessing zu den Ostjuden* [Lwow, 1910], p. 2.)

For an essay that stresses the Eastern origin and typology of Prussian Jewry, see Werner Cahnman, "A Regional Approach to German Jewish History," JSS (1943), pp. 216–24.

7. For a probing analysis of the ongoing German problem with people who do not conform, "who are not normal," see Ralf Dahrendorf, *Society and Democracy in Germany* (Garden City, N.Y., 1969), especially Chapters 5 and 22. References to the historical literature on Polish and other foreiogn workers will be cited below.

8. For two major studies presenting opposing interpretations, see Paul Massing, *Rehearsal for Destruction: A Study of Political Anti-Semitism in Imperial Germany* (New York, 1967), and Richard S. Levy, *The Downfall of the Anti-Semitic Political Parties in Imperial Germany* (New Haven, 1975).

In pointing to the continuity of German xenophobia and anti-Semitism from the Imperial era into the Third *Reich*, we are implicitly rejecting the views of those who regard Nazi policies as aberrant and discontinuous with earlier German behavior. The question of continuity has been raised afresh in David Blackbourn and Geoff Eley, *The Peculiarities of German History* (Oxford and New York, 1984), especially pp. 28–35. See also the important review essay of Robert G. Moeller, *"Die Besonderheiten der Deutschen? Neue Beiträge zur Sonderwegdiskussion," Internationale Schulbuchforschung*, IV, no. 1 (1982), pp. 71–80.

9. Steven E. Aschheim, "The East European Jew and German Jewish Identity," *Studies in Contemporary Jewry*, I (1984), pp. 21–22.

10. For some of the major works on the absorption of East European Jews in Western lands, see the references infra, the Conclusion.

Chapter 1

1. Early works generally dated the Jewish mass migration to the pogroms of 1881. (See, for example, Simon Dubnow, *History of the Jews in Russia and Poland* [Phila., 1918], II, p. 373.) But more recently historians have tended to view the migration as a response to economic strangulation in the Pale, and accordingly they pay attention to crises that occurred before the assassination of the tsar. Salo Baron writes that "the turning point came during the great famine and epidemics of 1868–69." (*The Russian Jews Under Czars and Soviets*, rev. ed. [New York, 1976], pp. 70, 72. See also Mark Wischnitzer, *To Dwell in Safety* (Philadelphia, 1948), pp. 29ff., and Elias Tcherikower, ed., *The Early Jewish Labor Movement in the United States* (New York, 1961), English text, pp. 54, 65.

For contemporary Jewish newspaper accounts that noted the upsurge of Jewish migration from western Russia, see the following numbers of the AZJ: May 18, 1869, pp. 390–91; Aug. 17, 1869, pp. 675; Aug. 24, 1869, p. 674; Sept. 7, 1869, pp. 716–17. In June

1869, several Christians joined in relief efforts (AZJ, June 15, 1869, p. 472) and by October 1869 there were calls to convene an international conference to organize the migration (ibid., Oct. 12, 1869). For some early discussions of programs to aid the refugees, see: AZJ, March 2, 1869, pp. 162–64; May 18, 1869, pp. 391ff.; June 1, 1869, pp. 425–27; July 6, 1869, pp. 535–37. During this period, Ludwig Philippson, the editor of the AZJ, submitted a memorandum to the *Deutsch-Israelitischer Gemeindebund* proposing solutions to the problems of Jews in western Russia (CAHJP M1/3/71–73). (Note: In these notes, all references to archival files will cite only file numbers; for the complete titles of all files utilized for this study, see the Bibliography.) In fact, the latter organization had been founded in response to the increased influx of Eastern Jews. (Ismar Schorsch, *Jewish Reactions to German Anti-Semitism.* [New York and Philadelphia, 1972], pp. 25–26.)

2. On the causes of Jewish emigration from Russia, see Salo Baron, pp. 70–71; Mark Wischnitzer, pp. 29ff.; Jacob Lestchinsky, *Jewish Migrations in Recent Generations* (in Hebrew) (Tel Aviv, 1965), pp. 41ff.

3. See the works cited in note 2, as well as the following on emigration from the Austro-Hungarian Empire: Marsha L. Rozenblit, *The Jews of Vienna: Assimilation and Identity, 1867–1914* (Albany, 1983), Chapter 2 and notes. (This book serves as a valuable introduction to the question of Jewish internal migration within the Austro-Hungarian Empire.); Raphael Mahler, "The Economic Background of Jewish Emigration from Galicia to the U.S.," *YIVO Annual of Jewish Social Science,* VII (1952), pp. 255–57. On Rumanian Jewry, see Joseph Kissman, "The Immigration of Rumanian Jews up to 1914," *YIVO Annual,* II/III (1947/48), pp. 160–66.

4. For an elaboration of this thesis, see Simon Kuznets, "Immigration of Russian Jews to the U.S.: Background and Structure," in *Perspectives in American History,* IX (1975).

5. There is a growing literature on anti-immigrant agitation in Western lands at the time of the Jewish mass migration. On the debate in England, see: John A. Garrard, *The English and Immigration* (London, 1971), and Bernard Gainer, *The Alien Invasion* (London, 1974). On French responses, Paula E. Hyman, *From Dreyfus to Vichy: The Remaking of French Jewry, 1906–1939* (New York, 1979). And on American debates, see especially John Higham, *Strangers in the Land: Patterns of American Nativism* (New York, 1972).

6. The laws are published in Ernst Rudolph Huber's *Dokumente zur deutschen Verfassungsgeschichte,* II (Stuttgart, 1964): the law of 1864 is on p. 241; that of 1869, on p. 248; and that of 1870, on p. 250. For an interpretation by a contemporary legal scholar, see Ludwig von Rönne, *Das Staats-Recht der Preussischen Monarchie,* IIb, p. 142, note 3, and ibid., pp. 54–55. See also Leopold Auerbach, *Das Judenthum und seine Bekenner in Preussen und in anderen deutschen Bundesstaaten* (Berlin, 1890), pp. 276–77.

7. On the Austrian trade treaty, see SBR, VIII Leg., I. Session, 1890–92 *Anlageband* V, p. 3218, and the addendum "Easing of Border Traffic," p. 3244. The Russian treaty and the German government's interpretation of its implications regarding border closings are in SBR, IX Leg., II Session, 1893–94 *Anlageband* II, pp. 952ff., and vol. II, p. 1733. It appears that the treaties also waved the requirement for Russians or Austrians to acquire German visas in order to cross into Germany for commercial purposes. (One may infer this from later proposals, in 1903, to introduce such a requirement as a means to keep out revolutionaries. [See Barbara Vogel, *Deutsche Russlandpolitik* (Düsseldorf, 1973), p. 95]). Finally, we must note that only commercial travelers were protected by these treaties, whereas manual laborers enjoyed no such protection. (See the comments of Prussia's minister of interior, DZA II, Rep. 77 Tit. 1176 No. 6 Bd. 1, p. 219 [letter of Aug. 14, 1912]).

8. On the growth of German shipping through the transport of transmigrants, see: Lamar Cecil, *Albert Ballin* (Princeton, 1967), pp. 41–42; as well as the dissertations by Bernhard Karlsberg (*Geschichte und Bedeutung der deutschen Durchwanderkontrolle*

[Hamburg, 1922], especially, p. 241) and Michael Just (*Transitprobleme der osteuro-päischen Amerikaauswanderung durch Deutschland Ende des 19. und Anfang des 20. Jahr-hunderts* [Hamburg, 1977], pp. 27, 36.) For statistics on this transmigration, see: ZfDS (July 1905), p. 12; Leon Sklarz, op. cit., p. 70; Mark Wischnitzer, op. cit., p. 70; and Walter F. Wilcox, ed., *International Migrations*, I, pp. 384–92.

9. On border controls, see the AZJ: May 1882, pp. 414–16 (article by Lina Morgen-stern); June 1882, p. 409; Dec. 19, 1893, *Beilage* 1; and the IR, May 2, 1902, p. 5. On the lobbying of German shipping companies to keep the borders open, see: Staatsarchiv Hamburg, Auswanderungsamt I, II EI 1a No. 4, and Karlsberg, pp. 188 and 193.

10. On border policies prior to 1885, see Helmuth Neubach, *Die Ausweisungen von Polen und Juden aus Preussen, 1885–86* (Wiesbaden, 1967), pp. 3, 15. The AZJ reports on orders given to border guards in 1885 (May 5, 1885, p. 303). For twentieth-century developments, see Vogel, pp. 101, 266, and Wilcox, II, p. 378. The *Königsberger Volks-zeitung* reported on the penalties faced by smugglers (clipping of Jan. 30, 1905 issue, DZA II, Rep. 77 Tit. 226 Nr. 130 vol. 1).

11. Selig Brodetsky, *Memoirs: From Ghetto to Israel* (London, 1960), p. 15.

12. See the following for accounts of Jews who crossed into Germany illegally: Ignatz Waghalter, *Aus dem Ghetto in die Freiheit* (Marienbad, 1936), pp. 61–64; Israel Sieff, *Memoirs* (London, 1970), pp. 9–10; J. P. Nettl, *Rosa Luxemburg*, I (London, 1966), p. 59; and *Ha-Melitz*, no. 134 (1895), pp. 2–3. (I am indebted to Shimshon Kirshenbaum's dissertation, op. cit., for most references cited in this work to the Hebrew periodicals *Ha-Magid, Ha-Melitz,* and *Ha-Tzephira*.) All of the above cases refer to the illegal entry of Russian Jews; entering Germany from the Austro-Hungarian Empire was considerably eas-ier and safer. Alexander Granach, a Galician, recalls in his memoirs how he entered Ger-many simply by posing as a worker crossing the border to purchase some good German beer (*There Goes an Actor*. [New York, 1945], p. 136). In order to stem the smuggling traffic, the government imposed a six-month prison sentence and 1,000-mark fine on any-one convicted of aiding Russians to cross illegally into Prussia. (See press clipping from the *Königsberger Volkszeitung*, Jan. 30, 1905, in DZA II, Rep. 77 Tit. 226 Nr. 130 vol. 1.)

13. See Johannes Nichtweiss, *Die ausländischen Saisonarbeiter in der Landwirtschaft der östlichen und Mittleren Gebiete des deutschen Reiches* (Berlin, 1959), p. 77, and Lawrence Schofer, *The Formation of a Modern Labor Force: Upper Silesia, 1865–1914* (Berkeley, 1975), pp. 23, 36, on the thousands of migrants who entered Prussia daily from the east. For the case of a Jewish ritual slaughterer who commuted two to three times weekly, see JP, Nov. 5, 1885, p. 456. Waghalter (op. cit., pp. 63–64) describes inns along the border that catered largely to smugglers and their human cargo.

14. For a summary of the powers exercised by state authorities and an outline of the administrative system, see Frank J. Goodnow, *Comparative Administrative Law* (New York, 1903), pp. 297ff., and Herbert Jacob, *German Administration Since Bismarck: Central Authority Versus Local Authority* (New Haven, 1963), pp. 1–66.

The present section provides a basic outline of state prerogatives regarding aliens. The specific application of these powers will be elaborated and more fully documented in Chap-ter 3.

15. P. Altmann, *Die Verfassung und Verwaltung im Deutschen Reiche und Preussen*, II (Berlin, 1908), p. 265. For an example of registration regulations in a Prussian district, including the requirement that an alien had to register with the local police within three days of his arrival and to keep them informed of his movements, see Hauptstaatsarchiv Düsseldorf, Zweigstelle Schloss Kalkum, Reg. Düsseldorf #30524.

16. For examples of regulations in Charlottenburg, Cologne, and Hamburg requiring

employers to give preference to native Germans over aliens, see Max Schippel, "Die Fremden Arbeitskräfte und die Gesetzgebungen der verschiedenen Länder," *Die Neue Zeit,* vol. 25 II, no. 41 (1907), pp. 60–63. See below, Chapter 3, for examples of restrictions placed upon certain categories of foreign Jews. On the law of public assembly, see Huber, IV, p. 296. And on restrictions placed upon political activities, see below, Chapter 7.

17. For the text of the law, Huber, II, #192. See also the English translation: *German Law Respecting the Acquisition and Loss of the Federal and State Nationality, June 1, 1870* (London, 1890).

18. Quoted from Generallandesarchiv. Karlsruhe, Abt. 233/11143. Letter from Staatsministerium of Hesse to Baden Foreign Ministry, Oct. 27, 1904.

19. On the grounds for expulsion, Werner Kobarg, *Ausweisung und Abweisung von Ausländern* (Berlin, 1930), pp. 50ff. and, especially, p. 66. On Bavarian policies specifically, Paul Scherber, *Die rechtliche Stellung der Ausländer in Bayern* (Würzburg, 1894), p. 5.

20. For estimates of the "Gain or Loss of Population in Germany" between 1871 and 1910, see Wilcox, II, p. 36. See below, Chapter 4, for more detailed statistics on aliens in the *Reich.*

21. Nettl discusses wage differences (*Rosa Luxemburg,* I, pp. 42–43). Hans-Ulrich Wehler refers to the attractiveness of Polish labor to Prussian estate owners (*Krisenherde des Kaiserreichs, 1871–1914* [Göttingen, 1970], p. 187). See also Nichtweiss, pp. 28–29. In recent years, Klaus J. Bade has published a series of essays on the importation of Polish workers. See especially *Transnationale Migration und Arbeitsmarkt im Kaiserreich: Vom Agrarstaat mit starker Industrie zum Industriestaat mit starker agrarischer Basis (Historische Arbeitsmarktforschung),* ed. Toni Pierenkemper and Richard Tilly (Göttingen, 1982), pp. 182–214; *'Preussengänger' und 'Abwehrpolitik.' Ausländerbeschäftigung, Ausländerpolitik und Ausländerkontrolle auf dem Arbeitsmarkt in Preussen vor dem Ersten Weltkrieg, Archiv für Sozialgeschichte,* vol. XXIV (1984); and his essays in the colloquium he edited, *Auswanderer, Wanderarbeiter, Gastarbeiter: Bevölkerung, Arbeitsmarkt und Wanderung in Deutschland seit der Mitte des 19. Jahrhunderts,* 2 vol. (Ostfildern, 1984). On the causes and dimensions of the emigration, see Mack Walker, *Germany and the Emigration, 1816–1885.* (Cambridge, Mass., 1964), pp. 181, 184, 192.

22. Wilcox, II, p. 387. On fears of Polish nationalism, see Hans Ulrich Wehler, *Sozialdemokratie und Nationalstaat: Nationalitätenfrage in Deutschland 1840–1914,* rev. ed., (Göttingen, 1971), p. 108. The Germanization policy has been studied by Richard W. Tims, *Germanizing Prussian Poland, 1894–1919.* (New York, 1941); Robert L. Koehl, "Colonialism Inside Germany, 1886–1918," *Journal of Modern History,* XXV (Sept. 1953); and Wehler, ibid. On the protests of Junkers and industrialists, see Neubach (Document 10, pp. 233–34) and Nichtweiss (pp. 34ff.).

23. For statistics on Poles in Germany, see Waldemar Mitscherlisch, *Die Ausbreitung der Polen in Preussen* (Leipzig, 1913), p. 21. Also Wehler, *Krisenherde,* p. 219, and *Sozialdemokratie,* pp. 103, 123. Richard Charles Murphy's *Guestworkers in the German Reich: A Polish Community in Wilhelmian Germany* (New York, 1983) examines the experience of Prussiasn Poles in Bottrop, a coal-mining city in the Ruhr. His findings, however, contradict the title of the book: Murphy argues that these Prussian Poles *were* absorbed into the pluralistic communities of the Ruhr; it is therefore unclear why he describes them as "guest workers."

24. Koehl (p. 262) discusses motives for the *Kulturkampf;* Wehler (*Sozialdemokratie,* pp. 110ff.) analyzes the stages of the Germanization policy as well as efforts to undermine the legal status of Prussian Poles (ibid., pp. 188–89, and *Krisenherde,* pp. 188, 234–36).

For a review essay that draws together much of the recent literature on the subject, see Geoff Eley, "German Politics and Polish Nationality: The Dialectic of Nation-Forming in the East of Prussia," *East European Quarterly* (Sept. 1984), pp. 335–59.

25. Nichtweiss, pp. 43–57, 138ff. Also J. Langhard, *Das Niederlassungsrecht der Ausländer in der Schweiz* (Zurich, 1913), p. 57.

26. For a good analysis of Prussian policies toward Polish seasonal workers, see Klaus J. Bade, "Politik und Ökonomie der Ausländerbeschäftigung im preussischen Osten, 1885–1914. Die Internationalisierung des Arbeitsmarkts im 'Rahmen der preussischen Abwehrpolitik,' " *Preussen im Rückblick, Geschichte und Gesellschaft, Sonderheft,* 6, pp. 273–99. See especially note 24, on the exclusion of Jews from seasonal labor.

In his memorandum admitting Polish seasonal laborers to Prussia, the minister of interior forbade the acceptance of Jews from Russia on the grounds that they are not workers. (GStA, Preussisches Justizministerium, Rep. 84a Nr. 14. Memorandum of Nov. 26, 1890.) This decision to discriminate between Jewish and Christian Poles in the recruitment of seasonal laborers was the decisive factor shaping the different experiences of these two groups in Imperial Germany. Until Bade underscored the point, German historians have overlooked the distinction and consequently have treated Polish Jews as merely an extension of the larger population of Poles in the *Reich*. For this reason, most German historians writing about the expulsions of Poles in the 1880s do not even mention that one-third of the victims were Jewish. (For more on this issue, see below, Chapter 3.)

Commissioner Madai's comment appears in a letter to the minister of interior (DZA II, Rep. 77 Tit. 1176 Nr. 1K Bd. 1, p. 20).

27. See below, Chapters 2 and 3, on lobbying to restrict Jewish immigration and on policies in Prussia's eastern provinces.

Chapter 2

1. German leaders repeatedly characterized Eastern Jews as an "unwanted element." Bismarck so described them in a cabinet meeting of May 22, 1881 (Neubach, p. 4). His minister of interior, Robert von Puttkamer, also employed the term (Albert von Puttkamer, *Staatsminister von Puttkamer: Ein Stück preussischer Vergangenheit* [Leipzig, 1928], p. 97). In 1905 government officials such as Chancellor von Bülow spoke of *"unliebsame Elemente"* (Leo Stern, ed., *Die Auswirkung der ersten russischen Revolution von 1905–07 auf Deutschland. Archivalische Forschungen zur Geschichte der deutschen Arbeiterbewegung* [East Berlin, 1955], 2/I, Document 52, pp. 138, 142). On officials depicting such Jews as a *"Landplage,"* see Neubach, p. 5, note 1, and SBR, IX Leg., II Session, 1893–94, vol. III, p. 1741.

2. On Bismarck's earliest statement, see Horst Kohl, *Die politischen Reden des Fuersten Bismarck* (Stuttgart, 1892; reprinted, 1969), I, p. 29; Heinrich von Treitschke, *History of Germany in the Nineteenth Century,* trans. Eden and Cedar Paul (New York, 1919), VII, pp. 449–57; Hans Wendt, *Bismarck und die Polnische Frage* (Halle, 1922), p. 3. For remarks dating to the 1880s, see Neubach, Document #20, p. 239. Bismarck on Russian Jews: AZJ, Nov. 11, 1892, *Beilage,* p. 1, and Albert von Puttkamer, p. 97.

3. The rationale for the expulsions was stated by Count Lerchenfeld (Neubach, p. 21 and also pp. 13, 20,). Puttkamer is quoted, ibid., p. 43; see also AZJ, March 2, 1886, p. 152. The term *Ueberläufer* and other pejorative epithets for Eastern Jews are discussed in Neubach, p. 1, note 2. Ambassadorial reports from Russia further strengthened the linkage of Jews and radicalism. (See ALBI, Microfilm #152, for examples.) Russian officials, of

course, encouraged such attitudes by constantly accusing Jews of radicalism; see, for example, Minister von Plehve's claim that "in the Russian South, Jews represent 90% and in the interior 40% of the revolutionaries" (AZJ, July 31, 1903, p. 362).

4. Two successors of Bismarck in the German chancellory, Caprivi and Hohenlohe-Schillingfürst, even took a more benign attitude toward Jews. Caprivi publicly attacked anti-Semitism during this period (SBR, IX Leg., 11 Session, 1893–94. vol. I, pp. 192–93, and Richard Levy, *The Downfall of the Anti-Semitic Political Parties in Germany* [New Haven, 1975], p. 74). And his successor even objected to the harsh treatment meted out to Eastern Jews: expulsions often occur, Schillingfürst wrote, "simply because an anti-Semitic representative of Germanism [*Deutschtum*] sees a threat when a few Polish-Jewish families seek out Posen or Upper Silesia in order to turn themselves from Polish Jews into civilized, international Israelites" (quoted in Neubach, p. 166).

5. On the linkage of Russian Jewish students with radicalism: Botho Brachmann, *Russische Sozialdemokraten in Berlin, 1895–1914* (East Berlin, 1962), pp. 15ff., and Leo Stern, 2/I. On the kaiser: Isaac Don Levine, *Letters from the Kaiser to the Czar* (New York, 1920), p. 224. Bethmann-Hollweg's speech is summarized in AZJ May 18, 1906, pp. 230–31, and MAV, XVI (May 16, 1906), p. 149. The "Mandelstamm-Silberfarb" speech is cited in Barbara Vogel, pp. 95–96. Robert C. Williams discusses the association of Russian Jews with revolution in *Culture in Exile* (Ithaca, N.Y., 1972), p. 50. Williams dates the linkage to 1905, but, as noted above, some German officials already associated Jews with subversiveness during the nineteenth century.

6. SBR, IX Leg., II Session, 1905–06, vol. IV, p. 2875. For an analysis of von Bülow's antipathy toward Eastern Jews, see Egmont Zechlin, *Die deutsche Politik und die Juden im Ersten Weltkrieg* (Göttingen, 1969), pp. 261–62. For the comments of the Bavarian Center Party leader, Hermann, on "Pushy beggars," see JR, Sept. 23, 1904, pp. 414–15. For the use of the term *Schnorrer* as a shorthand for Polish Jews, see the *Greifswalder Zeitung*, quoted in AZJ, Nov. 23, 1875.

7. On the delousing of transmigrants, AZJ, May 1882, pp. 409, 414–16, and Wiliams, p. 33. Hamburg epidemic: Helga Krohn, *Die Juden in Hamburg, 1848–1918* (Hamburg, 1974), p. 189. A few months prior to the outbreak there are reports stressing that "aside from a few streets in the city, the existence of Russian Jews is barely visible" (AZJ, Oct. 16, 1891, *Beilage*, p. 2). Marburg: AZJ, Sept. 14, 1894, p. 3. Even the *Vossische Zeitung*, a liberal newspaper, accused Polish Jews of infecting the Berlin city shelter with bugs; but no evidence of this was found (MAV III [Oct. 1, 1893], p. 372).

8. A worthwhile, though unpublished, collection of anti-Semitic cartoons was undertaken by S. Etlinger and is available in the CAHJP (Inv. 3109 [1–6]). See especially the numerous caricatures of East European Jews taken from from the *Megendorfer Blätter, Jugend, Lustige Blätter*, and *Simplicissimus*. (A few of these were reprinted by Eduard Fuchs, *Die Juden in der Karikatur* [Munich, 1921].) For a brief discussion of German popular stereotypes of Eastern Jews, see Aschheim, pp. 58–62. Particularly in light of the Nazis' subsequent demonization of Eastern Jews, the entire subject warrants further research.

9. For the minutes of the cabinet meeting, GStA, Rep. 91 Nr. 2253, Dec. 18, 1905. The need to protect native Germans from foreign Jews was expressed frequently; see, for example, the remarks of Münster's *Regierungspräsident* in DZA II, Rep. 77 Tit. 1176 Nr. 4a Bd. 1, pp. 106–08. In a letter dated Jan. 13, 1908, Prussia's minister of interior discusses the reasons for expelling a Jewish engineer named Kohn from Oppeln; aside from questions of policy, he aludes to the inferior quality of Eastern Jews (DZA II, Rep. 77 Tit. 1176 Nr. 7 Bd. 1, pp. 166–71).

10. For the opinion of leaders of the H-K-T Society on Poles and the Polish language,

see Tims, pp. 115, note 24, and on Herbert von Bismarck's remarks, see p. 134. On the link between Eastern Jews and Poles, see the anti-Semitic work by Gottfried Wolff, *Das Judentum in Bayern* (Munich, 1894), p. 62, and the *Norddeutsche Allgemeine Zeitung* as quoted in AZJ, April 15, 1885, p. 239. See also IR, Oct. 25, 1901, which quotes the *Posener Tageblatt* to the same effect. In the absence of more research on German stereotype of Poles, it is difficult to draw a more detailed comparison with stereotypes of Eastern Jews. (For a publication that begins to perform the former task, but mainly concentrates on the Weimar period, see Harry Kenneth Rosenthal, *German and Pole* [Gainsville, Fla., 1976].)

11. Treitschke's articles are reprinted in his *Deutsche Kämpfe* (N.F., Leipzig, 1896). They are translated into English in Helen Lederer, trans., *A Word About Our Jewry, Readings in Modern Jewish History*, ed. Ellis Rivkin (Cincinnati, 1958). Quotations are from Lederer, pp. 2, 3, 6, 7. Walter Böhlich, ed., *Der Berliner Antisemitismusstreit* (Frankfurt am Main, 1965), is a valuable compilation of polemical contributions to the Treitschke controversy. See also Michael Meyer, "Great Debate on Anti-Semitism—Jewish Reactions to New Hostility in Germany 1879–1880," YBLBI, XI (1966), pp. 137–70.

12. The *Preussische Jahrbücher* quotations are found in Lederer, pp. 2, 43. The 1883 article is in the *Preussische Jahrbücher*, vol. 52, pp. 534–38. See p. 538 for the quotation on the Polish character of Prussian Jews. On Posen Jews, see Treitschke, *History of Germany*, vol. VII, pp. 450, 452.

13. Adolf Wagner: *Zeitschrift für die gesamte Staatswissenschaft*, vol. XXXVI (1890), p. 779. See below, Chapter 9 on Neumann. Eugen von Bergmann, *Zur Geschichte der Entwickelung deutscher, polnischer und jüdischer Bevölkerung in der Provinz Posen seit 1824* (Tübingen, 1883), p. 317. Also see his "Die Jüdische Einwanderung in Deutschland," *Die Grenzboten*, vol. 43, I (*Erstes Quartal*, 1884), pp. 284, 286, for additional examples of the blurring of boundaries between Prussian subjects and Poles. For another anti-Semitic work that takes the same approach, see Richard Andre, *Zur Volkskunde der Juden* (Bielefeld and Leipzig, 1881), p. 260.

For two contemporary Jewish writers who clearly understood Treitschke's intention to attack Posen Jews and attempted to refute the historian's allegations, see Ludwig Bamberger, "Deutschtum und Judentum," in Böhlich, p. 163, and AZJ, Dec. 1883, pp. 830–31.

14. Euler is quoted in AZJ, Jan. 1895, p. 38. For a similar statement by another Reichstag deputy, see SBR, IX Leg., II Session, 1893–94, vol. II, p. 1746. A clipping of the Baden newspaper, dated April 19, 1898, is in CAHJP, Microfilm H.M. 9873. Hessen's article is quoted in AZJ, Dec. 19, 1898, p. 797.

15. Friedrich Wilhelm Grünow, *Israel und die Gojim. Beiträge zur Beurtheilung der Judenfrage* (Leipzig, 1880), pp. 222–26. The author, incidentally, is a racial anti-Semite who judged Treitschke too moderate (p. 304). Neubach claims that the book's real author was Busch (p. 9). Parts of the book were serialized in *Die Grenzboten*, vol. 139, Section I, (April–June 1880), under the title "The Polish Jews." The article also plays a variation upon a different motif when it pictures Germany as a way station for cultural transformation: The *Reich* thus becomes a "cleaning station" from whence "well-groomed and purified Jews" then move on to other Western lands.

16. For an overview of the key motifs developed by German anti-Semites, see Jacob Katz, *From Prejudice to Destruction.* (Cambridge, Mass., 1980), Chapters 4–7, 12–17. For an example of an anti-Semite who claimed that the German Jew "speaks the language of the nation in which he lives, but always speaks it as a foreigner," see Friedrich Dukmeyer, *Kritik der reinen und praktischen Unvernunft in der gemeinen Verjudung* (Berlin, 1892), p. 33. It is appropriate in this regard to recall Richard Wagner's association of

Yiddish with German Jewry's inability to grasp properly the essence of German culture. See also George Mosse's analysis of two popular novelists who "regarded the Jews of Poland as typically 'Jewish' " ("Felix Dahn and Gustav Freytag," YBLBI, II [1957], p. 2).

The metamorphosis of "Moses Pinkeles" appears in a Reichstag address (SBR, IX Leg., III Session, 1894–95, vol. II, p. 1290). *Simplicissimus* ran a cartoon about "Moische Pisch" in issue no. 10, 1903. For a Nazi version of this metamorphosis "from Ghetto Jew to Big Business," see the *Stürmer*, Feb., 1940. (Both of the cartoons are in Etlinger's collection, vol. II, unpaged.)

17. On the anti-Semitic petition, see Schorsch, p. 37, and Levy, p. 21. A clipping of the *Staatsbürgerzeitung* dated March 3, 1880, is in CAHJP P/52. See the same archive for copies of the petition (MI/5).

18. Leopold Auerbach, *Das Judenthum und seine Bekenner in Preussen und in anderen deutschen Bundesstaaten* (Berlin, 1890), p. 35. On the lapse in Prussian confessional tabulations, see Solomon Neumann, *Zur Statistik der Juden in Preussen von 1816 bis 1880* (Berlin, 1884), p. 7. Neumann contended in that work that the recent inclusion of confessional data in Prussian statistical works was the result of recent anti-Semitic agitation (p. 6). See SJDR, vol. I (1880), for evidence that the 1875 census questionnaire included questions on confession, but that data on this subject were not published. By contrast, local statistical bureaus never stopped publishing data on confessional matters during this period. See, for example, the *Statistisches Jahrbuch der Stadt Berlin*, 1878.

19. Levy, p. 166, and the broader discussion entitled "The Parliamentary Solution Is Tested."

20. Bills to prohibit Jewish immigration were introduced by Reichstag deputies during the following sessions: March 17, 1893 (SBR, VIII Leg., II Session, 1892–93, *Anlageband* II); Dec. 5, 1894 (SBR, IX Leg., III Session, 1894–95, *Anlageband* I, #54); 1896 (SBR, IX Leg., IV Session, *Anlageband* I, #44); Dec. 9, 1897 (SBR, IX Leg., V Session, 1897–98, *Anlageband* I); Dec. 15, 1898 (SBR, X Leg., I Session, 1898–99, *Anlageband* I); Nov. 23, 1900 (SBR, X Leg., II Session, 1900–02, *Anlageband* I, #58).

21. On the alliance between *Kreuzzeitung* Conservatives and anti-Semitic political parties, see Levy, Chapter Three, and especially pp. 70–73, 83, 173.

22. The Hammerstein/Manteuffel bill was dated March 17, 1893 (SBR, VII Leg., II Session, 1892–93, *Anlageband* II, *Aktenstück* 163); it was co-sponsored by twenty-eight of the sixty-four members of the Conservative Party. The bill was debated in the Reichstag on Feb. 27 and March 6, 1895 (see SBR, IX Leg., III Session, 1894–1895, vol. II, pp. 1304–05, on the vote). On the vote of 1909, Levy, p. 244.

23. Werner T. Angress, "The Impact of the *Judenwahlen* of 1912 on the Jewish Question—A Synthesis," YBLBI, 1983, p. 409. On the new right-wing coalition, see Geoff Eley, *Reshaping the German Right: Radical Nationalism and Political Change After Bismarck* (New Haven, 1980).

24. On Class' views, see Daniel Frymann (pseud. Heinrich Class), *Wenn ich der Kaiser wär* (Leipzig, 1912), pp. 74–76. While the Pan-German League did not embrace anti-Semitism publicly until Class assumed leadership, an earlier chairman, Professor Ernst Hasse, voted for the 1893 Hammerstein/Manteuffel bill, arguing that without it Germany would be deluged by a half-million Jews from the East. (On Hasse's stance, see SBR, IX Leg., III Session, 1894–95, vol. II, p. 1277, and X Leg., vol. III, p. 1735; see also, Levy, p. 167). For examples of efforts by right-wing lobbyists to promote restrictionism, see the petitions submitted to the Reichstag by the *Deutscher Volksbund* in Feb. 1906 with the support of the Pan-German League (SBR, IX Leg., II Session, *Achter Anlageband* #601,

pp. 3688–89). Similarly, in 1913 nationalists gathered in Eisenbach petitioned the chancellor to ban Jewish immigration (AZJ, Oct. 22, 1913, p. 507).

We may note in this context the long-standing efforts of agrarian forces to promote restrictionism. The most effective press organ of the Agrarian League, the *Deutsche Tageszeitung*, supported a bill banning Jewish immigration, and supporters of the league, such as Chairman von Wangenheim, von Mirbach, and Dr. Hahn, voted for restrictionist bills. On Wangenheim, Hahn, and the newspaper, see MAV, X (Nov. 28, 1900, pp. 380–81); on Mirbach, see AZJ, March 9, 1894, p. 111. For a general analysis of the league's anti-Semitism, see Hans Jürgen Puhle, *Agrarische Interessenpolitik und preussischer Konservatismus im Wilhelminischen Reich (1893–1914)* (Hanover, 1966), pp. 125–40.

25. See below, chapter 3, for a discussion of "The Special Case of Students," an analysis of the agitation and actions taken against Russian Jews at institutions of higher learning. I have discussed the entire issue at greater length and with fuller documentation in my essay "The 'Ausländerfrage' at Institutions of Higher Learning: A Controversy Over Russian-Jewish Students in Imperial Germany," YBLBI, XXVII (1982), pp. 187–215. For the Reichstag debates, see SBR, XII Leg., II Session, 1909–10, vol. 259, p. 1472, and vol. 262, p. 3590, and Resolution #83; see also AZJ, March 5, 1909, p. 110.

26. For restrictionist efforts in the Munich municipality, see BHA, Staatsarchiv München, Ministerium des Innern, #74140, press clippings from the *Augsburger Abendzeitung* (Oct. 21, 1904) and the *Neues Münchener Tageblatt* (Oct. 22, 1904). See also the collection in Stadtarchiv München, Einwohneramt Nr. 169, which includes the petitions of the anti-Semites and protocols of the debate in the *Gemeindekollegiums* of Sept. 9, 1904.

27. Leaflets: *Jüdische Volkszeitung*, Aug. 14, 1894, pp. 3–4. Shoe merchants: Hauptstaatsarchiv Düsseldorf, Zweigstelle Schloss Kalkum, Nr. 8892. Petitions dated Jan. 17, 1913, and Jan. 29, 1914. Bavarian workers: BHA Staatsarchiv München, Munich. Ministry of Interior, Nr. 74141, correspondence of Oct. 11, Nov. 5 and 15, 1900.

28. For a good introduction to the treaties and their impact on German agriculture and industry, see Levy, pp. 71–73. The *Grenzboten* article appeared in vol. 53 (Jan.–June 1894), pp. 417ff. The text of Article 1 is in SBR, IX Leg., II Session, *Anlageband* II, #190; the debate is in ibid., vol. II, pp. 1733ff. On the broader public debate over the treaties, see Kenneth Barkin, *The Controversy Over German Industrialization* (Chicago, 1970), pp. 73–89.

29. On Liebermann's role, see Levy, pp. 21, 203. For Liebermann's depiction of Russian Jews: SBR, XI Leg., II Session, 1905–06, vol. I, p. 232, and vol. 229 (Nov. 30, 1907, debate), p. 1940. For a few examples of the anti-Semites' inability to focus solely on alien Jews, see the speeches of Förster and Ahlwardt in SBR, IX Leg., II Session, vol. III, pp. 1296–97. And also note the speeches of Jacobskrötter and Bindewald, which eventually prompted the president of the Reichstag to rebuke the latter when he drifted from the stated topic of debate—immigration—to a diatribe against German Jewish judges (SBR, IX Leg., II Session, 1894–95, vol. II, pp. 114–48).

30. On the *Kreuzzeitung* circle, see Levy, p. 83. On Hammerstein's stance in 1884 and 1886, see Neubach, pp. 100–02. His opposition to the naturalization of Jews is stated in SBR, IX Leg., II Session, 1893–94, vol. III, p. 1742. On the role of anti-Semitism in the Conservative Party, see Dirk Stegmann, *Die Erben Bismarcks* (Cologne, 1970), pp. 22–24. The Free Conservatives, incidentally, were apparently not as hostile toward Eastern Jews: some restrictionist bills supported by Conservatives were rejected by the Free Conservatives (MAV, Nov. 28, 1900, pp. 380–81).

31. On the speeches of National Liberal deputies concerning the 1885 expulsions, see Neubach, pp. 99–101. See also von Bennigsen's comments quoted by the AZJ, March 9,

1894, p. 111. Bassermann: SBR XI Leg., II Session, vol. IV (May 3, 1906), p. 2888–89. Paasche: SBR IX Leg., III Session, vol. II, 1894–95 (Feb. 27, 1895), p. 1152.

32. On the inconsistent stance of the Center Party, see Marjorie Lamberti, *Jewish Activism in Imperial Germany: The Struggle for Legal Equality* (New Haven, 1978), pp. 79–80. The relationship of the Center Party to anti-Semitism has been reevaluated in David Blackbourn, "Roman Catholics, the Centre Party and Anti-Semitism in Imperial Germany," in Paul Kennedy and Anthony Nicholls, eds., *Nationalist and Racialist Movements in Britain and Germany Before 1914* (London, 1981), pp. 106–129. (See especially the distinction Blackbourn draws between the polite anti-Semitism of national leaders and the cruder expressions on the grass-roots level.) See AZJ for the Center's stance regarding the expulsions of the 1880s (Dec. 13, 1885, pp. 816–17). Lieber's speech is in SBR, IX Leg., III Session, 1894–95, vol. II, pp. 1286ff., and translated by Paul Massing in his *Rehearsal for Destruction* (New York, 1949), document IV, p. 295. No Center Party deputies voted for a ban on Jewish immigration. On Center Party opposition to the expulsions of 1905–06, see SBR, XI Leg., II Session, 1905–06, vol. IV, speeches by Spahn, etc. For an example of a local Center politician who lobbied for restrictions on Jewish immigrants, see our discussion of Munich's Councilman Herrmann earlier in this chapter.

Polish deputies in the Reichstag consistently urged resolutions that would require German governments to follow comprehensive guidelines regarding the residence of aliens. See, for example, Resolution #899 in SBR, XII Leg., II Session, 1909–11.

33. A debate over the Petition was prompted by the Progressives' challenge. (See *Die Judenfrage im preussischen Abgeordnetenhause* [Berlin, 1880].) On the Progressives' stand in 1885, see Neubach, pp. 97, 99. See also the following on the positions taken by Progressive deputies: SBR, IX Leg., III Session, 1894–95, vol. II, p. 1290 (Heine's speech); SBR, IX Leg., IV Session, 1894–95, p. 1283 (Rickert's address); Barbara Vogel, p. 102 (a challenge in the Prussian Diet regarding the expulsions of 1905–06); and AZJ, Feb. 7, 1908, p. 62 (a motion regarding naturalization).

34. On the role of Progressive leaders in the *Abwehrverein*, see Schorsch, pp. 86–88. The citation for Rickert's speech is in note 31. Georg Gothein also spoke out in defense of Eastern Jews and urged Christian Germans to join their Jewish compatriots in this cause (AZJ, Jan. 5, 1906, p. 2). Möller's articles appear in *Die Nation*, II, no. 50 and 51 (Sept. 12 and 19, 1885). The journal of the defense agency paid considerably more attention to the plight of Jews in the East than to the condition of Eastern Jews in the *Reich*. However, see the following exceptions in MAV: denunciations of government policies as discriminatory against foreign Jews (XII [Nov. 1902], p. 352, and XVIII [April 15, 1908], p. 127); opposition to existing naturalization policies (V [April 27, 1895], p. 136); rejection of restrictionist bills (X [Nov. 28, 1900]); and challenges to expulsion policies (XVI [May 9, 1906], p. 141, and [May 16, 1906], p. 149).

35. Massing, p. 151.

36. This highly generalized analysis of SPD attitudes is based upon the research of Edmund Silberner, a leading scholar of relations between socialists and Jews. See especially his "German Social Democracy and the Jewish Problem Prior to World War I," *Historia Judaica*, XV, Part I (April 1953), pp. 22–24. Marx's comments are quoted in Joseph Nedava, *Trotsky and the Jews* (Philadelphia, 1972), p. 245, note 44. Kautsky's views are discussed in Massing, p. 165. See also Donald Niewyck, "German Social Democracy and the Problem of Anti-Semitism, 1906–1914" (Unpublished M.A. Thesis, Tulane University, 1964), p. 30, which quotes an article from the Oct. 8, 1907, issue of *Vorwärts* praising the Bund and its use of Yiddish. Note, however, that Yiddish is praised for "making accessible to the Jewish masses the important treasures of international arts and sciences"—that is, it is a tool for assimilation, not a language of inherent value.

37. Vogther's speech is in SBR, IX Leg., III Session, 1894–95, vol. II, p. 1148. On Liebknecht's questionnaire, see Brachmann, Document #5, pp. 134–36. On Bebel and Bernstein, see IFH, Sept. 29, 1904, p. 3. On other SPD protests: JR, Aug. 17, 1906, p. 386, and *Neue Zeit*, vol. 25, no. 11 (1906–07), pp. 476ff; and SBR, XI Leg., II Session, 1905–06, vol. IV, pp. 2867ff. On Liebknecht's personal intervention to aid Eastern Jews, see JR, June 1, 1906, pp. 328–29.

The *Vorwärts* was particularly active in defense of Eastern Jews. According to Vogel, it was the first newspaper to break the story of Prussian expulsions in 1905 (p. 101). See also Niewyck, Chapter Two and especially p. 48. To give a sense of the tone of *Vorwärts* articles, we may cite its response to von Bülow's "*Schnorrer* and conspirator" speech of Feb. 29, 1904. Entitled "The Triumph of Kishenev," the newspaper's article argued that von Bülow had slandered all Jews, and it castigated the "so-called Jewish press," the *Berliner Tageblatt* and the *Vossische Zeitung,* for their silence in regard to official attacks upon Eastern Jews (GStA, Rep. 84a Nr. 14, clipping of March 2, 1904).

38. Bülow's talk at a cabinet meeting of Feb. 13, 1907, is in Brachmann, p. 85. Williams comments on the negative consequences of the association between Eastern Jews and social democracy (p. 34). For a discussion of the treatment of Jewish students from the East, see below, Chapter 3.

39. For an extended discussion of the "failure of the Reichstag," see Gordon A. Craig, *Germany, 1866–1945* (New York, 1978), Chapter VIII.

Chapter 3

1. Saxony: In an order dated Dec. 24, 1870, the heads of Saxonian districts *(Kreis-hauptmannschaften)* were instructed that "the naturalization of Jewish aliens was, in general, not to be favored." This order was still in effect in 1889 and, as we shall see, remained in force until World War I (Dresden, Ministerium des Innern, Nr. 9684, p. 89). (Note: Henceforth the abbreviation MINN will be employed for Ministry of Interior.) Bavaria: On Feb. 19, 1875, the state's Ministry of Interior decided not to permit any "Polish Jews from Russia" who arrive without means to receive a residence permit (BHA Staatsarchiv München, Landrat München, Nr. 9984a, memorandum of July 4, 1880). Prussian policies regarding "Polish-Russian deserters" were spelled out by the minister of interior on Nov. 11, 1871 (DZA II, Rep. 77 Tit. 226b Nr. 1 Bd. 4, pp. 80–85). For two examples of letters sent by Bismarck urging greater stringency in the naturalization of Poles, see DZA II, Rep. 77 Tit. 1176 No. 2a Bd. 4 (Bismarck to his *Regierungspräsidenten,* March 17, 1873; and Dresden, MINN #9682, undated letter of 1873 to the Saxon foreign minister, pp. 55–56).

2. For examples of reports sent by German ambassadors and consuls on the deteriorating status of Russian Jews in 1881–82, see DZA II, Rep. 77 Tit. 1176 No. 2a *Beiakten* 1, and CAHJP HM 9519B. We have given the date of the assassination according to the Gregorian (Western) calendar.

3. The correspondence appears in several files located in DZA II. For the May 11 letter, as well as Puttkamer's orders to his *Regierungspräsidenten* and *Oberpräsidenten,* see Rep. 77 Tit. 1176 No. 2a *Beiakten* 1, pp. 1–3; Puttkamer's correspondence with the statistical bureau is in Rep. 77 Tit. 1176 No. 2a gen. *Beiakten* 1, pp. 1–12; see also the subsequent response from the head of the bureau, Rep. 77 Tit. 1176 No. 2a *Beiheft* 1, Sept. 22, 1881.

Titles of Prussian officials are translated according to the terms employed by Henry Jacob (p. 13): *Oberpräsidenten, Regierungspräsidenten,* and *Landräte* are rendered as "provincial governors," "district officers," and "county executives," respectively.

4. Minutes of the cabinet meeting are in DZA II, Rep. 77 Tit. 1176 No. 2a *Beiakten* 1.

There is clear evidence that Prussian officials were intent on expediting Jewish refugees to America as early as February 1882. (See DZA II, Rep. 77 Tit. 1145 Nr. 114 Bd. 1, especially ministerial decrees dated Feb. 16 and May 17, 1882.) The role of German officials in channeling transmigrants to the United States is a subject worthy of more research.

5. For a copy of the directive, see DZA II, Rep. 77 Tit. 226b Nr. 1 Bd. 4, p. 238.

6. For copies of the reports from the *Oberpräsidenten*, see DZA II, Rep. 77 Tit. 226b Nr. 1 Bd. 4; see, for example, the report from the governor of Posen, pp. 224–26. For the decree of December 20, 1882, see DZA II, Rep. 77 Tit. 1176, Nr. 2a Bd. 4.

7. The correspondence concerning German Jewish women married to Polish Jews is in DZA II, Rep. 77 Tit. 226b Nr. 1 Bd. 4, pp. 238–39 (letter from Posen governor, dated April 17, 1882) and 240–41 (response of Puttkamer, dated May 21, 1882); see also Rep. 77 Tit. 226b No. 38 for copies of this exchange. The Posen governor referred to a circular dated March 2, 1871, that made it easier for Russian subjects to marry Prussian citizens. See below, Chapter 9 on the efforts of German Jewish groups to ameliorate the condition of these women.

8. A copy of the decree dated Sept. 30, 1884, is in Stadtarchiv Duisburg, *Bestand* 16/3600, pp. 6–10. Puttkamer's actions regarding synagogue functionaries are discussed by Auerbach, pp. 117–81, and Alfred Michaelis, *Die Rechtsverhältnisse der Juden in Preussen* (Berlin, 1910), pp. 215–16. The Jewry Law of 1847 stated that "foreign Jews may not be hired as rabbis and synagogue functionaries . . . without the approval of the minister of interior" (Michaelis, p. 214). See below, chapter 5, on the omnipresence of Eastern Jews as cantors, teachers, and ritual slaughterers. For a case study illustrating the willingness of Prussian officials to grant temporary approval for a Russian Jew to serve as a ritual slaughterer, see GStA, Rep. 180, #13550 (correspondence of Oct. 4–30, 1907, regarding a *Shochet* in Dirschau.) See my translation of this document in "Jewish Lobbyists and the German Citizenship Law of 1914: A Documentary Account," *Studies in Contemporary Jewry*, I (1984), pp. 147–49.

9. Rönne IIb, p. 142, note 3. The memoir of Elias Auerbach attests to the more lenient policy of the 1870s: Auerbach's Polish father was naturalized by a local Posen official one year after his arrival in Prussia. (See *Pionier der Verwirklichung* [Stuttgart, 1969], p. 19). On the court decisions supporting Puttkamer, see IDR, Nov. 1906, p. 621 (Wreschner article). For some of the numerous court cases in which German synagogue leaders were fined for hiring alien Jews without the proper permits, see Michaelis, pp. 559ff.; AZJ, Dec. 4, 1896, p. 579; Aug. 28, 1908, p. 410; March 19, 1909, p. 134; Oct. 6, 1909, *Beilage*, p. 3; and IFH, March 31, 1909, p. 3. There is strong evidence that rabbis who did receive work permits also acquired citizenship expeditiously. (See the statement to this effect in Felix Theilhaber, *Der Untergang der deutschen Juden* [Munich, 1911], p. 22, and *Der Israelit*, Aug. 21, 1913, p. 12, which quotes a Reichstag deputy to this effect).

10. See the extensive statistical compilation in DZA II, Rep. 77 Tit. 1176 No. 2a *Beiakten* 1, a file containing rich data on Polish Jews in Prussia between 1848 and 1884. See also DZA II, Rep. 77 Tit. 1176 No. 2a Bd. 4, for data on naturalizations between May 28, 1881, and Oct. 1, 1883 (p. 298). Note that 430 naturalizations were issued in this period to a population of some 15,000 Eastern Jews, most of whom had arrived only after 1881. Bismarck's orders are in DZA II, Rep. 77 Tit. 1176 Nr. 2a Gen. Bd. 5, dated Dec. 15, 1884, and March 11, 1885. (The latter is summarized in detail in the next two paragraphs.)

11. The order to expel "Russian Poles" from Berlin was dated April 13, 1884 (DZA II, Rep. 77 Tit. 1176 No. 2a Bd. 4). On the West Prussian and Berlin expulsions, see

Neubach, pp. 15, 19–20. Königsberg: AZJ, Aug. 1885, p. 542. Neubach refers to Prussian fears that Jewish immigrants would agitate for revolution (pp. 13, 20, 21). See also p. 22 for his analysis of the fundamentally anti-Semitic thrust of these early expulsions.

12. Bismarck set the expulsions in motion in his order to Puttkamer dated March 11, 1885. (See DZA II, Rep. 77 Tit. 1176 Nr. 2a Gen. Bd. 5, p. 88). See also Neubach, pp. 23–25 and 120–55, on individuals who departed as late as 1890. On the decision to include Galicians, see GStA, Rep. 84a Nr. 14, minutes of Prussian cabinet meeting of Sept. 24, 1885.

13. AZJ, June 7, 1888, p. 360, and Dec. 20, 1888, p. 808. Segall's estimate appears in an article in ZfDS, June 1912. Joachim Mai does not bother to discuss the Jewish identity of expulsion victims. (Joachim Mai, *Die preussisch-deutsche Polenpolitik 1885/87: Eine Studie zur Herausbildung des Imperialismus in Deutschland* (East Berlin, 1962), p. 205. Neubach, p. 129.

14. See the following memoranda to ministries in other German states: Baden—GLA Karlsruhe, Abt. 233 #11128, letters from Prussian ambassador dated July 27, 1885 and March 28, 1888; Saxony—Dresden, MINN #9683 (letter from Prussian ambassador in Dresden dated July 28, 1885) and 9684 (letter from the *Regierungspräsident* of Liegnitz, dated Feb. 12, 1888). Prussian efforts to keep track of expulsion victims who settled in other states are documented in DZA II, Rep. 77 Tit. 226b No. 38 Bd. 2; note especially the efforts to convince authorities in Hesse to reject Hirsch Peikert's application for citizenship. These files attest to the general acquiescence of states to Prussian requests: almost uniformly, ministries ordered local officials to tighten residence and naturalization regulations.

15. Neubach, p. 22.

16. The common plight of Christian Poles and Eastern Jews during the expulsions is illustrated in a short story by Mendele Mocher Seforim (pen name for S. Y. Abramowitz) entitled "Shem and Japtheth on the Train," originally published in 1890. (Translated in Robert Alter, *Modern Hebrew Literature* (New York, 1975), pp 19–38.

17. For a detailed account of Prussian border controls, see Karlsberg, pp. 55–135. Bavaria only instituted transmigrant controls in 1903 (Karlsberg, p. 201).

18. The most comprehensive English-language work on the Jewish mass migration is Mark Wischnitzer's *To Dwell in Safety*. See also Zosa Szajkowski, "Suffering of Jewish Emigrants to America in Transit through Germany," JSS, XXXIX (1977), pp. 105ff. For a report concerning 400 transmigrants who were stranded in Berlin because they had purchased counterfeit tickets, see AZJ, July, 1889, p. 435. In his memoir Samuel Chotzinoff recalls how his family settled in London because they had been swindled out of their fare to America (*A Lost Paradise* [New York, 1955], pp. 33–34). In his memoirs, Moshe Oved describes his family's transmigration through Germany and their one-week internment in Ruhleben (*Visions and Jewels* [London, 1952], pp. 32–40).

19. Mary Antin, *The Promised Land* (New York, 1912), pp. 172, 174–75, 177. See also her *From Plotzk to Boston* (Boston, 1899), pp. 23–62. For some photographs of the transmigration centers in Berlin and Hamburg, see the illustrations to my essay "The 'Unwanted Element': East European Jews in Imperial Germany," YBLBI, XXVI (1981), following p. 38. The efforts of German Jewish groups to aid transmigrants are discussed below in Chapter 9.

20. Statistics on the transmigrant traffic are cited above, Chapter 1, note 8.

21. We have already analyzed in Chapter 1 the legal and political structure for coping with foreigners in the *Reich;* the present chapter discusses specific measures utilized to manage Eastern Jews.

22. The Westphalian governor made his remarks in a memorandum dated June 18,

1900, which is located in Staatsarchiv Münster, Regierung Arnsberg, I Sta. Nr. 31. For remarks made by Bethmann-Hollweg and other ministers at a Prussian cabinet meeting, see Leo Stern, 2/I Document #52, pp. 137–39; and on the continued enforcement of these policies in the eastern provinces, see IFF, Nov. 4, 1910, pp. 2–3, and KB, Oct. 1910, p. 3. Such policies were directed at Jewish subjects of the Austro-Hungarian Empire, as well as at Russian Jews; see DZA II, Rep. 77 Tit. 1176 Nr. 7 Bd. 1, correspondence on pp. 166–71.

23. On Silesian policies, see DZA II, Rep. 77 Tit. 1176 Nr. 4 Bd. 1, letter from *Oberpräsident* of Silesia to minister of interior, dated Jan. 9, 1899, esp. pp. 222ff.; see also the last file cited in note 22. The situation in Oppeln is discussed in AZJ, Aug. 2, 1907, pp. 362–63, and Feb. 21, 1908, p. 86; see also IFH, Nov. 4, 1910, pp. 2–3, and the *Jüdisches Volksblatt* (Breslau), March 18, 1910, p. 109; on the uniquely anti-Jewish thrust of these policies, see KB, Oct. 1910, pp. 2–3; on the Poles in Oppeln, see W. Mitscherlisch, Table IVa, and Elizabeth Wiskemann, *Germany's Eastern Neighbors* (London, 1956), p. 26. For data on changes in the concentration of Eastern Jews in Prussia, see Rep. 77 Tit. 1176 Nr. 2a *Beiakten* 1.

24. Königsberg's policies were discussed in the Reichstag (SBR, IX Leg., III Session, 1894–95, II, p. 1282); see also the report carried by the *Berliner Tageblatt* in 1900 and the flurry of ministerial correspondence on the subject in DZA II, Rep. 77 Tit. 1176 No. 1M Bd. V, pp. 28ff. On expulsions: Vogel, p. 96; IFH, Feb. 16, 1911, p. 5, and *Die Welt*, Feb. 17, 1911, p. 153. The policy was still operative on the eve of the war (JR, Dec. 19, 1913, p. 549).

25. Munich and Chemnitz: *Die Welt*, April 27, 1906, p. 20, and April 3, 1914, p. 337, respectively. Offenbach: IDR, Sept. 1908, p. 529. On laws against *Betteljuden*, see Leopold Auerbach, p. 277 (Prussia), KB, Oct. 1910, p. 2 (Württemberg), and ALBI Microfilm #152 (Leipzig). On expulsions from particular localities, see ALBI microfilm #152 (Leipzig); Bund Archives, "Offenbach—Bundist Groups, Documents"; and BHA MINN #74140, clippings from the *Münchener Tageblatt* dated Nov. 12 and 18, 1909.

26. Stadtarchiv Offenbach, "Galizische und russische Juden, ihre Akten bis zum Kriegsausbruch, 1913–14." Police report dated Aug. 20, 1913.

27. I have learned from Professor Klaus J. Bade, an authority on the history of foreigners in Imperial Germany, about the reaffirmation of naturalization policies in the wake of Prussia's decision to import seasonal laborers from the East. For copies of decrees issued in 1892–93, see: DZA II, Rep. 77 Tit. 227 Nr. 4 Adhib. I, responses of *Oberpräsidenten* to decree of July 20, 1892; Rep. 77 Tit. 227 Heft I, letter of Jan. 16, 1893 from the minister of interior to the *Regierungspräsident* of Wiesbaden; and Staatsarchiv Münster #5802, Jan. 19, 1892, memorandum from the Prussian minister of interior to all *Regierungspräsidenten*. The ministerial order to submit regular reports on the confession of individuals naturalized in Prussia is in DZA II, Rep. 77 Tit. 227 No. 15, dated Jan. 19, 1892, and addressed to the *Regierungspräsidenten* and police commissioner of Berlin.

28. For an example of a reprimand issued by the minister of interior when too many Eastern Jews were naturalized, see the letter to Wiesbaden's *Regierungspräsident* cited in n. 27. On the new policy enacted in 1895 and revised in 1898, see Staatsarchiv Münster #5802, Prussian minister of interior to his *Oberpräsidenten*, dated Feb. 3, 1895, and July 4, 1898.

29. The following two documents directly confirm that the 1898 decree remained operative in subsequent decades: DZA II, Rep. 77 Tit. 226B Vol. 40 Nr. 1, correspondence between the *Regierungspräsident* of Pottsdam and his *Oberpräsident* dated Dec. 5, 1904; and Staatsarchiv Münster #5802, memo from the minister of interior to Prussian *Oberpräsidenten* dated Feb 7, 1911. (This document also refers to policies regarding children

of converts.) Prussian bureaucrats routinely noted the ban on naturalizing foreign Jews; see, for example, the comments of a *Landrat* regarding the application of a physician from the East in DZA II, Rep. 77 Tit. 227 Nr. 50 Bd. 3, p. 54. On the children of Polish immigrants, see DZA II, Rep. 77 Tit. 226B Vol. 40 Nr. 1, correspondence of July 11, 1907, which cites a ministerial decree of June 30, 1900. On Bethmann-Hollweg's report, see Leo Stern 2/I, Document #52, p. 138. On the utilitarian approach to naturalization questions, see the first document cited in this note.

30. Lange's memoir is in the ALBI; see especially pp. 33ff. Dr. Monika Richarz, the editor of *Jüdisches Leben in Deutschland*, a three-volume collection of memoir material gleaned from the ALBI, drew my attention to this and several other memoirs cited in this work.

31. See Schwartz's unpublished memoir in ALBI, p. 4. Schwartz also claimed that some foreign Jews were granted citizenship in Prussia upon their donation of 20,000 mark to a public foundation (p. 5).

32. The correspondence over Borg's applications is in DZA II, Rep. 77 Tit. 226B No. 1B, pp. 46–91. I have published several of these documents in Appendix I of my essay "The Unwanted Element," pp. 40–44.

33. Two noteworthy exceptions to the policy of not publicizing data on the naturalization of Jews both occurred shortly after mass expulsions, periods when many Eastern Jews had been swept out of the state; since most of those permitted to remain were naturalized foreigners, government figures distorted the true situation. For Prussian data on 1890 naturalizations, see AZJ, Jan. 25, 1894, and SBR, IX Leg., IV Session, 1894–95, vol. II, p. 1283. And on 1905 data, see Klara Eschelbacher, "Die Ostjüdische Einwanderungsbevölkerung der Stadt Berlin, ZfDS, XVI (1920), p. 7. On the campaigns of German Jews concerned about discrimination in naturalization procedures, see below, Chapter 9. For a case where naturalization is explicitly denied because of the applicant's Jewish confession, see Appendix II of my essay "The Unwanted Element," pp. 44–45 (the application of Dr. Jakob Rubin, DZA II, Rep. 77 Tit. 227 Vol. 3 Nr. 50, pp. 56–57).

34. The reports are all in DZA II, Rep. 77 Tit. 227: For 1892 data, see *Beiakten* I Nr. 4; 1896–Nr. 4 *Beihefte* IV; 1905–Nr. 4 *Beihefte* XIV; 1910–Nr. 4. Vol. XIX; 1914–Nr. 4 *Beiheft* XXIII. To put these trends into perspective, we must note the tiny populations that successfully acquired citizenship in Prussia: in 1892, out of 1,528 people naturalized, 36 were Jews, one-third of which originated in Russia or Austro-Hungary and the rest in the *Reich* or in Western Europe; in 1910, 2,594 foreigners were naturalized, of which 48 were Jews (34 from the East). We must also add in this context that some candidates were naturalized thanks to the efforts of local or district officials who supported their applications; not all Prussian officials were implacably opposed to the naturalization of a foreign Jew. See, for example, the efforts of Erfurt's *Regierungspräsident* in behalf of a local physician, Jakob Grünwald (DZA II, Rep. 77 Tit. 227 Nr. 50 Bd. 3, pp. 94–98).

35. The characteristics of successful applicants were much the same as in Prussia. For complete tallies of the number of naturalization certificates issued in Saxony between 1898 and 1916, with special breakdowns by religious confession, see Dresden #9701, pp. 49–50, 57–58. (These figures refer to certificates issued, not to the total number of individuals naturalized; some certificates granted citizenship to single people, whereas others naturalized an entire family.) For more detailed information on successful applicants, see Dresden #9702 and 9694. On the number of foreign Jews in Saxony, see *Kalender und statistisches Jahrbuch für das Königreich Sachsen* (1913), p. 17.

I am unable to locate copies of official ministerial orders outlining Saxony's naturalization policies toward Jews.

36. For an official overview of Bavarian naturalization policies, with reference to min-

isterial decrees issued in 1871, 1873, 1885, 1886, and 1907, see BHA MINN #74143, memorandum of July 27, 1914, from the Ministry of Interior to the various Bavarian district governors. The 1871 decree is quoted in BHA MINN #74140, memorandum of March 14, 1907. In drawing conclusions about actual naturalization practices, I reviewed all naturalization files for Regierung Oberbayern, RA 43484–43529.

For a clear admission in private correspondence that "Russian Jews are normally not naturalized" in Bavaria, see document #1 appended to my essay "Jewish Lobbyists and the German Citizenship Law of 1914," p. 146 (taken from BHA MINN #74140, correspondence of Feb. 13 and 15, 1913). It must be noted that Bavaria, like Prussia, prohibited the employment of foreign Jews as religious functionaries in order to prevent their swift naturalization under the *Reich*'s citizenship law.

37. KB, Oct. 1910, p. 3. See note 14, above, for early efforts by Prussia to pressure neighboring states not to naturalize foreign Jews. The archives of ministries of interior in Baden, Bavaria, and Saxony contain numerous requests by Prussian governments to reject the applications of foreign Jews. For a few examples, see: GLA Karlsruhe, 233/11129, letter of minister of interior dated Nov. 7, 1904, regarding Isidore Katz; BHA MINN #74140, the Bavarian minister of interior to his *Regierungspräsidenten,* dated Feb. 16, 1907; Dresden MINN #9684, letter from the Prussian government dated March 28, 1890.

38. For more on this law, see my essay "Jewish Lobbyists and the German Naturalization Law of 1914." The text of the new law is in Huber II, pp. 382–89. (The new law exempted individuals born in Germany to foreign parents from the need to gain the approval of all states, provided they applied for citizenship between the ages of twenty-one and twenty-three.) For some files illustrating abuses by Bavarian and Hamburg officials, see GStA Rep. 90/151, report of March 10, 1927, and DZA II, Rep. 120 C. IX. 19 Bd. 1–2, p. 232 (file of Isidor Horn).

39. Editorial article, AZJ, April 24, 1908, p. 193.

40. On the rights of foreigners, see Wilhelm Beutner, *Die Rechtsstellung der Ausländer nach Titel II der preussischen Verfassungsurkunde* (Tübingen, 1913), pp. 60–84.

41. For newspaper reports on expulsions at the end of the century, see AZJ, Sept. 18, 1896, p. 449, and July 9, 1897, *Beilage,* p. 1; and IDR, III, Sept. 1897, pp. 452–53 (these concern expulsions from Memel). For reports on expulsions from Saxony, Braunschweig, West Prussia, and Dortmund, see IDR, June 1897, p. 351, and March 1900, p. 147. The German press began to cover these "mass expulsions" (a term employed by the *Berliner Tageblatt*) when Austrian parliamentarians began to voice their concern over Polish and Czech expulsion victims. See the following press clippings in DZA II, Rep. 77 Tit. 1176 Nr. 4 Beiakten 1: *Frankfurter Zeitung,* Dec. 1, 1898, *Berliner Tageblatt* Dec. 5, 1898, *Vossische Zeitung* Nov. 11, 1898, and the *Kreuzzeitung,* Nov. 30, 1898.

42. On the expulsions of 1905–06, see Vogel, pp. 101ff.; AZJ, April 13, 1906, p. 170. For minutes of the Prussian cabinet meeting, see Leo Stern 2/I, passim. On the role of German Jewish groups, see AZJ, May 4, 1906, *Beilage,* p. 1, and JR, May 4, 1906, pp. 257–58.

43. *Die Welt* estimates that 2,000 Russian families were expelled from Berlin (April 27, 1906, p. 20). On expulsions from other areas, see JR, Aug. 24, 1906, p. 511, and Feb. 1906, pp. 82–83.

44. On the expulsion of wealthy Russian Jews, see JR, May 4, 1906, pp. 257–58, and SBR, XI Leg., II Session, vol. IV, May 3, 1906, pp. 2867ff.

45. Cassel's speech is cited in IFH, March 30, 1911, p. 1. Berlin expulsions, IFH, April 2, 1914, p. 13, and JR, May 1, 1914, p. 189. The request for additional data on Russian Jews in Berlin is in DZA II, Rep. 77 Tit. 1171 Nr. 1L Bd. 5, dated April 28, 1913, pp. 121–22.

46. The memorandum from Prussia' minister of trade is in GStA, Rep. 2II Nr. 2065, dated July 28, 1914, p. 228. Munich decrees: *Die Welt,* Sept. 22, 1911, p. 1011; IFH, Sept. 22, 1911, p. 3; JR, Sept. 8, 1911, p. 432, and *Ha-Ivri,* II (Sept. 8, 1911), p. 407. Rhineland decrees: AZJ, July 31, 1914, p. 363; *Der Israelit,* July 23, 1914, p. 7; and IFH, July 23, 1914, p. 5.

See the following for an overview of how the status of Eastern Jews in Germany changed with the outbreak of hostilities: on differences in the treatment of Russian and Austro-Hungarian subjects, see Zechlin, pp. 265–66, and S. Adler-Rudel, "East European Jewish Workers in Germany," YBLBI, II (1957), pp. 140ff. For some memoir accounts, see Kurt Katsch, "From Ghetto to Ghetto" (in German), ALBI, pp. 52ff.; Samuel Horodetsky, *Memoirs* (in Hebrew) (Tel Aviv, 1957), p. 107; and Bernhard Kahn, "Memoir of World War I" (in German), ALBI, pp. 5–7. For a well-documented file detailing the various measures taken against Russian subjects once war erupted, see Staatsarchiv Wiesbaden, Abt. 405 Nr. 2745.

47. On the citation of Bismarckian precedents: Vogel, pp. 96–97, and Leo Stern 2/I, p. 57.

48. The following section on the treatment of Jewish students from the East presents a modified and abridged version of my essay "The *'Ausländerfrage'* at Institutions of Higher Learning: A Controversey Over Russian-Jewish Students in Imperial Germany," YBLBI, XXVII (1982), pp. 187–215. The interested reader may wish to examine that essay, particularly for its more complete documentation of sources and statistical tables.

49. According to statistics compiled by the Prussian government, thirty-eight Russian Jews were enrolled at Prussian universities and nineteen at other German institutions during the summer of 1888. (DZA II, Rep. 76 Va Sekt. 1 Nr. 28, pp. 1–16.) For later figures, see ZfDSJ, XI, p. 83, and Tables I and II of my essay on the *Ausländerfrage,* pp. 209–11.

50. On the patterns of geographic distribution and faculty concentration, see Tables Ia and Ic of my essay cited in note 48. On developments in Karlsruhe, see GLA, Abt. 235 Nr. 4051, letter from the minister of education to the *Hochschule*'s Senate, Oct. 15, 1910. (These figures refer to all Russians but we can assume that seventy-five percent were Jews.)

51. For Prussian responses, see DZA II, Rep. 76 Va Sekt. 1 Nr. 28: minister of education to the chancellor, dated Feb. 12, 1890; chancellor's response, dated May 3, 1890; directive of minister to all university rectors, dated Nov. 23, 1890; and the Bavarian inquiry dated June 27, 1891. For Saxon responses, see Dresden, Ministerium für Volksbildung, Nr. 10084: minister of foreign affairs to education minister, dated January 10, 1889 (regarding inquiries from the tsarist government); education minister to academic administrators, dated January 12 and June 25, 1889.

52. Leo Stern 2/ I, p. XXV; Barbara Vogel, p. 87.

53. This theme is explored extensively in Botho Brachmann's *Russische Sozialdemokraten in Berlin, 1895–1914* (East Berlin, 1962), especially in Chapters I and V.

54. See Brachmann for numerous documents pertaining to the harassment and expulsion of Russian students. (Brachmann contends that these actions were motivated by anti-Russian, rather than anti-Semitic, motives.) Bundists: Stern 2/II, Document Nr. 2, pp. 61–62. Kirsch: DZA II, Rep. 77 Tit. 500 Nr. 38, letter from the Berlin office of the *Alliance Israélite Universelle,* May 28, 1907. Petition of 400: Brandenburgisches Landeshauptarchiv, Potsdam, Polizeipraesidium C, Rep. 30 Nr. 12708.

55. The following discussion synthesizes the key arguments and demands put forth in petitions submitted to *Hochschule* officials in: Berlin—AZJ, Aug. 12, 1898, *Beilage,* p. 1, and Brachmann, pp. 100ff.; Dresden—Ministerium für Volksbildung, Nr. 15804, petition from the *Verein deutscher Ingenieure,* dated Aug. 9, 1901; Munich—BHA, Staatsarchiv

München, Polizeidirektion München, Nr. 4115, especially press clippings from the *Münchener neuste Narchrichten*, July 3, 1901; Karlsruhe—GLA 235/7305, petitions of Sept. 15, 1904, from the *Verein Deutscher Chemiker*, May 1905, from the *Verband der deutschen Technischen Hochschulen*, and from the student organization at the local technical college dated July 18, 1902. (Our summary of these petitions will imitate their use of the terms "Russians" and "foreigners" interchangeably.)

56. As late as 1906 there were more foreigners in general, and Russians in particular, enrolled in technical *Hochschulen* than in universities. See, for example, data provided by the *Frankfurter Zeitung*, March 14, 1907. (Clipping in BHA Staatsarchiv München, Kultusministerium Nr. 19630.)

57. Fee structures at German institutions of higher learning can be gleaned from O. Koenen and W. Eicker, *Hochschulen-Führer* (Leipzig, 1911). Many schools already introduced higher fees for foreigners during the first years of the century. See, for example, CAHJP, TD/141, "Report of Self-Aid Committee for Jewish Students from Russia in Berlin, 1902," and the exchange of correspondence regarding fees for foreigners in various states in Dresden, Nr. 15804, especially pp. 110ff.

58. See press clippings from the *Münchener Allgemeine Zeitung* dated April 2, 1902, in GLA 235/4051 and Sept. 19, 1902, in GLA 235/7305. See also the correspondence between Bavaria's Education Ministry and Munich's technical school dated Sept. 18, 1901, and July 19, 1903, in BHA, Staatsarchiv München, MK 19630.

59. Protocols of the 1902 meeting are in GLA 235/7305 dated July 18–20, 1902; see also 235/4051 on the pressures exerted upon ministers to conform—for example, the Baden *Landtag*'s debate of March 6 and 22, 1902.

60. See Brachmann, p. 100, for statistics. For Karlsruhe and Darmstadt data, see the memorandum of Baden's minister of education dated May 10, 1907, in GLA 235/4051.

61. See the orders from Baden's education minister dated June 14, 1904, and Sept. 26, 1905, in the file cited in note 60.

62. See the same file for press clippings from the *Karlsruher Allgemeine Zeitung* (March 4, 1905) and the *Frankfurter Zeitung* (Oct. 19, 1907).

63. See the responses to a survey conducted by Baden's minister of education, dated May 10, 1907, in GLA 235/4051.

64. Baden: Printed report of April 1904 entitled "Anzahl der an den badischen Hochschulen Studierenden," in GLA 235/4051. Saxony: Dresden, Ministerium für Volksbildung, Nr. 10084 and 10085. See also the Appendix, Table III, of my essay on the *Ausländerfrage* to compare the relatively small number of students at technical colleges as opposed to universities by 1912–13. On the mounting influx of Russians after the 1905 revolution, see the memorandum submitted by the Senate of Munich's *Hochschule* to Bavaria's minister of interior, dated April 1, 1905 (in BHA, Staatsarchiv München, MK 19630).

65. Jena: JR, Dec. 1, 1905, p. 637. Darmstadt: AZJ, June 7, 1907, p. 267. Leipzig: AZJ, July 5, 1907, *Beilage*, p. 2. Berlin: AZJ, March 8, 1907, pp. 110–11. See above, Chapter 2, on Reichstag debates during this period. On tsarist demands, see Brachmann. And for correspondence between Bavarian and Russian officials regarding Russian requests, see BHA, Staatsarchiv München, Geheimes Archiv. MA 60 154, letter of May 5, 1911, from the interior minister and March 17 from the foreign ministry.

66. The Bavarian *numerus clausus* was imposed by the minister of education in an order dated April 11, 1911, to the rectorate of Munich's university. See BHA, Staatsarchiv München, MK 19630. See also *Israelitisches Familienblatt*, Frankfurt, April 11, 1913, p. 2. The Bavarians acted at a time of intensive pressure from the tsarist government.

67. On the Halle strike, AZJ, Feb. 7, 1913, *Beilage*, p. 1, and IFH, Jan. 16 and 30, 1913, p. 2 and p. 5, respectively. On other protests and petitions by medical students, see

K. C. Blätter, March 1, 1913, pp. 120–30, and *Der Jüdische Student,* 1913/14, pp. 60–61.

68. Citing figures in the *Statistische Korrespondenz,* the *Frankfurter Zeitung* (May 20, 1913) claimed that 1,486 foreigners enrolled in German medical schools in 1911–12; of these, 1,111 were Russians. On the number of Russian medical students in Germany who were Jews, see Table II of my essay on the *Ausländerfrage.* Abraham Flexner, *Medical Education in Europe.* (New York, 1912), pp. 18, 20.

69. Prussia's education and interior ministers admitted that Russian Jews did not deprive native students of places. (See AZJ, Oct. 10, 1913, *Beilage,* p. 1, and GStA, Rep. 91 Nr. 2253, Protocols of cabinet meeting, Dec. 20, 1905.) On the Prussian quotas, see GLA 235/7503, copy of order from the minister of education to university rectors dated Sept. 24, 1913.

70. See the decree of Bavaria's minister of education dated Oct. 6, 1913, in GLA 235/7503. This decree superseded the earlier quota imposed in April 1911 solely on Russians. The new decree did not single out Russians, but in practice Russians were most affected because they constituted the largest contingent of foreign students.

71. Saxon policies are spelled out in a letter from the Information Bureau of Leipzig's university dated April 16, 1913, in CZA, A126/29, Leon Motzkin Papers. See also *Die Welt,* Oct. 10, 1913, p. 1395, and AZJ, Oct. 15, 1913, pp. 495–96.

72. GLA 235/4051, memorandum of education minister to senates in Heidelberg and Freiburg, dated Oct. 6, 1913.

73. Quotas exceeded: *Die Welt,* Oct. 10, 1913, p. 395. Overall decline: *K.C. Blätter,* July, 1914, pp. 224–25. On developments in Prussia after the outbreak of the war, see DZA II, Rep. 77 Tit. 46 NR. 40 Vol. I, as well as SBR session of Oct. 31, 1916, for Dr. Lewald's report.

74. For the comments of the Berlin police official, see DZA II, Rep. 77 Tit. 46 Nr. 40, memorandum of Feb. 14, 1913. A clipping from the *Frankfurter Zeitung* dated Oct. 2, 1913 appears in GLA 235/7503.

75. The Russian government was even informed in advance of the impending expulsion of 1885 and, in the words of Prussia's ambassador to Moscow, the tsar "took these matters very calmly" (Neubach, p. 33). As the expulsions unfolded, the Russian consul in Warsaw complained to German officials that some Russian Jews were evading the decrees; as a consequence, Puttkamer was ordered to be even more vigilant in pursuing Russian Jews. (See DZA II, Rep. 77 Tit. 1176 Nr. 1G Bd. 5, p. 45, letter of August 17, 1885.)

In the twentieth century, Prussian officials had even fewer reasons to concern themselves about tsarist responses to new policies. In 1900, Prussia's minister of interior informed his colleagues that the expulsion of Russian Jews would not contravene Article 1 of the trade treaty because Russia also discriminated against Jews (Vogel, pp. 96–97). In anticipation of the 1905 expulsions, the Prussian cabinet discussed Russia's apathy to the fate of its subjects and resolved to enforce stricter curbs on migrating Russian Jews, since the tsarist government would not object. (See GSta 90-2253, Protocols of Cabinet Meeting of Dec. 18, 1905, p. 6.) During the next decade until the onset of World War I, tsarist officials and agents in fact pressured the German police to enforce ever greater restrictions on Russian Jews in the *Reich.*

76. Austrian officials protested the unfair treatment of some Jewish subjects throughout the Imperial era. See, for example, the intervention of Austrian consuls in Prussia in the following cases: DZA II, Rep. 77 Tit. 1176 Nr. 4 Bd. 4, letter dated Dec. 17, 1900, concerning a Hungarian Jew in Berlin and a letter dated July 8, 1900, concerning an Austrian Jew working in a coal mine in Silesia. Matters came to a head during the 1905–06 expulsions when Austrian officials protested the general tenor of Prussian policies: see DZA

II, Rep. 77 Tit. 1176 Nr. 7 Bd. 1, letter of protest from the Austrian foreign minister to Prussia's minister of interior dated March 17, 1906 (pp. 31–33); Germany's foreign minister to Prussia's minister of interior, warning that expulsions are damaging relations with Austro-Hungary, dated July 7, 1907; see also Nr. 6 Bd. 1 on correspondence of Jan. 9, 1909, Nov. 7, 1911, and Dec. 6, 1912. The exchanges were particularly extensive in November 1911, when Prussian expulsion policies were debated in the Austrian parliament. Prussian officials sought to assure their correspondents that Austrian Jews were barred only from the Eastern provinces and that subjects of Austro-Hungary would not be expelled en masse from Prussia. And, in contrast to the official attitude that it was possible to harass commercial travelers from Russia, Prussian bureaucrats felt constrained by the commercial treaty with Austria to tolerate Galician Jews peddling their wares in Germany. (See, for example, Staatsarchiv Münster, Nr. 6534, correspondence from the minister of interior to Münster's *Oberpräsident* regarding Osias Koppelman, dated Jan. 14, 1912.)

According to the press organ of German Jewry's leading defense agency, the *Central Verein,* there was a direct correlation between the treatment of East European Jews and the support they received from their native lands: thus, Russian Jews had no rights in Germany and Galician Jews were only slightly better off because tsarist Russia and Austro-Hungary were indifferent to the fate of these subjects; Hungarian Jews, by contrast, fared better because the Hungarian government protested when its subjects were unjustly driven from Germany. (See IDR, June 1914, p. 248.)

77. In response to the well-publicized case of Jannina Berson, the *Frankfurter Zeitung* stated in an editorial that "foreigners have no rights in Germany just as inhabitants of Russia have no rights." See press clippings from the *National-Zeitung* (Jan. 7, 1905), *Kölnische Zeitung* (Jan. 9, 1905), and *Frankfurter Zeitung* (Jan. 9, 1905) in GStA, Rep. 84a Nr. 14. The case of the Russian Jew in Posen is reported in the *Jüdisches Volksblatt,* Breslau, June 24, 1910, p. 247.

Despite their flimsy protection under the law, Eastern Jews actively sought to ameliorate their condition by appealing to local or state officials, and even the kaiser. These efforts ranged from hiring attorneys to draft appeals, to enlisting local Jewish groups, parliamentary deputies, and even newspapers to support an appeal, to submitting florid petitions beseeching the kaiser to intervene. For a good sampling of these appeals, see DZA II, Rep. 77 Tit. 1176 Nr. lL Bd. 1–6.

78. Recent historical scholarship has begun to explore the persistence of official anti-Semitism even after German Jewry was emancipated. Members of the judiciary, cabinet ministers, state bureaucrats, parliamentary deputies, military commanders, and university officials discriminated against Jews in matters that were not clearly defined or regulated by the law. For two major articles surveying the historiography of German anti-Semitism, see Ismar Schorsch, "German Anti-Semitism in the Light of Post-War Historiography," YBLBI, XIX (1974), pp. 257–71, and Shulamit Volkov, "Anti-Semitism as a Cultural Code. Reflections on the History and Historiography of Anti-Semitism in Imperial Germany," YBLBI, XXIII (1978), pp. 25–46. For several essays that explore official anti-Semitism in Imperial Germany, see my own article on the *Ausländerfrage,* as well as Marjorie Lamberti, "The Prussian Government and the Jews: Official Behavior and Policy-Making in the Wilhelminian Era," and Werner T. Angress, "Prussia's Army and the Jewish Reserve Officer Controversy Before World War I," both in YBLBI, XVII (1972).

Chapter 4

1. Jewish migration from Eastern Europe prior to the era of mass migration is a subject worthy of further study. For a brief examination of developments during the seventeenth

and eighteenth centuries, see Moses Shulvass, *From East to West* (Detroit, 1971). For detailed data on the naturalization of Polish Jews in Prussia between 1848 and 1880, see DZA II, Rep. 77 Tit. 1176 Nr. 2a *Beiakten* 1.

The reader interested in an overview of the kinds of statistics available on East European Jews in Germany is referred to Appendix A of my doctoral dissertation, "Statistics on Eastern Jews in Germany: An Introductory Essay." Appendices B–D provide some data and sources not available in the tables appended to this book. The figure for Leipzig is taken from Eugen von Bergmann, *Zur Geschichte der Entwicklung deutscher, polnischer, und jüdischer Bevölkerung in der Provinz Posen seit 1824* (Tübingen, 1883), p. 317.

2. For the sources of theses data, see Tables Ia–e in the Appendix of this book. (Unless noted otherwise, all references to tables refer to the tables appended to this book.)

3. Ibid.

4. J. Thon, "Berliner Brief," *Die Welt*, June 10, 1904, pp. 2–3.

5. See Table Ia. On the nationality composition of immigrant Jews in other Western lands, see: on the U.S.—*American Jewish Yearbook* (1914), p. 346; France—Paula E. Hyman, *From Dreyfus to Vichy*, pp. 65–73; England—Lloyd P. Gartner, *The Jewish Immigrant in England* (Detroit, 1960), p. 49.

6. These figures are extrapolated from Tables Ia–d.

7. For urbanization data, we must rely on statistics for settlement in the "large cities"; no complete information is available on the residence of foreign Gentiles and Jews in smaller cities. Still, it is reasonable to assume that virtually all Eastern Jews in Germany after the expulsions of the mid-1880s resided in cities. On residence in the "large cities," see Tables IIIa–b; and on populations in specific cities, see Tables Ia–j.

8. On the *Scheunenviertel*, see: Eschelbacher, ZfDS, 1920, p. 13–15; *Die Welt*, June 10, 1904, pp. 2–3; and the description in Chapter 6, below. For a description of this quarter after the outbreak of World War I, see the memoir of Mischket Liebermann, *Aus dem Ghetto in die Welt* (Berlin, 1979), and the interesting photographs collected by Eike Geisel, *Im Scheunenviertel* (Munich, 1982).

9. On the representation of Jews among foreign populations in the *Reich*, see Table IVa.

10. Urbanization data are in Tables IIIa–b; Berlin data are in Table IVb.

11. On the percentages of Russians in German localities who were Jews, see Tables Id–j (for cities) and IVb for the *Reich*.

12. See Table IIb.

13. Theilhaber, pp. 16, 24–25. German Jewish writers initially criticized Theilhaber's conclusions quite bitterly and denied evidence of demographic decline. By 1916, however, Henrietta Fürth published an article supporting Theilhaber's conclusions. In truth, the latter's figures were often inaccurate and his bias was strongly Zionist. Nevertheless, Theilhaber was correct in asserting that the German Jewish population was stagnating. For a bibliography on the controversy generated by Theilhaber's book, see Knöpfel, ZfDS, VIII (1912), pp. 43–44, and ZfDS, XII (July–Sept. 1916), pp. 79ff. for Fürth's article.

14. On the age composition of Eastern Jews in Munich in 1895, 1900, and 1905, see Jacob Segall, "Die Ausländischen Juden in München," ZfDS, V (1909), p. 20, and also A. Cohen, ZfDS, XV (1919), p. 125. Berlin: Eschelbacher, 1920, p. 8; Hesse: L. Knöpfel, "Die jüdische Bevölkerung im Grossherzogtum Hessen," ZfDS, VIII (1912), p. 102. Data on the age distribution of all Eastern Jews in Germany are not available.

The original computations of Leopold Knöpfel, a statistician in Hesse, provide rich data for historians of Hessian Jewry, particularly since manuscript census materials for that state have been destroyed. See Hessisches Staatsarchiv, Darmstadt, G 13. 4219/1.

15. For sex distribution, see Jacob Segall, *Die Entwicklung der jüdischen Bevölkerung in München, 1875–1905* (Berlin, 1910), pp. 8–49; *Statistisches Jahrbuch der Stadt Berlin,*

XXXII, pp. 30–31; A. Cohen, ZfDS, XV (1919), p. 122; and Jacob Segall, "Die Juden im Königreich Sachsen . . .", ZfDS, X (1914), p. 38.

16. Hanover data are based on Bruno Blau, ZfDS, X (1914), p. 133; Altona: Statsarchiv Hamburg, Jüdische Gemeinden, Nr. 160; Munich: BHA Staatsarchiv München, Kirchenbücher #12–13.

17. For several important files documenting cases of Eastern Jews seeking to marry in Prussia, see GStA, Rep. 84a Nr. 11896–11900. See especially the memoranda from the Foreign Ministry to the Ministry of Justice dated June 26, 1904, and Sept. 30, 1904, on tsarist policies regarding such marriages abroad, as well as the correspondence between ministries of Justice in Hesse and Prussia dated May 25, 1906, and between Prussia's ministries of Justice and Interior, dated Feb. 24, 1911 (one concerns the status of Russian draft dodgers and the other concerns German rabbis who do not hold officially sanctioned offices). See also Walter Breslauer, "Zum Recht der Eheschliessung und Ehescheidung der in Deutschland wohnenden ausländischen Juden," *Festschrift zum 70 Geburtstag von Moritz Schaefer* (Berlin, 1927), pp. 29, 36; Alexander Bergmann, *Internationales Ehe und Kinderschaftsrecht* (Berlin, 1926), p. 30. See Curt Rosenberg, "Ehescheidungen von Ausländern," *Rechtsfragen der Praxis* (Berlin, 1924), pp. 29ff., for the text of the Hague Convention. For reports on trials held to determine the marriage and divorce rights of Russian Jews in Germany, see *Strassburger Israelitische Wochenschrift,* April 1, 1909, p. 7; IFH, April 15, 1909, p. 5; AZJ, May 31, 1907, p. 225; and especially AZJ, Jan. 31, 1913, p. 55, which is entitled "Thirty Thousand People Outside of the Law" and deals with the situation of Russian Jews in France who faced barriers similar to those impeding their counterparts in Germany.

18. CZA 135/44, "Manuscript of Unpublished Part of S. Gronemann Memoir," p. 189.

19. For more detailed statistics on rates of marriage, see Tables 4.3, 4.4, and 4.5 in Chapter Four of my doctoral dissertation. Data for Munich are based on A. Cohen, ZfDS, XV (1919), pp. 123, 126; Hesse—Knöpfel, ZfDS, VIII (1912), pp. 102, 104; Hanover—Blau, ZfDS, X (1914), p. 115. See also A. Cohen, p. 127, on the marital patterns of Hungarian versus Russian men in Munich.

20. For statistical tables on the fertility of native and foreign Jewish women in Berlin, Munich, Hesse, and Hanover, see Tables 4.6–4.9 of my doctoral dissertation. Data on fertility of Jewish women in Berlin are based on Eschelbacher, 1920, p. 3. For data on Munich, Hesse and Hanover, see the sources cited in note 19. To cite one more example: in 1890 in the city of Altona, there were thirty-four married couples among the Jewish residents from Russia, Austro-Hungary, and Rumania; these thirty-four couples had 105 children between them, with a few families numbering 6, 7, and even 8 children. (Staatsarchiv Hamburg, Jüdische Gemeinden, Nr. 160.)

21. Eschelbacher, 1920, p. 3; Theilhaber, p. 65. On the low level of fertility that characterized German Jewry, see John Knodel, *The Decline of Fertility in Germany, 1871–1939* (Princeton, 1974), pp. 130ff. See Calvin Goldscheider, "Fertility of the Jews," *Demography,* IV (1967), pp. 196ff., for a discussion of the possible factors causing the low fertility of Jews in the United States, factors that may well hold true also for German Jewry prior to the Holocaust.

22. The demographic impact of Eastern Jews on German Jewry cannot fully be appreciated without information on the role of the second generation: What percentage of children of immigrants married children of native Jews? And how large were their families? Unfortunately, it is impossible to gather data on this subject. A study of the Weimar era might well glean information on the behavior of second-generation Eastern Jews after they had come of age.

23. There were only 152 more Eastern Jews in Prussia in 1890 than there had been in 1880; and during the same period, Saxony's population of Eastern Jews grew by 1,800 souls. Since these two states contained the preponderant majority of Eastern Jews during the nineteenth century, it appears that growth in the population of immigrant Jews was limited to about 2,000 individuals during the 1880s. (Adler-Rudel asserts without evidence that the population of alien Jews grew by 7,000 persons [p. 164].)

24. See Tables Ia–j.

25. See Table Ib. Note the observation of Josef Kruk: Jewish emigrants from the East "all know that a Jew—especially a Russian Jew—will not find anything in Germany. . . . One can never get in, let us not even mention finding work there." *Die Handlung enwickelt sich* (Offprint, Jewish Territorial Organization) (Zurich, 1910), n.p.

26. Data are culled from Tables Ia–c.

27. On the distribution of Jews in Prussia, see Table 4.12 of my dissertation. Of the 48,000 foreign Jews in Prussia in 1910, only some 5,500 resided in the four eastern provinces of East and West Prussia, Posen, and Silesia (see Table IIa).

28. On Berlin, see Table Ie; on Offenbach, see ZfDS, VIII (May 1912), p. 77.

29. For detailed data on the dispersal of Eastern Jews in Prussia in the early 1880s, see the material compiled by the Prussian Ministry of Interior in DZA II, Rep. 77 Tit. 1176 Nr. 2a *Beiakten* 1.

Chapter 5

1. The data from each locality deal with only one census year. Statistics for Berlin and Hesse cover the year 1910, for Munich, 1907, and for Hanover, the year 1913. In this chapter all references to the occupational structure and economic activities of Jews in these four areas refer to these census returns—unless noted otherwise. Note also that the Berlin and Hesse data deal with Eastern Jews, while the Munich and Hanover information does not differentiate between Eastern and other foreign Jews. (Because the latter were overwhelmingly from the East, these data are highly reliable.) For a discussion of the sources available on occupational patterns among Eastern Jews, see Appendix A of my dissertation. Occupational data from the above-mentioned localities are based on: Berlin—Eschelbacher, 1920; Hesse—L. Knöpfel, "Die jüdische Bevölkerung im Grossherzogtum Hessen nach dem Ergebnisse der Volkszählung vom I. Dezember 1910," ZfDS, VIII (1912), pp. 106–07; Hanover—Bruno Blau, "Zur Statistik der Juden in Hannover," ZfDS, X (July/August 1914); Munich—Paula Wiener-Odenheimer, "Die Berufe der Juden in München," ZfDS, XII (1916). (In this chapter, references to these works will cite only the authors and relevant page numbers; when citations refer to other works by these same authors, such works will be identified in greater detail.)

2. Eschelbacher, p. 17; Knoepfel, pp. 106–07; Blau, p. 115; Wiener-Odenheimer, p. 39. See Table Va for the percentages of nonworking Gentile aliens and Jewish and Gentile natives.

3. On Bethmann-Hollweg's speech, see Leo Stern 2/I, Document 52, p. 137. Bebel: SBR, XI Leg., II Session, 1905–06, vol. IV, pp. 2867ff. See also the report carried by the *Vorwärts*, cited in JR, May 14, 1908, pp. 257–58. Fraustädter, p. 40. A listing of the occupations of Eastern Jews in Danzig includes several Russian bank directors, an Austrian engineer, as well as less wealthy individuals. (See GStA, Rep. A 180 Nr. 13506, report of April 1906.)

4. See Table Va for a breakdown by occupational category. See Chapter Five of my dissertation for an elaboration of the reasons I conclude that most Eastern Jews engaged in

commerce. Note also the observation of Felix Goldmann that the proletarianization of Eastern Jews in German was a post–World War I development. (*Aus Geschichte und Leben der Juden in Leipzig* [Leipzig, 1930], p. 76.)

5. For a correlation of occupations and nationality among Eastern Jews in Germany, see Table Vb. I have not found a similar table for the occupations of Eastern Jews in other Western lands.

6. See Neubach, pp. 19, 21, 55–56, 64, 144.

7. Gustav Karpeles already in the mid-1890s characterized Russian immigrants as manual workers (AZJ, Feb. 1, 1895, pp. 49–50). Eschelbacher, 1920, p. 14.

8. For occupational patterns in other lands, see: England—EJ, VI, column 759; France—Paula Hyman, pp. 73–77; U.S.–L. Hersch, "Jewish Immigration During the Last Hundred Years," *The Jewish People: Past and Present*, I (New York, 1946), pp. 425–27.

9. On efforts to prohibit Eastern Jews from serving as apprentices and artisans, see Michaelis, pp. 214–23, and *Statistisches Jahrbuch des DIGG*, 1897, p. xx. In 1878 a number of craftsmen in Königsberg were fined for having taken on foreign Jews as apprentices; but in that more liberal era, courts overthrew the fines (AZJ, July 16, 1878, pp. 455–56). Despite the tough government policies, there is evidence from Berlin and Hanover that some Eastern Jews served as apprentices and journeymen (see Eschelbacher, 1923, pp. 12–13, and Blau, p. 115).

10. The role of Eastern Jews in these industries is discussed below in this chapter.

11. On the lack of Sabbath observance, see Eschelbacher, 1920, p. 19. The quotation on self-employment is from Thomas Kessner, *The Golden Door: Italian and Jewish Immigrant Mobility in New York 1880–1915* (New York, 1977), pp. 171–72, which discusses a similar drive among immigrant Jews in New York.

12. Wilhelm Harmelin, "The Jews in the Leipzig Fur Trade Industry," YBLBI, IX, pp. 250, 262; idem., "Juden in der Leipziger Rauchwarenwirtschaft," *Tradition*, XI, no. 6 (1966), pp. 262–63. (Harmelin tends to exaggerate Jewish control over this industry; quite a number of non-Jews owned fur concerns.)

13. On the existence of traders in eastern Prussia, see Shmaryahu Levin, *Youth in Revolt* (New York, 1930), p. 287; *Ost und West*, column 27–34; Neubach, p. 56. On the protests of chambers of commerce, for example, DZA II, Rep. 77 Tit. 1176 Nr. 20 Bd. 6, which contains an appeal from the Königsberg *Kaufmannschaft* to Bismarck asking him to spare 150 Russian Jews who had been ordered to leave (July 5, 1885). The father of Israel Sieff, an import-export agent, was one such merchant expelled in 1885 (*Memoirs* [London, 1970], p. 7.)

Russian Jews in Danzig were especially active in the lumber trade. In the year 1910, 147 Russian traders applied for a residence permit in Danzig, almost all had Jewish-sounding names. (See GStA, Rep. A180 Nr. 14182, pp. 249–61.)

14. Berlin: Eschelbacher, 1923, p. 16; Hanover: Blau, p. 115; Munich: Wiener-Odenheimer, *Die Berufe der Juden in München* (Munich, 1918), p. 64. Eggs: *Die Welt*, June 10, 1904, pp. 2–3. Odd-lot business: Wiener-Odenheimer, p. 41. On the expulsion, see above, Chapter 3.

15. On the advantages of import-export work, see Levin, p. 287. On self-employment in Berlin, Eschelbacher, 1923, p. 14. In Munich, forty-six percent of foreign Jews, versus fifty-one percent of native Jews, in business were self-employed (Wiener-Odenheimer, p. 88).

16. On the history of cigarette production in Germany, see Max Josef Graf, *Der Werdegang der Zigarette und die Entwicklung der deutschen Zigarettenindustrie* (Dissertation, Erlangen, 1932), especially pp. 8–9, on the role of Russian Jews. See also Eschelbacher,

1920, pp. 21ff., and 1923, pp. 10–15. The AZJ reports on the expulsion of cigarette workers from Königsberg (Nov. 1885, p. 753).

17. Eschelbacher, 1923, p. 14. Alexander Granach, p. 187. On cigarette workers in Hesse, Knöpfel, pp. 106–107; and Munich, Wiener-Odenheimer, p. 40. On the expulsions of these workers in the spring of 1914, see IFH, April 2, 1914, p. 13; AZJ, March 27, 1914, *Beilage*, p. 1; and JR, May 1, 1914, p. 189.

18. Eschelbacher, 1920, p. 20; see also pp. 12–13, on self-employment among these workers. Odenheimer (*Die Berufe* . . . . , p. 81) refers to the number of self-employed workers in Munich.

19. The Offenbach and Mannheim files in the Bund Archives suggest that many bag-makers and garment workers had already engaged in the needle trades prior to their emigration from the East. There are references to individuals arriving in Germany with their own sewing machines.

20. In Berlin fifty-three percent of Jewish immigrants employed in industry worked in the garment trades (Eschelbacher, 1920, p. 19); in Hesse the figure was sixty-one percent (Knöpfel, pp. 106–07); but in Munich and Hanover the figure was a bit under fifty percent (Wiener-Odenheimer, p. 40). Eschelbacher's observations are in ZfDS, 1920, pp. 20–21.

21. Cleaning business: IFH, Sept. 22, 1911, p. 3. Photography: JR, June 1, 1906, p. 329. Metalworkers: AZJ, April 27, 1906, p. 194. See also the lists of occupations practiced by immigrant workers: in Munich—Wiener-Odenheimer, p. 40; in Hesse-Knöpfel, pp. 106–07; in Hanover—Blau, p. 115; and in Mannheim—"Mannheim File" in the Bund Archives (handwritten survey of the activities of immigrant workers).

22. See Jacob Toury, "Ostjüdische Handarbeiter in Deutschland vor 1914," BLBI, VI, no. 21 (1963). See also Andrzej Brozek, "Attempts to Employ Jewish Workers in Upper Silesia Before World War I" (Polish, n.d.). On this program, see also IFF, Sept. 11, 1912, pp. 2–3, and JR, Aug. 30, 1912, p. 332. According to government memoranda, the initial plan envisaged the importation of 6,000 such workers. The program was dissolved at the direct order of Prussia's minister of interior on the grounds that it contravened long-standing policies aimed at keeping out "Austrian and Galician Jews from the *Regierungsbezirk* of Oppeln." (See the minister's order to the *Oberpräsident* of Upper Silesia, dated Aug. 14, 1912, in DZA II, Rep. 77 Tit. 1176 Nr. 6 Bd. 1, pp. 218ff.) On forced conscription during World War I, see Z. Szajkowski, "East European Jewish Workers in Germany During World War I": *Salo Baron Jubilee Volume*, II (Jerusalem, 1975).

23. On the position of SPD leaders, see above, Chapter 2. The statutes of Bundist groups in Mannheim and Offenbach contain statements of support for German workers. See also the appeals in Yiddish to join German trade unions put out by the local labor movement. The fact that the bag-makers' union took the trouble to prepare flyers outlining benefits and insurance compensation available to members suggests that the union viewed foreign Jews as likely to join. The Offenbach workers also permitted Bundists to hold their meetings in the Workers' House (*Gewerkschafthaus*) and the local socialist newspaper urged German workers to attend the Founder's Day celebration of the Bund as a gesture of solidarity. (See the Offenbach and Mannheim files in the Bund Archives.) We may note parenthetically that given Germany's policy of importing hundreds of thousands of seasonal laborers, the presence of some Jewish workers from the East would not have evoked the concern of the German labor movement.

24. The "Offenbach File" at the Bund Archives contains press clippings on this conflict. See especially the article from the *Offenbacher Abendblatt*, Jan. 5, 1909, and also AZJ, Jan. 1, 1909, *Beilage*, p. 3. There is no report on the resolution of this conflict. (I have found no other examples of clashes between German workers and Eastern Jews.)

25. See the "Offenbach File" on the entrepreneurial activities of Eastern Jews.

26. Eschelbacher, 1920, p. 18. Herberg is quoted in Kessner, p. 88. Unfortunately, it is not possible to find statistical data on the mobility patterns of the second generation. The following excerpt from the memoirs of Josef Lange, an immigrant cantor/teacher, provides some support for Eschelbacher's assessment. Describing his children's education, Lange wrote: "The girls went to high school and the boys to a *Gymnasium*. When they were finished with school, I wanted them to learn something, to become *Menschen*. This was our greatest worry. Bertha . . . learned millinery work in Berlin . . . and finally became a saleslady. . . . Goldschen wanted to become a nurse, and because she received excellent grades on her exams, she worked in the Jewish hospital for ten years. My oldest son David I apprenticed . . . as a businessman. Eventually he worked for Wertheim [stores]. Two other sons also became businessmen" (*Memoir*, ALBI, pp. 39–40).

27. Cigarette manufacturer: Sammy Gronemann, *Memoirs of a Yekke* (in Hebrew) (Tel Aviv, 1946), p. 73–74. Lange: *Memoir*, ALBI, pp. 17–18, 31–33. Granach: *There Goes An Actor*, passim.

28. References to all individuals may be found in Siegmund Kaznelson, *Juden im deutschen Kulturbereich* (Berlin, 1959). A few of the academics were Mark Lidzbarski and Eduard Glaser, who taught Semitics; Ignaz Jastrow lectured on medieval German history; and Hermann Schapira professed mathematics at Heidelberg.

29. These conclusions are based on an examination of reports issued by the seminaries: *Jahresberichte des Rabbiner-Seminars für das orthodoxe Judenthum* (Berlin, 1873–1914); *Die Lehranstalt für die Wissenschaft des Judentums in Berlin. Rückblick auf ihre ersten fünfundzwanzig Jahre, 1872–97* (Berlin, 1897); Marcus Brann, *Geschichte des jüdischen theologischen Seminars in Breslau* (Breslau, 1904), pp. 140–207; and Guido Kisch, ed., *Das Breslauer Seminar* (Tübingen, 1963), pp. 395–442. (Note the *Hochschule* data cover only until 1897. Also, we are only discussing those Jewish students from the East who occupied German pulpits; many others found positions outside of Germany.) On rabbis in Frankfurt, see Paul Arnsberg, *900 Jahre Mutter-Gemeinde in Israel* (Frankfurt am Main, 1974), pp. 112–13. Fried and Porges are listed in the works on Breslau cited above.

30. On the role of Polish Jews as teachers and cantors during the seventeenth and eighteenth centuries, see Shulvass, p. 27. Karpeles: AZJ, July 8, 1892, lead article. The figures on cantors expelled in 1885 appear in Lion Wolff, *Fünfzig Jahre Lebenserfahrungen eines jüdischen Lehrers und Schriftstellers* (Leipzig, 1919), pp. 180–81. Wolff headed various cantors' groups and admitted to being one of the few natives in these societies. On the cantors' school, see AZJ, April 27, 1900, pp. 197–98. For the remarks by the Berlin leader, see Wolff, p. 179.

31. *Der Israelit* reported in 1913 that ninety percent of all teachers in German Jewish schools also served as cantors (Oct. 15, 1913, p. 12). See also AZJ, Feb. 18, 1879, p. 117, and IFH, July 9, 1908, p. 9. Heinemann Stern proudly noted that *Landjuden* in Hesse did not have to rely on Polish teachers, in contrast to other areas in Germany. *Warum hassen sie uns eigentlich.* (Düsseldorf, 1970), p. 32.

32. The cantor H. Fabisch opposed hiring Eastern Jews as synagogue functionaries, but nonetheless admitted that they were desperately needed as ritual slaughterers (IFH, Aug. 7, 1913, p. 11). See also *Der Israelit* to this effect (Sept. 4, 1913, p. 12). On communal odd jobs, see the reports of the rabbinical schools on the placement of some students. On the *Klausrabbiner* of Hamburg, O. A. Reichel, *Issac Halevy: Spokesman and Historian of Jewish Tradition* (New York, 1960), p. 32. For information on other rabbinic offices held by Eastern Jews in Berlin, see Max Sinasohn, *Die Berliner Synagogengemeinden* (Jerusalem, 1971), p. 29. Goldman: N. Goldman, *The Autobiography of Nahum Goldman* (New York, 1969), p. 11. Publisher of IFH: JR, Feb. 21, 1913, p. 231, on Max

Lessman, born Marek Rubin. Statistical Bureau: Alfred Nossig, ed., *Jüdische Statistik* (Berlin, 1903), p. 146, and *The Letters of Chaim Weizmann*, I (London, 1968), p. 264, note 7.

33. Berlin: Eschelbacher, 1923, p. 17; Munich: Wiener-Odenheimer, p. 55.

34. See Table 5.1 in my dissertation on women's occupations in Berlin and Hesse. These data are based on Eschelbacher, 1920, pp. 12–17, and Knoepfel, pp. 106–07.

35. See Eschelbacher, 1923, p. 15, and 1920, p. 14.

In this context, it is appropriate to comment on the involvement of Jewish women from the East in prostitution. While this vice was a major problem during the era of Jewish mass migration, there is little evidence that such prostitutes plied their trade in Germany. See Marion A. Kaplan, *The Jewish Feminist Movement in Germany: The Campaigns of the Jüdischer Frauenbund, 1904–1938* (Westport, Conn., 1979), which mainly discusses efforts to prevent women from falling into the hands of traffickers (pp. 127–29, 134–36). On Jewish procurers who were caught traveling through Germany, sometimes with Jewish prostitutes, see Edward Bristow, *Prostitution and Prejudice: The Jewish Fight Against White Slavery 1870–1939* (London, 1982), pp. 53, 57, 128, 130–35. (Aside from reports about pimps, there are few other noteworthy cases of Eastern Jews tried for criminal activities.)

36. Eschelbacher, 1923, p. 16; AZJ, April 30, 1897, pp. 208–09, and May 7, 1897, p. 228. The Zionist Fabius Schach proposed training Russian and Galician women as maids in order to combat prostitution and to meet the need for Jewish maids (*Ost und West*, June 1903, col. 423–424).

37. See Tables Va–d.

38. Jacob Lestchinsky, "Economic and Social Development of American Jewry," *The Jewish People: Past and Present*, IV (New York, 1946), p. 82. England: EJ, VI, col. 759.

39. See Chapter 8 for German Jewish perceptions of the immigrants.

Chapter 6

1. Jacob Toury refers to a number of these individuals, see *Die politischen Orientierungen der Juden in Deutschland* (Tübingen, 1966), pp. 216–17. Braun on Luxemburg: Friedrich Stampfer, *Erfahrungen und Erkenntnisse* (Cologne, 1957), p. 89. Needless to say, there were also many non-Jews among the Russian radical intellectuals in Germany; these have been discussed by other scholars, especially East Germany historians. On the political orientation of Russians versus Austrians, see the memoirs cited in notes 2–4, below.

2. "Parvus" Helphand: Robert C. Williams, p. 35. Luxemburg: Nettl, I, pp. 137–62. Stampfer: *Erfahrungen und Erkenntnise*, p. 56. Buchholz: Brachmann, pp. 10ff. Braun: Stampfer, p. 73. "Unpleasant Tone": Quoted in Williams, p. 36. Noske: quoted in Robert S. Wistrich, *Revolutionary Jews from Marx to Trotsky* (London, 1976), p. 90.

3. Williams, pp. 34–35. Buchholz: Brachmann, p. 73. Apparently even the Austrians felt rejected by their German colleagues. Max Reiner wrote in his memoirs that he "was viewed in Germany as a foreigner not only formally," but also by his peers and comrades (unpublished memoir, ALBI, p. 8).

4. Brachmann, Chapter I; Leo Stern, 2/II, document 13e, p. 71, and pp. XXVI–VII. On the Bundists, see Franz Kursky, *Gesamelte Shriftn* (in Yiddish) (New York, 1952), pp. 204–05; see also below in this chapter.

5. Granach, *There Goes An Actor* (New York, 1945), pp. 141–43.

6. On expulsions, see Leo Stern, 2/II, document 10, pp. 39ff., and 13e, p. 71; Z. A. B. Zeman and W. B. Scharlau, *The Merchant of Revolution* (London, 1965), p. 25;

Stampfer, p. 73; Williams, pp. 34–35; and Rosa Leviné-Meyer, *Leviné: The Life of a Revolutionary* (Hampshire, England, 1973), p. 17. We should note that all of these individuals were assimilated Jews who generally lacked any Jewish education; and, in turn, the leaders of German Jewry had little patience for revolutionary politics. (See Ludwig Philippson's tirade against Jewish "Nihilists" in Russia [AZJ, April, 1877, p. 231–32] and Arthur Ruppin's critique of the Bund [AZJ, Oct. 30, 1903, pp. 523–24]).

7. Tchernichowsky: Eisig Silberschlag, *Saul Tchernichowsky: A Poet in Revolt* (Ithaca, N.Y., 1968), pp. 16–18. Bernfeld: Elias Hurwicz, "Shai Ish Hurwicz and the Berlin *He-Atid,*" YBLBI, 1967, pp. 87–88.

8. Itamar Ben Avi, *At the Dawn of Our Independence: Memoirs of the First Hebrew Child* (in Hebrew) (Tel Aviv, 1961), p. 146. On the Hebraists, see especially Stanley Nash, *In Search of Hebraism. Shai Ish Hurwitz and His Polemics in the Hebrew Press* (Leiden, 1980), p. 175.

9. On some of these Hebrew periodicals, see Meir Bar Ilan, *From Volozhin to Jerusalem* (in Hebrew) (Tel Aviv, 1971), pp. 391–95; and the statements of purpose of *Ha-Ivri* (vol. I, no. 1, Dec. 2, 1910, pp. 11–12); *Ha-Shiloach,* Oct. 1896; on *He-Atid,* see Hurwicz, pp. 91–93. On the Hebraist convention in Berlin, see *Minutes of the Meeting of the Association for the Hebrew Language and Culture in Berlin* (in Hebrew) (Warsaw, 1910). Menachem Ussishkin noted the absence of local Jews from this congress (p. 34).

10. E. Werner, "The Tragedy of Ephraim Moses Lilien," *Herzl Yearbook,* II (1959), p. 98; Arnold Band, *Nostalgia and Nightmare* (Berkeley, 1968), p. 93, on the aid Agnon received from German Jews. I have visited the Weissensee cemetery where Berdichevsky's grave is in the honorary row.

11. Weizmann, *Trial and Error,* I (Philadelphia, 1949), pp. 31ff; for the first detailed account of Weizmann's educational sojourn in Germany, see Jehuda Reinharz, *Chaim Weizmann: The Making of a Zionist Leader* (New York and Oxford, 1985), Chapter III. Levin, *Youth in Revolt* (New York, 1930), pp. 225–26, 234; Klatzkin, *Trifles* (in Hebrew) (Berlin, 1925), pp. 134ff.

12. Shulvass, pp. 13, 21.

13. For some reports on beggars—and especially swindlers—see AZJ, May 1874, p. 353; Nov. 7, 1876, p. 730; July 1879, pp. 489–91; Jan. 1884, p. 24; Oct. 27, 1885, p. 706; July–Aug. 1893, articles in numbers 28, 29, and 31 on Russians posing as scions of famous rabbis, April 2, 1897, p. 158. Rahel Straus, *Wir lebten in Deutschland* (Stuttgart, 1961), p. 20.

14. On efforts to centralize philanthropy, see AZJ, Aug. 6, 1872, pp. 623–25, and Dec. 2, 1873, p. 803. See also Schorsch, p. 27. Some German Jews gave to the beggars because they feared that if these indigents would have no other recourse, they would seek aid from Christian missionaries. (See AZJ, Feb. 1867, p. 151, and Nahum Goldman, p. 24.)

15. Gronemann, *Memoirs of a Yekke,* pp. 16–17; Strauss, p. 20. On aid extended by small-town Jews, see also Lion Wolff, *Fünfzig Jahre Lebenserfahrungen eines jüdischen Lehrers und Schriftstellers* (Leipzig, 1919), pp. 171ff; Heinemann Stern, p. 30; and Jakob Lowenberg, *Aus zwei Quellen* (Berlin, 1914), p. 89.

16. This section is based on my essay "Between Tsar and Kaiser: The Radicalization of Russian-Jewish University Students in Germany," YBLBI, XXVII (1983), pp. 329–49. See that essay for more complete documentation and details, especially on the political activities of various factions which eventually led to the formation of national and international organizations of Jewish students from Russia.

17. AZJ, Jan. 24, 1871, p. 67; March 21, 1871, p. 234; and April 9, 1872, p. 288–

89. The statutes of both societies are in the library of the Leo Baeck Institute, New York City.

18. BHA, Staatsarchiv München, Polizeidirektion, München, Nr. 524 and 571. The Berlin incident appears in Levin, p. 234. Unless noted otherwise, all references in this section to supporters of various political factions pertain solely to Jews; we are not concerned here with the relatively small group of Gentile Russians affiliated with these factions.

19. On Bolshevik and Menshevik factions, see Brachmann and Leo Stern. On the Bund, see B. Hofmann, *Zivion* (in Yiddish) (New York, 1948), pp. ix-xi; Yankev Sholem Hertz, *Di geshikhte fun Bund,* II (in Yiddish) (New York, 1962), pp. 422–23; and the Berlin file in the Bund Archives.

20. Samuel Portnoy, trans., *Vladimir Medem: The Life of a Legendary Jewish Socialist* (New York, 1979), pp. 268–69.

21. For the statutes of *Bildung,* see Jehuda Reinharz, ed., *Dokumente zur Geschichte des deutschen Zionismus 1882–1933* (Tübingen, 1981), p. 18. See also *Weizmann Letters and Papers,* I, p. 58, note 1. On the Cartel, see Motzkin Papers, CZA A126/19, "Matters Relating to Jewish Students," and *Die Welt,* July 18, 1913, p. 920.

22. On the Rumanian *Ivriah* clubs, see IR, Aug. 8, 1892, p. 5, and March 21, 1902, p. 4. In both the GLA Karlsruhe and BHA Staatsarchiv München there are well over a dozen files on various Russian Jewish groups at local institutions of higher learning.

23. Levin, pp. 242–43, 248–49. Even in the tiny Russian student colony in Coethen (Anhalt) propaganda battles raged between at least five different political factions—a remarkable divisiveness considering that there were only fifty Jews and fifty Gentiles in the entire population of Russians. (See *Di Yidishe Studentenshaft,* Dec. 1913, p. 2.)

24. See student organization files numbers 524, 529, 568, and 571 in BHA, Staatsarchiv München. On police harassment, see Leo Stern and Brachmann. Writing in 1913, a student lamented the brief, seven- to eight-year life span enjoyed by most societies; each student cohort maintained its own clubs and when it departed, most societies disintegrated (*Di Yidishe Studentenshaft,* Dec. 1913, pp. 11–12). On the greater tolerance of police for the Zionists, see Levin, p. 238.

25. See pp. 342–47 of my essay "Between Tsar and Kaiser" for a more complete treatment of the *Farband fun Mizrekh Yidishe Studenten-Fareynen in Mayrev Europe* and the *Allgemeine Organisation russischer Studierender in Deutschland,* their constituents, goals, and programs.

26. Our discussion of life in the "student colonies" will focus on the experiences of male students. This is so because women could not matriculate until just a few years before the outbreak of World War I, and also because it appears from membership lists that women generally did not join student societies. For more on the isolation of women students, see note 17 in my "Between Tsar and Kaiser."

27. The following memoirs depict the immediate absorption of new arrivals into the life of the "colonies": Joseph Klausner, *My Path Toward the Revival and Redemption: An Autobiography, 1874–1944* (in Hebrew) (Tel Aviv, 1950), pp. 68–86 (Klausner left Berlin for Heidelberg to escape the "commotion" of the Berlin "colony"); Ben Zion Dinur, *In a World That Has Passed* (in Hebrew) (Jerusalem, 1958), pp. 360–411; Levin, p. 235.

28. On lectures given by Hebraists and Yiddishists such as Sholom Aleichem, Chaim Zhitlovsky, and Sholem Asch, see *Di Yidish Studentenshaft,* Dec. 1913, p. 7. On lectures by radicals, see Leviné, p. 17; Brachmann, pp. 10ff. 73, and Nettl, pp. 137–62.

29. Dinur, pp. 366–67, and Levin, p. 222, describe the meager quarters in which students lived. Weizmann, pp. 38–39.

30. Levin, pp. 237–39.

31. Levin, p. 235.

32. See *K.C. Blätter,* Nov. 1, 1913, p. 331, and *Der jüdische Student,* Aug. 24, 1910, pp. 130–32, on East European members. (The latter, a nationwide Zionist organization, listed only eleven and three students from Russia in 1907 and 1910, respectively, out of a membership exceeding 400.) The quotation is in CZA, A15/VII/4, letter from Dr. J. Hurwitz, dated March 9, 1898.

33. Schach, "The Russian Jews in Germany," *Ost und West,* Oct./Nov. 1905, col. 724.

34. Levin, p. 235.

35. Important works describing these key centers are Gartner, passim; Hyman, pp. 66–72; and Moses Rischin, *The Promised City* (New York, 1961).

36. *Hassidim* and *Mitnagdim* were two major religious factions that emerged in Poland in the eighteenth century; these groups survive to the present day—albeit in different form. On the formal German temple, Mordechai Ehrenpreis, *Between East and West* (in Hebrew) (Tel Aviv, 1953), p. 35. On synagogues for *Landsleit,* see Lion Wolff, pp. 183–224. Eschelbacher also describes mutual aid societies in Berlin, including some numbering 300 members (Eschelbacher, 1920, p. 17).

In all of Germany, the most dense concentration of immigrant aid stations, restaurants, hostels, and prayer halls was clustered in Berlin's *Scheunenviertel.* See the descriptions of Granach, p. 8; advertisements in the JR for kosher pensions (Jan. 1909, p. 35); and a chapter on the Grenadierstrasse in Salamon Dembitzer, *Aus Engen Gassen* (Berlin, n.d.). (Eschelbacher [1920], p. 11] claims the book appeared in 1915 and therefore would reflect prewar conditions.) We must stress, however, that this area took on its strong "ghetto" flavor only after World War I.

37. There are references to East European synagogues in the following sources: Berlin—Max Sinasohn, pp. 45–53; Königsberg—AZJ, Nov. 18, 1873, p. 770, and *Ha-Melitz,* Feb. 26, 1896, p. 5; Memel—A. Carlebach, *Adass Jeshurun of Cologne* (Belfast, 1964), p. 25; Nuremberg—Max Freudenthal, *Die Israelitische Kultusgemeinde Nürnberg, 1874–1925,* p. 11; Stuttgart—M. Zelzer, *Weg und Schicksal der Juden in Stuttgart* (Stuttgart, n.d.), p. 99; Chemnitz—JR, June 26, 1914, p. 82; Leipzig—Felix Goldman, p. 77; Duisburg—CZA, A101/21 (letter from Harry Epstein to Dr. Unna, dated Jan. 30, 1914). Sometimes these congregations were incorporated into the official Jewish community: see Freudenthal, p. 11, and *Ost und West,* Jan. 1907, col. 27–34, for examples. On private synagogues in Berlin run by German Jews, see Sinasohn, pp. 1–2, and in Leipzig, see Gustav Cohn, "Die Entwicklung der gottesdienstlichen Verhältnisse bis zur Entwicklung der Synagogue," *Aus Geschichte und Leben der Juden in Leipzig* (Leipzig, 1930), p. 47.

38. On the founding of the Bund, see Henry Tobias, *The Jewish Bund in Russia* (Stanford, 1972). These paragraphs on Bundist groups in Germany are based on files in the Bund Archives named after the following cities: Berlin, Karlsruhe, Kelten-Friedberg, Leipzig, Mannheim, Offenbach. The late Mr. H. Kempinski, archivist, and Mr. S. Hertz, historian of the Bund, graciously advised me during my work at the Bund Archives.

39. See Offenbach File at the Bund Archives for the handwritten statutes of the "General Jewish Workers Bund, Offenbach Section."

40. Shelly's article appeared in *Morgen-Freiheit,* April 5, 1961; a clipping is in the "Offenbach File." See also the following memoirs of Bundists who briefly lived in Germany: *Zivion,* p. ix–xi; Medem, p. 11; Franz Kursky, pp. 202ff.

41. Granach, p. 187, and *Alexander Granach und das Jiddische Theater des Ostens* (Berlin, 1971), which refers to Yiddish troupes passing through Germany during the interwar era. The JR contains an advertisement for the *Jargon Theater* located on the corner of

Muenzstrasse and Grenadierstrasse (Dec. 9, 1910, p. 567). *Eisik Sheftel:* JR, Sept. 22, 1905, p. 488.

42. Waxman, *A History of Jewish Literature* (New York and London, 1936), III, p. 335, and IV, p. 444. I have compiled a list of all Yiddish and Hebrew newspapers published in Germany between 1868 and 1914 and have managed to locate copies of all but three. (See Chapter Eight, note 17, of my dissertation for this listing.)

43. I have located references to two societies that may have represented immigrants: According to a 1926 source, the *Verband der Ostjuden in Deutschland, Ortsgruppe Berlin,* was founded in 1908; since there are no newspaper or other references to this group, it could not have been terribly significant. (See *Jüdisches Jahrbuch für Gross-Berlin,* 1926.) A second group, named the *Jüdische Volksverein,* was founded by a small group of Russian laborers in Berlin mainly to aid transmigrants. (See *Ost und West,* July 1906, col. 479–88, and JR, Oct. 1905, p. 509.)

Chapter 7

1. On medieval *Kehilot* see, Salo Baron, *The Jewish Community,* I–III (Philadelphia, 1942), and especially II, p. 356–63, on the role of absolutist states. For a concise analysis of the structure and function of modern *Gemeinden,* see Kurt Wilhelm, "The Jewish Community in the Post-Emancipation Period," YBLBI, II, 1957, pp. 47–75. The communities were given different names by various state governments: *Jüdische Gemeinde, Synagogengemeinde, Israelitische Gemeinde, Israelitische Kultusgemeinde, Israelitische Religionsgemeinde.* But they all shared three common characteristics: (1) they were recognized public bodies; (2) membership in them was compulsory; (3) they had the right to levy taxes (Wilhelm, pp. 47–48). It is therefore possible to refer to them generically as *Gemeinden.*

2. Wilhelm, op. cit. On the development of Orthodox secessionism, see Robert S. Liberles, "Between Community and Separation: The Resurgence of Orthodoxy in Frankfurt, 1838–1877" (Dissertation, The Jewish Theological Seminary of America, 1980), Chapters 6 and 7.

3. Wilhelm, op. cit. On the power of Jewish notables, see Marjorie Lamberti, "The Attempt to Form a Jewish Bloc," *Central European History,* III, no. 1/2 (1970), pp. 89ff.

4. The role of government officials in approving and vetoing statutes will be clearly demonstrated in our discussion of the voting rights controversy (see infra).

5. The 1847 law is quoted and translated by Walter Breslauer, "Notes on Organizational Problems of German Jewry," YBLBBI, XIV, p. 260. See infra in this chapter on different interpretations of this article. On Saxon laws, see Curt Graf, *Das Recht der Israelitischen Religions-Gemeinschaft im Königreich Sachsen* (Frankfurt am Main, 1914), especially p. 35 on the vagueness of Saxon laws regarding voting rights. I have found no information explaining why Saxon governments maintained neutrality on the question of voting rights. On the exclusion of noncitizens from voting, but not membership, in Leipzig and Dresden, see *Statut der Israelitischen Religions-Gemeinde zu Dresden* (1869, 1905, 1913) (CAHJP TD/120), *Revidierte Gemeindeordnung für die Israelitische Religiongemeinde zu Leipzig von Jahre,* 1884 (CAHJP TD/91), and *Der Israelit,* Aug. 14, 1913, p. 6. On developments in Chemnitz, see below.

On laws in Württemberg, see Alfred Gunzenhausen, *Sammlung der Gesetze, Verordenungen, Verfügungen, und Erlasse betreffend die Kirchenverfassung und die religiösen Einrichtungen der Israeliten in Württemberg* (Stuttgart, 1909), esp. pp. 27–28, where the law of 1851 is quoted. (According to Article One, the active and passive vote belongs to all Jews.) Baden: The law of March 21, 1894, does not exclude noncitizens from voting

(*Statistisches Jahrbuch der D.I.G.B.*, 1896, pp. 129–30). See also, Siegfried Wolff, *Das Recht der Israelitischen Religions-Gemeinschaft des Grossherzogtums Baden* (Karlsruhe, 1913), pp. 54–58, 97–98, 140. Bavaria: Joseph Heimberger, *Die staatskirchenrechtliche Stellung der Israeliten in Bayern* (Tübingen, 1912), p. 131. Hesse: Leopold Katz, *Die rechtliche Stellung der Israeliten nach dem Staatskirchenrecht des Grossherzogtums Hessen* (Giessen, 1906).

6. The statutes of the following *Gemeinden* were randomly chosen for perusal. (Their archival file numbers in the CAHJP are given and the dates in parentheses indicate the years of publication. Since all of the statutes are entitled *"Statzung der . . ."* or *"Statut der . . ."* titles are not cited in their entirety.)

Bad Kissingen, TD/1002 (1888)
Bamberg, TD/ 16 (1873, 1888, 1910)
Berlin, D/GSA #148 (1898/1901) and TD/100-16 (1907)
Beuthen, TD/18 (1880)
Bochum, GA/Bochum 52 (1886)
Cologne, INV 627 (1896)
Erfurt, TD/4 (1889)
Halle, TD/6 (1858 and 1886)
Halberstadt, TD/59 (1886)
Hamburg, TD/352 (1867) and AHW 297, vol. 15 (1906)
Königsberg, INV 627 (1903)
Secessionists in Frankfurt am Main, TD/593 (1876)
Nuremberg, "Nuernberg 19/38" (1897)
Berlin, TD/796 (n.d.)

DIGB survey: *Mitteilungen* May, 1903 (no. 60), pp. 1–2, and note the correction regarding Würzburg in no. 61, p. 20. (No. 60 claims that in Würzburg aliens did not have the vote; this was corrected in the next issue.)

7. Fabius Schach claimed that aliens only began to exercise their franchise in the twentieth century (*Ost und West*, Jan. 1914, col. 13). See below on the voting behavior of Eastern Jews.

8. For references to *Shtibls* especially in smaller cities, see supra, Chapter 6. Eschelbacher (1920, p. 19) stresses the lack of ritual obervances and absence of Zionism among immigrant Jews in Berlin. Bamberg: AZJ, April, 1888, p. 297; Cologne: *Die Welt*, May 18, 1906, p. 9.

9. *Bericht über die Lehranstalten der jüdischen Gemeinde zu Berlin* (April 1914), pp. 81ff. Describing the religious schools on the Grenadier and Dragoner streets, Eschelbacher claimed that Eastern Jews sent their children "exclusively" to these schools. Yet a few paragraphs later she commented on the difficulty in discerning differences between Eastern and foreign-born children attending *Gemeinde* schools (Eschelbacher, 1920, p. 19). She also noted that some of the latter institutions enrolled more alien than native students. Hamburg: *Talmud Torah Realschule: Bericht über das Schuljahr 1898–99,* CAHJP INV. 1025; "Reports of the *Talmud Torah Realschule.*" Frankfurt: *Program der Realschule der israelitischen Gemeinde (Philanthropin) Frankfurt am Main* (1888, 1892), CAHJP INV. 1544.

10. Frankfurt: *Jahresbericht der Realschule der Israelitischen Religionsgesellschaft in Frankfurt am Main* (1911–12, 1913–14), CAHJP TD/594/2. For an earlier report, see *Einladungschrift zu der öffentlichung Prüfung der Realschule der Isr. Religionsgesellschaft,* 1891. Goldman: *The Autobiography of Nahum Goldman* (New York, 1965), p. 19. Rahel Strauss also refers in her memoirs to Eastern children attending the Karlsruhe secessionist

school even though their parents were not members of the *Austritt Religionsgesellschaft* (*Wir lebten in Deutchland* [Stuttgart, 1961], p. 34). According to Paul Arnsberg, the Frankfurt secessionists under Salamon Breuer took an "ur-German identity and socially excluded the *Polacken.*" For this reason, most Eastern Jews, aside from Hungarians, joined the Orthodox *Gemeinde* synagogue of Marcus Horovitz (*900 Jahre Muttergemeinde in Israel* [Frankfurt am Main 1975], p. 140).

11. The statutes of B'nai Brith lodges contain no stipulation against admitting foreigners. See, for example, the statutes of lodges in Berlin (TD/1000), Coblenz (TD/634), Cologne (TD/632), Düsseldorf (TD/672), Frankfurt am Main (TD/671), all in the CAHJP. See also the regulations of the *Verein für jüdische Geschichte und Literatur* (CAHJP TD/69). (Albert Katz from Lodz was the secretary of this society.) Women's League: Marion A. Kaplan, "German Jewish Feminism: The Jüdischer Frauenbund, 1904–1938" (Dissertation, Columbia University, 1977), pp. 199ff. Zionist Federation: *Statuten der Berliner Zionistischen Vereinigung*, CZA A142/181. C.V.: *Mitglieder Verzeichniss*, 1899, CAHJP TD/24 (*Satzung* published in rear of pamphlet.) See also IFH for a report on the founding of a *"Deutscher Verein zur Unterstützung notleidender Russen,"* a society that admitted only German citizens (Sept. 3, 1908, p. 4).

12. Eschelbacher, 1920, p. 17; Kaplan, pp. 202, 204, on the *Frauenbund;* for references to the B'nai Brith, see note 11.

13. Assessing the Zionist allegiance of immigrants poses special problems to the historian. Most writers and memoirists draw no distinction between generational groups or pre- and postwar events. While it appears that Eastern Jews—especially of the second generation—played an important role in German Zionism during the interwar period, we simply do not have sufficient evidence on the period before World War I to draw any generalizations. It is particularly unfortunate that the membership lists of German Zionist groups have not survived.

We do, however, know several things about the participation of Eastern Jews in German Zionism. They rarely played a leadership role. (Max Bodenheimer even urged foreigners not to seek prominent positions since such exposure would endanger their status in Germany [CZA A15/I/A8, letter dated Aug. 9, 1899].) Russians such as Shmaryahu Levin and Nahum Sokolow often addressed local groups (JR, vol. XIX, p. 27). And in several localities, Eastern Jews augmented the ranks of Zionists: In Berlin, 120 foreign Jews belonged to *Ahawath Zion,* a club specifically for foreign Zionists (IR, Nov. 28, 1902, p. 68). Two similar societies, known as *Dorsche Schlom Zion* and *Ahawath Zion,* functioned in Hanover (IR, May 31, 1901, and JR, Jan. 16, 1903, p. 22). Heinemann Stern recalled the numerical and intellectual contributions of Eastern Jews to Upper Silesian Zionist groups (*Warum hassen sie uns eigentlich?* [Düsseldorf, 1970], p. 86). And Nahum Goldmann recalled the same for Frankfurt am Main (p. 19). Moreover, at a meeting of the Berlin Zionist Federation one speaker charged that three-quarters of those attending were from Poland (MAV, Jan 23, 1901, p. 27). Finally, we shall see that the immigrants voted for Zionist and Orthodox slates in several communities. Despite these fragmentary pieces of evidence, we still know very little about the political and ideological commitments of the immigrants.

14. For more on these ideological differences, see Ismar Schorsch, *Jewish Reactions to German Anti-Semitism* (New York, 1972), Chapter Seven; Jehuda Reinharz, *Fatherland or Promised Land: The Dilemma of the German Jew, 1893–1914* (Ann Arbor, 1975), Chapters Two and Six; and Sanford Ragins, *Jewish Responses to Anti-Semitism in Germany, 1870–1914* (Cincinnati, 1980), especially pp. 88–103 on Orthodox groups. Thus far, we have little information on the social composition of these factions or the actual political campaigns waged on the local level.

15. Cologne: *Die Welt,* Feb. 8, 1907, pp. 405, and *Handbuch der jüdischen Gemeindeverwaltung und Wohlfahrtspflege,* XIX (1909), p. 218. (Interestingly, the foreigner elected in Cologne had resided there for eighteen years but was still not naturalized.) Prussian officials in Cologne and the Rhineland rejected this challenge. On developments in Duisburg, see the last section of this chapter.

16. For reports on immigrants threatened in Hanover: JR, March 8, 1907 (letter from Meyer); also June 15, 1906, p. 356. On similar activities in Chemnitz: JR, Jan. 3, 1913, p. 5. The JR accused elders in Chemnitz of instigating the government's closing of an immigrant prayer room as a way of intimidating vulnerable newcomers.

17. IFF, Dec. 12, 1913, p. 13; JR, Nov. 28, 1913, p. 515; and CZA A101/Box 21 (letter from Dr. Ascher of Dessau dated Jan. 28, 1914).

18. Hamborn: CZA A101/Box 15 contains reports submitted by the Hamborn representatives to the city's mayor (dated Feb 8, 1911), as well as petitions and letters opposing the statute revision. Additional correspondence in the archive of the district governor makes plain that both proponents and opponents of the three-tier system viewed it as a means to limit the electoral influence of aliens, who constituted thirty-seven percent of eligible voters in Hamborn. See Haupstaatsarchiv Düsseldorf, Zweigstelle Schloss Kalkum, Regierung Düsseldorf (hereafter noted as "Düsseldorf") #30562.

19. Neustadt: MDIGB, May 1902, pp. 1–2. The Prussian minister of interior rendered a decision on this case. For the text of the final decision handed down by the governor in Oppeln, see CZA A101/Box 9 (letter from the governor to the mayor of Neustadt dated July 12, 1897). Chemnitz: *Statut für die israelitische Religionsgemeinde zu Chemnitz,* 1905, p. 11. Stuttgart: *Die Welt* May 1, 1908, pp. 8–9, and July 17, 1908, p. 15. The files of Harry Epstein contain a copy of a decision rendered in 1880 in which the Prussian minister of interior upheld the right of aliens to hold office in representative assemblies and on executive boards. The community of Russ in Gumbinen (East Prussia) apparently had raised the issue, but there is no evidence that this *Gemeinde* actually attempted to disenfranchise aliens. (See CZA A101/Box 9, letter from the office of the minister of interior to the *Oberpräsident* in Königsberg, dated Feb. 21, 1880). The IFH also reported that communities in eastern Prussia such as Eydtkuhen and Tilsit had found ways of circumventing the law by not placing foreigners on polling lists (Jan. 9, 1913, p. 10).

20. Bochum: IFF, Aug. 2, 1912, p. 3; on the consequences, see CZA A101/Box 21 (letter from Epstein to M. Loeb dated March 6, 1914) and Naomi Katzenberger, *"Dokumente zur Frage des Wahlrechts ausländischer Juden in den preussischen Synagogengemeinden,"* Michael, II (Tel Aviv, 1973), p. 109. See infra this chapter on Duisburg. Cologne: IFH, p. 5. Danzig: *Der Israelit,* Jan 2, 1913, p. 1, and Elijahu Stern, "The History of the Jews in Danzig from Emancipation Until Their Deportation in the Nazi Era" (in Hebrew) (Dissertation, Hebrew University, 1978), pp. 54–63. Dortmund: IFH, Aug 8, 1912, pp. 2–3. Chemnitz: *Der Israelit,* Aug 7, 1913, p. 3. According to the revised statutes, aliens could only vote if they had resided in Chemnitz for at least ten years and had earned over 4,000 mark annually. Hamm and Muenster: CZA A1442/79 Alfred Klee Files (letter by H. Epstein of Duisburg to A. Hantke, dated May 26, 1914, and letter by Moses Schwitz of Hamm to the editor of the JR). It is not clear why most of these statute revisions were initiated by Rhenish communities. As we shall see, their populations of foreigners were not unusually large.

21. AZJ, May 24 and 31, 1912, pp. 241ff. and 251ff., respspectively. It should be noted that Michaelis lived in Hamm and was therefore personally involved in efforts to disenfranchise aliens in that city, as well as in neighboring Rhenish towns.

22. See the exchange of letters between Michaelis (letter of Dec. 24, 1912) and Harry Epstein (dated Dec. 23 and Dec. 30, 1913) in CZA A101/Box 7. Epstein refers to the

rejection Michaelis' radical conclusions by many liberals (ibid., letter to ZVfD dated Nov. 24, 1913, p. iv).

23. See the writings of Siegfried Schwarzschild: *Der Israelit,* March 6, 1913, and March 13, 1913; Harry Epstein: JR, Aug 22, 1913, p. 353; Joseph Heimberger: *Jüdischer Volksfreund,* cited in Epstein, JP, Aug. 22, 1913, and *Der Israelit,* Aug 14, 1913. Dr. Victor: *Jüdisches Gemeindejahrbuch* 1913/14. Michaelis' response to his critics appeared in AZJ, Dec. 5 and 12, 1913, which in turn was answered by H. Epstein in JR, Jan. 1914 (no. 3).

It is interesting that the "conservatives," as they styled themselves, turned typically liberal arguments against the liberals: In order to prove that a Jew's nationality was irrelevant to *Gemeinde* status, they defined *Gemeinden* as confessional rather than political organizations. But it was the liberal ideology that defined Jewish identity as a matter of religion, not nationality. Zionists, by contrast, usually stressed the national and ethnic components of Jewish identity.

24. On the decision rendered by the Prussian minister of interior, see CZA A142/79, Alfred Klee Files. A copy of this decision was sent to the provincial governor in Königsberg and probably to all other Prussian governors. (I found this document in Göttingen *Archivlager,* Rep 2, No. 212, vol. I, p. 374, but it is now in GStA with the rest of the Prussian materials formerly in Göttingen.) After the minister's decision, the *Oberpräsident* of the Rhine Province rejected various statute revisions proposed by Rhineland *Gemeinden.* For the text of the decision by the Rhenish governor, see *Der Israelit,* Jan 29, 1914, *Beilage,* and JR, May 1914, p. 232, as well as Naomi Katzenberger, pp. 201–202. Hamborn decision: CZA A101/Box 2 (letter from the mayor of Hamborn dated March 30, 1912). Cologne: see references in note 15.

25. IFH, Jan 16, 1913, p. 1.

26. See the article cited in note 25, as well as IFH, Jan. 30, 1913, p. 1, and Feb. 13, 1913, p. 3; also *Liberales Judentum,* VI, no. 1 (1914), pp. 10ff.

27. Residency requirements: IFH, Jan. 16, 1913, p. 1. The liberal Rabbi Ziemels of Baden opposed statute changes in 1908 (*Die Welt,* May 1, 1908, pp. 8–9). The response of IDR illustrates the division among *Central Verein* members: the paper defends Duisburg liberals from Zionist criticism, but it takes pains to show that C.V. members were divided even in Duisburg on the principle of disenfranchisement. According to IDR, the C.V. was not informed of developments in Duisburg, the issue was not even discussed at the C.V. meetings held in Duisburg, and its C.V. members were found on both sides of the controversy (IDR, Feb. 1914, pp. 71–73). Another C.V. member wrote to the JR claiming that his organization did not support disenfranchisement (JR, Dec. 12, 1913, p. 536). See also *Die Welt,* Aug. 22, 1913, p. 1093, for a C.V. attempt to remain neutral. DIGB and *Verband:* CZA A101/Box 7, Harry Epstein's letter of Nov. 24, 1913, to the Zionist Federation of Germany.

The Orthodox also did not present a monolithic front. An Orthodox rabbi named Brader informed a Prussian official that he saw no reason to oppose disenfranchisement (Katzenberger, p. 20), and some Orthodox communities in South Germany were criticized by *Der Israelit* for discriminating against foreigners (Jan. 2, 1913, p. 2).

28. *Der Israelit,* Jan. 2, 1913, p. 1, and Feb. 20, 1913, pp. 2–3 (source of quotation): *Die Jüdische Presse,* XVIII, p. 84; and IFH, Aug. 1, 1912. It is odd that the separatist newspaper *Der Israelit* preached for unity among Jews and berated liberals for dividing Jew from Jew! (Note also that the IFH article of Aug. 1912 is extremely hostile toward the Bochum statute revision; a half a year later the paper became far more sympathetic to the cause—if not the methods—of the liberals.)

29. JR, Jan. 31, 1913 (lead article).

30. Cited in IFH, Feb. 13, 1912, p. 1.

31. On the meeting in Hamburg, see JR, Feb. 14, 1913, p. 61. Fight in Dessau: IFF, Dec. 12, 1913, p. 3. CZA A101/Box 7 on plans to hold a protest meeting in Duesseldorf (letter from the *Verein für die jüdischen Interessen*). Due to the intemperate outbursts of participants in the controversy, libel suits were occasionally initiated: The Dessau Zionist leader Dr. Ascher sued a liberal member of the Prussian Diet (IFH, Dec. 12, 1913, p. 2) and Harry Epstein sued a liberal Duisburg Jew.

32. Saul, *Liberales Judentum*, VI, no. I (1914), pp. 10ff.; Geiger: quoted in JR, Nov. 7, 1913, pp. 482–83. Katz: AZJ, Jan. 30, 1914, p. 51. See also IFH, Feb. 13, 1913, p. 3.

33. *Die Welt*, Feb. 21, 1913, p. 231; JR, Jan. 24, 1913, p. 35; and especially the *Weckruf* published by the *Neuer Jüdischer Gemeindeverein* (n.d., but by internal evidence can be dated to 1913) in CAHJP Inv. 1430 (1).

34. See Table IIb in the Appendix of this book for the percentage of foreign Jews in Danzig, Bochum, Cologne, Duisburg, Hamborn, Chemnitz, and Baden in 1910. Nearly nineteen percent of the Jews in the "large cities" were aliens. (In the above-cited localities, this figure was exceeded only in Duisburg—and there only slightly.)

35. This paragraph and the ensuing discussion of the growing rift between Zionists and liberals are based upon Ismar Schorsch, Chapter Seven, and Jehuda Reinharz, Chapters Four and Five.

36. Reinharz alludes to struggles between opposing political factions in Berlin, Munich, and Posen (pp. 189ff.). Since a systematic account of electoral politics in Jewish *Gemeinden* remains to be written, the following comments of necessity must be sketchy. On the *Neuer Jüdischer Gemeindeverein* in Chemnitz: CZA A101/Box 7 (memorandum by to a Saxon official dated August 19). Königsberg: Reinharz, p. 199; Dessau: IFF, Dec. 12, 1913, p. 3.

37. Epstein's letter is published by Naomi Katzenberger, p. 201. See also *Jahresbericht über die Tätigkeit der Zionistischen Vereinigung für Deutschland* (Berlin, 1913), p. 11. Interestingly, the sole published response I have seen by an Eastern Jew portrays the controversy in the same light. The Galician author contends that Zionists used foreigners only as a means to their political ends (IFH, Feb. 13, 1913, pp. 2–3). For examples of memoranda sent to government officials by Zionist groups, see the letter of Nov. 30, 1913, in CZA A101/Box 7 and JR, Feb. 14, 1913, p. 1.

38. Reports on the Synod are found in *Die Welt*, May 1, 1908, pp. 8–9, and JR, July 17, 1908, p. 282. For the background to the conference, see Adolf Lewin, *Geschichte der badischen Juden* (Karlsruhe, 1909), pp. 474ff. and 487. See also the correspondence in GLA, Abt. 233/27731.

39. *Die Welt*, April 7, 1911, p. 320.

40. For the background, see CZA A101/Box 7 (memorandum to the government by members of the *Neuer Jüdischer Gemeindeverein* in Chemnitz, dated Aug. 19, 1913). See also the Chemnitz communal statutes of 1914.

41. On the efforts to disenfranchise aliens in Cologne, see Landeshauptarchiv Koblenz, Bestand 403, Nr. 16011. Katzenberger refers to the formation of an Orthodox/Zionist alliance in Cologne already at the beginning of the twentieth century. The first disenfranchisment proposals were suggested in the wake of the quick success scored by this alliance (p. 195). Dessau: in 1913 the liberals won fifty-six to forty-three, but only because they frightened ten aliens into voting with them (*Liberales Judentum*, VI, no. 1 [1914], pp. 10ff.)

42. For an account that is primarily concerned with the political ramifications of this affair, see my "The Duisburg Affair: A Test Case in the Struggle for 'Conquest of the Communities,' " in *AJS Review*, VI (1981), pp. 185–206.

43. See Düsseldorf #30567 for a series of petitions dated December 1909–April 1910.

A memorandum from the mayor of Duisburg is especially useful in clarifying the major issues. Additional memoranda on this election are available in Landeshauptarchiv Koblenz, Bestand 403, Nr. 16011. See Rabbi Neumark's appeal, *"Die Bürgschaftspflicht. Ein Mahnruf an die Gemeinde,"* in CZA A101/Box 9.

44. On the election campaign, see CZA A101/Box 4 (Epstein's memorandum of April 10, 1913) and a letter from the mayor of Duisburg dated December 30, 1912, in Düsseldorf #30567. By comparing the names of successful candidates with names on liberal and "conservative" petitions, I have been able to identify the allegiances of newly elected representatives.

45. A copy of the petition is in Düsseldorf #30567.

46. The memorandum (dated December 28, 1912) is located in CZ A101/Box 4.

47. See the same file for the memorandum sent by "conservatives." For additional memoranda sent to the district and provincial governors, see CZA A101/Box 7, dated January 23, 1913, and signed by M. Kolsky and Max Levy. An additional petition, dated January 6, 1913, deals especially with the charge of vote fraud; see Düsseldorf #30567.

48. Both the mayor's letter to the *Regierungspräsident* (February 17, 1913) and the governor's letter to the *Gemeinde* (Feb. 24, 1913) are in Düsseldorf #30567.

49. On the meeting and its consequences for Rosenthal, see CZA A101/Box 4 (legal correspondence between Epstein and his attorney) and JR, February 6, 1914, p. 59. Rosenthal's attorney threatened that Siegmund Epstein and Emanuel Lowe would testify against Harry Epstein. See letter dated April 10, 1913, in the above-cited file.

50. The article appeared on the front page of the JR of November 21, 1913, pp. 501–02.

51. The minister's decision is in CZA A142/79 (letter from the *Oberpräsident* to Rabbi Wolff). For the directive sent by the *Oberpräsident* to the *Gemeinde,* see the letter dated May 18, 1914, from Rabbi Munk to E. Strauss in the same file; see also JR, May 1914, p. 232.

52. On the implications of developments in Duisburg for the larger conflict between liberals and Zionists, see my essay on the affair, pp. 202–06.

53. The JR reports on a public meeting in Duisburg at which liberals openly spoke of *"Polacken"* (Feb. 6, 1914, pp. 58–59).

Chapter 8

1. These assessments are taken from Shmaryahu Levin, *Youth in Revolt* (New York, 1930), p. 226; and Chaim Weizmann, *Trial and Error,* I (Philadelphia, 1944), p. 39. See supra, Chapter 6 for Jacob Klatzkin's depiction of the contempt displayed by German Jews.

For a different account of German Jewish attitudes toward Eastern Jews, which focuses particularly on the views of intellectuals throughout the modern era, see Steven Aschheim, *Brothers and Strangers: The East European Jew in German and German Jewish Consciousness, 1800–1923* (Madison, Wisc., 1982).

2. Karpeles returned to this theme often during his tenure as editor of the AZJ: see Feb. 1, 1895, pp. 49–50; May 20, 1898, lead article; Sept. 7, 1906, pp. 421–22; June 28, 1907, pp. 301–02. Zionists: *Die Welt,* Feb. 8, 1907, pp. 405; JR, Nov. 21, 1913, p. 501, refers to the history of German Jews "looking upon their Eastern coreligionists with mocking arrogance." Galicians: IFH, Feb. 13, 1913, pp. 2–3.

3. Jacob Lowenberg, *Aus zwei Quellen* (Berlin, 1914), p. 89; Kurt Blumenfeld, *Erlebte Judenfrage* (Stuttgart, 1962), p. 27. Galician children: recounted by Dr. Fred Grubel, interview of April 6, 1976.

4. Blumenfeld, p. 37; JR, Nov. 6, 1902, p. 37; JR, Nov. 20, 1902, p. 47.

5. *Ha-Melitz,* 1885, p. 269, and No. 134, 1895, pp. 2–3.

6. On the use of the term by German Jews in different regions, see *Die Welt,* Sept. 22, 1911, p. 1011 (Bavaria); Heinmann Stern, *Warum hassen sie uns eigentlich?* (Düsseldorf, 1970), p. 30 (Hesse); CZA A101 Box 21, letter of Jan. 28, 1914, from Dr. Acher of Dessau (Rhineland); Isaac Rülf, *Die russischen Juden* (Memel, 1892), p. 209 (eastern Prussia). For indications that the term was used for all Poles and foreigners, see A. Granach, *There Goes an Actor* (New York, 1945), p. 152; and Ernst Toller, *I Was a German* (New York, 1934), p. 12. I have not found any studied dealing with the use of this term in German literature, a subject that would illuminate German attitudes toward Poles. The term was used already by south German Jews in the United States by the mid-nineteenth century. (Rudolf Glanz, "The 'Bayer' and 'Pollack' in America," JSS, 1954, p. 29). It appears already in a dramatic poem written around 1675, "Die Beschreibungen fun Ashkenaz un Polack," M. Shulvass, *From East to West* (Detroit, 1971), p. 129, note 2. See also Max Weinreich, "Two Yiddish Satirical Poems About Jews," *Philologishe Shriftn,* III (1929), pp. 537ff.

7. The following newspapers utilize some of these terms: AZJ, July 3, 1891, pp. 313–15; *Ha-Ivri,* Jan. 20, 1911, p. 35; IFH, July 23, 1908, p. 6; AZJ, Dec. 23, 1892, p. 624.

8. Teachers: AZJ, April 22, 1910, p. 187. Renegades: AZJ, May 28, 1872, pp. 432–33.

9. School visit: AZJ, June 12, 1908, pp. 282–84. Maids: AZJ, April 30, 1897, pp. 208–09, and May 7, 1897, p. 228. Prayer for the kaiser: *Die Welt,* May 18, 1906, p. 9.

10. Orthodox rabbi: *Die Welt,* Sept. 22, 1911, p. 1011; Frankfurt: Jacob Rosenheim, *Erinnerungern 1870–1920* (Frankfurt am Main, 1970), p. 42. South German communities: *Der Israelit,* Jan. 2, 1913, p. 2. Braude: *Memoirs* (in Hebrew) (Jerusalem, 1960), p. 127, and pp. 140, 143 on Zionist bigotry. On the polemic regarding *Ost und West Judentum,* see Ismar Schorsch, *Jewish Reactions to German Anti-Semitism* (New York, 1972), p. 186; *Die Welt* March 18, 1910 (lead article), and Michael Heymann, *The Uganda Controversy,* I (Jerusalem 1970), pp. 21–23. See especially the bitter letter of Leo Winz, editor of *Ost und West,* to Adolf Friedemann (ibid., pp. 68–71).

11. Lissauer quoted in Max Marcuse, "Die christliche-jüdische Mischehe," *Sexual-Probleme: Zeitschrift fuer Sexualwissenschaft und Sexualpolitik* (Oct. 1913), p. 746.

12. Our description in this section will rely heavily upon the AZJ because it was the most prominent and oldest continuously publishing organ of German Jewry. Since, admittedly, this survey of attitudes is not exhaustive, we can use the AZJ to get a sense of the major issues that bothered native Jews. See: AZJ, Dec. 7, 1869, *Beilage;* AZJ, July 10, 1883, p. 448. The short stories of Karl Emil Franzos especially stress the dangers of arranged marriages and thwarted love.

13. Hugo Ganz, *Land of Riddles* (New York, 1904), pp. 167–68. Lessing: AZJ, Dec. 3, 1909, pp. 587–88, 620–22, 634–35.

14. AZJ, Nov. 7, 1891, *Beilage,* p. 1, and July 1889, p. 438.

15. AZJ, Jan. 31, 1871, pp. 93–95; ibid., Feb. 27, 1883, pp. 142–44; on Salanter's sojourn in Germany, see Immanuel Etkes, *Rabbi Israel Salanter and the Beginning of the "Mussar" Movement* (in Hebrew) (Jerusalem, 1982), pp. 255–70. Rülf: *Der Israelit,* Oct. 20, 1869, pp. 804–08.

16. AZJ, June 30, 1868, pp. 538–39, and Sept. 25, 1891, pp. 458–59.

17. Fuchs: *Um Deutschtum und Judentum* (Frankfurt am Main, 1919), p. 216. (The remark was made in 1905.) Bund: AZJ, Oct. 30, 1902, pp. 523–24. (Note that Arthur Ruppin, a Zionist, penned the article.)

18. AZJ, Feb. 1869, pp. 1103–07; July 1889, p. 438; and Sept. 25, 1891, pp. 4458–59.

19. For a brief analysis of attitudes during the seventeenth and eighteenth centuries, see Shulvass, pp. 47–48, 74, 129. Mendelssohn and his circle: Dan Miron, *A Traveler Disguised* (New York, 1973), pp. 36ff. Miron interprets the passage we have quoted as an attack upon the language itself; it may only refer to Yiddish translations of the Bible.

20. Hirsch: I. Heinemann, "Samson Raphael Hirsch: The Formative Years," *Historia Judaica*, April 1951, pp. 44, 47. Graetz: Joseph Meisels, "Graetz und das Ostjudentum," JP, Nov. 23, 1917, p. 494ff., and especially p. 505. Use of Graetz: CZA A101/Box 21, copy of letter sent by Harry Epstein dated Jan. 30, 1914.

21. For a brief English survey of "ghetto literature," see Mary Lynn Martin, "Karl Emil Franzos: His Views on Jewry, as Reflected in his Writings on the Ghetto" (Unpublished Dissertation, University of Wisconsin, 1968), especially Chapter II. For a German survey of ghetto writings, see K. E. Franzos' series of articles in AZJ, 1895, pp. 5ff. and 98ff. For a reinterpretation of this literature, see Ismar Schorsch, "Art as Social History: Moritz Oppenheim and the German Jewish Vision of Emancipation," in *Danzig, Between East and West: Aspects of Modern Jewish History*. ed. Isadore Twersky (Cambridge, Mass., 1985), pp. 164–67.

22. On Franzos, see Martin, pp. 5–14. *The Jews of Barnow,* trans. M. W. Macdowall (Edinburgh and London, 1892). The quotations are from pp. vii and viii. The themes I have outlined are apparent especially in the stories of "Chane" and "The Shylock of Barnow."

23. Martin, p. 267. Karpeles: AZJ, Feb. 5, 1904, pp. 64–65. Franzos often spoke before native Jewish audiences and eventually was buried in the honorary row in the *Gemeinde* cemetery in Berlin.

24. On the *Verlag,* see *Jüdischer Almanach* (Berlin, 1902); and *Jüdischer Verlag: Almanach,* 1902–1964 (Berlin, 1964), p. 10. The quotation from Eliaschoff is in Robert Weltsch's "Introduction" to YBLBI, IX, p. xxiii. On the Statistical Bureau: AZJ, Jan. 1, 1904, *Beilage,* p. 1, and Jan. 29, 1904, *Beilage,* p. 1.

25. Loewe article: JR, Jan. 22, 1904, p. 35. *Die Freistatt,* I (1913). See Max Mayer, "A German Jew Goes East," YBLBI, III, p. 349.

26. On its founders and purpose: *Ost und West,* Jan. 1901, col. 4, and Sept. 1901, col. 673.

27. A perusal of the first several volumes plainly indicates which Yiddish and Hebrew scholars were published. For the quotations see, March 1901, pp. 181–83, and Sept. 1901, pp. 653–54. The journal also sponsored Jewish Folk-Song Evenings in cities throughout Germany, which featured the music and poetry of East European Jewry (see report, December 1912, col. 1169–1200).

28. AZJ, June 1874, pp. 444–45; June 20, 1882, pp. 414–16; and Sept, 7, 1906, pp. 421–22. For examples of stories by Sholom Aleichem, see Jan. 31, 1902, pp. 57ff.; by Sholem Asch, March 6, 1908, pp. 119ff.; for a historical article by Mayer Balaban, Sept. 16, 1910, pp. 488–89.

29. Dembitzer: *Schwarze Blätter* (Berlin, 1913). Buber: Hans Kohn, *Martin Buber: Sein Werk und seine Zeit* (Hellerau, 1930), pp. 68–74. Heinrich Grünau (pseud. Grünzweig), *Exil: Drama aus dem jüdischen Leben* (Dresden and Leipzig, 1902).

30. On the postwar revival, see Adler-Rudel, pp. 47–56; Eva Reichmann, "Der Bewusstseinswandel der deutschen Juden," *Deutsches Judentum in Krieg und Revolution, 1916–1923,* ed. Werner E. Mosse (Tübingen, 1971), pp. 537–45; and Aschheim, Chapter 7.

31. Residency requirement and Berlin aid: Eschelbacher, 1920, p. 16. *Frauenbund:* Marion A. Kaplan, *The Jewish Feminist Movement in Germany: The Campaigns of the Jüdischer Frauenbund, 1904–1938* (Westport, Conn., 1979), p. 129. B'nai Brith lodges and *Verband:* S. Adler-Rudel, "East European Jewish Workers in Germany, YBLBI, II, p. 156. Cologne: AZJ, May 3, 1901, *Beilage,* p. 3.

32. Weissensee, MDIGB, No. 53 (1900), p. 4; also AZJ, Feb. 21, 1913, *Beilage,* p. 1. Pankow: Frederick Grubbel, "From Kiev via Brody to Pankow," *Jubilee Volume Dedicated to Curt C. Silberman,* ed. Herbert Strauss (New York, 1969), pp. 15–16; also AZJ, March 1887, p. 152, and March 21, 1890, pp. 148–50. *Frauenbund:* Kaplan, pp. 134ff. Schools in Munich: Elisabeth Kitzinger, *"Jüdische Jugendfürsorge in München, 1904–1943," Von Juden in München,* ed. Hans Lamm (Munich, 1958), p. 75. Offenbach: AZJ, June 12, 1908, pp. 282–84.

33. *Ost und West,* April, 1901, col. 291–98 on the programs of Toynbee Halls. *Jahres-Bericht der jüdischen Toynbee-Halle der Berliner Bnei Briss-Logen,* 1912/13. Maximillan Stein, *Zur Eröffnung der jüdischen Toynbee-Halle in Berlin* (Berlin, n.d.). Frankfurt: IFF, Oct. 15, 1913, pp. 12–13.

34. *Frauenbund:* Kaplan, p. 129. *Lesehalle: Die Welt,* Jan. 8, 1909, p. 34. Silesian miners: see supra, Chapter 5; on reading Graetz, IFH, July 18, 1912, p. 1.

35. For statistical tables on the nationality composition of students at German rabbinical schools, see Appendix E, especially Table IV, of my dissertation. There I note that each school drew foreigners from different countries: the *Rabbinerseminar* mainly attracted Hungarians, the *Hochschule* had a particularly large contingent of Russians, and the Breslau seminary drew most of its students from Bohemia, Moravia, and Galicia. Levin, pp. 229–30. Mordechai Ehrenpreis shared this assessment, *Between East and West* (Tel Aviv, 1953) p. 45. And Mordecai Braude complained of the ignorance of German students at the Hildesheimer Academy (p. 119).

36. Levin, pp. 229–30, and p. 232 on Maybaum. Also Ehrenpreis, p. 36. Caesar Seligmann "Mein Leben: Erinnerungen eines Grossvaters" (Unpublished Memoir, ALBI, p. 54). Hildesheimer: Bernard D. Perlow, "Institutions for the Education of the Modern Rabbi in Germany" (Unpublished Dissertation, Dropsie College, 1954), p. 113.

37. Levin, p. 233.

38. Levin, p. 289, and AZJ, Nov. 1878, p. 583.

39. Königsberg: AZJ, Nov., 1878, p. 583; Eschelbacher, 1920, pp. 18–19; Tuerk: M. Sinasohn, *Die Berliner Privatsynagogen und ihre Rabbiner 1671–1971* (Jerusalem, 1971), p. 26.

40. Eschelbacher, 1920, pp. 18–19. The assessment from the interwar period in *Jüdische Welt,* I (1928), p. 3.

41. On positive views of Germany (and Westernization) in the literature of Eastern Jewry see, Miron, pp. 99–118. Kurt Katsch, an Austrian, recalled his excitement at the prospect of immigrating to Germany: "that was, afer all, the land where our language originated, the land whose increasing might we admired from afar" (Unpublished Memoir, ALBI, p. 27).

There was also a high regard for the achievements of German Jewry. Even writers who scorned such Jews still could not help admiring their cultural attainments. As he departed Germany, Moses Eisenstadt conceded his awe, for "one will find no land where the science of Judaism and its literature flourish and bloom as in Germany" (*Ha-Melitz,* 1895, no. 134, pp. 2–3). According to Meir Bar Ilan, most orthodox immigrants "preferred German Jewish religious life and say it is superior to the religious spirit of Russian Jewry" (*From Volozhin to Jerusalem,* II (in Hebrew) [Tel Aviv, 1971], pp. 374–79).

42. Peter Gay, "Encounter With Modernism: German Jews in German Culture, 1888–1914," *Midstream*, Feb. 1975, p. 50.

43. *Ha-Melitz*, 1895, No. 134, pp. 2–3.

44. Bernfeld: *Ha-Maggid*, Jan. 22, 1885, pp. 27–28; Wolf: *Ha-Maggid*, July 22, 1891, pp. 227–28, 236–37. Wolff's comments are translated into Hebrew from his pamphlet *Ein Stiefkind der jüdischen Gemeinde* (Berlin, 1891). It is difficult to reconcile these statements with Wolff's later description of his efforts to aid and protect Polish cantors in Germany. See his *Fünfzig Jahre Lebenserfahrungen eines jüdischen Lehrers und Schriftstellers: Kulturbilder aus den jüdischen Gemeinden* (Leipzig, 1919), pp. 179–80. Max Marcuse, "Die christliche-jüdische Mischehe," *Sexual-Probleme: Zeitschrift für Sexualwissenschaft und Sexualpolitik* (Oct. 1912), p. 748.

45. Gordon W. Allport is one distinguished social psychologist who has alluded to the question at hand. During the course of a discussion about "Trait Due to Victimization," he refers to the behavior of German Jews as "aggression against one's own group" (*The Nature of Prejudice* [Reading, Mass., 1954], pp. 152–53).

46. Already when Jews were readmitted into Prussia during the seventeenth and eighteenth centuries laws distinguished between native and alien Jews, see Jacob R. Marcus, *The Jew in the Medieval World* (New York, 1975), #16 and 18, for two translated texts that illustrate how German Jews were forced to cooperate in keeping out aliens. For more such texts, see Selma Stern, *Der preussische Staat und die Juden,* I–IV (Tübingen, 1962).

47. Chaim Weizmann, *Trial and Error,* I, p. 32.

48. The term *Bildung* has connotations that go beyond those described here. W. H. Brufford writes of "self-cultivation" in defining *Bildung*. And Thomas Mann claimed that the "inwardness, the culture *[Bildung]* of a German implies introspectiveness, and individualistic cultural conscience; consideration for the careful tending, the shaping, deepening and perfecting of one's own personality. . . ." W. H. Buford, *The German Tradition of Self-Cultivation* (Cambridge, U.K., 1975), p. i and vii. It is doubtful from the ways German Jews used the term *Bildung* that they had all these qualities in mind. Rather, they wanted Eastern Jews to Germanize, acquire a Western education, outlook, and value system, and behave in a refined manner. On the changing meanings of *Bildung* for German Jewry, see George Mosse, *German Jews Beyond Judaism* (Cincinnati, 1985), Chapter one.

The following are a few of the numerous articles that exhort Eastern Jews to acquire *Bildung,* or criticize them for lacking this quality: AZJ, May 19, 1868, p. 417; May 26, 1868, pp. 438–39; Oct. 1869, *Beilage* to #45; as well as most of the references in notes 12–18 of this chapter. Interestingly, the emphasis on *Bildung* is strongest in articles from the 1860s and then lessens in the twentieth century. This may reflect the realization that *Bildung* alone would not solve the problems of Jewry—whether Russian or German.

49. For one of the numerous articles analyzing German Jewry's belief that education was a means of achieving emancipation and becoming better citizens, see Adolf Kober, "Emancipation's Impact on the Education and Vocational Training of German Jewry," JSS, 1954. On the new type of Jewish education pioneered by the leaders of the German *Haskalah,* see Mordechai Eliav, *Jewish Education in Germany in the Period of the Enlightenment and Emancipation* (in Hebrew) (Jerusalem, 1960).

50. On charges by anti-Semites that German Jews were "Oriental" and alien to the German *Volk,* see George L. Mosse, *The Crisis of German Ideology* (New York, 1964), Part I. Jacoby: quoted by Eleanor Sterling, "Jewish Reactions to Jew-Hatred in the First Half of the Nineteenth Century," YBLBI II (1958), p. 105.

51. The history of intergroup tensions among Jews remains to be written. Evidence of such tensions during the Middle Ages is attested by the widespread use of the "ban of

residence" *(Herem-Ha-Yishuv)* by medieval communities in order to keep out unwanted fellow Jews, including aliens; see Baron, *The Jewish Community,* passim, and especially II, pp. 7–8. On tensions between native and immigrant Jews in the modern era, see references in this book's Conclusion. On the critique of ghetto culture by *Maskilim* and Yiddish authors, see Israel Zinberg, *A History of Jewish Literature,* trans., Bernard Martin (New York, 1976–78), especially vol. IX, Chapter Nine, and vol. XI–XII; and Dan Miron, *A Traveler Disguised: The Rise of Modern Yiddish Fiction in the Nineteenth Century* (New York, 1973), especially Chapters One and Two.

Chapter 9

1. On the gradual emergence of organizations for Jewish self-defense in imperial Germany, see Ismar Schorsch, *Jewish Reactions to German Anti-Semitism, 1870–1914* (New York, 1972), especially pp. 103–04, 116.

2. In his analysis of Jewish press reactions during the expulsions of the 1880s, Helmuth Neubach is highly critical of the feeble protests issued by the AZJ, "the mouthpiece of German Jews" (see p. 148–51). In fact, the Jewish press gradually shifted its stance during the 1880s and 1890s.

3. The first reference to an expulsion order appears in the Feb. 17, 1885, issue of the AZJ (p. 124); during the subsequent four months, there were few reports on Prussian expulsions. See the issue of July 21, 1885, for a bland report on developments (p. 478). For examples of articles contending that Jews are indirect victims of Polish expulsions, see Sept. 29, 1885, p. 663; Oct. 6, 1885, p. 655; Nov. 24, 1885, p. 763; Dec. 1, 1885, pp. 784, 786; Dec. 15, 1885, pp. 784, 786. For a critique of Puttkamer, see Sept. 22, 1885, p. 619. A January 1, 1886, article objects to the expulsion of Jews who have lived in Prussia for years and labels critics of the movement from eastern into western Germany as anti-Semites (p. 6). (It is intriguing that during the expulsions, the Russian press played down the suffering of Russians, the Vatican press said little of Catholic suffering, and the Jewish press reported scantily on Jewish misery.)

It is not immediately apparent what motivated the AZJ's frequent changes in policy. Perhaps, as the expulsions unfolded and were defended publicly by Prussian officials, German Jews became aware of the anti-Semitic character of government actions. Since the newspaper's boldest refutation of Puttkamer came after the expulsions had already been debated publicly in the Prussian Chamber of Deputies and the Reichstag, perhaps its new candor stemmed from the knowledge that prominent Gentiles also opposed the expulsions. Also, the forthright defense of Polish Jews published by *Die Nation* greatly impressed the editors of the AZJ; the paper reprinted Möller's articles in their entirety. (On these articles, see supra, Chapter 2.) While this is all speculative, the variety of responses in the AZJ is, in itself, noteworthy,

4. On the AZJ's opposition to restrictionist legislation, see Jan. 12, 1885, pp. 37–38; Jan. 30, 1895, p. 49; Nov. 30, 1900, p. 566; and Jan. 5, 1908, p. 276. The Karpeles quotation is from the May 20, 1898, issue (lead editorial). On the AZJ's reaction to the debate over Article I, see March 16, 1894, pp. 121–22. Undoubtedly, a major factor motivating the paper's championing of immigrant Jews was Gustav Karpeles' assumption of the editorship in 1890. Karpeles, a Moravian-born immigrant to Germany, was an outspoken critic of those German Jews who mistreated immigrant coreligionists.

5. JP, May 14, 1885, pp. 201, 500. On this paper's harsh critique of the 1906 expulsions, see May 11, 1906, pp. 239–42; May 18, 1906, p. 255. See also AZJ, May 25, 1906, pp. 242–43, and Oct. 1907, p. 506; IDR, XII (April 1906), p. 241, and Sept. 1907,

pp. 510–11. For the vehement opposition to the expulsions by the JR, see its May 4, 1906, issue (pp. 257–58).

6. On attitudes toward naturalization policies, see IFH, Aug. 18, 1904 (lead article), and AZJ, April 24, 1908, p. 193. On concern over the new naturalization law, see June 10, 1913, p. 7, and IFH, April 5, 1914 (lead article). On opposition to residence policies see, IFH, Feb. 16, 1911, p. 5; JR, Dec. 19, 1913, p. 549; *Jüdisches Volksblatt* (Breslau), March 18, 1910, p. 109, and AZJ, Aug. 2, 1907, pp. 362–63.

7. On German Jewry's traditional "preference for the intercession of Christian spokesmen on their behalf," see Schorsch, pp. 79–80. For a few examples of reports that quoted Gentiles, see AZJ, Nov. 30, 1900, p. 566, which quotes the *Kölnische Zeitung;* JR, May 1906, p. 287, quotes the *Österreichische Wochenschrift;* IDR, XIII (Sept., 1907), pp. 510–11, quotes the *Breslauer Zeitung* and *Frankfurter Zeitung.* Also see quotations from the speech of an unnamed "non-Jewish politician" in AZJ, May 25, 1906, pp. 242–43. For an indirect attack upon government policies that is couched as an expression of sympathy for Jewish victims, see AZJ, July 14, 1893, *Beilage,* p. 1.

8. For a few articles refuting charges of a "mass immigration," see AZJ, Nov. 1869, p. 923; AZJ, May 13, 1884, p. 309; AZJ, Dec. 1869, p. 590; AZJ, May 20, 1898, *Beilage,* p. 1. The repeated denials by this paper give a sense of how seriously this charge rankled.

In its references to the "fable" of Jewish mass migration, the paper relied heavily upon the work of Solomon Neumann, a statistician who tried to prove that the Jewish population of Prussia was not growing due to an influx from the East. See *Die Fabel von der jüdischen Masseneinwanderung* (Berlin, 1880) and *Zur Statistik der Juden in Preussen von 1816 bis 1880* (Berlin, 1884), which brings the former study up to date by utilizing 1880 statistics. It should be added that the statistican was hampered by a dearth of data and therefore could not fully prove his case that the mass immigration was a "fable." I have found no evidence that Neumann was working on behalf of a Jewish organization.

9. On the economic activities of Eastern Jews, see AZJ, March 16, 1894, pp. 121–22. The following articles denied the existence of any links between Russian Jews and revolutionary activities: AZJ, Oct. 12, 1906, p. 483; April 5, 1881, pp. 217–18; June 14, 1907, p. 279. On investigations clearing transmigrant Jews of responsibility for cholera outbreaks, see AZJ, Sept. 14, 1894, *Beilage,* p. 3, and AZJ, Sept 22, 1905, pp. 446–47.

10. Articles denying any links between Eastern Jews and Polish nationalism appear in AZJ, April 1885, p. 239, and IR, Oct. 25, 1901. The activities of these Jews as agents of Germanization in Poland are discussed in AZJ, Dec. 9, 1879, p. 786; AZJ, April 13, 1906, pp. 172–73; see also IDR, XII (March 1911), pp. 169–71, for a summary of Davis Trietsch's book *Das Deutschtum im Ausland,* which claims that any German traveler in Eastern Europe can converse with Jews but will not be able to carry on a conversation with Slavs. On the anthropology of these Jews, see ZfDS, II (Sept. 1906), p. 144. Karpeles: AZJ, April 24, 1908, p. 194.

11. Threats: see AZJ, Jan. 1, 1886, pp. 5–6; AZJ, Jan. 26, 1886, pp. 67–69. Humanitarian and religious appeals: see *Der Israelit,* April 26, 1906, p. 1, and AZJ, March 23, 1906, pp. 133–34. Jannasch's appeal: AZJ, Dec. 8, 1905, pp. 58–81.

12. On the absence of a German tradition of welcoming strangers and refugees, see Ralf Dahrendorf, *Society and Democracy in Germany* (New York, 1967), Chapter 22. For some examples of newspapers goading Jewish groups to act on behalf of Eastern Jews, see AZJ, Feb. 1895, p. 49; IFH, Aug. 18, 1904, p. 1; IFH, Sept. 29, 1904, p. 3; IFH, March 23, 1911, p. 5; IFH, May 17, 1914, p. 1. The JR criticized Jewish representatives in the Prussian *Landtag* for not fighting against the 1906 expulsions (May 1906, p. 287).

13. Ottmar von Mohl, *Fünfzig Jahre Reichsdienst: Lebenserinnerungen* (Leipzig, 1920),

p. 171; on the DIGB, see Schorsch, pp. 24–26; AZJ, Jan 18, 1870, p. 41; AZJ, May 14, 1872, pp. 392–93.

14. On the importance of the C.V., see Schorsch, Chapter Five. 1894 meeting: AZJ, Jan. 25, 1895, p. 49. 1897 protest: IDR, III (Sept. 1897), pp. 452–53.

15. IDR published numerous articles on the expulsions: see, for example, XII (April 1906), p. 241; (June 1906), pp. 358–60; XII (Sept. 1907), p. 506; the quotation is from vol. XIII (Sept. 1907), pp. 510–11.

16. On the critique of Austria, IDR, XIII (Sept. 1907), p. 506, and Offenbach, vol. XIV (Sept. 1908), p. 529. For examples of protests over naturalization policies, see vol. XIII (Jan. 1907), p. 52; vol. XIII (Sept. 1907), p. 510–11; vol. XX (June 1914), pp. 246–51; and especially AZJ, Jan. 21, 1910, Beilage, p. 2. The last quotation is from a speech by Dr. Cohn of Dessau, IDR, vol. XVIII (1912), p. 185.

17. JR, June 1, 1906, p. 329; AZJ, October 18, 1907, p. 495; Walter Breslauer, "Der Verband der deutschen Juden (1904–1922)," BLBI, VII (1964), p. 370, and JR, Nov. 7, 1913, p. 479. Horowitz's address is recorded in Stenographischer Bericht über die fünfte Hauptversammlung des Verbands der Deutschen Juden (Berlin, 1914), p. 17; according to the report, his remarks were applauded warmly.

18. On the Verband's areas of concern, see Schorsch, p. 158, and Marjorie Lamberti, Jewish Activism in Imperial Germany, p. 112. On the system of correspondents, see AZJ, June 19, 1908, Beilage, p. 1. See Achter GB of the Verband, p. 18, on the disputed statistics.

19. The text of the eighth report contains information on these actions; see pp. 17–18, 36.

20. On the joint commission, see the fifth and sixth GB of the Verband, pp. 20 and 27–28, respectively. For protests raised at the commission's January 23, 1910, meeting, see CAHJP KN, IIa II/s, pp. 244–45. On the unwillingness to take up individual cases, see the controversy in the IFH. (Also cited in AZJ, June 5, 1914, p. 266.)

Jewish communities did, however, file suits to challenge Puttkamer's use of the 1847 Jewry Law in regard to synagogue functionaries. Since German Jews were fined for hiring functionaries lacking proper permits, they could challenge this particular measure in the courts. Similar opportunities to file lawsuits were unavailable to foreigners who wished to challenge naturalization proceedings. (On suits regarding the 1847 law: IDR, XII [Nov. 1906], pp. 621–22.)

21. For a broader discussion of Jewish efforts in regard to the new law, see my "Jewish Lobbyists and the German Citizenship Law of 1914: A Documentary Account," Studies in Contemporary Jewry, I (1984), pp. 140–142. On Verband lobbying, see AZJ, June 5, 1914, p. 266. Siebenter GB, pp. 23–24; Achter GB, pp. 16–18, 31–39, 40–43; and Schorsch, pp. 163–64. SBR, XIII Leg., I Session, June 25, 1913, pp. 5773–75.

22. SBR, XII Leg., I Session, June 25, 1913, pp. 5773–75, and Der Israelit, Aug. 21, 1913, p. 12. Minister of Interior Delbrueck opposed the new wording on the grounds that states must maintain their prerogative over naturalizations. On German Jewry's dependence upon alien religious functionaries, see infra, Chapters 5 and 9.

23. On lobbying for the Gröber revision, see IFH, July 4, 1913, Beilage, p. 102, and JR, July 4, 1913, p. 274. On the intercession of Berlin's Gemeinde, see SBR, IX Leg., II Session, vol IV, 1905–06, p. 2872. On later intercessions, see IFH, April 3, 1914, p. 2; and AZJ, March 27, 1914, Beilage, p. 1. This article reveals a nonaltruistic motive for the intense Jewish concern over the pending expulsions: Gemeinde members feared that the community would have to support the Jews who were thrown out of their jobs. On 1897 protests, see IDR, III (Sept. 1897), pp. 452–53; and AZJ, Aug. 6, 1897, Beilage, p. 1. See also Donald Niewyck, "German Social Democracy and the Problem of Anti-Semitism,

1906–1914'' (Unpublished M.A. Thesis, Tulane University, 1964), p. 52, which refers to the intercession of the Frankfurt am Main community on behalf of expelled poets and artists; see also Lion Wolff's account of the deputation sent by the Cantor's Welfare Fund *(Cantor Hilfskasse)* on behalf of two seminary students ordered to leave in 1885 *(Fünfzig Jahre Lebenserfahrungen eines jüdischen Lehrers und Schriftstellers: Kulturbilder aus den jüdischen Gemeinden)* [Leipzig, 1919], pp. 179–80), and the petitions submitted by the *Alliance* office in Berlin to save individuals who had been ordered to leave Germany (DZA II, Rep. 77 Tit. 1176 Nr. 1L Bd. 5, pp. 10, 23, 29, 38, 73). These examples indicate that some German Jewish groups acted to protect Eastern Jews from harsh German policies. There is no way, however, to gauge whether only a handful of Jewish groups acted or whether many organizations were engaged in behind-the-scenes lobbying.

24. AZJ, Nov. 30, 1968, pp. 963–64. The AZJ of 1868 and 1869 contains numerous reports on the activities of these border and fund-raising committees. See also Wischnitzer, pp. 29–30. (The latter work provides only a scanty survey of German Jewish activities from 1880 until the founding of the *Hilfsverein;* see pp. 70–72.) On the facilities established in ports, see AZJ, June 22, 1906, *Beilage,* p. 1; *Bericht der Bremer Komitees für hilfsbedürftige durchreisende Juden . . . 1907,* pp. 405, in CAHJP TD/879, and AZJ, Jan. 10, 1902, *Beilage,* p. 3. On some activities of the Berlin Committee: AZJ, May 1882, pp. 414–16, and Nov. 6, 1891, pp. 529–36; see also ''Deutsches Central-Komitee für die russichen Juden in Berlin: Die Organisation in Ostpreussen und Oberschlesien, May–Sept., 1892,'' for a report that describes the hierarchy of committees operating in East Prussia alone (ALBI, AR-A598 2023, ''Emigration, 1881–1914''). Aid to vulnerable travelers: AZJ, May, 1882, pp. 414–16.

25. On the work and goals of the *Hilfsverein:* Wischnitzer, pp. 100–04: Sklarz, pp. 69, 71; Moshe Rinott, *Hilfsverein der deutschen Juden: Creation and Struggle* (in Hebrew) (Jerusalem, 1971), p. 28, and James Simon's speech, reported in AZJ, Feb. 11, 1910, *Beilage,* p. 1.

26. Historians: Shimshon Kirschenbaum, for example, makes the following statement: ''German Jews . . . tried their best to relieve themselves of the burden of caring [for needy Eastern Jews].'' ''The Immigration of Russian and Polish Jews to Germany. . . .'' (Unpublished Dissertation, Hebrew University, 1950), p. 290.

For lists of contributors, see AZJ, 1869, pp. 35, 176. Contributions of German Jewry compared to other Jewries: Wischnitzer, pp. 78–115. *Alliance* membership: Zosa Szajkowski, ''Conflicts in the *Alliance Israélite Universelle* and the Founding of the Anglo-Jewish Association, the Vienna *Allianz* and the *Hilfsverein,''* JSS, 1957, pp. 30–31. The author does not account for the stupendous growth of German members in the late 1860s. Several Eastern Jews have acknowledged the sincere kindness of German Jews to the transmigrants: Mary Antin interrupts her long tale of mistreatment at the hands of German officials to recall the generous help extended by a German Jew who negotiated on behalf of the Antin family and ''entertained us in his house, shabby immigrants through we were'' *(The Promised Land,* pp. 171–72). Shmaryahu Levin, a Russian Jew intimately involved with aiding the transmigrants, wrote at length about the brotherly love extended by native Jews—even the wealthy *(Youth in Revolt* [New York, 1930], pp. 252–57).

27. Orthodox Jews in Germany have been largely ignored by social historians. (For an important exception, see the Liberles dissertation cited above, in Chapter 7, note 2.) It is therefore difficult to present more than a sketchy outline of their stances vis-à-vis anti-Semitism. On JP's position in 1885–86, see May 7, 1995, p. 191; no. 20 (May 14, 1885, p. 210) interprets the expulsions as directed solely at religious functionaries; no. 50 (Dec. 10, 1885, p. 500) accepts Windthorst's claim that ninety percent of the victims were Catholics. In the nineteenth century, *Der Israelit* ignored the problems of immigrant Jews. See

also the forthright critique of twentieth-century German policies: JP, May 18, 1906, p. 255, and May 11, 1906, pp. 239–42. On Rabbi Joseph Carlebach's letter to a Reichstag deputy who had claimed that German Jewry supported border restrictions against Eastern Jews, JP, Feb. 21, 1913, pp. 75–77; *Der Israelit*, Jan. 15, 1914, p. 5, defends the Prussian officials. See IFH, June 18, 1914, p. 6, on the hiring of an attorney in Halberstadt.

28. For some examples of Zionist criticism of liberal organizations, see *Die Welt*, Sept, 22, 1911, p. 1011; JR, May 14, 1906, pp. 257–58. For an example of a protest resolution, see JR, May 1906, p. 300. On the lobbying against planned expulsions, see CZA 142/47/4 (Alfred Klee files—letter of July 29, 1914). On the *Reichsverein:* Schorsch, p. 200 and p. 266, note 82.

29. *Die Grenzboten*, vol. I (1880), p. 45. *Judentaufen*, A. Landsberger, ed. (Munich, 1912), pp. 15–16, 38, 76.

30. IDR, XIX (March 1913), pp. 125–26. SBR, IX Leg., III Session, 1894–95, vol. II, pp. 1145D and 1303 for speeches by Jacobskröter and Manteuffel.

31. Haase's charge is in SBR, IX Leg., II Session, 1894–95, *Anlageband* VIII, p. 5688. For a similar attack on Jewish solidarity, see AZJ, Dec. 19, 1889, p. 797 (article on the views of Robert Hessen). See also JR, Jan. 12, 1906, p. 19. Hans Heilbronner quotes Richthofen's letter in "Count Aehrenthal and Russian Jewry, 1903–1907," *Journal of Modern History*, vol. 38 (Dec. 1966), p. 402, note 32.

32. In the Conclusion, German Jewry's strategy for defending immigrant coreligionists will be compared to the approach of other Jewries.

33. Leo Kreindler in *Jüdishe Welt*, I (1928), p. 3 (Clipping found in CZA 101/Box 15.) While the article dates to the interwar period, it reflects an approach that already was evident in the imperial era.

Conclusion

1. Our comparison focuses on developments in England, France, and the United States because these societies were most analogous to Germany and because an important historical literature is available on the experiences of East European Jews in these countries. On England, see Lloyd P. Gartner, *The Jewish Immigrant in England 1870–1914* (London, 1960); France—Paula E. Hyman, *From Dreyfus to Vichy: The Remaking of French Jewry, 1906–1939* (New York, 1979); the U.S.—Moses Rischin, *The Promised City* (New York, 1970), and Irving Howe, *World of Our Fathers* (New York, 1976).

2. On England's failure to sign the treaty, see Barbara Vogel, p. 88.

3. On restrictionism in the United States, see John Higham, *Strangers in the Land: Patterns of American Nativism, 1860–1925*, sec. ed. (New York, 1963), and Thomas J. Curran, *Xenophobia and Immigration, 1820–1930* (Boston, 1975). On England, John A. Garrard, *The English and Immigration, 1880–1910; A Comparative Study of the Influx* (London, 1971), and Bernard Gainer, *The Alien Invasion: The Origins of the Aliens Act of 1905* (London, 1972).

4. The comments of Germany's foreign minister in 1894 appear in SBR, IX Leg., II Session, 1893–94, vol. III, p. 1772. Bülow's assessment is quoted in Leo Stern 2/I, document #52, p. 143. Egmont Zechlin claims that Bülow decided against supporting such legislation because he feared adverse press reaction; see *Die deutsche Politik und die Juden im Ersten Weltkrieg* (Göttingen, 1969), pp. 261–62.

5. See the works of Klaus J. Bade (cited above) for recent works drawing such parallels.

6. According to the sociological theories of Samuel Stouffer, intervening opportunities

often attract immigrants to settle in a locality that was not their planned destination. See "Migration and Intervening Opportunities," *American Sociological Review,* V (December 1940). Germany should have offered such opportunities, but official policies rendered the *Reich* inhospitable.

7. Joseph Kruk, "Die Handlung entwickelt sich" (Offprint, Jewish Telegraphic Agency), Zurich, 1910.

8. On the national composition and occupations of Eastern Jews in England, see Gartner, Chapters II and III; in France, Hyman, Chapter 3; and the U.S., see Rischin's appendices.

9. On the cultural and political institutions in France, see Hyman, Chapter 4; in England, Gartner, Chapters V–IX; and the U.S., see Howe.

10. See the references in note 9 on organizations for self-defense.

11. The term is employed by Lucy Dawidowicz in her highly sympathetic portrait of East European Jewry in the modern era. See *The Golden Tradition* (Boston, 1967).

12. Whereas the children of immigrants entered the rabbinate and communal organizations of native Jews in other Western lands, it was relatively uncommon for immigrants to provide such a service for native Jews—except perhaps in lower-status occupations such as ritual slaughtering and teaching Hebrew.

13. The anti-Jewish thrust of restrictionism in Germany prompted native Jews to express their opposition as a protest against religious discrimination. In England and the United States restrictionists did not single out Jews for special legislation and avoided the public appearance of anti-Semitism. As a consequence, native Jews in the United States and England fought restrictionism on the more general ground that the immigration of all people should be free. On the responses of native Jews in the United States, see Sheldon M. Neuringer, *American Jewry and United States Immigration Policy, 1881–1953* (New York, 1980); and on the leadership of Anglo-Jewry, see Todd M. Endelman, "Native Jews and Foreign Jews in London, 1870–1914," in *The Legacy of Jewish Immigration: 1881 and Its Impact,* David Berger, ed. (New York, 1983), pp. 109–30.

14. Rosenzweig, *Briefe* (Berlin, 1935), p. 95, is cited in Z. Szajkowski, "The Struggle for Yiddish During World War I," YBLBI, IX (1964), p. 147. Endelman argues that the nature of the Jewish Question in England, France, and the United States accounts for different responses by native Jewries in those countries to the challenge of Jewish mass migration (pp. 124–25).

Bibliography

Archival Sources

Archives of the Leo Baeck Institute, New York (ALBI)

Microfilm #152. "Aus. Amt: Stuttgart—Polizeibericht betr. Juden (österreichischer und russischer Nationalität).
Unpublished Memoirs:
Bernhard Kahn
Kurt Katsch
Josef Lange
Max Reiner
Oskar Schwartz
Caesar Seligmann

Bayerisches Hauptstaatsarchiv, Munich (BHA)

Abt. III: Staatsarchiv München
Kultusministerium:
#19630, #19631. K. Technische Hochschule München. Aufnahme der Studierenden, Zuhörer, u. Hospitanten (Ausländer—Generalia) 1900–1912, 1913–1921.
Landratsamt München
Nr. 9984a. Generalia: Aufsicht über herumziehende Zigeuner, Italiener, Juden. . .
Ministerium des Innern:
#52131. Heimat und Staatsangehörigkeit, 1889–92.
#71648. Ausweisungsmassregelung in Preussen, 1885–1911.
#74140. Einwänderung und Aufenthalt von Ausländern. Generalia, 1871–1919.
#74741–42. Gesetz über den Ewerb und Verlust der Reichsangehörigkeit, 1870–1911, 1912–1913.
#74143. Reichs und Staatsang.-Gesetz.
Polizeidirektion München:
Nr. 524. Wissenschaftlicher Verein polnischer Studenten.
Nr. 571. Polonia.
Regierung Oberbayern:
RA 43484–43529. Naturalisationen.
Kirchenbücher #12–13. Trauungen.

Brandenburgisches Landeshauptarchiv, Potsdam

Pr. Br. Rep. 30 Berlin C Polizeipräsidium Berlin.
#12707/1–2. Russenausweisungen, 1903–06.

#12708. *Vernehmungen in Sachen der russischen Protestresolutionen gegen die Ausführungen des Reichskanzlers am 29.2.1904.*

Bund Archives, New York

Files Entitled:
"Berlin"
"Gera"
"Leipzig"
"Karlsruhe"
"Kelten-Friedberg"
"Mannheim
"Offenbach Bundist Groups"
"Seventh and Eight Conventions of Bundists in Western Europe"

Central Archives for the History of the Jewish People, Jerusalem. (CAHJP)

HM 9520a-b. *Acta Nihilisten* (Microfilm)
HM 9873. *Die Agitationen gegen die Juden betr. 1898–1904.*
HM 9519B. *Juden in Russland.*
INV. 1412/12. Anti-Semitism and the Fight Against It.
INV. 3109 (1–6). Collection of Caricatures on German Jewry.
KN IIa II/s. Königsberg.
M I/5. *Deutsch. Isr. Gemeindebund*—Anti-Semitic Petitions, 1879–81.
P/52. *Nachlass Sanitätsrat Dr. Solomon Neumann.*
TD/141. Report of Self-Aid Committee of Jewish Students from Russia in Berlin.
Communal Ordinances:
TD 1002. Bad Kissingen, 1888.
TD/16. Bamberg, 1873, 1888, 1910.
D/GSA #148 and TD/100–16. Berlin, 1898, 1901, 1907.
TD/18. Beuthen, 1880.
GA/Bochum 52. Bochum, 1886.
INV. 627. Cologne, 1896.
TD/120. Dresden, 1869, 1905, 1913.
TD/4. Erfurt, 1889.
TD/6. Halle, 1858, 1886.
TD/59. Halberstadt, 1886.
TD/352 and AHW 297, vol. 15. Hamburg, 1867, 1906.
INV. 627. Königsberg.
TD/91. Leipzig, 1884.
TD/593. Secessionists in Frankfurt am Main, 1876.
Nürnberg 19/38. Secessionists in Nürnberg, 1897.
TD/ 796. Secessionists in Berlin, n.d.
INV. 627. Würzburg, n.d.
Reports of B'nai Brith Lodges: Berlin, Coblenz, Cologne, Düsseldorf, Frankfurt am Main.
TD/ 879. Bremen Committee to Aid Transmigrant Jews.
TD/24. *Central Verein. Mitglieder Verzeichnis, 1899.*
INV 1430-(1). *Neuer Jüdischer Gemeindeverein.*
TD/69. *Verein für Jüdische Geschichte und Literatur.*

Central Zionist Archives, Jerusalem (CZA)

A142. *Berlin. Zionistische Vereiningung.* . .
A15. Max Bodenheimer.
A101. Harry Epstein.
A135 Sammy Gronemann.
A42. Heinrich Klee.
A146. Heinrich Loewe.
A126. Leo Motzkin.

Deutsches Zentralarchiv, Merseburg (DZA II)

Kultusministerium:
Rep. 76 Va Sekt 1 Tit. I Nr. 28. *Der Andrang russischer Staatsangehöriger jüdischen Bekentnisses zu dem Universitäts-Studium in Preussen und zum ärztlichen Stande, 1890–1911.*
Ministerium des Innern:
Rep. 77 Tit. 46 Nr. 40 Bd. 1. *Das Studium russischer Staatsangehöriger an den preussischen Hochschulen.*
Rep. 77 Tit. 226 No. 130 Bd. 1. *Erlass von Polizeiverordnungen über den Verkehr von ausserdeutschen Auswanderen über die preussisch-russische Grenze.*
Rep. 77 Tit. 226B Nr. 66 Bd. 1. *Die Einwanderung und der Aufenthalt ausländischer Juden—Generalia.*
Rep. 77 Tit. 226b No. 1A and 1B Bd. 2 and Bd. 4, and Bd. 5, and Bd. 40 Nr. 1 *Die Einwanderungen aus Russland.*
Rep. 77 Tit. 226b No. 38. *Verhinderung der Naturalisation aus dem preuss. Staatsgebiet ausgewiesener russ.—polnischer u. galizischer Juden seitens anderer Bundesstaaten.*
Rep. 77 Tit. 226b No. 38. Heft I. *Nachweisungen*
Rep. 77 Tit. 227 No.4. Beihefte (1891–92).
Rep. 77 Tit. 227 Nr. 4 Adh. XXIII.
Rep. 77 Tit. 227 Nr. 15. *Naturalisation ausländischer Gewerbetreibender.*
Rep. 77 Tit. 227 Nr. 50 Bd. 1 and Bd. 3. *Die Naturalisation ausländischer Ärzte.*
Rep. 77 Tit. 500 No. 38. *Ausländerwesen, Miscellan.*
Rep. 77 Tit. 874K Nr. 20. *Dr. Adolph Kohut.*
Rep. 77. Tit. 1145 Nr. 114 Bd. 1. *Die Massregeln in Folge das Übertritts jüdischer Ausfliege aus Russland nach Preussen.*
Rep. 77 Tit. 1176 No. 1G Bd. 5. *Massregeln zur Verhütung des Anwachsens des polnischen Elements in Preussen.*
Rep. 77 Tit. 1176 Nr. 1K Bd. 1, Bd. 2, Bd. 4, Bd. 5. *Massnahmen zur Verhütung des Anwachsens des polnischen Elements in Preussen.*
Rep. 77 Tit. 1176 Nr. 1L Bd. 1–6. *Massregeln zur Verhütung des Anwachsens des polnischen Elements in Preussen.*
Rep. 77 Tit. 1176 No. 2a Gen. Bd. 4 and Bd. 5. *Über den Aufenthalt poln. Flüchtlinge in den preuss. Staaten sowie über deren Ausweisungen.*
Rep. 77 Tit. 1176 No. 2a Bd. 6. *Über die Aufenthalt polnischer Flüchtlinge.*
Rep. 77 Tit. 1176 No. 2a Biakten 1. *Die Einwanderung aus Russland und Juden Verfolgung daselbst.*
Rep. 77 Tit. 1176 No. 2a gen. Beiheft 1.
Rep. 77 Tit. 1176 Nr. 4 Bd. 1. *Die Ausweisungen öster. Staatsangehöriger aus Preussen.*
Rep. 77. Tit. 1176 No. 6. Bd. 1. *Ausweisung ausländisch-polnischer Saisonarbeiter aus Preussen.*

Rep. 77 Tit. 1176 No. 7 Bd. 1. *Das bei Landesverweisungen oester.-ungarischer Staatsan-gehöriger zur beobachtende*. . .

Rep. 77 Tit. 1176 No. 23 Adhib. I. *Die Sammlung auf das Circ. Resc. von 22 Feb., 1885 eingenomenen Berichte wegen der Ausweisungen von Ausländern aus dem Reichs-gebiet*.

Preussisches Staatsministerium:

Rep. 90a B III 2b Nr. 6 Bd. 151. *Protokolle*.

Ministerium für Handel und Gewerbe:

Rep. 120 C. IX 19. Bd. 1–2. *Die Anträge fremder Juden wegen Niederlassung im Preuss-ischen Staate und Verleihung des Staatsbürgerrechts*.

Geheimes Staatsarchiv Preussischer Kulturbesitz, Dahlem (West Berlin) (GStA)

Regierung Bomberg:

Rep. 30 I Nr. 1090 Bd. 1. *Ausweisungen polnischer Überlaufer*.

Regierung Danzig:

Rep. A 180 Nr. 13506, Nr. 13550, Nr. 13752, Nr. 14182. *Aufenthalt von Ausländern*.

Rep. 1 180 #13627, 13372, 13731. *Ausweisungen*.

Regierung Königsberg:

Rep. 2 I Tit. 30 Nr. 43. *Auswanderung der ausgewiesenen russischen Juden, 1882–93*.

Rep. 2II Nr. 2065. *Hausiererhandel polnischer Juden, 1831–1931*.

Preussisches Justizministerium:

Rep. 84a Nr. 14. *Ausweisungen von Ausländern, 1855–1906*.

Rep. 84a Nr. 11896–900. *Ehe zwischen Inländern und Ausländern, 1871–1914*.

Generallandesarchiv, Karlsruhe (GLA)

Kultusministerium:

Abt. 235/4051. *Die Aufnahme russischer Studierender an der Technischen Hochschule, 1902–1921*.

Abt. 235/7305. *Die Zulassung von Ausländern zum Studium an den badischen Hoch-schulen*.

Staatsministerium:

Abt. 233/ 11128 and 11129. *Staatsbürgerrecht*.

Abt. 233/11143. *Staatsbürgerrecht. Der Erwerb und Verlust der Staatsangehörigkeit*.

Abt. 233/11454. *Bürger-Heimats- und Niederlassungsrecht, 1872–1927*.

Abt. 233/27731. *Judensachen. Die Vertretung der israelitischen Religionsgemeinschaft be-sonders durch eine Synode*.

Abt. 233/31326. *Judenrechte. Die Constituierung des jüdischen Oberrates*.

Hauptstaatsarchiv Düsseldorf, Zweigstelle Schloss Kalkum

Regierung Düsseldorf:

Nr. 8768. *Das Verfahren gegen die in diesseitigen Bezirken sich aufhaltenden nicht natu-ralisierten Ausländer*.

Nr. 8892. *Ausweisung aus dem preuss. Staatsgebiete*.

Nr. 30524. *Meldewesen*.

Nr. 30562. *Synagogengemeinde zu Hamborn*.

Nr. 30567. *Synagogengemeinde in Duisburg, 1891–1916*.

Hessisches Hauptstaatsarchiv, Wiesbaden

Preussische Regierung:

Abt. 405 Nr. 2745. *Russische Staatsangehörige während des Krieges im Regierungsbezirk Wiesbaden, 1914–1919.*

Abt. 405 Nr. 8416. *Anschuldigung gegen die aus Russland und Polen kommenden und in Deutschland vagabundierenden Juden, 1881.*

Abt. 405 Nr. 9005. *Klage der Sarah Koralnick . . . 1894–99.*

Hessisches Staatsarchiv, Darmstadt

Hess. Landesstatistisches Amts in Darmstadt.

G 13. 4219/1. *Statistik der Juden.*

Jewish National and University Library and Archives, Jerusalem. (JNL&A)

v. 768. Association of East European Students in Western Europe.

Landeshauptarchiv Koblenz

Oberpräsidium Koblenz:

Nr. 16010. *Abfassung und Genehmigung der jüdischen Synagogengemeindes-Statuten im Regierungsbezirk: Köln, 1901–1930.*

Nr. 16011. *Beschwerden und Anträge in Verwaltungsangelegenheiten der jüdischen Synagogen-Gemeinden, 1902–1929.*

Sächsisches Landeshauptarchiv, Dresden (Dresden)

Ministerium des Innern:

Sekt. V. *Staats und Heimatsangehörigkeitssachen.*

Nr. 9682–99. *Aufnahme und Naturalisationangelegenheiten, 1871–1913.*

Nr. 9700–02. *Verzeichnisse der Naturalisation, 1899–1917.*

Sekt IX. *Politische Polizei, Sicherheitspolizei, Gendarmerie. 7. Pass- und Fremdenpolizei. Grenzpolizei.*

Nr. 11691–94. *Ausweisung russischer Staatsang. aus Sachsen und sächs. Staatsangehörige aus Russland, 1870–1922.*

Nr. 11697–1700. *Ausweisungen von Ausländern aus d. Deutschen Reich, 1904–1923.*

Ministerium für Volksbildung.

A. Hochschulen. I 10. Ausländische Studierende.

Nr. 15804. *Ausländische Studierende, 1901–1918.*

II. Universitätsgericht.

Nr. 10084 and 10085. *Die an der Universität zu Leipzig und am Politechnikum Studierende russischer Nationalität, 1889–1915.*

IX. Sachen die jüdischen Glaubensgenossen betr.

Nr. 1149/3 *Die isr. Religionsgemeinde zu Dresden, 1904–20.*

Staatsarchiv der Freien und Hansenstadt Hamburg

Auswanderungsamt:

II C I 8. *Auswanderung aus Russland, 1906–1938.*

II E I 1a No. 4. *Gesuch der Hamburg-Amerika Linie um Aufhebung der Grenzsperre, 1893.*

II E III P 53. *Schriftwechsel mit Bremer Behörden, die Gefahr der Einschleppung der Cholera durch russische Auswanderer betreffend 1905.*

II E III P 5. *Behandlung der Auswanderer bei den Volkszählung 1895, 1900, 1905.*
II F 14. *Massnahmen gegen den Mädchenhandel, 1889–1937.*
Jüdische Gemeinde:
151 2). *Statistisches Material.*
160. *Verzeichnis der isr. Einwohner Altona, 1890.*

Staatsarchiv Münster

Oberpräsidium:
#5802. *Ewerb und Verlust der Bundes-bzw. Staatsangehörigkeit, 1871–1912.*
#6534. *Aus-und Einwanderer.*
Regierung Arnsberg:
I Sta Nr. 31. *Ausländern . . . russischer u. galizischer Arbeiter, 1874–1905.*

Stadtarchiv Duisburg

Bestand 16/3600. Hamborn. *Jüdische Kultusangelegenheiten, 1817–1929.*

Stadtarchiv Offenbach am Main

Angelegenheiten der isr. Religionsgemeinde Akt. 251 Abt. XIII/1:
Fasc. 4. *Galizische und russische Juden, 1913–14.*
Fasc. 5. *Polnische Juden, 1905.*
Fasc. 7. *Ausländische jüdische Händler, 1905.*

Stadtarchiv München, Munich

Einwohneramt Nr. 169. *Juden-Aufnahme, 1857–1906.*
Wohlfahrtsamt Nr. 1183. *Unterstützung, Beteiligung der Isr. an den Armenflege, 1858–1909.*

Yiddish Scientific Institute, New York

"Die Entwicklung, der jüdischen Bevölkerung in Deutschland, 1880–1945. Unpublished mss. by Bruno Blau.

Government Publications

Beiträge zur Statistik der Stadt Frankfurt am Main.
Die Bevölkerungs- und Wohnungsaufnahme in der Stadt Berlin, 1900.
Die Ergebnisse der Volkszählung von 1. Dezember 1900 in der Stadt Leipzig.
Kalender und Statistisches Jahrbuch für das Königreich Sachsen.
Statistisches Jahrbuch für das Deutsche Reich.
Statistisches Jahrbuch für das Grossherzogtum Baden.
Statistisches Jahrbuch für den Preussischen Staat.
Statistisches Jahrbuch für die Königliche Haupt- und Residenzstadt Königsberg in Preussen.
Statistisches Jahrbuch für das Königreich Bayern.
Statistisches Jahrbuch der Stadt Berlin.
Statistisches Handbuch der Stadt Dresden.
Statistik des Deutschen Reiches.

Stenographische Berichte über die Verhandlungen des Hauses der Abgeordneten.
Stenographische Berichte über die Verhandlungen des Reichstags.
Vierteljahrshefte zur Statistik des Deutschen Reichs.
Zeitschrift des K. Sächs. Statistischen Landesamts.
Zeitschrift des Königlich Preussischen Statistischen Landesamts.
Zeitschrift des Königliche Bayerischen Statistischen Bureaus.

Newspapers and Periodicals

Allgemeine Zeitung des Judentums.
American Jewish Yearbook.
Frankfurter Israelitisches Familienblatt.
Die Freistatt.
Die Grenzboten: Zeitschrift für Politik, Literatur, und Kunst.
Ha-Ivri.
Ha-Maggid.
Ha-Melitz.
Hashiloach.
Ha-Tzephira.
Im deutschen Reich.
Der Israelit.
Israelitische Rundschau.
Israelitisches Familienblatt (Hamburg).
The Jewish Chronicle.
Di Jidische Studentenschaft.
Der Jüdische Grenzbote.
Jüdische Rundschau.
Der Jüdische Student.
Jüdischer Almanach.
Jüdisches Volksblatt.
K.C. Blätter.
Korrespondenz-Blatt des Verbandes der Deutschen Juden.
Liberales Judentum.
Mitteilungen aus dem Verein zur Abwehr des Antisemitismus.
Mitteilungen des Deutsch-Israelitischen Gemeindebund.
Neue Zeit.
Ost und West.
Preussische Jahrbücher.
Selbst-Emancipation.
Serubabel.
Strassburger Israelitische Wochenschrift.
Veröffentlichungen des Bureaus für Statistik der Juden.
Die Welt.
Zeitschrift für Demographie und Statistik der Juden.
Zeitschrift für die gesamte Staatswissenschaft.
Zion: Monatsschrift für die Nationalen Interessen des Jüdischen Volkes.

Reports and Yearbooks

Bericht über die Lehranstalten der jüdischen Gemeinde zu Berlin (April 1914).

Geschäftsberichte des Verbandes der deutschen Juden.

Jahres-Bericht der jüdischen Toynbee-Halle der Berliner Bnei Briss Logen, 1912/13. Berlin, 1913.

Jahresberichte des Rabbinerseminars für das orthodoxe Judenthum.

Jahresbericht der Realschule der Israelitischen Religionsgesellschaft in Frankfurt am Main.

Jahresbericht über die Tätigkeit der Zionistischen Vereinigung für Deutschland. Berlin, 1913.

Jüdisches Jahrbuch für Gross Berlin. Berlin, 1927.

Statistisches Jahrbuch des Deutsch-Israelitischen Gemeindebundes.

Stenographische Berichte des Verbandes der deutschen Juden.

Handbuch der jüdischen Gemeindeverwaltung und Wohlfahrtspflege. Berlin, 1909.

Minutes of the Meeting of the Association for the Hebrew Language and Culture in Berlin (in Hebrew). Warsaw, 1910.

Programm der Realschule der Israelitischen Gemeinde (Philanthropin) zu Frankfurt am Main. Frankfurt, 1888, 1892.

Talmud Torah Realschule: Bericht über das Schuljahr 1898–99. Hamburg, 1899.

Printed Primary Sources

Albumblätter gespendet für die Selbstschriften-Tombola des Sommernachts-Festes zum Besten ausgewiesener russischer Juden. Berlin, 1892.

Andree, Richard. *Zur Volkskunde der Juden.* Bielefeld und Leipzig, 1881.

Antin, Mary. *From Plotzk to Boston.* Boston, 1899.

———. *The Promised Land.* New York, 1912.

Auerbach, Elias. *Pionier der Verwirklichung.* Stuttgart, 1969.

Bar-Ilan, Meir. *From Volozhin to Jerusalem* (in Hebrew), 2 vol. Tel Aviv, 1971.

Ben Avi, Itamar. *At the Dawn of Our Freedom: Memoirs of the First Hebrew Child* (in Hebrew). Tel Aviv, 1961.

Bergmann, Eugen von. "Die jüdische Einwanderung in Deutschland." *Die Grenzboten* XLIII *Erster Quartal* (1884).

———. *Zur Geschichte der Entwicklung deutscher, polnischer, und jüdischer Bevölkerung in der Provinz Posen seit 1824.* Tübingen, 1883.

Berkowitz, Isaac. *Ha-Rishonim K'Vnai Adam* (in Hebrew). Tel Aviv, 1943.

Blumenfeld, Kurt. *Erlebte Judenfrage.* Stuttgart, 1962.

Böhlich, Walter, ed. *Der Berliner Antisemitismusstreit.* Frankfurt am Main, 1965.

Brachmann, Botho, ed. *Russische Sozialdemokraten in Berlin, 1895–1914.* Berlin (East), 1962.

Braude, Mordechai. *Memoirs* (in Hebrew). Jerusalem, 1960.

Brodetsky, Selig. *Memoirs: From Ghetto to Israel.* London, 1960.

Buber, Martin, et al. *Eine Jüdische Hochschule.* Berlin, 1902. Reprinted, Jerusalem, 1968.

Chotzinoff, Samuel. *A Lost Paradise.* New York, 1955.

Class, Heinrich. *Wenn ich der Kaiser wär.* Leipzig, 1912.

Dembitzer, Salamon. *Aus engen Gassen.* Berlin, n.d.

———. *Schwartze Blätter.* Berlin, 1913.

Dinur, Ben Zion. *In a World That Has Passed* (in Hebrew). Jerusalem, 1958.

Dohm, C. W. *Über die Bürgerliche Verbesserung der Juden.* Berlin, 1783.

Dukmeyer, Friedrich. *Kritik der reinen und praktischen Unvernunft in der gemeinen Verjudung*. Berlin, 1892.

Ehrenpreis, Mordechai. *Between East and West* (in Hebrew). Tel Aviv, 1953.

Feiwel, Berthold. *"Enquete unter den Westeuropäischen jüdischen Studierenden."* In Alfred Nossig, ed., *Jüdische Statistik*. Berlin, 1903.

Franzos, Karl Emil. *The Jews of Barnow*. Trans. M. W. Macdowall. Edinburgh and London, 1892.

Fuchs, Eugen. *Um Deutschtum und Judentum*. Frankfurt am Main, 1919.

Ganz, Hugo, *Land of Riddles*. New York, 1904.

German Law Respecting the Acquisition and Loss of Federal and State Nationality, June 1, 1870 (London, 1890).

Geise, Wilhelm, *Die Juden und die deutsche Kriminal Statistik*. Leipzig, 1893.

Geisel, Eike. *Im Scheunenviertel*. Munich, 1982.

Goldmann, Nahum. *The Autobiography of Nahum Goldmann*. New York, 1969.

Granach, Alexander. *There Goes an Actor*. New York, 1945.

Gronemann, Sammy. *Memoirs of a Yekke* (in Hebrew). Tel Aviv, 1946.

Grünau, Heinrich. *Exil: Drama aus dem jüdischen Leben*. Dresden and Leipzig, 1902.

Grünow, Friedrich Wilhelm. *Israel und die Gojim: Beiträge zur Beurtheilung der Judenfrage*. Leipzig, 1880.

Hermoni, Aron. *B'ikvot Ha-biluim* (in Hebrew). Jerusalem, 1952.

Hoffman, B. *Zivion*. New York, 1948.

Horodetsky, Samuel Abba. *Memoirs* (in Hebrew). Tel Aviv, 1957.

Huber, Ernst Rudolph. *Dokumente zur Deutschen Verfassungsgeschichte*, II. Stuttgart, 1964.

Jüdischer Verlag: Almanach, 1902–1964. Berlin, 1964.

Jungman, Max. *Erinnerungen eines Zionisten*. Jerusalem, 1959.

Katzenberger, Naomi. "Dokumente zur Frage des Wahlrechts Ausländischer Juden in den preussischen Synagogengemeinden." *Michael*, II. Tel Aviv, 1973.

Klatzkin, Jacob. "Germans of the Mosaic Persuasion." *Zutot* (in Hebrew). Berlin, 1925.

Klausner, J. *My Path Toward the Revival and Redemption. An Autobiography 1874–1944* (in Hebrew). Tel Aviv, 1950.

Koenen, O., and Eicker, W., ed., *Hochschulen-Führer*. Leipzig, 1911.

Kohl, Horst, ed. *Die politischen Reden des Fürsten Bismarck*, I. Stuttgart, 1892. Reprinted, 1969.

Kruk, Joseph. *Die Handlung entwickelt sich, das Finale näht*. Offprint, Zurich, 1910.

Kursky, Franz. *Gesammelte Shriftn* (in Yiddish). New York, 1952.

Landsberger, A., ed. *Judentaufen*. Munich, 1912.

Die Lehranstalt für die Wissenschaft des Judentums in Berlin. Rückblick auf ihre ersten fünfundzwanzig Jahre, 1872–97. Berlin, 1897.

Levin, Shmaryahu. *Youth in Revolt*. New York, 1930.

Levine, Isaac Don. *Letters from the Kaiser to the Czar*. New York, 1920.

Levinsohn, Abraham, ed. *Dr. Isaac Rülf: Selected Works* (in Hebrew). Tel Aviv, 1950.

Liebermann, Mischket. *Aus dem Ghetto in die Welt*. Berlin, 1979.

Löwenberg, Jacob. *Aus zwei Quellen*. Berlin, 1914.

Marcus, Jacob R., ed. *The Jew in the Medieval World*. New York, 1965.

Marcuse, Max. "Die christlich-jüdische Mischehe." *Sexual-Probleme: Zeitschrift für Sexual wissenschaft und Sexualpolitik* (Oct. 1912).

Mayer, Max. "A German Jew Goes East." YBLBI, III (1958).

Mohl, Ottmar von. *Fünfzig Jahre Reichsdienst: Lebenserinnerungen*. Leipzig, 1920.

Neumann, Solomon. *Die Fabel von der jüdischen Masseneinwanderung*. Berlin, 1880.

————. *Zur Statistik der Juden in Preussen von 1816 bis 1880*. Berlin, 1884.

Nossig, A., ed. *Jüdische Statistik*. Berlin, 1903.

Oved, Moshe. *Visions and Jewels*. London, 1952.

Portnoy, Samuel, trans. *Vladamir Medem: The Life of a Legendary Jewish Socialist*. New York, 1979.

Puttkamer, Albert. *Staatsminister von Puttkamer: Ein Stück preussischer Vergangenheit*. Leipzig, 1928.

Radin, Adolph. *Offener Brief eines polnischen Juden an Herrn Heinrich von Treitschke*. New York, 1885.

Reinharz, Jehuda, ed. *Dokumente zur Geschichte des deutschen Zionismus 1882–1933*. Tübingen, 1981.

Rosenheim, Jacob. *Erinnerungen 1870–1920*. Frankfurt am Main, 1970.

Rosenzweig, Franz. *Briefe*. Berlin, 1935.

Rülf, Isaac. *Die russischen Juden*. Memel, 1892.

Segel, Benjamin. *Die Entdeckungsreise des Herrn Dr. Theodor Lessing zu den Ostjuden*. Lwow, 1910.

Sieff, Israel. *Memoirs*. London, 1910.

Stampfer, Friedrich. *Erfahrungen und Erkenntnisse*. Cologne, 1957.

Statuten des russisch-juedischen Vereins "Concordia" zu Berlin. Berlin, 1870.

Statuten des Vereins "Amicitia" zu Berlin. Berlin, 1870.

Stein, Maximillian. *Zur Eröffnung der jüdischen Toynbee-Halle in Berlin*. Berlin, n.d.

Stern Heinemann. *Warum hassen sie uns eigentlich?* Düsseldorf, 1970.

Stern, Leo, ed. *Die Auswirkungen der Ersten Russischen Revolution von 1905–07 auf Deutschland*, 2 vol. Berlin, 1955.

Stern, Selma. *Der preussische Staat und die Juden*, I–IV. Tübingen, 1962–.

Strauss, Rahel. *Wir lebten in Deutschland*. Stuttgart, 1961.

Theilhaber, Felix. *Der Untergang der deutschen Juden*. Munich, 1911.

Toller, Ernst. *I Was a German*. New York, 1934.

Treitschke, Heinrich von. *A Word About Our Jewry*. Trans. Helen Lederer. *Readings in Modern Jewish History*, ed. Ellis Rivkin. Cincinnati, 1958.

————. *Deutsche Kämpfe*. N.F. Leipzig, 1896.

————. *History of Germany in the Nineteenth Century*, VII. Trans. Eden and Cedar Paul. New York, 1919.

Waghalter, Ignatz. *Aus dem Ghetto in die Freiheit*. Marienbad, 1936.

Weizmann, Chaim. *The Letters and Papers of Chaim Weizmann*, I. Oxford, 1968.

————. *Trial and Error*, 2 vol. Philadelphia, 1949.

Wolff, Gottfried. *Das Judentum in Bayern*. Munich, 1897.

Wolff, Lion. *Ein Stiefkind der jüdischen Gemeinden*. Berlin, 1891.

————. *Fünfzig Jahre Lebenserfahrungen eines jüdischen Lehrers und Schriftstellers: Kulturbilder aus den jüdischen Gemeinden*. Leipzig, 1919.

Zweig, Arnold. *Das Los der Geflüchteten*. Berlin, 1930.

Secondary Sources

Abramowitz, S. Y. (Mendele Mocher Seforim). "Shem and Japheth on a Train." In Robert Alter, ed. *Modern Hebrew Literature*. New York, 1975.

Adler-Rudel, Shalom. *Ostjuden in Deutschland, 1880–1940*. Tübingen, 1959.

Alexander Granach und das Jiddische Theater des Ostens. Berlin, 1971.

Allport, Gordon W. *The Nature of Prejudice.* Reading, Mass. 1954.

Altman, P. *Die Verfassung und Verwaltung im Deutschen Reiche und Preussen,* 2 vol. Berlin, 1908.

Angress, Werner T. "Prussia's Army and The Jewish Reserve Officer Controversy Before World War I." YBLBI, XVII (1972).

———. "The Impact of the *Judenwahlen* of 1912 on the Jewish Question—a Synthesis," YBLBI, XXVIII (1983), pp. 367–412.

Arendt, Hannah. "Privileged Jews." JSS, VIII (Jan. 1946).

Arnsberg, Paul. *900 Jahre Muttergemeinde in Israel.* Frankfurt am Main, 1974.

Aschheim, Steven. *Brothers and Strangers: The East European Jew in German and German Jewish Consciousness, 1800–1923.* Madison, 1982.

———. "The East European Jew and German Jewish Identity." *Studies in Contemporary Jewry,* I (1984), pp. 3–25.

Auerbach, Leopold. *Das Judenthum und seine Bekenner in Preussen und in anderen deutschen Bundesstaaten.* Berlin, 1890.

Bade, Klaus. ed. *Auswanderer, Wanderarbeiter, Gastarbeiter: Bevölkerung, Arbeitsmarkt und Wanderung in Deutschland seit der Mitte des 19. Jahrhunderts,* 2 vol. Ostfildern, 1984.

———. "Politik und Ökonomie der Ausländerbeschäftigung im preussischen Osten, 1885–1914. Die Internationalisierung des Arbeitsmarkts im 'Rahmen der preussischen Abwehrpolitik.' " In *Geschichte und Gesellschaft, Sonderheft,* VI (1982).

———. " 'Preussengänger' und 'Abwehrpolitik.' Ausländerbeschäftigung, Ausländerpolitik und Ausländerkontrolle auf dem Arbeitsmarkt in Preussen vor dem Ersten Weltkrieg." *Archiv für Sozialgeschichte,* XXIV (1984).

———. *Transnationale Migration und Arbeitsmarkt im Kaiserreich: Vom Agrarstaat mit starker Industrie zum Industriestaat mit starker agrarischer Basis. Historische Arbeitsmarktforschung.* Ed. Toni Pierenkemper and Richard Tilly. Göttingen, 1982.

Band, Arnold. *Nostalgia and Nightmare: A Study of the Fiction of S. Y. Agnon.* Berkeley, 1968.

Barkin, Kenneth. *The Controversy over German Industrialization.* Chicago, 1970.

Baron, Salo W. *The Jewish Community,* 3 vol. Philadelphia, 1942.

———. *The Russian Jews Under Tsars and Soviets,* revised edition. New York, 1976.

———. *A Social and Religious History of the Jews,* II. New York, 1937.

Berger, Erich. *Das nationale und konfessionelle Gefüge der Bevölkerung im Königreiche Sachsen.* Halle, 1912.

Bergmann, Alexander. *Internationales Ehe-und Kinderchaftsrecht.* Berlin, 1926.

Bernard, William S., ed. *American Immigration Policy—a Reappraisal.* New York, 1950.

Beutner, Wilhelm. *Die Rechtsstellung der Ausländer nach Titel II der preussischen Verfassungsurkunde.* Tübingen, 1913.

Blackbourn, David. "Roman Catholics, the Centre Party and Anti-Semitism in Imperial Germany." In Paul Kennedy and Anthony Nicholls, ed. *Nationalist and Racialist Movements in Britain and Germany Before 1914.* London, 1981, pp. 106–29.

——— and Geoff Eley. *The Peculiarities of German History: Bourgeois Society and Politics in Nineteenth Century Germany.* Oxford and New York, 1984.

Blau, Bruno. "Sociology of the Jews." *Historia Judaica,* XI (Oct. 1949).

———. "Zur Statistik der Juden in Hannover." ZfDS, X (July–August, 1914).

Brann, Marcus. *Geschichte des jüdische Theologisch Seminars in Breslau.* Breslau, 1904.

Breslauer, Walter. "Notes on the Organizational Problems of German Jewry." YBLBI, XIV (1969).

————. "Der Verband der deutschen Juden (1904–1922)." BLBI (1964).

————. "Zum Recht der Eheschliessung und Ehescheidung der in Deutschland wohnenden ausländischen Juden," *Festschrift zum 70 Geburstag von Moritz Schaefer*. Berlin, 1928.

Bristow, Edward. *Prostitution and Prejudice: The Jewish Fight Against White Slavery, 1890–1939*. London, 1982.

Brozek, Andrzej. "Attempts to Employ Jewish Workers in Upper Silesia Before World War I" (in Polish). Offprint, n.d.

Bruford, W.H. *The German Tradition of Self-Cultivation*. Cambridge, U.K., 1975.

Cahnman, Werner. "A Regional Approach to German Jewish History." JSS, V (1943).

Carlebach, Alexander. *Adass Jeshurun of Cologne*. Belfast, 1964.

Cecil, Lamar. *Albert Ballin*. Princeton, 1967.

Cohen, Arthur. "Die jüdische Bevölkerung in München im Jahre 1910, mit besonderer Berücksichtigung der Gebürtigkeit." ZfDS, VI (May/June/July, 1919).

Cohen, Naomi W. *Not Free to Desist: The American Jewish Committee, 1906–1966*. Philadelphia, 1972.

Cohn, Gustav. "Die Entwicklung der gottesdienstlichen Verhältinisse bis zur Entwicklung der Synagoge." *Aus Geschichte und Leben der Juden in Leipzig*. Leipzig, 1930.

Craig, Gordon. *Germany, 1866–1945*. New York, 1978.

Curran, Thomas J. *Xenophobia and Immigration, 1820–1930*. Boston, 1975.

Dahrendorf, Ralf. *Society and Democracy in Germany*. New York, 1967.

Dawidowicz, Lucy, ed. *The Golden Tradition*. Boston, 1967.

Diamant, A. *Chronik der Juden in Dresden*. Darmstadt, 1973.

Dubnow, Simon. *History of the Jews in Russia and Poland*, 3 vol. Philadelphia, 1918.

Elazar, Daniel. "Sephardim and Ashkenazim: The Classic and Romantic Traditions in Jewish Civilization." *Judiasm*, vol. 33 (Spring 1984).

Eley, Geoff. "German Politics and Polish Nationality: The Dialectic of Nation-Forming in the East of Prussia." *East European Quarterly*, XVIII, no. 3 (September 1984), pp. 335–59.

————. *Reshaping the German Right: Radical Nationalism and Political Change After Bismarck*. New Haven, 1980.

Eliav, Mordechai. "German Jews' Share in the Building of the National Home in Palestine and the State of Israel." YBLBI (1985), pp. 255–64.

————. *Jewish Education in Germany in the Period of Enlightenment and Emancipation* (in Hebrew). Jerusalem, 1960.

Endelman, Todd. "Native Jews and Foreign Jews in London, 1870–1914." In David Berger, ed., *The Legacy of Jewish Immigration: 1881 and Its Impact*. New York, 1983, pp. 109–30.

Eschelbacher, Klara. "Die Ostjüdische Einwanderungsbevölkerung der Stadt Berlin." ZfDS, XVI (1920) and XVII (1923).

Etkes, Immanuel. *Rabbi Israel Salanter and The Beginning of the "Musar" Movement* (in Hebrew). Jerusalem, 1982.

Flexner, Abraham. *Medical Education in Europe*. New York, 1912.

Fraustädter, Werner. *Die ostjüdische Arbeitereinwanderung im Rheinisch-westfälischen Industriegebiet*. Dissertation. Frankfurt am Main, n.d.

Freudenthal, Max. *Die Israelitische Kultusgemeinde in Nürnberg, 1874–1924*. Nürnberg, 1925.

Froehlich, Paul. *Rosa Luxemburg: Gedanke und Tat*. Paris, 1939.

Fuchs, Eduard. *Die Juden in der Karikatur*. Munich, 1921.

Gainer, Bernard. *The Alien Invasion*. London, 1974.

Garrard, John A. *The English and Immigration*. London, 1971.

Gartner, Lloyd. *The Jewish Immigrant in England, 1870–1914*. Detroit, 1960.

Gay, Peter. "The Berlin Jewish Spirit: A Dogma in Search of Some Doubts." Leo Baeck Memorial Lecture #15. New York, 1972.

———. "Encounter With Modernism: German Jews in German Culture, 1888–1914." *Midstream*, Feb. 1975.

Glanz, Rudolf. "The 'Bayer' and the 'Pollack' in America." JSS (1954).

———. *Geschichte des Niederen Jüdischen Volks in Deutschland*. New York, 1968.

Goldman, Felix. "Der Charakter der Leipziger Gemeinde." *Aus Geschichte und Leben der Juden in Leipzig*. Leipzig, 1930.

Goldscheider, Calvin. "Fertility of the Jews." *Demography*, IV (1967).

Goodnow, Frank J. *Comparative Administrative Law*. New York, 1903.

Goren, Arthur. *New York Jews and the Quest for Community*. New York, 1970.

Graf, Curt. *Das Recht der Israelitischen Religionsgemeinschaft im Königreich Sachsen*. Frankfurt am Main, 1914.

Graf, Max Josef. *Der Werdegang der Zigarette und die Entwicklung der deutschen Zigarettenindustrie*. Dissertation. Erlangen, 1932.

Greenberg, Louis. *The Jews of Russia*, 2 vols. New Haven, 1944, 1951.

Grubel, Fredrick. "From Kiev to Brody to Pankow." *Jubilee Volume Dedicated to Curt C. Silberman*. Ed. Herbert Strauss. New York, 1969.

Grund, P. *Die ausländischen Wanderarbeiter und ihre Bedeutung für Oberschlesien*. Leipzig, 1913.

Gunzenhausen, Alfred. *Sammlung der Gesetze, Verordnungen, Verfügungen, und Erlasse betreffend die Kirchenverfassung und die religiösen Einrichtungen der Israeliten in Württemberg*. Stuttgart, 1909.

Hamerow, Theodor. "Cravat and Caftan Jews." *Commentary*, vol. 77 (May 1984).

Harmelin, William. "Jews in the Leipzig Fur Industry." YBLBI, IX (1964).

Harmelin, Wilhelm. "Juden in der Leipziger Rauchwarenwirtschaft." *Tradition: Zeitschrift für Firmengeschichte und Unternehmerbiographie*, XI (December 1966).

Heid, Ludger. "East European Jewish Workers in the Ruhr, 1915–1922." YBLBI (1985), pp. 141–68.

Heimberger, Joseph. *Die staatskirchenrechtliche Stellung der Israeliten in Bayern*. Tübingen, 1912.

Heinemann, I. "Samson Raphael Hirsch: The Formative Years." *Historia Judaica*, XIII (1951).

Hersh, L. "Jewish Migration During the Modern Period." *The Jewish People: Past and Present*, I. New York, 1946.

Herz, Y. S. *Die Geshikhte fun Bund*, II (in Yiddish). New York, 1962.

Higham, John. *Strangers in the Land: Patterns of American Nativism*. New York, 1972.

Howe, Irving. *World of Our Fathers*. New York, 1976.

Hurwicz, Elias. "Shai Ish Hurwicz and the Berlin He-Athid." YBLBI, XII (1967).

Hyman, Paula. *From Dreyfus to Vichy: The Remaking of French Jewry, 1906–1939*. New York, 1979.

Jacob, Herbert. *German Administration Since Bismarck: Central Authority versus Local Autonomy*. New Haven, 1963.

Jacobs, Joseph. "Jewish Population in the United States." *American Jewish Yearbook*, XVI (1914).

The Jewish Encyclopedia. New York, 1905.

Jüdisches Lexikon. Berlin, 1927–1930.

Just, M. "Transitprobleme der osteuropäischen Amerikaauswanderung durch Deutschland Ende des 19. und Anfang des 20. Jahrhunderts." Thesis. Hamburg, 1977.

Kaplan, Marion. "German-Jewish Feminism: The *Jüdischer Frauenbund, 1904–1938.*" Unpublished Dissertation. Columbia University, 1976.

————. *The Jewish Feminist Movement in Germany: The Campaign of the Jüdischer Frauenbund, 1904–1938.* Westport, Conn., 1979.

Karlsberg, Bernhard. "Geschichte und Bedeutung der deutschen Durchwanderkontrolle." Dissertation. Hamburg, 1922.

Katz, Leopold. *Die rechtliche Stellung der Israeliten nach dem Staatskirchenrecht des Grossherzogtums Hessen.* Giessen, 1906.

Kaznelson, Siegmund. *Juden im deutschen Kulturbereich.* Berlin, 1959.

Kessner, Thomas. *The Golden Door: Italian and Jewish Immigrant Mobility in New York 1880–1915.* New York, 1977.

Kirshenbaum, Shimshon. "The Immigration of Jews from Russia and Poland into Germany, France, and England in the Last Quarter of the 19th Century" (in Hebrew). Dissertation. Hebrew University, Jerusalem, 1950.

Kisch, Guido, ed. *Das Breslauer Seminar.* Tübingen, 1963.

Kitzinger, Elisabeth. "Jüdische Jugendfürsorge in München, 1904–1943." *Von Juden in München.* Ed. Hans Lamm. Munich, 1958.

Knodel, John. *The Decline of Fertility in Germany, 1871–1939.* Princeton, 1974.

Knoepfel, L. "Die Geburtenrückgang und die Sterblichkeit bei der jüdischen Bevölkerung." ZfDS, IX (Jan. 1913).

————. "Die jüdische Bevölkerung im Grossherzogtum Hessen nach dem Ergebnisse der Volkszählung vom I. Dezember 1910." ZfDS, VIII (July–Aug. 1912).

Kober, Adolf. "Emancipation's Impact on the Education and Vocational Training of German Jewry." JSS, XVI (1954).

Koehl, Robert L. "Colonialism Inside Germany, 1886–1918." *Journal of Modern History,* XXV (Sept. 1953).

Kohn, Hans. *Martin Buber: Sein Werk und seine Zeit.* Hellerau, 1930.

Korburg, Werner. *Ausweisung und Abweisung von Ausländern.* Berlin, 1930.

Krohn, Helga. *Die Juden in Hamburg, 1848–1918.* Hamburg, 1974.

Kuznets, Simon. "Immigration of Russian Jews to the U.S.: Background and Structure." *Perspectives in American History,* IX (1975).

Lamberti, Marjorie. *Jewish Activism in Imperial Germany: The Struggle for Civil Equality.* New Haven, 1978.

————. "The Attempt to Form a Jewish Bloc: Jewish Notables and Politics in Wilhelminian Germany." *Central European History,* III (1970).

————." The Prussian Government and the Jews: Official Behaviors and Policy-Making in the Wilhelminian Era." YBLBI, XVII (1972).

Langhard, J. *Das Niederlassungsrecht der Ausländer in der Schweiz.* Zurich, 1913.

Lestchinsky, Jacob. "Economic and Social Development of American Jewry." *The Jewish People: Past and Present,* IV. New York, 1946.

————. *Jewish Migrations in Recent Generations* (in Hebrew). Tel Aviv, 1965.

Leviné-Meyer, Rosa. *Leviné: The Life of a Revolutionary.* Hampshire, England, 1973.

Levy, Richard. *The Downfall of the Anti-Semitic Political Parties in Imperial Germany.* New Haven, 1975.

Lewin, Adolf. *Geschichte der badischen Juden.* Karlsruhe, 1909.

Liberles, Robert S. "Between Community and Separation: The Resurgence of Orthodoxy in Frankfurt, 1838–1877." Dissertation. The Jewish Theological Seminary of America, 1980.

Lipman, V. D. *Social History of the Jews in England*. London, 1954.

Mahler, Raphael. "The Economic Background of Jewish Emigration from Galicia to the U.S." *YIVO Annual of Jewish Social Science*, VII (1952).

Mai, Joachim. *Die preussisch-deutsche Polenpolitik 1885/87: Eine Studie zur Herausbildung des Imperialismus in Deutschland*. Berlin (East), 1962.

Martin, Mary Lynn. "Karl Emil Franzos: His Views on Jewry as Reflected in His Writings on the Ghetto." Dissertation. University of Wisconsin, 1968.

Massing, Paul. *Rehearsal for Destruction*. New York, 1949.

Maurer, Trude. "The East European Jew in the Weimar Press: Stereotype and Attempted Rebuttal." *Studies in Contemporary Jewry*, I (1984), pp. 176–200.

Meisels, Josef. "Graetz und das Ostjudentum." JP, Nov. 23, 1917.

Meyer, Michael. "Great Debate on Anti-Semitism—Jewish Reactions to New Hostility in Germany, 1879–1880." YBLBI, XI (1966).

Meyers Deutscher Städteatlas. Leipzig and Vienna, 1913.

Michaelis, Alfred. *Die Rechtsverhaeltnisse der Juden in Preussen*. Berlin, 1910.

Miron, Dan. *A Traveller Disguised*. New York, 1973.

Mitscherlisch, Waldemar. *Die Ausbreitung der Polen in Preussen*. Leipzig, 1913.

Moeller, Robert G. "Die Besonderheiten der Deutschen? Neue Beiträge zur Sonderwegsdiskussion." *Internationale Schulbuchforschung*, vol. 4, no. 1 (1982), pp. 71–80.

Mombert, Paul. *Studien zur Bevölkerungsbewegung in Deutschland*. Karlsruhe, 1907.

Mosse, George. *The Crisis of German Ideology*. New York, 1964.

———. "Felix Dahn and Gustav Freytag." YBLBI, II (1957).

———. *German Jews Beyond Judiasm*. Cincinnati, 1985.

Murphy, Richard Charles. *Guestworkers in the German Reich: A Polish Community in Wilhelmian Germany*. New York, 1983.

Nash, Stanley. *In Search of Hebraism. Shai Hurwitz and His Polemics in the Hebrew Press*. Leiden, 1980.

Nedava, Joseph. *Trotsky and the Jews*. Philadelphia, 1973.

Nettl, J. P. *Rosa Luxemburg*, 2 vol. London, 1966.

Neubach, Helmut. *Die Ausweisungen von Polen und Juden aus Preussen 1885/1886*. Wiesbaden, 1967.

Neuringer, Sheldon M. *American Jewry and the United States Immigration Policy, 1881–1953*. New York, 1980.

Nichtweiss, Johannes. *Die ausländischen Saisonarbeiter in der Landwirtschaft der östlichen und mittleren Gebiete des deutschen Reiches*. Berlin, 1959.

Niewyck, Donald. "German Social Democracy and the Problem of Anti-Semitism, 1906–1914." M.A. Thesis. Tulane University, 1964.

Odenheimer, Paula. "Die Berufe der Juden in München." ZfDS, XII (1916).

Oncken, Hermann. "Preussen und Polen im 19 Jahrhundert." In *Deutschland und Polen*. Ed. Albert Brackmann. Munich and Leipzig, 1933.

Perlow, Bernard D. "Institutions for the Education of the Modern Rabbi in Germany." Dissertation. Dropsie College, 1954.

Poppel, Stephen M. *Zionism in Germany*. Philadelphia, 1977.

Puhle, Hans-Jürgen. *Agrarische Interessenpolitik und Preussischer Konservatismus im wilhelminischen Reich (1893–1914)*. Hanover, 1966.

Reich, Jacob. "Eine Episode aus der Geschichte der Ostjuden Münchens." *Von Juden in München*. Ed. Hans Lamm. Munich, 1958.

Reichel, O. A. *Isaac Halevy: Spokesman and Historian of Jewish Tradition*. New York, 1960.

Reichmann, Eva. "Der Bewusstseinswandel der deutschen Juden." *Deutsches Judentum in Krieg und Revolution, 1916–1923*. Ed. Werner E. Mosse. Tübingen, 1971.

Reinharz, Jehuda. *Chaim Weizmann: The Making of A Zionist Leader.* New York and Oxford, 1985.

———. "East European Jews in the *Weltanschauung* of German Zionists, 1882–1914." *Studies in Contemporary Jewry,* I (1984), pp. 55–95.

———. *Fatherland or Promised Land: The Dilemma of the German Jew, 1893–1914.* Ann Arbor, Mich., 1975.

Richarz, Monika. *Der Eintritt der Juden in die akademischen Berufe.* Tübingen, 1974.

———, ed. *Jüdisches Leben in Deutschland,* II. Stuttgart, 1979.

Rinott, Moshe. *Hilfsverein der deutschen Juden: Creation and Struggle* (in Hebrew). Jerusalem, 1971.

Rischin, Moses. *The Promised City.* New York, 1970.

Rönne, Ludwig von. *Das Staats-Recht der Preussischen Monarchie,* 2 vol. Leipzig, 1870.

Rosenberg, Curt. "Ehescheidungen von Ausländern." *Rechtsfragen der Praxis.* Berlin, 1924.

Rosenthal, Erich. "Trends of the Jewish Population in Germany, 1910–1939." JSS, VI (1944).

Rosenthal, Harry Kenneth. *German and Pole.* Gainsville, Fl., 1976.

Rozenblit, Marsha L. *The Jews of Vienna: Assimilation and Identity, 1867–1914.* Albany, N.Y., 1983.

Ruppin, Arthur. *The Jews of Today.* London, 1913.

———. "Die Juden auf den preussischen Universitäten." ZfDS, I (1905).

Scherber, Paul. *Die rechtliche Stellung der Ausländer in Bayern.* Würzburg, 1897.

Schippel, Max. "Die fremden Arbeitskräfte und die Gesetzgebungen der verschiedenen Länder." *Die Neue Zeit,* XXV, no. 41 (1907).

Schofer, Lawrence. *The Formation of a Modern Labor Force: Upper Silesia, 1865–1914.* Berkeley, 1975.

Schorsch, Ismar. "Art as Social History: Moritz Oppenheim and the German Jewish Vision of Emancipation." *Danzig Between East and West: Aspects of Modern Jewish History.* Ed. Isidore Twersky. Cambridge, Mass., 1985.

———. "German Anti-Semitism in the Light of Post-War Historiography." YBLBI, XIX (1974).

———. *Jewish Reactions to German Anti-Semitism.* New York and Philadelphia, 1972.

Schulze, F., and Sysmanik, P. *Das deutsche Studententum,* fourth revised edition. Munich, 1932.

Segall, Jacob. "Die ausländischen Juden in München." ZfDS, V (Feb. 1909).

———. *Die beruflichen und sozialen Verhältnisse der Juden in Deutschland.* Berlin, 1912.

———. "Die Entwicklung der jüdischen Bevölkerung in Berlin von 1811–1910." ZfDS, IX (Jan. 1913).

———. *Die Entwicklung der jüdischen Bevölkerung in München von 1875–1905.* Berlin, 1910.

———. "Die Entwicklung der jüdischen Bevölkerung in Württemburg von 1820 bis 1910." ZfDS, IX (April 1913).

———. "Die Juden in Gross-Berlin." ZfDS, X (Sept.–Oct. 1914).

———. "Die Juden im Königreich Sachsen von 1832 bis 1910." ZfDS, X (March 1914).

———. "Stand der jüdischen Bevölkerung in Deutschland auf Grund der Volkszählung von 1. Dez. 1910." ZfDS, VII (Nov. 1911).

———. "Die wirtschaftliche und soziale Lage der Juden in Deutschland." ZfDS, VII (June 1911).

Sempell, Charlotte. "Leo Caprivi." *Journal of Modern History,* XXV (Sept. 1953).

Shatzker, Chaim. "Jewish Youth Movements in Germany Between the Years 1900–1933" (in Hebrew). Dissertation. Hebrew University, 1969.

Shulvass, Moses. *From East to West*. Detroit, 1971.

Silbergleit, Heinrich. *Die Bevölkerung und Berufsverhältnisse der Juden in Deutschland*. Berlin, 1930.

Silberner, Edmund. "German Social Democracy and the Jewish Problem Prior to World War I." *Historia Judaica*, XV, Part I (April 1953).

Silberschlag, Eisig. *Saul Tchernichowsky: A Poet in Revolt*. Ithaca, N.Y., 1968.

Sinasohn, Max. *Die Berliner Privatsynagogen und ihre Rabbiner*. Jerusalem, 1971.

Sklarz, Leon. *Geschichte und Organisation der Ostjudenhilfe in Deutschland seit dem Jahre 1914*. Dissertation. Rostock, 1927.

Stegman, Dirk. *Die Erben Bismarcks*. Cologne, 1970.

Sterling, Eleanor. "Jewish Reactions to Jew-Hatred in the First Half of the Nineteenth Century." YBLBI, III (1958).

Stern, Elijahu. "The History of the Jews of Danzig from Emancipation until Their Deportation in the Nazi Era" (in Hebrew). Dissertation. Hebrew University, 1978.

Stevens, Austin. *The Dispossessed*. London, 1975.

Stouffer, Samuel. "Migration and Intervening Opportunities." *American Sociological Review*, V (December 1940).

Suchy, Barbara, "The *Verein zur Abwehr des Antisemitismus*(I)—From Its Beginning to the First World War." YBLBI, XXVIII (1983), pp. 205–40.

Szajkowski, Zosa. "East European Jewish Workers in Germany During World War I." *S. Baron Jubilee Volume*, II. Jerusalem, 1975.

———. *Jews, Wars, Communism*, I–III. New York, 1972–1976.

———. "The *Komité für den Osten* and Zionism." *Herzl Yearbook* (1971).

———. "The Struggle for Yiddish During World War I." YBLBI, IX (1964).

———. "Suffering of Jewish Emigrants to America in Transit through Germany." JSS, XXXIX (1977).

Tcherikower, Elias, ed. *The Early Jewish Labor Movement in the United States* (in Yiddish). New York, 1961.

Tims, Richard W. *Germanizing Prussian Poland, 1894–1919*. New York, 1941.

Tirrel, Sarah. *German Agrarian Politics after Bismarck*. New York, 1951.

Toury, Jacob. "Ostjüdische Handarbeiter in Deutschland vor 1914." BLBI, VI, no. 21 (1963).

———. *Die politischen Orientierungen der Juden in Deutschland*. Tübingen, 1966.

Vogel, Barbara. *Deutsche Russlandpolitk*. Düsseldorf, 1973.

Volkov, Shulamit. "Anti-Semitism as a Cultural Code: Reflections on the History and Historiography of Anti-Semitism in Imperial Germany." YBLBI, XXIII (1978).

Walker, Mack. *Germany and the Emigration, 1816–1865*. Cambridge, Mass., 1964.

Waxmann, Meyer. *A History of Jewish Literature*, III and IV. New York and London, 1936.

Wehler, Hans-Ulrich. *Krisenherde des Kaiserreichs, 1871–1914*. Göttingen, 1970.

———. *Sozialdemokratie und Nationalstaat: Nationalitätenfrage in Deutschland 1840–1914*, revised edition. Göttingen, 1971.

Weinreich, Max. "Two Yiddish Satirical Poems About Jews." *Philologishe Shriftn*, III (in Yiddish) (1929).

Weltsch, Robert. "Introduction." YBLBI, IX (1964).

Wendt, Hans. *Bismarck und die polnische Frage*. Halle, 1922.

Werner, E. "The Tragedy of Ephraim Moses Lilien." *Herzl Yearbook*, II. New York, 1959.

Wertheimer, Jack. "Between Tsar and Kaiser: The Radicalization of Russian Jewish University Students in Germany." YBLBI, XXVIII (1983).

————. "Jewish Lobbyists and the German Citizenship Law of 1914." *Studies in Contemporary Jewry,* vol. I (1984).

————. "The *Ausländerfrage* at Institutions of Higher Learning: A Controversy Over Russian Jewish Students in Germany." YBLBI, XXVII (1982).

————. "The Duisburg Affair: A Test Case in the 'Struggle for Conquest of the Communities.' " *Association for Jewish Studies Review,* VI (1981).

————. " 'The Unwanted Element': East European Jews in Imperial Germany." YBLBI, XXVI (1981).

Wertheimer, Mildred. *The Pan-German League.* New York, 1924.

Wilcox, Walter F., ed. *International Migrations,* 2 vol. New York, 1929 and 1931.

Wilhelm, Kurt. "The Jewish Community in the Post-Emancipation Period." YBLBI, II (1957).

Williams, Robert C. *Culture in Exile: Russian Emigres in Germany, 1881–1941.* Ithaca, N.Y., 1972.

Wischnitzer, Mark. *To Dwell in Safety: The Story of Jewish Migration Since 1800.* Philadelphia, 1948.

Wiskemann, Elizabeth. *Germany's Eastern Neighbors.* London, 1956.

Wistrich, Robert S. *Revolutionary Jews from Marx to Trotsky.* London, 1976.

Wolff, Siegfried. *Das Recht der Israelitischen Religions-Gemeinschaft des Grossherzogtums Baden.* Karlsruhe, 1913.

Yoffe, L. *Professor Hermann Schapira* (in Hebrew). Tel Aviv, 1936.

Zelzer, M. *Weg und Schicksal der Juden in Stuttgart.* Stuttgart, n.d.

Zeman, Z. A. B. and Scharlau, W. B. *The Merchant of Revolution: The Life of Alexander Israel Helphand (Parvus).* London, 1965.

Index

DATE DUE
